JAPANESE COST MANAGEMENT

Series on Technology Management

SERIES ON TECHNOLOGY MANAGEMENT – VOL. 4

JAPANESE COST MANAGEMENT

YASUHIRO MONDEN

University of Tsukuba, Japan

Imperial College Press

Published by

Imperial College Press
57 Shelton Street
Covent Garden
London WC2H 9HE

Distributed by

World Scientific Publishing Co. Pte. Ltd.
P O Box 128, Farrer Road, Singapore 912805
USA office: Suite 1B, 1060 Main Street, River Edge, NJ 07661
UK office: 57 Shelton Street, Covent Garden, London WC2H 9HE

British Library Cataloguing-in-Publication Data
A catalogue record for this book is available from the British Library.

JAPANESE COST MANAGEMENT

ISBN 1-86094-185-0

Printed in Singapore.

Preface

This book deals with the systems of cost reduction that originated in Japan. These are mostly new systems that did not exist in western practices before they were utilized in Japan. The book also presents the Japanese ways of carrying out the globally popular cost reduction practices.

It introduces new ideas to the current management accounting that is being developed.

The structure of the book is as follows:

(1) It describes the *strategic cost management* conducted by top management through alliances between companies and/or between government and industry.
(2) It shows the functional cost reduction systems along *the various phases of the product life cycle* as follows: R&D → Product development → Manufacturing → Administration and indirect operations.
(3) It conducts some *humanistic or behavioral aspects* of Japanese cost reduction systems.

More specifically this book is composed of the following eight parts:

Part 1: The **strategic decisions of organizational change** for cost reduction, that includes new business alliances.
Part 2: **R&D cost** reduction systems in research activities.
Part 3: Cost reduction systems in new product development, that is, the **target costing** system. Parts 2 and 3 are very important from the viewpoint of technology and innovation management.

v

Part 4: Cost management techniques in the manufacturing phase, that include Japanese **Just-in-Time**, **TPM** (total productive maintenance) and **Kaizen costing** systems.

Part 5: Cost management systems in the **administrative and indirect departments**. This part includes Japanese application of **ABM** (activity-based management) and **BPR** (business process reengineering).

Part 6: Cost management from the viewpoint of **marketing strategy**.

Part 7: **Humanistic elements** in the Japanese cost management.

Part 8: Cost management in the **decentralized organization**.

This book describes the cost management techniques in a realistic manner as it tries to be useful in the practical world. Further, it covers not only the systems or techniques, but also the economic, organizational or behavioral aspects behind them. I hope this book would be beneficial to both practitioners as well as academicians.

Here, I also wish to express my gratitude to Dr. Joe Tidd, Imperial College Management School, who is the editor-in-charge of the Series on Technology Management of the Imperial College Press, for proposing the publication of this book. I am also grateful to Ms. Geetha Nair, Editor, Imperial College Press, for her support in publishing this book. Last but not least, many help extended by Ms. Lakshmi Narayan, World Scientific Publishing Co., in the production of this book is greatly appreciated.

Yasuhiro Monden
University of Tsukuba

Contents

List of Contributors

Henry Aigbedo
Department of Logistics, Operations
and Management Information Systems
College of Business
Iowa State University, USA

Mahmuda Akter
Institute of Policy and Planning Sciences
University of Tsukuba, Tennodai 1-1-1
Tsukuba, Ibaraki 305-8573 Japan

Takayuki Asada
Graduate School of Economics
Osaka University
Toyonaka, Osaka 560-0043 Japan

Kazuki Hamada
Faculty of Commerce
Seinan Gakuin University
Fukuoka, Fukuoka 814-8511 Japan

Shufuku Hiraoka
Department of Business Administration
Soka University
Hachioji, Tokyo 192-8577 Japan

Mahfuzul Hoque
Institute of Policy and Planning Sciences
University of Tsukuba, Tennodai 1-1-1
Tsukuba, Ibaraki 305-8573 Japan

Noriko Hoshi
Hakuoh University Women's College
Oyama, Tochigi 323-8588 Japan

Norika Ikeda
Tohmatsu Consulting Co., Ltd.
MS Shibaura Building
13-23, Shibaura 4-chome
Minato-ku, Tokyo 108-0023 Japan

Kentaro Koga
School of Commerce, Waseda University
1-6-1 Nishi-waseda
Shinjuku-ku 169-8050 Japan

Gun-Yung Lee
Department of Business Administration
Osaka Sangyo University
Nakagaito, Daito-city 574-8530 Japan

John Y. Lee
Lubin School of Business
Pace University
Pleasantville, NY 10570 USA

Shunzo Matsuoka
Faculty of Business
Hannan University
5-4-33 Amami-Higashi, Matsubara
Osaka 580-8502 Japan

Yoshio Matsushita
Tohmatsu Consulting Co., Ltd.
MS Shibaura Building
13-23, Shibaura 4-chome
Minato-ku, Tokyo 108-0023 Japan

Kazuhito Miura
Tohmatsu Consulting Co., Ltd.
MS Shibaura Building
13-23, Shibaura 4-chome
Minato-ku, Tokyo 108-0023 Japan

Yasuhiro Monden
Institute of Policy and Planning Sciences
University of Tsukuba
Tsukuba, Ibaraki 305-8573 Japan

Yoshiyuki Nagasaka
Faculty of Business Management
Osaka Sangyo University
Daito, Osaka 574-8530 Japan

Noboru Ogura
Institute of Socio-Economic Planning
University of Tsukuba
3-29-1 Otsuka, Bunkyo-ku
Tokyo 112-0012 Japan

Kozo Suzuki
Tokyo Metropolitan Government
Research Office
In-Service Training Institute
Aomi 2-38, Koto Tokyo, 135-8070 Japan

Susumu Ueno
Professor of Accounting
Faculty of Business Administration
Konan University, Japan

Sachie Yamada
Institute of Policy and Planning Sciences
University of Tsukuba, Tennodai 1-1-1
Tsukuba, Ibaraki 305-8573 Japan

Part 1
Strategic Cost Management

Chapter 1

Strategic Cost Decisions in the Industry as a Whole

KOZO SUZUKI

1. Introduction

1.1. *The purposes of Part 1*

Part 1 describes the following: the reality of strategic cost management in today's manufacturing industry in Japan; and the behaviour styles practised by companies, industry and government concerning mergers and other inter-company relationships. These are shown as being the characteristics of decision making at a strategic level for cost reduction in the Japanese manufacturing industry.

The main method of approach in this chapter is thus: following the construction of relationships between independent companies, such as mergers, acquisitions and tie-ups and, through them, drawing conclusions on cost reduction as practised in a specified industry as a whole. Mergers, acquisitions and tie-ups are all classified as relationships between companies. Competition is intensifying on an international scale, and it has become very important for companies to produce and supply good products cheaply; so cost reduction is always needed. Therefore, it is becoming increasingly common for companies to construct new relationships with other companies. This is because swift and reliable cost reduction can be realised by making use of the management resources of another company.

A merger is the direct acquisition of outside management resources, and a tie-up is an in-between way of achieving inside growth, merger and acquisition.[1] In these ways, we can see a more conspicuous company management strategy. Internal cost reduction strategies are harder to see, but they tend to appear when a relationship with another company is created, and there are many cases where this reflects strategy of the highest level of a company.

Part 1 describes the process of decision-making at a strategic level for cost reduction.

1. Cost reduction through mutual relationships with other companies;
2. Cost reduction through relationships with the industry group, company group and government-led (MITI) cost reduction strategy.

First of all, in Chap. 1, cost reduction strategies through the construction of relationships between current Japanese companies are discussed, on the basis of newspaper news between 1996 and 1997. The reality of cost reduction strategies is also described, through forms of reorganization such as mergers, habitat segregation, share distribution, technology alternating current and production adjustment in Japanese industry groups or company groups.

The government-led reorganization of the industry and industrial groups is discussed in Chap. 2, along with production adjustment, the historical progress of scale-merit investigation by entry regulation and the behaviour style of each sector.

1.2. *Points of view for consideration*

In decision-making at a strategic level for cost reduction in Japanese industry as a whole, the following four characteristics are important:

1.2.1. *The existence of cost reduction by historic company reorganization*

The first, merger and tie-up in the manufacturing industry in this country for cost reduction purposes was several years after World War II. This was followed by many other cases in different types of industry in the same company groups. The major purposes of cost reduction in these cases were the compression of manufacturing costs, distribution costs, sales and management costs. These were achieved mainly by an investigation of scale merit. The integration and joint disposal of production facilities was also carried out, along with co-existence and habitat segregation in a domestic market with a limited growth.

Japanese growth has been based on these types of positive cost reduction efforts taken by each company. Those factors are common to times of post-war revival, advanced economic growth, the oil crisis, and after the collapse of an asset-inflated economy.

At the same time, the company group and the industry group as a whole tried to reduce costs. Competition between individual companies and competition was seen, and it was often seen that industry groups made inside adjustments for such opposition. There were many cases where industry groups led cost reduction strategies for the whole industry. These efforts were made through mergers, acquisitions, tie-ups, production adjustment, and the continuous movement of labour between companies. On the other hand, this was not for cost reduction, but the development of keeping stocks from one another which is one of the characteristics of post-war relationships between Japanese companies.

1.2.2. *Cost reduction by government or industry group participation*

Secondly, there were many cases of cost reduction which were government-led, by the Ministry of International Trade and Industry (MITI). The MITI led the reorganisation of the industry and industrial groups, through advancement of production efficiency in the industry by scale merit, production adjustment and entry regulation. This influenced the cost reduction that was practised by the industry as a whole. From post-war revival to a time of rapid economic growth, key industries and structural depression type of industries were watched over carefully by the government, and were the object of an advancement policy. The advancement of medium and small-sized businesses by the Machine Industry Promotion Temporary Step Law was also advocated by the MITI.

However, each company and individual interest did not always agree with the government's intentions, which may have occurred as a result of being contrary to government expectations. However, the cost reduction efforts of each company intensified the competitive power of Japanese companies, and this helped to bring about the growth of each company. Thus, cost reduction in the Japanese manufacturing industry came about by the inside efforts of each individual company, as well as being realized by the industry as a whole and the participation of government in addition to the efforts of each individual company.

1.2.3. *Cost reduction in relationships between companies today*

Thirdly, relationships between modern companies have become more common recently in order to encourage cost reduction. This is different from former relationships between companies that were mentioned earlier. This aims at a high cost reduction within a short period by the practical use of outside management resources, thus the compression of research and development expenses in a market ruled by the industry standard formation are regarded as important, and a reduction of the whole manufacturing costs is pursued by constructing an international parts supply system.

The background to this includes the intensification of international competition, the increasing globalization of economy, and changes in the management environment such as the speeding up of progress in advanced technology and the shortening of product life cycle.

The most important reason is also that the former relationships between companies are inadequate for cost reduction today. Cost reduction strategies of individual companies are proving impossible to be equivalent to the maintenance and expansion of competitive power in today's market.

1.2.4. *The existence of overlapping relationships between companies*

Fourthly, the overlapping relationships between companies of the former type and current type are observed. This is related to a characteristic of the constitution of current Japanese companies. This characteristic is that various companies are located in every part of the industrial life cycle.

For example, growth type industries establish relationships of the current type. Companies that are superior in international competition follow a former pattern. In depressed industries, there are many forms of reorganization currently taking place.

And in cases of reorganisation of the former type, mergers are frequently used for getting management resources of another company. On the other hand, in reorganization of the current type tie-up is often selected. Tie-up is the in-between way of inside strategic growth of company and merger or acquisition. A position in an Industrial Life Cycle (ILC)[2] of a specific company has a close connection with a position on a Product Life Cycle (PLC)[3] of its main product. And the characteristics of the ILC of a specific industry are based on the economy environment, industry structure, etc. So, the position of a specific industry influences its approach to cost reduction, innovation and advancement of competitive power.

The ways of achieving cost reduction also vary with such differences. For example, there is an infinite variety of manufacturing costs, sale-costs, management costs, distribution costs and research and development expenses in any type of industry that wishes to achieve cost reduction. However, in most cases, the construction of relationships between companies for drastic cost reduction is realized as an outcome of strategic decision-making of the highest level of a company.

2. Strategies of Relationships Between Japanese Companies

2.1. *Strategic decision-making for cost reduction in the manufacturing industry*

Today, the frequency of mergers, acquisitions and tie-ups is increasing beyond existing series groups or industrial groups. On the other hand, existing industrial groups indulge in much reorganisation and integration. (Here, industrial groups mean series or company groups.)

Mergers and tie-ups have increased internationally. However, the former type of relationships can be seen in some industries. Price adjustment and production adjustments constitute some of them.

In this chapter, an analysis of recent mergers, acquisitions and tie-ups is presented, in order to clarify the trend of cost reduction strategies that do not remain in one company and general cost reduction plans in the recent history of the Japanese manufacturing industry.

In the Japanese manufacturing industry, through industrialization after the Meiji ages, post-war revival and advanced economic growth, various types of industry have grown up. These include growth industries such as the semiconductor industry. At the same time, other industries have declined in power, such as the iron and steel industry and the pulp industry. These were typical growth industries until an age of advanced economic growth.

In this way, ILC and PLC are distributed over various types of industry throughout Japanese manufacturing industries, and these become a source of the various relationships between companies in Japan. However, the current trend is towards a rise in mergers, acquisitions and tie-ups, for the purpose of constructing relationships between companies with the aims of cost reduction and increasing research and development. In this way, companies form mutual relationships.

A. Terms and purposes of related constructions between companies in one industry have a fixed tendency by their position of the industrial ILC or PLC (Fig. 1.1).
B. In the case of relationships between companies for cost reduction, the target of cost reduction is settled by their position on the industrial ILC and PLC (Fig. 1.2).

Through the following pattern, the factors prescribing strategic decision making for cost reduction in company mergers are seen and described:

1. Terms (1: merger; 2: acquisition; 3: tie-up);
2. Purposes (1: cost reduction, 2: research and development, 3: market correspondence);
3. Partners of relationships between companies (1: inside the same company group or part of a series, 2: outside the group or a different series, 3: international combination);

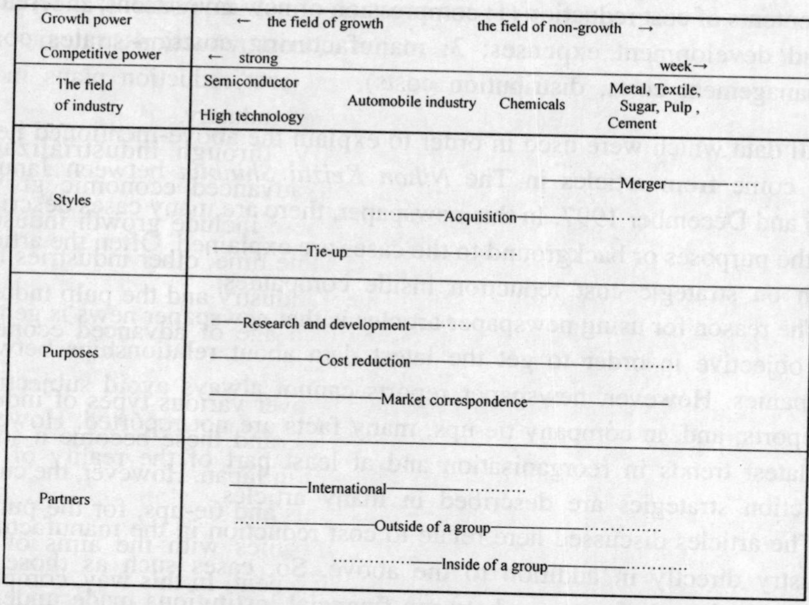

Growth power	← the field of growth		the field of non-growth →	
Competitive power	← strong			week→
The field of industry	Semiconductor High technology	Automobile industry	Chemicals	Metal, Textile, Sugar, Pulp, Cement
Styles		Tie-up ··········	········· Acquisition ···········	————— Merger ·········
Purposes	————Research and development——······	———————Cost reduction——·········	——————Market correspondence————————	
Partners	—————International———··········	·········——Outside of a group——··········	·········——Inside of a group———·········	

Fig. 1.1. Styles, purposes and partners of relationships between companies.

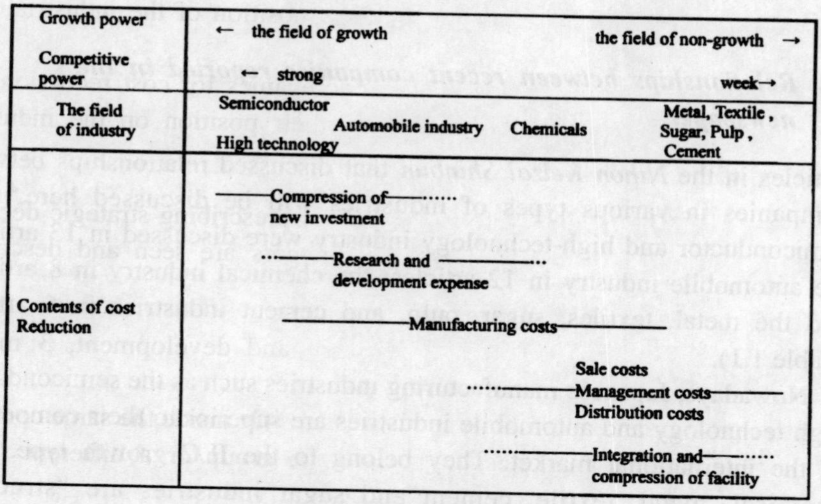

Growth power	← the field of growth		the field of non-growth →	
Competitive power	← strong			week→
The field of industry	Semiconductor High technology	Automobile industry	Chemicals	Metal, Textile, Sugar, Pulp, Cement
Contents of cost Reduction	Compression of new investment			
	·········Research and development expense·······			
	————Manufacturing costs————			
			Sale costs ········Management costs Distribution costs	
			·········Integration and compression of facility·········	

Fig. 1.2. Contents of cost reduction.

4. Contents of cost reduction (1: compression of new investment; 2: research and development expenses; 3: manufacturing costs; 4: sales costs, management costs, distribution costs).

All data which were used in order to explain the above-mentioned items have come from articles in The *Nihon Keizai Shinbun* between January 1996 and December 1997. In this newspaper, there are many cases described and the purposes or background to the cases are explained. Often the articles touch on strategic cost reduction inside companies.

The reason for using newspaper articles is that newspaper news is general and objective in order to get the latest data about relationships between companies. However, newspaper reports cannot always avoid subjectivity in reports; and, in company tie-ups, many facts are not reported. However, the latest trends in reorganisation and at least part of the reality of cost reduction strategies are described in many articles.

The articles discussed here relate to cost reduction in the manufacturing industry directly in addition to the above. So, cases such as those that seemed to be relief mergers between financial institutions made under the leadership of the Ministry of Finance and M&A for investment purposes have been excluded.

2.2. *Relationships between recent companies reported in the newspaper*

Articles in the *Nihon Keizai Shinbun* that discussed relationships between companies in various types of industries will be discussed here.[4] The semiconductor and high-technology industry were discussed in 13 articles; the automobile industry in 12 articles; the chemical industry in 8 articles; and the metal, textiles, sugar, pulp, and cement industries in 6 articles (Table 1.1).

Nowadays, Japanese manufacturing industries such as the semiconductor, high technology and automobile industries are superior to their competition in the international market. They belong to the ILC growth type.[5] The chemical, metal, textile, cement and sugar industries are "structural

Table 1.1. Relationships between companies (by industry).

Industry	Mergers	Acquisitions	Tie-ups	Total
Semiconductor and High technology	0 (0.0)%	0 (0.0)%	13 (100.0)%	13 (100.0)%
Automobile industry	0 (0.0)%	1 (8.3)%	11 (91.7)%	12 (100.0)%
Chemicals	1 (12.5)%	2 (25.0)%	5 (62.5)%	8 (100.0)%
Metal, Textile, Sugar, Pulp, Cement	3 (50.0)%	1 (16.7)%	2 (33.3)%	6 (100.0)%

depression" type of industries and have the common characteristic of being depressed in ILC.[6] Those were the "star" industries that led the Japanese economy in the past.

Many articles also reported on the machine industries, information and communication, and other commerce. These are excluded here because the object of this chapter is to look at the manufacturing industry. Moreover, in the machine industry, the kinds of products made are very wide-ranging, for example, from nuclear electric power generation to bicycles, so it is not appropriate to take these *en masse*.

The background to building relationships between companies includes intense international competition in the case of both types of industry. The construction of relationships between companies profits them both by leading to immediate cost reduction and innovation in order to fight successfully against competition, and in the development of new products.

Repetitions of fields is often found by the classification of the type of industry in this chapter. For example, the automobile industry is in the same class as the semiconductor industry in that the automobile industry introduced the production know-how to semiconductor companies and thus went into semiconductor production. Companies are classed by the products that are made in the relationships built between companies.

Table 1.2. Relationships between companies as in the newspaper.

Industry	Cases			Date of articles	Products	Forms of relationship		
	No	Company	Partner			(a)	(b)	(c)
(A)	①	Inotec	Credence Systems(US)	Nov.27,1997	Tester of semiconductor			O
	②	Toshiba	Siemens Medical(Ger)	Nov.21,1997	Nuclear medical equiment			O
	③	Mitsubishi Electric	NEC	Oct.28,1997	Factory automation			O
	④	Seiko Exson	Mitsubishi Electric	Oct.23,1997	DRAM			O
	⑤	Bull(France)	NEC	Oct.20,1997	Personal computer			O
	⑥	Toshiba,IBM,Siemens(Ger),Motorola(US)		Oct.19,1997	DRAM			O
	⑦	Toyota Motor Groups	Sony	May 28,1997	Liquid crystal display			O
	⑧	NEC	Samsung(Koria)	Jan.15,1996	DRAM			O
	⑨	Fuji Photo Film	Eastman Kodac(US)	Sep.8,1996	Digital photograph			O
	⑩	Toyota Motor Groups	Texas Instrument(US)	Aug.7,1996	DRAM			O
	⑪	Hitachi	Robotic Vision(US)	Jul.26,1996	Personal computer			O
	⑫	Fujitsu	TSMC(Taiwan)	Jun.15,1996	DRAM			O
	⑬	Top makers of semiconductor(Japan and USA)		Feb.23,1996	Standardize productive technology			O
Automobile Industry	①	GM(US)	Suzuki Motor	Oct.2,1997	Mini-car for Europe			O
	②	Toyota Motor	Montel(Netherland)	Aug.20,1997	Synthetic resins			O
	③	Mazda	Parts Makers	Aug.18,1997	Parts of car			O
	④	Toyoda Automatic Loom Works	Nissan Motor	Jul.26,1997	Charger for electric-car			O
	⑤	GM(US)	Isuzu Motors	Jul.10,1997	Diesel engine			O
	⑥	Mitsubishi Heavy Industries	GM(US)	May.16,1997	Parts of Car air-conditioner			O
	⑦	Toyota Motor	Danar(US)	Apr.12,1997	Parts of car engine			O
	⑧	Mazda Motor	Ford(US)	Jan.23,1997	Engine			O
	⑨	Hashimoto Forming Industries	Toyoda Gosei	Jun.18,1996	Technology of changeable forming			O
	⑩	Mitsubishi Heavy Industries	GM(US)	Jun.15,1996	Car air-conditioner			O
	⑪	Ford(US)	Mazda	Apr.12,1996	Cars		O	
	⑫	Mitsubishi Motor	Netherlands Car B.V.	Apr.15,1996	Minicar(RV)			O
Chemicals	①	Nisseki Petrochemical Industries	Dow Chemical(US)	Nov.12,1997	Ethylene			O
	②	Idemitsu Petrochemical Industries	Dainippon Ink Chemicals	Oct.15,1997	Polystyrene			O
	③	Mitsui Petrochemical Industries	Mitsui Toatsu	Sep.9,1996	Phenol	O		
	④	BSAF(Germany)	Hokuriku Seiyaku	Mar.15,1996	Medicines		O	
	⑤	Japan Systhetic Rubber	Mitsubishi Chemical	Mar.12,1996	ABR resins			O

Table 1.2 (*Continued*)

Industry	Cases			Date of articles	Products	Forms of relationship		
	No	Company	Partner			(a)	(b)	(c)
	⑥	Eastman Kodac(US)	Konica	Feb.22,1996	Compact camera			○
	⑦	Toray Industries	Rhone-Poulene(France)	Jan.23,1996	Polyester film		○	
	⑧	E.I.du Pont(US)	Mitsubishi Rayon	Jan.23,1996	Dry film			○
Metal, Textile, Sugar, Pulp, Cement	①	Nippon Steel	Nisshin Steel	Nov.7,1997	Cooperative transport			○
	②	Alcan Aluminium	Nippon Light Metal, Toyo Aluminium	Jul.26,1996	Aluminium		○	
	③	Nissinbo Industries	Teijin	Nov.14,1997	Deying			○
	④	Nihon Suger Refining	Meiji Suger Refining	Jan.17,1996	Sugar	○		
	⑤	New Oji Paper	Honshu Paper	Mar.30,1996	Paper	○		
	⑥	Chichibu Onoda Cement	Nihon Cement	Oct.3,1997	Cement	○		

Note: (A) Semiconductor and High-technology
    (a) Merger (b) Acquisition (c) Tie-up
Source: Nihon Kezai Shinbun

2.3. *Terms of relationships between companies*

At first, tie-ups made up the greater part in terms of relationships between companies such as mergers, acquisitions and tie-ups. However, there are now increasing numbers of articles in the news about mergers and acquisitions. In particular, there is much reorganization by merger in structurally depressed industries. On the other hand, many tie-ups are entered into by strong growth industries in ILC, and this is similar to the industry having strong competitive power in the international market, like the semiconductor and high-technology industries. There are many mergers taking place in fields such as chemicals and metal, and these industries belong to mature or non-growth fields (Fig. 1.3).

All relationships between companies in the semiconductor and high-technology industries are tie-ups, as well as in the automobile industry. However, there are most tie-ups in the chemical industry, and mergers and acquisitions are also seen here. In the metal industry, the merger is the major form of reorganization. Thus, in companies where growth is high and there is a strong competitive power in ILC, there are many opportunities

Industry	Mergers	Acquisitions	Tie-ups
Semiconductor and High technology			① ④ ⑦ ⑩ ⑬ ② ⑤ ⑧ ⑪ ③ ⑥ ⑨ ⑫
Automobile industry		⑪	① ④ ⑦ ⑩ ② ⑤ ⑧ ⑫ ③ ⑥ ⑨
Chemicals	③	④ ②	④ ⑥ ② ⑧ ⑤
Metal, Textile , Sugar, Pulp, Cement	④ ⑤ ⑥	②	① ③

Note.
1. A number referred to each type of industry in the figure inside copes with a number according to a type of industry in Table 1.2.
2. One circled number in the figure shows the case of a merger, an acquisition or a tie-up.

Fig. 1.3. Relationships between companies.

when the gradual combination of enterprises in tie-ups is selected. It is the same for two companies which have some products that are similar in PLC, too.

Thus, even if the outward appearances of company reorganizations seem to be similar forms of merger or acquisitions, the characteristics of strategic decision-making behind these mergers are not the same. For example, in a limited market, mergers take place to plan for both companies surviving by preventing excessive competition. Otherwise, powerful companies merge in order to conquer the world market. Judging from company management strategy, these two aims contrast with each other.

2.4. *The purposes of relationships between companies*

Figure 1.4 shows various types of relationships between companies according to the purposes of each relationship. We can see that the purposes of cost

Industry	Cost reduction	Research and development	Market correspondence
Semiconductor and High technology	① ⑥ ⑫ ② ⑦ ⑬ ④ ⑩	① ⑤ ⑨ ② ⑦ ⑪ ③ ⑧ ⑬	⑤ ⑪ ⑧ ⑩
Automobile industry	③ ⑦ ⑪ ④ ⑧ ⑫ ⑤ ⑨	②	① ⑩ ⑤ ⑪ ⑥ ⑫
Chemicals	① ④ ② ⑤ ③ ⑧	① ③	② ⑦ ④ ⑥
Metal, Textile, Sugar, Pulp , Cement	① ⑥ ④ ⑤		② ③ ⑤

Note.
1. A number referred to each type of industry in the figure inside copes with a number according to a type of industry in Table 1.2.
2. One circled number in the figure shows the case of a merger, an acquisition or a tie-up.

Fig. 1.4. Purposes of construction of relationships between companies.

reduction and market correspondence are distributed through the whole figure. Thus, the main aims in the construction of relationships between companies are cost reduction and market correspondence.

The circled numbers of each industry in Fig. 1.4 coincide with those in Table 1.2 (recent relationships between companies in the newspaper). And it is the same for Fig. 1.5, and Fig. 1.6.

There are also many cases where semiconductor and high-technology industries are put together for increased research and development, and there are some cases which have several purposes simultaneously. But, even if cost reduction is a shared purpose of those, the types of costs to reduce are different depending on the part of ILC that the industry is located in.

In industries in growth fields, the expansion of market rule power to contain the world market is "Market correspondence". The rejection of

Industry	Internal combination		International combination
	Inside of a group	Outside of a group	
Semiconductor and High technology		③ ④ ⑦	① ⑥ ⑩ ⑬ ② ⑧ ⑪ ⑤ ⑨ ⑫
Automobile industry	③	④ ⑨	① ⑥ ⑩ ② ⑦ ⑪ ⑤ ⑧ ⑫
Chemicals	③	② ⑤	① ⑦ ④ ⑧ ⑥
Metal, Textile, Sugar, Pulp, Cement	④	① ⑥ ③ ⑤	②

Note.
1. A number referred to each type of industry in the figure inside copes with a number according to a type of industry in Table 1.2.
2. One circled number in the figure shows the case of a merger, an acquisition or a tie-up.

Fig. 1.5. Combination partners (by industry).

	Compressions of New investment	Research and development expense	Manufacturing costs	Sale costs, Management costs, Distribution costs	Integration or compression of facilities
Semiconductor and High technology	④ ⑩ ⑥ ⑫ ⑦ ⑬	① ⑥ ⑬	① ② ⑫		
Automobile Industry	⑧ ⑨	④ ⑨ ⑤ ⑫ ⑧	③ ⑦ ⑫ ④ ⑧ ⑤ ⑥		
Chemicals	①	④ ⑧	③ ⑥ ⑧ ⑤	② ③ ⑤	② ③
Metal, Textile, Sugar, Pulp, Cement			④ ⑤	① ⑥ ④ ⑤	⑥

Note.
1. A number referred to each type of industry in the figure inside copes with a number according to a type of industry in Table 1.2.
2. One circled number in the figure shows the case of a merger, an acquisition or a tie-up.

Fig. 1.6. Contents of cost reduction (by industry).

excessive competition and survival in a market are, conversely, main aims in non-growth fields. Thus, aggressiveness in management in the purpose of market correspondence becomes the form that has followed the ILC stage and the position on PLC of the industrial main product.

In addition to the above, research and development, technology development, technology grants and technical supplements are also incentives for companies to merge. This also leads to the reduction of research and development expenses. There are chances for companies to advance to new fields, and a technology supplement to a company gives increased diversity. Research and development for the establishment of the industry standard is also contained, seeking the expansion of market rule and power. "Market correspondence" includes joint management with a shift to the actual market place. It included the maintenance of a domestic industry share or the expansion of an international market, too.

This will be discussed in relation to ILC and PLC. The pace of innovation rises rapidly in growth fields. In that case, the success or failure of the realization of values added by the application of advanced technology directly controls the profit structure of a company. So a market can be lost or sales can be lost to another company if there is a delay in production. This can be an advantage to a competing company if the opposite happens.

Therefore, in companies in high technology fields, competition in research and development is more intense. In such companies, there are many opportunities when the unexpected development of relationships between companies can be found.

2.5. *Partners in relationships between companies*

The combinations of relationships with partner companies are shown in Fig. 1.5. The combination of relationships between companies that are in different company groups and different subsidiaries are widely distributed. However, there is an international combination of prosperous companies in growth industries that are strong in competitive power in ILC and PLC. However, there are also a few company reorganizations in the same groups when they are growth companies, and there are many reorganizations in the non-growth field.

There is no figure for this but, in the newspaper, there are articles on examples of reorganisation with existing series and company groups. Combinations between unexpected industry types by technical mutual agreement in a market are also shown. If there is agreement of a profit relationship between both companies even if two companies compete, these companies may become active in a tie-up. This is conspicuous in growth fields.

2.6. *Motives behind the combination of enterprises*

Next, the motives for forming relationships between enterprises are explained. Table 1.3 shows the various motives behind mergers and acquisitions, based on the Fair Trade Commission Annual Report of each year.[7] Only the facts of mergers and acquisitions are discussed here, and the backgrounds or purposes to these mergers are not touched on; also, tie-ups are not mentioned. Therefore, there is not enough information here to be aware of the total strategic decision making behind company reorganizations, but this information is useful enough to investigate the motives of these enterprises.

Table 1.3. Motives of merger and acquisition.

Year	Agreement of partners	Policy of a parent company	Policy of common chief shareholders	Recommend by main bank	Recommend by client	Lesson by an administrative agency	The others	Total
1975	124 (11.5)%	370 (34.4)%	523 (48.6)%	12 (1.1)%	16 (1.5)%	31 (2.9)%	1 (0.0)%	1,077 (100.0)%
1980	200 (23.0)%	363 (41.7)%	293 (33.6)%	1 (0.1)%	1 (0.1)%	8 (0.9)%	5 (0.6)%	871 (100.0)%
1985	599 (52.0)%	307 (27.6)%	176 (15.8)%	11 (1.0)%	6 (0.5)%	15 (1.4)%	19 (1.7)%	1,103 (100.0)%
1990	796 (45.5)%	597 (34.1)%	282 (16.1)%	14 (0.8)%	8 (0.5)%	18 (1.0)%	36 (2.1)%	1,751 (100.0)%
1993	866 (45.2)%	637 (33.2)%	291 (15.2)%	11 (0.6)%	10 (0.5)%	6 (0.3)%	96 (5.0)%	1,917 (100.0)%

Source: An annual report of the Fair Trade Commission (each year).

It is because their strategic decision-making is shown plainly that these companies have been selected to be discussed.

Table 1.3 shows the chronological order of changes in the motives behind mergers and acquisitions. As "agreement of partners" increases, we can see that "policy of common chief shareholders" decreases. It is a characteristic of mergers that the reverse phenomenon is not seen. That is to say, there is an increase in independent combinations of companies that do not depend on government and the leadership of a common chief shareholder. The reason for this is because the advancement of competitive power cannot be anticipated in company reorganization inside existing company groups or series companies.

2.7. Cost reduction strategies in relationships between Japanese companies

2.7.1. Cost reduction and ILC/PLC

ILC and PLC and the cost reduction strategies in relationships between Japanese companies will be explained next. The objectives of cost reduction change depending on where the types of industries or companies are located in ILC; or the characteristics of products change depending on what kinds of PLC are produced. These are classified as "Compression of new investment", "Research and development expenses", "Manufacturing costs", "Sale costs", "Management costs", "Distribution costs" and "Integration or compression of facility". Figure 1.6 shows this classification that is based on the classification of the Value Chain.

The compression/dispersion of new investment risks is called "Compression of new investment"; and "Manufacturing costs" in this chapter means the reduction of general manufacturing costs. This is realised by utilising a shared product supply, parts supply, and by practising joint production. This contains product promotion of efficiency by scale merit investigation. "Integration or compression of facility" means the joint disposal of surplus production facilities or bringing product facilities together. Companies can also have two or three simultaneous objectives for cost reduction.

Figure 1.6 shows the characteristics of cost reduction that are distributed throughout ILC and PLC. In the growth industries or strong competitive industries, "Compression of new investment", and "Research and development expenses" appear several times. In non-growth industries, the appearance of "Sale costs", "Management costs", and "Distribution costs" increase adversely, and the integration of facilities is common.

Thus we can see that the contents and purposes of cost reduction are different even if the fact of the construction of the relationships between companies is the same. Thus in high-technology industries or in existing industries, the objects of cost reduction effort are different. In the same way, the goals of cost reduction in growth industries are different from those in non-growth industries.

2.7.2. *Cost reduction for new investment, research and development expenses*

In industries such as the semiconductor industry, there is a reason for "new investment" becoming a target of cost reduction. The burden of new equipment investment and the dispersion of investment risks become topics for management in industries such as this.

Even if a company is provided with technology and its technical knowledge is cultivated by research and development, this knowledge may not be promptly translated to the production stage. This is research and development in a fundamental or applicable field. In order for a switchover to the production stage to be effected, there is a need for a large amount of equipment investment. This increases the compression of new investment to be turned into a target of cost reduction, along with research and development expenses. Because of rapid increases in research and development expenses, the pressure for increased equipment investment becomes an increasing burden for a company.

For example, in the fields of memory and medical supplies of a semiconductor, such trends are strong. In the case of research and development of memory for a personal computer, a large amount of investment is necessary. In such companies, tie-ups for research and development in a new field are common. There are also many tie-ups in order to seek reductions in research and development costs. It is quite common that the partners in such tie-ups are foreign or rival companies, especially in fields where the establishment of an industry standard would realise overwhelming superiority in the world market.

2.7.3. *Strategy reduction of manufacturing costs*

A major aim in each industry is to reduce manufacturing costs. This promotion of efficiency becomes the basis of cost reduction in manufacturing industries.

Manufacturing costs are also a target of cost reduction in the automobile industry. This is related to the accumulation of effort for manufacturing costs reduction in this industry which has continued from the past. Its strong competition in today's international market has been cultivated and aided by steady cost reduction. Therefore, the automobile industry, which leads current Japanese exports, is continuing to make an effort to reduce manufacturing costs by tie-ups.

The objectives of tie-ups are not limited to a field of peripheral parts. There are tie-ups for the standardization of mainstay parts represented by engines or a frame integration. International tie-ups take place for the specialization on products or sales.

2.7.4. *Sales, management costs and distribution costs*

On the other hand, industries that turn sale costs, management costs and distribution costs into targets of reduction are seen in the non-growth field of ILC. This is similar to the integration or compression of facilities. In such industries, one can see many relationships between companies for the reduction of costs such as management and distribution costs, as well as for production adjustments and the integration of production facilities.

The background to this is that production systems or demand structures cannot anticipate dramatic changes in these industries, and it is difficult for new companies to enter these fields. Accordingly, for cost reduction in the whole enterprise, sale costs, management costs and distributing costs must be reduced. These are balanced by reductions in costs through the integration of facilities and so on.

2.8. *Relationships between companies*

2.8.1. *The semiconductor industry*

The semiconductor industry is a strong growth field in the Japanese manufacturing industry, and it is strong in competition in the international market. In this field, intense share expansion competition over the world market is prosperous, and influential companies in developed nations compete fiercely for innovation and research and development. So, forms of relationships between companies in this field are dramatic.

All 13 cases referred to here deal with tie-ups (see Table 1.1). The aims of these tie-ups are as follows: Cost reduction (9), Research and development (8), Market correspondence (4) (Fig. 1.3). There are three companies which have partners outside their company group, while there are ten international combinations (Fig. 1.4). However, reorganization within a group is not seen.

In this case, the major objects of cost reduction are manufacturing costs and new investments, followed by research and development expenses (Fig. 1.6). In tie-ups concerned with research and development and technological knowledge, the establishment of industry standards are a major incentive (Fig. 1.5), and, in market correspondence, the incentives are the expansion and maintenance of an international market, and the reinforcement power of market control by established international industrial standards.

In this way, in relationships between companies in the semiconductor industry, we can see that the advancement of competitive power in the international market is important. The aim of this is the establishment of a production system which is more technologically advanced, therefore the introduction of technology from a partner company and joint research and development are important considerations. In these cases, it becomes part of company strategy to lead the formation of the international industry standard together with partner companies.

2.8.2. *The automobile industry*

In the automobile industry, Mergers and purchases (1), as well as Tie-ups (11) are seen (Table 1.1). The merger and tie-up of Mazda by U.S. Ford is an example of the right of management acquisition.

Cost reduction (8), and Market correspondence (6) are found to be the most important reasons for seeking tie-ups. The objects of cost reduction are manufacturing costs, research and development expenses, and the compression of new investment (Fig. 1.6). In Market correspondence, relationships are mainly between the companies that aim at the expansion and maintenance of international markets. There are two partnerships of companies outside the company group, but mainly we see International combinations of companies (9) (Fig. 1.4). Thus, in this industry, relationships between companies are created as a cost reduction strategy to secure predominance in international markets. In tie-ups, product and parts supply are the major objectives; and there is most construction of relationships between companies of different nationalities (7).

2.8.3. *The chemical industry*

The industries described until now represent growth industries. Non-growth industries are described next. The petrochemical industry is an example of a heavy, large type of processing industry, which is exposed to low home demand and severe international competition with influential foreign companies.

The different forms of relationships between these companies are as follows: Merger (1), Acquisition (2), Tie-up (5). The occurrence of specific relationships such as mergers or acquisitions is high compared with the types of industry that discussed earlier (Table 1.1).

A merger (1) is a company reorganization within the same company group. The acquisitions (2) are cases of Japanese companies being purchased by strong foreign competitors. Cost reduction and market correspondence are the main purposes here (Fig. 1.4).

On the other hand, "combination" partners are next most common, viz. "Inside a group" (1), "Outside a group" (2), "International combination" (5). Compared with the two types of industry discussed earlier, there are few international relationships formed (Fig. 1.5).

The objectives of cost reduction are mainly distribution costs, manufacturing costs, sale costs and management costs; but research and development expenses and facility integration and compression are also seen (Fig. 1.6). The chemicals industry is inferior in competition in the international market and has little growth power compared with the two industries discussed before. One cost reduction strategy in such a case is applied to the existing manufacturing costs. This is because investments in a new field that depends on research and development are weaker than in growth fields.

In market correspondence and the maintenance of share in a home market, survival has become a major theme in the construction of relationships between domestic companies. On the other hand, in the cases of acquisition by foreign companies, Japanese companies are appointed to be one part of the partner.

2.8.4. *The metal, textile, sugar, pulp and cement industries*

Finally, declining industries which have large-scale facilities will be discussed. There are few newspaper articles on these (6). However, in the past they were large, important industries and were regularly discussed in the newspaper.

The forms of relationship found between these companies are Mergers (3), Acquisitions (1) and Tie-ups (2), so the relative importance of mergers is high (see Table 1.1). The purposes of these relationships are cost reduction and market correspondence (Fig. 1.4).

The objects of cost reduction are sale costs, management expenses and distribution costs. This trend is stronger than in the chemical industry, and this is a characteristic of relationships in these industries (Fig. 1.6). We have thus seen that the objectives of cost reduction in declining, "sunset" industries are focused on production systems more than in the chemical industry. It is one of the characteristics of sunset industries to have such positions on ILC and PLC.

3. Conclusion

The globalisation of markets and innovation in industry is rapidly increasing, and competition intensifies daily. A rapid realisation of this is demanded from cost reduction strategies in such a management environment. Therefore it is likely that, in future, the combination of enterprises such as mergers or tie-ups will increase. These are influential techniques for strategic cost reduction in Japanese companies, but only in an ambiguous way to take in outside management resources, as the combination of enterprises may not be useful for cost reduction. In aiming strategic cost reduction at a combination of enterprises, the important criteria must not be forgotten.

This important factor is the understanding of relative company positions on ILC and PLC of each company and its partner companies. The objects or purposes of cost reduction to meet ILC or PLC are fixed. The partner companies will be selected which fit the other company's requirements, and it will thus be possible to achieve effective cost reduction.

It is thought generally that a common approach to ILC and PLC is effective in combination with a new partner. However, there is a way of combining companies when this common approach is not found. This can clarify whether the costs of various parts can be reduced by comparing a company's own ILC and PLC with its partner's ILC and PLC. Paying attention to ILC and PLC can increase the possibility of the success of cost reduction in the strategic construction of relationships between companies.

References

1. Wakasugi, A., M & A no Zaimu Kaikei Senryaku (Bijinesu Kyouiku Shuppansha, 1989), 4–7.
2. Morikawa, H. & Yonekura, S., Nippon Keieisha 5 (Iwanami Shoten, 1995), 14–17.

3. Nakamura, J. & Takayanagi, A., Keieigaku Education, Third Edition (Yuhikaku, 1987), 262–266.
4. The Nihon Keizai Shinbun; Date or abstracts of newspaper articles are printed in Table 1.2.
5. Morikawa & Yonkers, Nippon Keieisha 5 (Iwanami Shoten, 1995), 12–13.
6. Morikawa & Yonekura, Nippon Keieisha 5 (Iwanami Shoten, 1995), 11–12.
7. Fair Trade Commission, Fair Trade Commission Annual Report (1975,1980,1985,1990,1993).

Chapter 2

Strategic Cost Reduction Through Mutual Relationships Between Companies, Industry Groups and Government

KOZO SUZUKI

1. The Structure of Strategic Cost Reduction in Japan Today

In Chap. 1, cost reduction strategies by the construction of relationships between companies was discussed. In this chapter, cost reduction by traditional company relationships is discussed, along with the behaviour styles of Japanese companies today are also considered, along with the historical point of view. Cost reduction strategies on the basis of traditional company relationships have the following characteristics: the existence of cost reduction by government-led lessons and instructions to companies, industry groups and company groups. Figure 2.1 shows this structure, showing cost reduction in the Japanese manufacturing industry and the relationship between each sector. The mutual functions of a company, industry groups, company groups and government are shown.

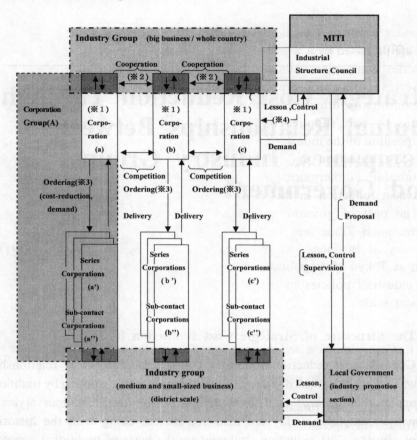

Fig. 2.1. The mutual relationships between the industry group, company group and the MITI on cost reduction.

1.1. *Cost reduction strategies by industry groups and company groups*

In Japan, industry groups have promoted the cost reduction in an individual company belonging to these groups. They are formed from companies belonging to the same type of industry. Between member companies, sometimes there is no relationship of bargaining and there are several cases of rival companies joining up together. On the other hand, under the policies of leader companies of the group, there are some cost reduction strategies that are practised by a whole company group. This company group consists of series companies mainly.[1]

Series companies are constituted, based on hierarchical business relationships to affect processes of production. There are many company groups by part supplies in manufacturing industry. Cost reduction by interposition of the industry group can be shown as a horizontal relationship, and cost reduction put into practice in company group by a vertical relationship. Furthermore, government participation is found in other matters than cost reduction in this horizontal and vertical relationship.

The part of government being discussed here is the Ministry of International Trade and Industry (MITI) and it is an antecedent of the Ministry of Business and Industry. It is made up of local governments, such as Tokyo Metropolitan Government and some prefectures, which put the industrial policies of the MITI into operation in various districts on a local scale.

1.1.1. *Cost reduction led by the industry groups*

It is assumed that the industry groups today have the following functions:[2]

1. Pressure group function
2. Trustee or operator of policy and accomplishment function
3. Cartel function
4. Information creation function.

By acting as a pressure group, industry groups demand concessions such as the grant of a subsidy or the regulation of imports from the MITI. The promotion and marketing of the industry as a whole is also demanded.

These are actions which demand profitable policy for the specific industry. The cartel function tries to limit competition. On the other hand, cost reduction is also realized through product agreement, price adjustment and some industry adjustments. The progress of production efficiency has been attempted by co-operation between companies that belong to the same industry group.

A major purpose of this production efficiency investigation is quality improvement and the reduction of production costs which will extend to the whole industry. As a result, companies in many different industrial sectors have been able to achieve both quality progress and the reduction of production cost.

In the continuing process of Japanese industrialization, cost reductions of the kinds shown in Fig. 2.1 that the industry groups led have been continued (Fig. 2.1, ※1). These include the improvements in methods of supplying raw materials and manufacturing technology, simplification of products, efficiency of facilities and technical promotions, research and development, increased productivity of labour, improvement of selling, and rearrangement of capital. These factors raised the competitive powers of all subsidiary companies of the industry group.

These are carried out together by one company and another company, when there is no leadership of the industry group, thus aiming at co-existence and co-prosperity in the existing market. Co-operation is attempted if both companies agree, even if the companies are rivals. (Fig. 2.1, ※2). Conversely, the importance of limiting competition in the industry group shows that competition between companies is intense. Therefore, inside control by the industry groups is necessary. Such industry groups and mutual dependence relationships between the industry group and government have existed in Japan from the old days. As will be described later, such partnerships can date back to the Edo period, the pre-war period or the Meiji era.[3]

There are the following factors in a background of such industry groups in Japan. Historically, in many cases, the whole industry has been turned into a constitution of excessive competition that intensifies the competition between existing companies and new companies entering the market. Those practises destroyed customs in a business transaction, and the management of each such company belonging to the same type of industry was threatened.

Such circumstances were linked with the behaviour pattern of the company and the industry. It is true that the enterprises planned to limit competition between and reject outsiders, using the influence of the government and the insider control of the industry as the alliance of individual companies.

1.1.2. *Cost reduction in company groups*

On the other hand, the core companies in company groups (makers of the finished product) always demand cost reduction, better quality, shorter appointed date of delivery times for subsidiary subcontracting companies. Therefore reduction of production cost has been investigated in many subcontractors (Fig. 2.1, ※3).

Dual structure is a characteristic of the structure of Japanese industry. This means that under a few big businesses, many medium size or small size contractors exist. In this dual structure, cost reduction of the subcontractors is connected directly with cost reduction strategies in the parent factory.

Therefore, strategic decision-making for cost reduction in the parent factory is applied to cost reduction of the subcontractors. The most effective cost reduction for makers of the finished products is to reduce the cost of parts delivered by the subcontractors.

In this way, cost reduction of the whole company group has been realized. Such cases are often seen in a field where the specialization system has been established between makers of the finished product and part makers, and in fields of intense competition. The automobile industry is a good example.

1.2. *Cost reduction in industry as a whole by government participation*

The MITI has promoted the efficiency of industries by preparing some new acts and industrial policies (Fig. 2.1, ※4). The Temporary Promotion Measures on Mechanical Industry Law (the first such law) in 1956 was one of these. By increasing standards in technology across the whole machine industry, it realized improvements in management in medium and small-sized business, the promotion of production efficiency, and this in turn guided cost reduction.

The purpose of this law was to increase standards in technology in the whole mechanical industry. This in turn led to management efficiency, productivity and cost reduction of medium and small-sized businesses. The development of the part makers and the peripheral industries were also important for assembly makers. For example, the automobile industry is supported by the accumulation of many part makers and machine tool makers. In Japan, most of these part makers and machine tool makers are medium or small-sized businesses. So, the promotion of medium or small-sized businesses is indispensable to technological progress and cost reduction in the whole industry. The requirements for the advancement of assembly makers in big-businesses were prepared by a law.

The government also promoted company reorganization as mergers. It saw this as a means to make use of the scale merit in order to realize rationalization and modernization in each industry. The Temporary Promotion Measures on Mechanical Industry Law (the second, in 1961), set out measures on the taxation system for mergers and co-operation between enterprises.[4] This was in order to establish the system of large-scale production that was necessary for reinforcement of competition in the international machine industry market. Furthermore, by the Temporary Promotion Measures on Mechanical Industry Law (the third, in 1966), the MITI emphasised the reinforcement of export competitive power. In this law, the grouping of companies was prescribed in order to promote specialization of production and concentration of production. Limitations were placed on some kinds of produce (by cartel), and the standardization and co-operation of production and sale were introduced.[5]

Industry groups consisting of medium or small-sized businesses are usually organized in range of the Metropolis or prefectures. There are many groups that are made up of subcontract groups of the larger groups in Japan.

Thus, local public entities gave lessons and guidance to district groups and local groups, and the national industry groups also acted in the same way. However, local public entities and the whole country groups put those functions into operation under supervision and guidance of the MITI.

1.3. *Functions of Industrial Structure Council*

The MITI, in drafting industrial policy, made enquires to the consultative body, the Industrial Structure Council. The opinions expressed in the council are made use of in the MITI for future policy making. The Industrial Structure Council was established in April 1964, as the permanent consultative body of the MITI. Their purpose is to "discuss important matters about industrial structure". It has the following functions:[6]

1. The function of deliberation for making important policies.
2. The function of investigation and deliberation for directional long-term or fundamental policies.

Members of council are selected from representative people of the business and the specified industries, bureaucratic alumnus, journalists, scholars and men of experience. They are appointed by the MITI. In the council, opinions of interest of the business are discussed. The policies are assessed by scholars and men of experience. By such methods, the council also justifies the policies of the MITI.[7]

Two phases of co-ordination[8] exist between the MITI and companies, the Industrial Structure Council and the industry groups that form this structure. Because of this system, the co-operation and joint ownership of information and consensus to policy has been formed between government and companies.

2. Case Study of the Automobile Industry

The MITI has not always been able to put such policies into operation. The MITI tried to reorganise the automobile industry, but it strongly resisted this reorganization. Therefore there was little realization of mergers or tie-ups of existing makers.

After the 1950s, the MITI established its economic advancement policy that laid emphasis on the automobile industry, and it had started to gain support for its policies. It was based on the recognition that the progress of the automobile industry was necessary for the advancement of the Japanese industrial structure and the acquisition or saving of foreign currency. The above-mentioned Temporary Promotion Measures on Mechanical Industry Law, was one of these such policies.

During the age of advanced economic growth, the policy for the automobile industry of the MITI consisted of conservation systems, subsidy policies and reorganization of the industry. Upon reorganization of the industry, the following policies were announced.[9]

1. A plan to increase production of a popular-priced car (in 1955),
2. The design of the grouping of the automobile makers (in 1961),
3. The proposition to the Congress of the "Special Industrial Promotion Measures Bill" (in 1962),
4. Restriction of tie-ups or joint capital with foreign makers (after 1964).

By (1), the MITI established conditions such as price, displacement volume, and the highest speed per hour. It let each make. design a car in a trial manufacture in line with the above conditions. It also subsidised the makers who made trial cars which were classed as "excellent" cars. So, the mass production of cars was attempted. (2) was a target of the MITI to reorganise the automobile industry in the following three groups:[10]

1. A group which would produce mass produced cars,
2. A group to produce vehicles with a large carrying capacity,
3. A group to produce small cars.

The purpose for policies were to prepare for a domestic industrial system by co-operation between public agencies and private enterprise, so that it could cope with the liberalization of trade and of capital transactions. The automobile industry had become the subject of increased reinforcement of competition in the international market. Therefore, expanding the scale of production and management was aided by company mergers, specialization of production and cooperation between enterprises.[11]

The purposes of these changes were the reinforcement of competition in the international automobile industry. Therefore, the combination of companies to realize scale merit was regarded as important. However, each maker strongly objected to (1), for they thought this was contrary to equal opportunities and free competition. Makers, except Toyota and Nissan, opposed (2) so neither option happened;[12] (3) was withdrawn because the industry regarded the independent adjustment as being more important than co-operation between public agencies and private enterprise.

On the other hand, by the leadership of the MITI, the reorganization of some existing makers was brought about. Examples include the merger between Nissan and Prince Motor in 1965, the tie-up between Toyota, Hino and Diahatsu in 1966–67 and the tie-up between Nissan and Fuji Juko in 1969. But all other mergers and tie-ups ended in failure and, in spite of the policy of restraint of new entry, Honda and Diahatsu entered the car market.

Similarly, (4) was broken in 1969 by the establishment of Mitsubishi Motors with joint capital from Mitsubishi Heavy Industries and Chrysler.

In times of advanced economic growth, the abolition of conservation policies for the Japanese automobile industry could not be avoided. For example, the government had decided on a basic policy to liberalize exchange trade, in 1958, and the liberalization of trade in participation with OECD (in 1964) increased because of the internal demand for the liberalization of the automobile industry.

Under such environments, competition for capital investment developed between each automobile maker. Japanese automobile makers hurried the construction of mass-production factories for new large-scale cars. This was necessary in order to compete with European and American makers. It could be seen every time that when the MITI proposed a new policy, newcomers rushed into the market one after another. As a result, the Japanese automobile industry consisted of 11 companies by the latter half of the 1960s. This rapid completion of building was not seen in any rival advanced industry country.[13] Because of intense competition with other internal makers and foreign makers, cost reduction has been always the important subject in management of the Japanese automobile industry, in order to reinforce Japanese competitive powers. This became a driving force behind the formation of the just in time (JIT) system.

3. Cost Reduction in the Iron and Steel Industry

In Japan, cost reduction was practised in the field of many industries for about 50 years after World War II. In the case of the iron and steel industry, co-operation between government and private enterprise and movements in the industry for cost reduction were keenly watched. Strategies of cost reduction that suited the industrial life cycle (ILC) and processes of evolution were eventually found. Strategies for cost reduction of government, the industry group and individual companies have also been found, and the industry conditions that those change into, according to different stages of industrial evolution, are seen below in chronological order.

3.1. *Plans for rationalization*

The Japanese iron and steel industry had been under the conservation and control of the government for a long time. The first modern ironworks in Japan were the Yahata Ironworks managed by the government that started operation in 1897. During World War II, iron and steel makers were gathered into the Japan Steel Corporation by government policy. Especially in the war, government control over the industry was strengthened remarkably as follows:

A ration system of iron and scrap steel was started in 1938 and in 1941 the Iron and Steel Control Society was established. The Ministry of Business and Industry had also directly managed major iron manufacture factories in 1943.

After the war, the government adopted the "priority production system". It was their policy to bring about increases in production by the prior injection of resources in an attempt to revive the economy. The steel industry was positioned as a key industry with the coal industry, the electrical industry and the shipping industry. However, under the retrenchment policies of Dodge-line, the independence of the Japanese economy through industrial rationalization and increasing exports became the policy of the government. By the policy, the government urged each industry to prevent the decrease of their operation and product.

The MITI submitted the "Rationalization of Iron and Steel Industry Law" Bill to Congress in 1949. This included permission for the new equipment investment to a limited scale and the exclusion of the application of Antitrust Law and the re-organization of the company by leadership of the government. The iron and steel industry group welcomed the relaxing of the restraint of cartel. The investment into equipment of each iron and steel maker was excellent. Therefore, the industry group objected to this together, and the government's policy failed.[14]

On the other hand, the boom period of special procurement demands was brought on by the Korean War (1950–51). At this time, each iron and steel makers made "Plans for Rationalization of Facility" to a total of 1,200 hundred million yen. This led to the Iron and Steel Section of the Industrial Rationalization Council report "The report on rationalization of iron and steel industry" for 1951–53. These contents were compressed by half of the plan that the industry had made, and the plan called "The First Plan of Rationalization of Iron and Steel" was extended until 1955.

The Industrial Rationalization Council is the antecedent of the Industrial Structure Council. According to the report above, the rationalization plans of each iron and steel maker were made. The pursuit of scale merit by making larger and more modern facilities was begun in earnest. As for the system of iron manufacture, the conversion from the old-type of pullover to the strip mill (a rolling mill of continuous type) was attempted. By "The First Plan", the iron and steel industry had achieved a large cost reduction of 14% in the iron sector.[15] Similarly, a cost reduction of 12% had been achieved in the pig iron sector. By "The Second Plan of Rationalization of Iron and Steel" (1956–60), every company had built full-scale facilities of continuous production which converted pig iron to steel. Japanese factories and equipment, such as the strip mill and the pure oxygen converter, were the newest and most modern in the world in those days. Because of this investment into plant and equipment, production on a larger scale became possible, such as producing car bodies and decoration of household electric appliances. This made the production of iron and steel in Japan equal to that of the U.S. and West Germany.[16]

"The Second Plan" formed the grand total of every company's investment programs.

"The Third Plan of Rationalization of Iron and Steel" was set out in 1961. In the first and second plans, the government had built on industry trends and had made the rationalization plans. Based on those, each company planned their facilities and investment programs. However, in "The Third

Plan", the independent opinions and plans of the industry were regarded as important. This time, the Social Gathering of Iron and Steel Industry led the making of the plan, with backup from the MITI.

The Japan Iron and Steel League and the Club of Iron and Steel then became the secretariat, and the investigation staff of the iron and steel companies began to prepare the plan, which included the following:[17]

1. The designs of the new ironworks (superior in scale and production)
2. The realization of the design of the industrial complex
3. The enforcement of self-adjustment of facilities
4. The enlargement of the investment into facilities.

In this plan, the role of the MITI was to act as watchdog over the implementation of the adjustments to the iron and steel industry.[18]

3.2. *The limits of co-operation and the MITI's change of function*

The investment into equipment by the iron and steel industry increased rapidly, through the first to the third rationalization plans, thus triggering the investigation of cost reduction through equipment investment. For example, the cost reduction gained by increasing the quantity of heavy oil and reducing of ratio of coke; the increase in efficiency of iron and steel production by the spread of strip mills; the speeding up of production by automation and the use of computers.

On the other hand, recession influenced the industry and led to over-production and excessive competition. As anti-depression measures, the Open Sale System of Iron and Steel was organized under the administrative guidance of the MITI in 1958. At a time of depression in 1962, the market price of steel materials fell heavily. However, this system did not work, because a lot of makers sold cheaply in the depression, even if industry co-operation was kept and a price was agreed on at the time of prosperity. The MITI decided on new measures in June of the same year. These measures included the reinforcing of the reduced output and supervision of the agreed price, as well as financial support to medium or small size companies which were sold cheaply when they became unprofitable.

The Japan Iron and Steel League was one of the industry groups that decided that supervision on the Open Sale System too should be practised; but despite these measures, the bearish tone of the market continued. The effect of adjustment of the MITI was limited, having the effect of the adjustment of production and the agreement of sale by industry co-operation. However, measures to decrease the production of crude steel, in order to conquer the depression, were adopted by MITI-led lessons over 1962–63 and 1970–71.

During 1962–63, counter-measures to the market were put into operation to decrease the production of steel materials and crude steel. This was done after the MITI approved the plan of reducing output which was agreed by 40 companies joining to the Open Sale System. Between 1970 and 1971, this was done under the guidance of the MITI.

However, the Sumitomo Metal Industries objected to the method of reducing output by independent adjustment of the industry group, and it refused administrative guidance of the MITI and the attempted persuasion of other iron manufacture makers, and continued with its original production. The MITI punished this company by limiting the company's allotment on imports of coal and raw materials. In this way, the independence adjustment over prolonged planning of facilities had become difficult. This was because every company wanted to invest in equipment with economic growth. As a result, in 1961, eight blast furnaces entrusted their adjustment to the MITI.

In this way, the industry co-operation became more workable, so the adjustment of some product field was taken and series companies were developed. This product field was made of blast furnace makers, flat converter makers and medium or small-sized makers. In addition to this, in 1966, the Industrial Structure Council made a report to the Minister of International Trade and Industry. It was important to gain future international competitive power by gathering investment and improving management.[19]

3.3. *Merger of the Yahata Iron Manufacture and the Fuji Iron Manufacture*

The merger of Yahata and Fuji was announced in 1968. This is known as the greatest merger in Japan after the war. It was the merger of the top two companies in the iron and steel industry, and in March 1970 the merger went through. In 1950, Japan Iron Manufacture has been dissolved by the Decentralization Law established in 1948 by indication of the General Headquarters (GHQ), and both companies were established from JIM. This merger was selected as a result of the independent strategy of both companies and, as a result, the greatest company in Japan today was born. Their market share exceeded 30% for about 20 items. Capital stock was 2,294 hundred million yen. Their total assets were 12,587 hundred million yen. Annual turnover was 8,000 hundred million yen. One of the reasons why both companies had selected each partner to merge with was because both companies had demanded a return to old Japan Iron Manufacture. But it was more important that the products of those companies and the scale of each company had been resembled. Thus, by the merger, the loss of JIM had been combined into one company which shared productive facilities, the facilities of circulative processing, and research facilities.[20] Both companies announced that their purposes behind the merger had been:[21]

1. An increase in efficiency of equipment investment, such as investment by priority system, construction of large-sized facilities and its effective operation,
2. The reinforcement of technological developing powers by concentrating the research systems and the promotion of efficiency of a large amount of research and development investment,
3. The effective distribution of raw materials by prolonged contracts and rationalization of conveyance,
4. The rationale of concentration and distribution of the product and measurement of the standard,
5. The rejection of mixture conveyance of products by the regional regulation of supply and demand,
6. The integration and reinforcement of the sales section, and a simplification of the circulative processing section,
7. The increased use of computers and the development of the computer system.

Many kinds of purposes can thus be seen in the construction of relationship between these companies for strategic cost reduction.

Beside, the merits shown in (1) and (2) are common in the purposes of constructing relationships between companies in fields of growth, such as the semiconductor industry and the automobile industry today. In relationships between companies in the current iron and steel industry, (3) and (6) are seen, but the positive combinations of (1) and (2) have not been very common. Here, a contrast is seen between the iron and steel industry of the past and the industry today. Thirty years ago, this industry was one of growth but today, the industry has fallen into a decline.

The iron and steel industry in 1968 was the leading industry and had strong competition in the international market. There was great technical advancement in iron manufacture, and research and development for promotion of efficiency. As mentioned in Chap. 1, when relationships between companies are created for cost reduction, the kinds of costs to become objects of reduction are decided to suit the stage of Industrial Life Cycle (ILC) that the industry belongs to. The iron and steel industry can be used as an example here; by comparing the cost reduction in this industry in chronological order, the relationship between the objects of cost reduction and the ILC is proved.

The targets of relationships between companies and of cost reduction must be appropriate for the degree of industrial evolution that the company has undergone. If the industry is strengthened by growth, the leadership or intervention of the government to make relationships between companies will decrease. Thus, strategic decision-making in the enterprise becomes more important.

4. Mutual Relationships between Government and the Industry Group

4.1. *The chronological continuation of behaviour patterns of the companies, the industry groups and government*

Before World War II, the function of the Japanese industry groups included the restriction of competition, keeping of labour forces on the basis of co-operation, the supply of raw materials, expansion of the market, financing and collection of information. Collectively, these functions were "the Industrial Rationalization". These have also continued as the functions of the industry groups after the war.[22] Nevertheless, some people are of the opinion that the characteristics of the industry group after the war are different from pre-war characteristics. For example, one opinion is that "There is a Japanese industry group between government and individual companies, which has a function to reduce non-symmetry of information. It is a characteristic of the controlled economy in the wartime."[23]

There is also the opinion that the "two phases of co-ordination", as mentioned above, occurred after the latter half of the 1940s.

The latter opinion can be affirmed. Certainly, it was in the latter half of the 1940s that the mutual relationship between the government, the industry groups and companies became what it is today. The antecedent of the Industrial Structure Council was established in those ages. But the organization of enterprises in the same profession has functioned as a trustee or operator of policy of government for a long time. The organization of those enterprises in the same profession has had the function of autonomous adjustment. Traditionally in Japan, industry groups such as autonomous organizations work as subcontractors of the government.

Of course, the kind and the character of companies constituting the industry group marches with the times. Most of the industry group were based in the circulation business and the finance business until the first half of the Meiji era, but the behaviour styles of each sector in the mutual relationship between the government, the industry group, and companies have been one part of the style of the Japanese economical system since the Edo period.

4.2. *Relationships between companies during industrial rationalization*

A publication that shows cost reduction in the industry group, and the relationship between it and the government from before World War II to after the war in Japan is "autonomous industrial control in the industrial rationalization times" published in 1951 by the MITI.[24]

It reproduces the magazine which The Japan Chamber of Commerce and Industry published in 1933. It also contains the commentary of Dr. Takao Tsuchiya, who edited the History of Business and Industry Administration of the MITI in 1951. The Ministry of Business and Industry took some measures against the world financial crisis in 1929. These major measures were the encouragement of industrial rationalization and the increased use of domestic product.[25]

This policy had consisted of two main points. The first was a cost reduction in product engineering and management by each individual company. The second was the control by a cartel and the control of guild that had been done mutually by similar companies. The latter is the rationalization by autonomous industrial control described in the book I mentioned above. It also describes the core of industrial policy of this country in the time of panic in the early years of the Showa era (1929–32).[26]

The next two points were characteristics of the policy by the "Autonomous industrial control". The first was that, the industry groups of each field made autonomous adjustment of production such as cartel. The second was that, those groups worked as trustee or operator of the Ministry of Business and Industry, and put its policies into practice.

4.3. *Techniques in cost reduction of the industrial group*

This book described next is on cost reduction in the steel industry in the 1930s:[27]

"As the policy of rationalization of the iron industry in this country, there are rationalizations over organizations of companies like the agreement of control on products or sales and the rearranging and combining of enterprise."

"The rationalization of management is important, such as centralization of capital or simplification of products, and rationalizing on facility or technology."

"In particular the government and the private supplier have made efforts to enforce those policies."

Similarly, in the chapter entitled "The Cotton Yarn and Cotton-spinning Industry" in the book, the reasons why the industry had grown up remarkably since the Meiji era in Japan were deemed as follows.[28]

The first reason is that the, "manufacture of superior goods and reduction of product cost had been attempted by paying attention to always improving the buying methods of raw cotton, technology of manufacture and labour productivity", and that the "rationalization of management has been done effectively because of improvements in selling methods".

The second reason is that, "The industry turned its attention to control, and some measures had been taken to make sound developments in, and peaceful progress of, the business". The Japan Spinning Alliance Society was formed, and any waste by useless competition was removed by industry control. The whole industry had put cost reduction into operation co-operatively, which meant cost reduction by competition of individual enterprises. Those were connected directly with reinforcement of export competitive power. It was the most strategic field in Japan at that time.

On the other hand, it was said, "the history of control was the history of the development of the spinning industry in Japan". This expression shows the outcome of this problem, that the Ministry of Business and Industry had made much of the control by cartel through inside adjustment of the industry.

Besides, it is assumed that "if this industry had not paid attention to control, flooding of the business would have occurred, and the industry would have fallen into miserable confusion as a result of excessive competition, which may have destroyed it." That is to say, the government had recognized that the decline of the whole industry would be brought about by free competition shifting to excessive competition. Other people recognised this too. Therefore, the industry had put "inside adjustment through the group" into operation independently and co-operatively.

In this way, the relationship between the government and industry is seen, lying between the present age and the pre-war age, the Showa era and the Meiji era besides the Edo period. The success of Japanese industrialization after the Meiji era was accomplished through the existence of the companies that had continued investigating growth by their constant efforts to promote the efficiency of management. At the same time, it was very important that co-operation and specialization between the government, the industry groups and each private sector continued. So there was competition between companies, and opposition between each sector. However, as a whole, that had been instigated by the rise in the competitive power of export.

It is common to the Japanese government that it uses the industry groups that are based on autonomous inside control for its indirect control. And, in the private sector, it has also been a common practise to attempt the promotion of efficiency of management, and the co-existence and co-prosperity of each individual company by inside adjustment of its industry group.

5. Conclusion

The intensification of competition has progressed internationally, and the necessity of cost management has risen accordingly to produce well manufactured products cheaply. Therefore the costs that are necessary for the fundamental research and development for products and the industrialization of those products have risen rapidly, and it has become more important strategically to raise the ruling power in the world market. This is achieved by technology and cost reduction that are more superior to some companies than in others. However, these costs for that purpose are becoming enormous, and realising this quickly has become more important, too. And the cases are increasing so much so that individual companies cannot catch up with the competition within themselves. Such circumstances have invented significance in the present age, such as the construction of relationships between companies, co-operative behavior in the industry and government participation.[29]

Of course, now, there are a lot of problems in the relationship between the government and industry in Japan. There is much restriction of free competition, such as the administrative guidance and "The Escort Fleet System", which have produced a lot of structural rigidity and problems. But it is necessary to regard the function of cost reduction, that Japanese companies, industry groups and government have had as their behavior pattern, as important, after having conquered such problems, since for the continuing growth of companies, every management resource which can be utilised must be utilised. Therefore, in strategic decision-making for cost reduction, there is now an increasingly popular point of view that it is beneficial to get management resources from outside a company. The "outside" means companies taking partners, and co-operating with the whole industry and government. Thus we have seen how constructing relationships between companies, while retaining the behaviour patterns of Japanese companies, industry and government, has become useful and accepted as the method for strategic cost reduction.

References

1. Yamazaki, H. & Kikkawa, T., Nippon Keieishi 4 (Iwanami Shoten, 1995), 233–236.
2. Okazaki, T. & Okuno, M., Gendai Nihon Keizai Shisutemu no Genryu (Nihon Keizai Shinbunsha, 1993), 207.
3. Suzuki, K., Edo no Keizai Shisutemu (Nihon Keizai Shinbunsha, 1995), 92–93.
4. Tsusho Sangyo Seisakushi Hensan Iinkai, Tsusho Sangyo Seisakushi 10 (1990), 193.
5. Tsusho Sangyo Seisakushi Hensan Iinkai, Tsusho Sangyo Seisakushi 10 (1990), 197.
6. Tsusho Sangyo Seisakushi Hensan Iinkai, Tsusho Sangyo Seisakushi 10 (1990), 31.
7. Morikawa, H. & Yonekura, S., Nippon Keieishi 5 (Iwanami Shoten, 1995), 255.
8. Okazaki, T., Nihon no Seifu-Kigyou kan Kankei, Soshiki Kagaku, Vol. 26, No. 4, 1993, 188.
9. Morikawa, H. & Yonekura, S., Nippon Keieishi 5 (Iwanami Shoten, 1995), 266.
10. Tsusho Sangyo Seisakushi Hensan Iinkai, Tsusho Sangyo Seisakushi 10 (1990), 298–299.
11. Tsusho Sangyo Seisakushi Hensan Iinkai, Tsusho Sangyo Seisakushi 10 (1990), 74.
12. Morikawa, H. & Yonekura, S., Nippon Keieishi 5 (Iwanami Shoten, 1995), 266.
13. Morikawa, H. & Yonekura, S., Nippon Keieishi 5 (Iwanami Shoten, 1995), 268.
14. Morikawa, H. & Yonekura, S., Nippon Keieishi 5 (Iwanami Shoten, 1995), 262.

15. Morikawa, H. & Yonekura, S., Nippon Keieishi 5 (Iwanami Shoten, 1995), 260–261.
16. Yasuba, Y. & Inoki, T., Nippon Keizaishi 8 (Iwanami Shoten, 1989), 10–12.
17. Kawasaki, M., Sengo Tekkougyou Ron (Tekkou Shinbunsha, 1968), 193–194.
18. Tsusho Sangyo Seisakushi Hensan Iinkai, Tsusho Sangyo Seisakushi 10 (1990), 134–135.
19. Tsusho Sangyo Seisakushi Hensan Iinkai, Tsusho Sangyo Seisakushi 10 (1990), 170–172.
20. Tsusho Sangyo Seisakushi Hensan Iinkai, Tsusho Sangyo Seisakushi 10 (1990), 173–175.
21. Yahata Seitetsu & Fuji Seitetsu, Gappei Shushi (Yahata Seitetsu & Fuji Seitetsu, 1968).
22. Yamazaki, H. & Kikkawa, T., Nippon Keieishi 4 (Iwanami Shoten, 1995), 254.
23. Okazaki, T. & Okuno, M., Gendai Nihon Keizai Shistemu no Genryu (Nihon Keizai Shinbunsha, 1993), 207.
24. Tsushosangyo Daijin Kanbo Chosa Tokei bu, Sangyo Gourika Jidai no Jichiteki Sangyo Tosei (MITI, 1951).
25. Tsushosangyo Daijin Kanbo Chosa Tokei bu, Sangyo Gourika Jidai no Jichiteki Sangyo Tosei (MITI, 1951), 1.
26. Tsushosangyo Daijin Kanbo Chosa Tokei bu, Sangyo Gourika Jidai no Jichiteki Sangyo Tosei (MITI, 1951), 3.
27. Tsushosangyo Daijin Kanbo Chosa Tokei bu, Sangyo Gourika Jidai no Jichiteki Sangyo Tosei (MITI, 1951), 163–164.
28. Tsushosangyo Daijin Kanbo Chosa Tokei bu, Sangyo Gourika Jidai no Jichiteki Sangyo Tosei (MITI, 1951), 6.
29. Kawai, T., Nihon ni Okeru Seifu to Kigyo no Bimyo na Kankei, Soshiki Kagaku, Vol. 26, No. 4, 1993, 106–107.

Part 2
Cost Management in R&D

Chapter 3

Cost Management in R&D: A Side of Japanese Management

SHUNZO MATSUOKA

1. Introduction

I study the cost of basic research activity and applied research activities of Japanese corporations and investment management. I compare different methods of research and development management in companies such as Yukizirusinyuugyou Co., Ltd. and Nihonnseikousyo Co., Ltd. with traditional methods. I then examine their research and development budgets, their themes of research and development, project evaluation, budget distribution, the execution, management and activation of research and development activity, in order to let companies utilize their resources effectively and to increase their research and development activities.

2. Basic Research, Applied Research and Development Research

Research and development is classified into basic research, applied research, and development research by distinguishing various stages of activity and the manpower involved. The results of research and development activity are influenced by the time spent on research and by the ability of the research personnel required.

E. Maruyama is a chief engineer at the research and development headquarters of Hitachi Seisakusyo Co., Ltd., and he decides on what research

51

and development can be classified into basic research, application research, and development research in term of manpower.

Basic research is the source which gives life and vitality to the management of tomorrow. It has the possibility of bringing prospective profit to a company, and it may be said that the general purpose of basic research activities is to accumulate scientific knowledge with no relation to a specified commerce purpose.

If the manpower effect is represented with E (person × year), when an expression of inequality where

E (ten people × 1 year) < E (one person × 10 year) = research
becomes dependent on having the research manpower to carry
out basic research activities.

Basic research is the foundation of applied research and development research, but branch selection of applied research and development research may not necessarily be discovered in basic studies. One branch of basic research comes from applied research and is born from development research and production activity. Areas for applied and research development are not always necessarily derived from basic studies, there is no time to pursue this interesting branch traditionally. Interesting though this area of research is, it is not possible nowadays to focus on production only. Basic research must not be neglected in application research and development research from now on. This is what can act as the seedbed in a corporation whose strength is in their basic research section which brings up themes discovered from applied research, development research and production activity.

Applied research sets out to discover whether or not a product can utilize a principle that has been provided by basic physical and mechanical research. It may be said that application research consists of the research activity of research manpower which is located in between basic studies manpower and development research manpower, if it is classified in terms of manpower as follows:

E (ten person × 1 year) > research > E (one person × 10 year).

Development research is the overall experimental research for the development of a new product, and is a comparatively short-term research and development activity. This is the research and development that has an impact on the market if it is successful. Development research is an important base supporting basic research in today's management and supporting the future of a corporation.

It may be said that research is development research if it is classed from the point of manpower as follows:

$$\text{research} = E \text{ (ten people} \times 1 \text{ year)} > E \text{ (one person} \times 10 \text{ years)}.$$

As a means and an aim become clear, the manpower on a project is increased and the research and development period are thus shortened. Accordingly, when development research is carried out based on customer needs, the result is shown in the short term.

The results of research studies are inherited by applied research, and the results of any applied research are handed to development research, and the research that then becomes a product is handed over to the marketing section of the business. But, for such a 'baton pass' system, the probability of a new product being successful is low in intense innovation. Development aims are decided by market needs, and are researched and developed for the realization of these needs. The formation of a new product concept begins with market insight, and the research knowledge layer gets feedback at the design, production, and circulation stages as well as at each stage of sale, and so new technology and new product are born. In Nittoudennkou Co. LTD, the engineers in the development section go to see a customer together with a member of the business department. And together they discuss the needs of a customer. Customer needs become a source of wisdom and can be how the idea of a new product is invented.

3. Evaluation of Research and Development Activity

It is assumed that qualitative assessment is good for the evaluation of activity at an early stage of research. Research and development activity concentrates more on quantitative evaluation as it gets closer to the production, sale, application and development research stage.

3.1. *Evaluation of basic research stage*

Basic research creates the future. The foundations for the technology of an optical disk were drafted in a plan room of the central research institute of Matsushita Electric Industrial Co., Ltd. in 1973. This project has now come to fruition. Technology sowed the seed of a topic 10 or 20 years ago, and this seed may flower today.

The value of an area of basic research is judged according to how useful it might be to the future of the enterprise, according to whether or not, if put into practice, it can generate patents and industrial know-how, and thirdly according to the extent to which it has wider economic repercussion. The potential effect of the research on corporate image and the degree of investment required in human resources, materials, and plant facilities must also be taken into consideration. One must depend on the subjectivity of evaluation personnel for the evaluation of essential basic research. This is a difficult problem to evaluate economically because there are many parts where application development is uncertain, as is also the case for basic research. Therefore, quantity evaluation should be avoided. As for the evaluation in this company, top management believes that promoting self-evaluation among researchers leads to good results.

3.2. *Project evaluation in applied research*

Because one can see a concrete product at the application research stage, it is possible to grasp the marketability, the predicted amount of production and competing products, and a person understanding the research can fundamentally evaluate a product even at this stage from a management and technical viewpoint. At this stage a graded evaluation method is introduced in the interests of more precise measurement.

The points of evaluation will be discussed next.

1. The elements of management:
A. Industrialization
   a. Does it go along with the long-term management plan and corporation policy?
   b. Is it useful for world needs and corporation image?
B. Marketability
   a. Are there any similar products, or substitute products?
   b. Is there a safe sale route?
C. Degree of investment
   a. Are research and development expenses necessary?
   b. Suitability of plant and facilities
D. Legal regulations
   a. Potential legal and environmental problems
2. Technical element
A. Possibility
   a. Is there the possibility of realization of the product?
   b. Are development periods and technical correspondence possible?
B. Originality
   a. Has the company acquired a basic patent?
   b. Accumulation of nucleus technology is possible
C. Predominance
   a. Will the company be ahead of other technical establishments, will it produce the product on time with the best technology?
   b. Is the basic patent or the know-how acquired?

In order to evaluate a new product, it is rated according to the answers to the questions above, and its quality evaluation is completed.

3.3. *Evaluation at the development research stage*

Development research is evaluated from the following points:

* The "newness" of development research,
* Industrialization of an epoch-making product,

* The number of technological developments that eventually become industrial property,
* The degree of technology granted for another company,
* The degree of adaptation for social needs.

Evaluation at this stage needs to be more quantitative than at the applied research stage. Evaluation items will be discussed next, and these are the likelihood of market demand, sale share, prospective costs, the necessary labor force required, facility, profit, the income and expenditure, the management efficiency, productivity, investment recovery period, influence effect, patent and technical predominance, corporation image, and any risks for industrialization. Schedule management is carried out for the research personnel required between the injection time and the other resources of consumption.

4. Cost Management in Research and Development Activity

Resources are assigned to the R&D budget according to the short-, mid- and long-term plans. The short-term plan is the research and development budget, and it is a characteristic of the research and development compilation of the budget that will be allotted according to each segment of research and development. The key to managing any research and development activity is budget management.

4.1. *Significance of research and development expenses budget*

Research and development budgets function in order to adjust research and development plans to the long-term and short-term financial affairs of a corporation. It is difficult to evaluate a patent, a new product, or a new manufacturing process by an amount of money because the output of the research and development activity is not yet reality. The output of research and development activity needs a long-term realization and this theme budget and project budget do not always agree with the annual budget of a corporation. Because a "special" element has to be calculated, this calculation becomes difficult, and it can be impossible for the management to evaluate the efficiency of research and development activity. Accordingly, although the normal functions of budgeting are planning, adjustment and control, in the case of research and development, budgeting is principally focussed on the area of planning. In the case of R&D Budgeting no attempt is made to assess efficiency. Therefore research and development expenses budgets attempt a balance between various research and development programs and plans for adjustment with the research and development section.

4.2. *Managing the allotment of R&D costs*

A Corporation seeks for predominance over its competitors in high-risk, high-return environments, and uses research and development as a corporate strategy. If a corporation does not achieve its mid-term or long-term plan, its research and development will not move forward and thus there are few good chances for success. Research and development funds are increasingly limited, and in the present situation funds are allocated by prior order by resources domains and project. This is necessary so that a company's middle- and long-term plans divide resources between fields that have been shown to yield a reliable prospective profit. There are no objective foundation data, that can be surveyed for a plan of research and development activity. Production activity is a matter of personal subjective judgement and cannot establish a standard for research and development activity. One characteristic comes out in budget distribution for research and development whether you develop aggressive research and development or whether you develop defensive research and development activity. Because a plan functions for a whole research and development expenses budget, research and development expenses must be managed at each stage of the plan. Managing the allotment of funds must be done successfully. Research and development expenses are managed costs, and most are capacity costs. The total sum of research and development expenses to be divided for product development themes and technology development themes is decided by the policy of the research and development section.

For example, the total sum of research and development expenses in Yukijirusi Nyuugyou Co., Ltd. is divided into new product development themes and technology development themes, and the distribution ratio is decided 45 : 55 by the policy of top management.

Seven projects are run by a president as CTO (Chief Technology Officer) in Nittou Denko Co., Ltd. The CTO has the right to distribute research and development expenses budgets, and he judges 80% of R&D budget and divides it. This is called a "policy cost", and therefore research and development expenses are called "discretionary costs". With discretionary costs there is no perceivable relationship of cause and effect between input and output. Therefore research and development expenses are costs which occur as strategic and tactical decision making. Research and development expenses are managed costs, and committed costs occupy an important part of these costs. Research material costs, articles of consumption costs, service costs and other information costs are all managed costs. Depreciation costs, property tax on a research facility, and personnel expenses are committed costs and these are the costs that have occurred by the decision making of past investment and experience. Accordingly, in management, managed cost appears as a minus to an achievement in the short term and is easy to become an object for reduction in recession; thus a long-term point of view is sought for by management. As for committed costs, management for primitive cost outbreak stages such as long term plan or decision of investment is required, and in the short term, management procedures concentrate on the full utillization of plant and stuff.

4.3. *Compilation of the research and development expenses budget*

The research and development expenses budget is different from the production budget or sale budget, and items to be added up for this cost include the number of research personnel required (whom a corporation employs currently). The research facility becomes the starting point for the compilation of the budget. The amount of research and development budget is adjusted in line with the company profit plan along management policy and is examined. The research and development budget total sum adds up the amount allotted for each project, and this is calculated. The project method, option increase and decrease method and competition opposition methods are examined to find out if the company can bear the costs from a financial point of view. Finally the total sum is decided. But one method of research and development expenses rate for sales is widely used by business with the arbitrary increase and decrease method. The quality and specialist technology of the research personnel required might itself threaten research and development plans, and special consideration is necessary for the research personnel required.

Therefore, primarily a research and development expenses budget attempts to maintain former conditions and the maintenance of research and development ability and, secondly, must be aimed towards the growth and future prosperity of the business. First, improvements to an existing product, and improvements in the production manufacturing process are made.

4.4. *The importance of basic research*

In Japan, the levels of resources applied to basic research have been lower than those devoted to applied and development research and this "cost-free" approach has been a source of trade and technological friction with overseas country. As for Japanese corporations, creative or original technology was sought for as a research and development strategy. In the 21st century, basic research in Japanese corporations will be more active in activity plans of research and development. A program that can provide new knowledge for each of basic research, application research and development research must be sought after. It is difficult to logically decide the amount of budget for basic research. A budget for basic research costs may be decided by a constant ratio of sales and a constant ratio of research and development investment. As for the distribution of resources to a basic research budget, this is asserted to be half of the research and development budget, but the amount of money injected into basic scientific research is much less.

Application research budgets and development research budgets will be decided along corporate strategy and a company's mid-term and long-term plans while keeping a balance with the short-term management plan.

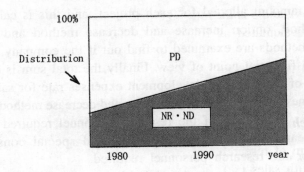

Fig. 3.1. Apportion guidline of NR · ND · PD.

Figure 3.1 shows the distribution of resources of the mid-term management plan for basic technical research in new fields (NR), product development in new fields (ND) and the existing enterprise product reinforcement research (PD) in Nihon Seikousyo Co., Ltd. Nihon Seikousyo Co., Ltd. establishes a high-oriented field strategically along the annual policy of the research and development headquarters, and established their budget frame in order to divide research and development expenses between NR and ND pre ponderantly.

5. Decision of Total Budget for Research and Development Expenses

5.1. *From the required number of research personnel*

When the amount of budget that one person uses in a year is added up for a research and development expenses budget, a total R&D budget wil then be prepared; thus the morale of the research personnel involved i raised. Therefore we come to the next equation. If N is the number o research personnel required; T is the amount of research in man-hours tha one person does in a year; a is the sum total of wages, overhead cost and general administrative costs per hour, in other words, a is the procesin costs per hour; A is total personnel expenses and others; r is the rati of direct expenses and direct materials costs in all to the personnel expense and others (A), and S is the total sum of research and development expenses, then this is calculated as follows:

$$A = a \cdot T \cdot N$$
$$S = A(1 + r)$$

5.2. *Research and development expenses ratio to sales*

The total sum of research and development expenses is often represented as a ratio with sales (%). In the world of medical supplies, the research and development expense to sales ratio is high and, in electrical machinery and appliances companies, this ratio is relatively low. The ratio of the total sum of research and development expenses to profit is also sought, but this is not much used. Calculating the research and development expenses to sales ratio and the research and development expenses to profit ratio is not a logical method on which to decide a research and development expenses budget. A research and development expenses to sales ratio is useful in deciding when to make arbitrary increases in such expenses but it is only of value as a reference guideline. Nihon Seikousyo Co., Ltd. decides their total sum of research and development expenses by calculating their research and development expenses to sales ratio, and 50% of Japanese companies decides their research and development expenses by calculating their research and development expenses to sales ratio.

5.3. *New product sales targets*

From a long-term growth viewpoint of a corporation, its prospective target sales are established, and this section will explain how the total sum of research and development expenses is decided.

T. Tanaka, Professor at Tohoku University shows the next method as a method of estimating the research and development expenses of the mid-term and long-term. If current sales are So, and target sales after T years are S_t, and the increase in sales rate during T years is π, then:

$$S_t = So(1 + \pi)$$

Necessary sales (N) of a new product can be estimated by a calculation, with Δ standing for the rate decrease from decreasing sales by a fall of competitive power after T years, thus:

$$S_t = So(1 - \Delta) + N$$

From the above two expressions,

$$N = So(\pi + \Delta)$$

The necessary sales of a new product after T years are thus calculated. There is a new product, N, a plural number $N = N_1 + N_2 + \cdots + N_m$. If we take RD_1, RD_2, ... RD_m to be the Research and Development expenses corresponding to the new product plan's $N_1 + N_2 + N_3 + \cdots + N_m$, then total R&D costs may be said to be $RD = RD_1 + RD_2 + RD_3 + \cdots + RD_m$. The total sum of research and development expenses for the compilation of the budget is calculated as research and development expenses led from target sales. Of course, because all research and development projects may not be successful, space is sought for in π and Δ.

5.4. *Project portfolio management*

New products can emerge from many technical combinations, and a new product that is based on technology and innovation is born from technical boundary domain and technological know-how. Resources cast into one technology and the development of a new product are increased research costs and an increase in the number of researchers. A decreased development period is pressed for by severe competition, and companies are forced to inject a large quantity of resources in the short term. This means an increased risk in product development. Accordingly, an improvement in the efficiency of research and development is demanded, along with the management of portfolio selection.

K. Kagoya, who is a partner in the Strategic Decision Group, describes the total sum of research and development investment decision by an application of R&D portfolio management in the medical supplies corporation ABC company as follows.

Based on DCF (Discounted Cash Flow) and the expectations of the project, its enterprise value is calculated as in Fig. 3.2. This is plotted using the first highest projected ratio of enterprise value to development cost for every project (investment productivity); and investment productivity is set from a high project by order, and it is accumulated along the axis ordinates and the axis of abscissas line development cost and expectation enterprise value. In Fig. 3.3, a curve is drawn to show the accumulation of enterprise value. Accumulation enterprise value is worth about $10,000,000,000 for

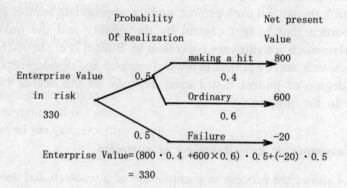

Enterprise Value = (800 · 0.4 + 600 × 0.6) · 0.5 + (−20) · 0.5

= 330

Fig. 3.2. Risk and enterprise value.

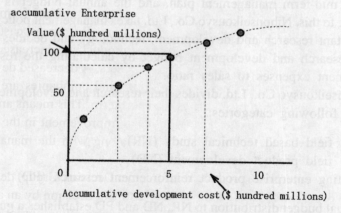

Fig. 3.3. Project portfolio.

development cost and $500,000,000 accumulated with an existing portfolio in the next figure. When a strategy is established for an R&D project, a decision must be made about how much of the enterprise value is created by the whole R&D portfolio and how much of the budget is divided between those portfolios. What is a reasonable amount of budget and how do various projects raise their total enterprise value? This is controlled by budget management. Budget management of research and development expenses is divided into three phases. Each item of expenditure of a fund is totaled for the management of a period, and this is divided between each research section, each theme and each project, and the appropriate control is exerted. It is important that budget control by the quality and the quantity that individual research activities are equivalent to. Budget is organized by subject in basic research, and by project in applied research and development research. A prior degree of budget distribution depends on the degree of strategy involved in the project.

5.5. *An example of how a budget is compiled*

Figure 3.4 shows the process of compilation of a research and development budget for Nihonseikousyo Co., Ltd. and the management of this. A general guideline or frame of research and development expenses is established with the mid-term management plan, and the annual budget is organized according to this. Nihonseikousyo Co., Ltd. takes management policy regarded as important research and development, technology and decides total sum of the research and development budget by calculating the research and development expenses to sales ratio.

Nihonseikousyo Co., Ltd. divides their research and development activity into the following categories:

(1) New field based technical study (NR)
(2) New field product development (ND)
(3) Existing enterprise product reinforcement research (PD)

The annual budget distribution to NR, ND and PD establishes a guideline for a frame of NR < ND < PD in the mid-term. The headquarters research institute

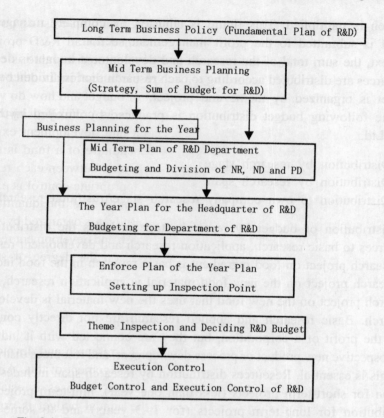

Fig. 3.4. Budgeting process of R&D in Nihonseikousyo Co., Ltd.

is responsible for NR and ND overall, and the enterprise department research institute mainly researches and develops PD. The enterprise department research institute researches and develops a fixed ratio of ND : NR for prospective enterprise department products.

6. Budget Distribution to Projects and to Subjects

In compiling a research and development budget, research groups must be broken down into themes and projects, and the amount of budget necessary for each is multiplied. This figure is adjusted by company management, and it is submitted to the profit management section.

Next, the sum total of the research and development budget is decided. Resources are distributed according to each research section. In other words, budget is organized by theme and project.

The following budget distribution is practiced by Yukijirusinyuugyou Co., Ltd.

(1) Distribution by research stage
(2) Distribution by research span
(3) Distribution to own company research stage/trust/joint research

Distribution of budget by research stage includes the distribution of resources to basic research, application research and development research. A research project on food ingredient is basic research in the food industry; a research project on the new food material is application research, and a research project on the new food that uses the new material is development research. Basic research and applied research are not directly connected with the profit of a corporation, but they are connected with it indirectly, in prospective new product or process development, and resources distribution for this is essential. Resources distribution by research span includes distribution for short-term projects (less than one year), mid-term projects and distribution for long-term projects (for 1–3 years) and to some extent distribution is linked to research stage distinction.

In Yukijirusinyuugyou Co., Ltd., various research and development themes are divided as follows:

(1) New product development
(2) Technology development

New product development is directly carried out according to new product development, whereas technology development themes need basic research and applied research to be connected with the new product and the manufacturing process.

6.1. *Evaluation of projects*

Evaluation of projects by subject is done so that a budget can be divided into both research and development themes, and a prior distribution of resources must be decided. Research efficiency is shown by results gained from resources spent. Resources spent need to be added up for every project. In Yukijirusinyuugyou Co., Ltd., project evaluation and research and development subjects are all evaluated and they are classed as follows:

(A) important projects,
(B) general projects,
(C) close inspection projects,
(D) re-examination projects.

The period necessary for the completion of a project, technology power, the possibility of success, a function and system, originality of materials, composition, technical influence, effect and accumulation must be examined closely and judged in this subject evaluation. It must be examined whether the project is connected with scale expansion in the reclamation of new enterprise, whether it is connected with quality improvement and reducing costs, and whether the project fits consumer needs.

A standard of synthesis evaluation. An important project (A) is a high profit, high technology product. Evaluation is needed for early detection of product defect, and is connected with important technology development.

General project (B) bolster up low profit and high technology products and these are currently connected with technical application and expansion.

Close inspection project (C) cannot be dealt with by existing facilities and their basic concept and basis for improvement are unclear.

Re-examination projects (D) may not properly be treated as research themes.

7. The Execution and Management of R&D

Research and development investment is a strategic arrangement that looks to the future. It may be thought that these costs should not be built into current profit evaluation, but in terms of cost recognition, they should not be deferred. Strategic investments in the future should be examined while grasping current profit.

7.1. *Management by segment*

Half of all research and development budget is spent on personnel and salary expenses. Development research cost occupies 70% of total research and development expenses, and it is comparatively easy to be tied to an existing device and product. However, the ratio of fixed cost to total cost is high, and it is difficult to be clearly assigned to each segment, accordingly getting a firm grasp of cost suppressing profit by customer and by product is not feasible.

It is practical to assign increasing research and development expenses to an existing product group, from the point of view of investment manage-ment. When sales are calculated according to a product group, basic research costs as a total cost of a corporation are assigned to each product group. However, current sales and profit may be the result of past research and development expenses, and this technique is flawed because prospective sales and profit are not the overall result of current accurate research and development expenses. If the cost of a series of products is calculated from the viewpoint of management accounts, it is useful for cost management, profit management and price setting. In Nissan Motor Co., Ltd., the accounts

	Sale	XXXXX
-)	Material Cost	XXXXX
	Material Contribution Margin	XXXXX
-)	Direct Labor	XXXXX
-)	Direct expense	XXXXX
-)	Depreciation(model cycle)	XXXXX
-)	Development cost(model cycle)	XXXXX
	Contribution Margin by A Series of Products	XXXXX

Fig. 3.5. Contribution margin by series of products.

system has responsibility for a particular product; development costs are calculated for a fixed length of model cycle, and these costs are assigned to a series of products as in Fig. 3.5. Development costs can be managed in relation to a series of products by doing this.

8. Conclusion

Basic research activities used to be denigrated in Japan, but the importance of basic research has been recognized in recent years. Japanese corporations are beginning to invest more in basic and applied research. Budgetary control of R&D constitutes a nucleus of R&D Management. R&D budgets function mainly for planning, regulating and controlling costs.

As competition becomes more intense, R&D management will change from budget control to investment control in future.The spread involved in R&D evaluation is becoming increasingly broad. The coming trend even in basic research is toward quantitative valuation. To activate R&D, a reasonable budget must be drawn up. Budget will have to be executed elastically if R&D are to be accomplished efficiently.

References

1. Ezaki, G., To Reconstruct R&D Organization, R&D MANAGEMENT (Abanpurodyusu, 1992), 3.
2. Kobe University. A Large Dictionary of Business Administration Chuoukeizaisha, 1988.
3. Maruyama, E., How Should be Basic Research for a Private Enterprise, R&D MANAGEMENT (Abanpurodyusu, 1992), 5.
4. Hujimori, T., R&D Budget is Decided Like This. In Nihonseikousyo Co., Ltd., R&D MANAGEMENT (Abanpurodyusu, 1991), 4.
5. Sakuma, Y., Changing R&D Organization, R&D MANAGEMENT (Abanpurodyusu, 1996), 8.
6. Tanaka, T., Management of R&D Investment, Advertisement Investment and Discretionary Cost, ACCOUNTING (Chuoukeizaisha, 1997), 8.
7. Kobayashi, K., A Fundamental Knowledge of Budget Control Tokyojohoushuppan, 1991.

8. Hukui, T., R&D MANAGEMENT (Abanpurodyusu, 1991).

9. Kato, M., Management Accounting System of Our Company: Nissan Automobile Co., Ltd., ACCOUNTING (Chuoukeizaisha, 1990), 10.

10. Kagoya, K., Decision Making and Strategy Establishment by Decision Management, R&D MANAGEMENT (Abanpurodyusu, 1997), 10.

11. Hirabayashi, T., Application of Activity Based Costing for R&D Investment, R&D MANAGEMENT (Abanpurodyusu, 1997), 10.

Chapter 4

R&D Management and Management Accounting in Japan: Case Studies of Selected Japanese Pharmaceutical Companies

TAKAYUKI ASADA

1. The Current State of Research and Development of Pharmaceutical Manufacturing Companies in Japan

The output objectives of research activity and development activity are very different, even if we could say that research and development activity are one subject. The output of research activity is usually a thesis, containing new findings and the results of the patent and the report of the research activity. This does not have direct management value for an enterprise. Of course, this might have business value in a venture enterprise in realizing such a result on an individual contract base. However, it is usually necessary to convert products that only have intellectual value to those with market value in the manufacturing industry. On the other hand, results produced from development activities have an immediate market value. Product developments such as transistors and diodes are typical examples. Some inventions are not easily acknowledged in the enterprise as value. However, the basic paradigm of R&D activity has changed, and many companies are said to be defeated in product development competition in a new market

71

if they cannot find the seeds of new idea and technology by their own effort in the present manufacturing industries. One good example of this is in manufacturing semiconductors. As the time of development of competition in semiconductors is called a 'dog year', it is said that time does not pass on the axis of 'man-time' but will usually pass with the axis of 'dog-time'. Therefore, a new product is developed in the semiconductor industry within six months. In various companies, in order to maintain the speed of product development, companies only develop their strongest components by themselves; any potentially 'weak' parts are developed in alliance with another company or companies. This could be called a semi-open strategy. The same way of working can be developed even in the pharmaceutical industry. This industry is strongly influenced by the policy restrictions with regard to government public policy, because of the direct effect of products to human health and life. Pharmaceutical companies need a lot of funds to operate, and take a long time for new products to develop. However, the latest results of research are made public one after the other through the media of industry journals, journals related to medical treatment and academic research journals. It is so published that product development is encouraged now up to a certain developmental step in various enterprises, so that development research activity can be seen to be open to the public to a considerable degree. Moreover, because the market for a new drug which has been born as a result of this effort matures rapidly the price of new drugs also decreases rapidly, the enterprise cannot enjoy the same profit as the developer if the market is not entered as one of the first three manufacturers. It is extremely important to know what kinds of medicine will receive attention, and to identify whether it is possible to enter a new medicine into the market at a certain time. When a company holds the seeds of a new research project, other companies are limited to entering a similar area which belongs to basic research. To create such a barrier each company makes an effort to establish a method of chemical compound synthesis or generation which is called making new medicine, and to acquire the patent for the method of manufacturing the new element and the peripheral patents. As a result, each company forms their own good field or core competence, so that one enterprise may be good at developing medicine in the area of geriatric diseases and another enterprise is good at developing medicine to treat diseases of circulatory organs. However, the know-how for this, accumulated in the past, forms the core of the competing power of each enterprise and this influences the basic research area of a company from its ability to 'generate seeds' in a clinical development. Perhaps such a tendency can be seen in the pharmaceutical industries in many countries, but in Japan each drug manufacturer also specializes in diagnosis and hospital treatment to some degree. This tendency with constraining scale up by owner management company has encouraged focusing strategy of pharmaceutical enterprise (in 1985, 1,400 companies existed in Japan). Thus, up to now the Japanese pharmaceutical industry has enjoyed an oligopoly position owing to the stability of medical charges and public policy from the government health and welfare regulations.

However, in the middle of 1980s, Japanese government began to reduce medical charges with the abolition of the entry barrier of the medical services between advanced countries because of the downturn in economic growth and a chronic deficit of the health insurance fund due to an increasing aged population; thus the environment which surrounds this industry has changed greatly in recent years.

On examining the financial performance of the Japanese pharmaceutical industry, the average ROE (return on equity) of the main six companies (Takeda, Sankyo, Ezai, Yamanouchi, Sionogi and Taisho) is about 8.7%. The top ROEs are 12.3% (in Sankyo pharmaceutical company in March 1996), and the bottom ROEs are 5.6% (in Sionogi pharmaceutical company). On the other hand, the USA's six main companies in 1995 averaged an ROE of 32.8%. However, 20% of the world's annual medicines are now being consumed in Japan, and this ranking order of world medicine's consumption quantity is second behind the USA. Also, Japan has relatively more number of pharmaceutical companies than any other economically advanced country. Up until now, there have been many restrictions and now it has been requested that the research efficiency be improved in enterprise activity in the future. Moreover, domestic sale competition was a central concern for such companies and the export ratio was very low. It could thus be said to be a typical domestic demand industry. However, since the pharmaceutical industry entered into the global industry in the 1990s, many characteristics of this domestic demand industry are disappearing, and companies are beginning to rush into new stages of competition. The Japanese pharmaceutical industry has changed into a global industry.

The pharmaceutical manufacturing industry in Japan is positioned in the age of strategic management. Moreover, it is the high profit rate in the pharmaceutical manufacturing industry that makes this situation accelerate further in comparison with other industries. The ROEs of the pharmaceutical manufacturing industry are 2 or 3% higher than those of a general manufacturing industry. The numbers of some new entry companies from other industries have recently increased. However, each such newcomer does not carry out clinical development on its own even if they have the chemical knowledge to do this.[3] As the case with Showa Denko K. K. shows, even if the company has approval for manufacturing specific medicines, and if any defect in GDP (Good Drug Practice) was noticed, it would be fatal for the company. It can also be pointed out that the development of medicine is important in management with chemical knowledge, not only for basic research but also for safety inspections and manufacturing inspections, etc.

How is management then developed in a laboratory, especially one that is responsible for 'seed development' in research investigating the current state of the pharmaceutical enterprise in Japan? Moreover, it is the main motive of this research to examine whether there is an area where management accounting can have an effect on management and to which area can it contribute. In European and American research, a necessary management process for the improvement in efficiency during the research process was investigated by Ellis (1997). International research and development control was examined by Yamanouchi (1992) and in the clinical development process by Kuwajima *et al.* (1997).

2. The Environment Around Japanese Pharmaceutical Companies

The reason why pharmaceutical companies have been chosen as research objects is due to the following: they have the research and development management that can provide them with the core of competing power, a already described. A considerable difference between each pharmaceutical company can be observed in their R&D management. Very few such practices have been observed and there might be a unique practice of R&D management very different from the production control which became public. I believe that R&D management will become more and more important owing to the increasing internationalization of R&D activity.

First of all, three pharmaceutical manufacturing companies and one chemical company will be examined here.

2.1. Problems of pharmaceutical research and development

The general development process in that industry is similar to that shown in Fig. 4.1.

There is a move towards standardization between countries for medical research and development. It is now necessary to carry out all processes from clinical development to the acquisition of manufacturing approval according to each country's policies and it takes a long time and costs a lot of money to do this. A clinical standard that extends over all countries

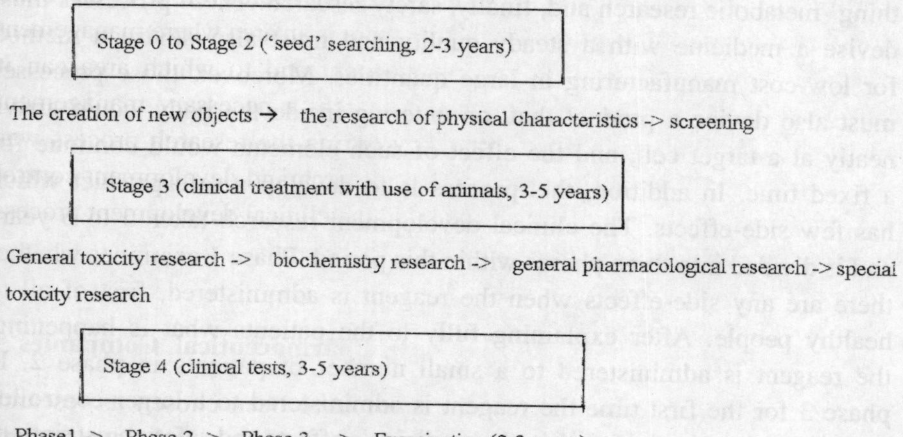

Stage 0 to Stage 2 ('seed' searching, 2-3 years)

The creation of new objects → the research of physical characteristics -> screening

Stage 3 (clinical treatment with use of animals, 3-5 years)

General toxicity research -> biochemistry research -> general pharmacological research -> special toxicity research

Stage 4 (clinical tests, 3-5 years)

Phase1 -> Phase 2 -> Phase 3 -> Examination (2-3 years)

Fig. 4.1. Pharmaceutical research and development processes.

has not yet been completed, although ICH (International Congress of Harmonization) is to be established as an international organization for standardizing the pharmaceutical industry. Eisai Co., Ltd. has carried out its research and development activity in foreign countries for a relatively long time, when most Japanese enterprises did not consider basing their R&D activities in a foreign country. Figure 4.1 above shows R&D activities in Eisai Co. It takes on an average three years for clinical research, 5–6 years for clinical development, and 2–3 years for the application and examination processes. Only medicine approved at the end of these processes can be marketed and sold. Various devices to reduce the development risk are performed for new projects during this long period. The most important thing to decide is what kind of synthetic material is to used to manufacture the medicine. When the idea materializes, 5 to 7 years are spent on chemical and synthetic experiments which are carried out in test tubes, and after this the living evaluation is repeated. The former clinical tests are repeated for new medicines if they have any toxicity problems but the manufacturer would still want to go ahead with producing them. Research is also carried out by Eisai Co. to find out the optimum dosage of medicine to administer for safety and efficacy. This is sometimes done by carrying out animal experiments. This former clinical research consists of process research, 'living thing' metabolic research and, finally, safety research. These processes must devise a medicine with a steady quality and must also devise a method for low-cost manufacturing in large quantities. Moreover, those processes must also device a product that, on entering inside the body, could arrive neatly at a target cell, and the effect of such elements would continue for a fixed time. In addition, this process is to develop a safe product which has few side-effects. The clinical development research takes 5 to 6 years and is divided into three phases within this period. Phase 1 examines whether there are any side-effects when the reagent is administered, first of all to healthy people. After explaining fully to the patients what is happening the reagent is administered to a small number of patients in phase 2. phase 3 for the first time the reagent is administered to a larger controlled study of patients and, after that, the medicine's effects and safety prescription are completed.

The cost of a clinical development test increases greatly between the three phases. The reason for this is that costs increase according to the hospital numbers involved as well as the numbers for administering the medicine and the accumulating examination and organization charges. Products are often developed jointly with other companies although producing new products only by its own development efforts is a kind of basic principle for a company. Moreover, to get patents for medicines or the manufacturing method patented is important because this clinical test process is open to the public. The establishment of intellectual property ownership is important for a medicine, because getting some patents is necessary also to obtain licences from other enterprises. Highly efficient development and production are increasingly hoped for and aimed at in the pharmaceutical industry.

3. Examination of Each Company Individually

Case 1: Ezai Co., Ltd. (Company A)

Data:
Founded in: 1941
Capital: 23 billion 440 million yen (in March 1996)
Sales volume: 253 billion 640 million yen
R&D ratio: 14.3%

This figure (Fig. 4.2) shows the organization of four laboratories and staff. The Tsukuba drug discovery research center is composed of an administration section with three laboratory business units which are treated as companies and laboratory units. The main business of these 'companies' is to carry out the most topical and current activities at this center. Drug elements which emerge are examined with each unit organized along function lines. Support for the center activities is carried out by the administration department and this includes the research planning section. Laboratories other than the Tsukuba research center are divided into the process research center and pre-clinical technical research center and the safety laboratory, which takes charge of clinical test activities. Besides these, there is also

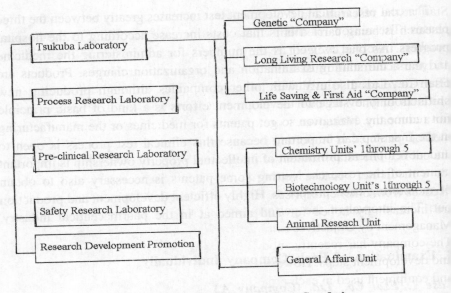

Fig. 4.2. R&D organization of Ezai Co., Ltd.

an organization that takes charge of the planning of all research and the protection of intellectual property and patents as a research and development promotion department. Here, companies also take charge of joint activities in collaboration with research organizations on the outside, and they have independent budgets for such activities.

The organization of 'units' is activated by comparatively young researchers and is based on the latest scientific information. This organization is composed of chemistry, biology and animal research units, and is functionally-oriented with no formal lines between units. These units carry out joint research by project.

The performance evaluation

As a rule, the research center manpower organization is 'flat', and the person who comes up with an idea becomes a team leader for that project. The wall between 'units' is lowered to facilitate more flexible project formation

Staff at the research and development promotion department monitor what research is being carried out where, and also monitor and control research progress. As one cycle of research and development process takes about 10 years, the staff must have a long-term approach to all this. However, Esai Co., Ltd. also evaluates projects for the short term. In research that shifts from one stage to the next, there are often research errors. We do not reduce the evaluation score of the researcher in principle if the research at the first step can be seen to be scientifically rational. Staff in the research and development promotion department should thus be familiar with the content of the research. Moreover, there is one member of staff in charge of monitoring each project as a rule because so many projects are carried out. The interval of the performance evaluation is every six months and Management by Objectives is implemented at this interval for each researcher. The company has recently subdivided more and has controlled the research and development steps. However, there is a considerable difference of capital and equipment used in each project. Here we abolish such uniform evaluation systems because this does not give researchers any appropriate motivation.

Project plan and control

The project leader discusses the report evaluation of the research theme in the development conference. Some projects need capital in an emergency, while other projects need more later research, on the other hand. Budget control is flexible because these kind of situations often happen, and because of the research activity and changes in the distribution of the capital in every case. This is called milestone control and it evaluates the degree of achievement of the research project against its targeted progress level. However, the success or failure of each project is not directly related to the evaluation of the researcher's achievement.

The international conference, GRC (Global Research Committee) is used as one of the progress controls in this company. This conference is a review conference for 'discovery' research and pre-clinical research steps. The research representative in each laboratory (in Boston, Tsukuba and London) attends this GRC and one of the representative directors works as a conference chairman. There is a GRC headquarters in Boston amongst three research bases. It is situated there because it is central to many advances in research. The research Institute of Ezai in Boston was set up in 1986 and the Research Institute of London was set up in 1992. Conferences have been carried out using video-phones since 1996.

There is also another conference, called GCC (Global Critical Committee) as well as the GRC. This takes charge of reviewing the clinical side of the development project from phase 1. In this way, Eisai Co., Ltd. executes progress control in the drug discovery steps of its research as well as in a clinical step of its development by reviewing different staff and organizations.

The research and development budget in Japan is decided at a company' headquarters except for the personnel expense budgets. Because personne expenses for the researchers and general employees are not treated differently they are the same. In a foreign country, a local subsidiary independently decides his master budget along some guidelines from the headquarter and decides the expense budgets including personnel expenses with the aid of company headquarters.

Global research activity

In global research activity, the allotment of the base and the applicatio is different. The Research Institution in Boston and The Research Cente in London are geared towards basic research and application research. Tukut Research Center is responsible for development research and other Japane laboratories are responsible for clinical research.

Case 2: *Yamanouchi Pharmaceutical Co., Ltd.* (*Company B*)

General Data:
Founded in: 1923
Capital: 56 billion 949 million yen (March 1997)
Employees: 3,946
Sales Volume: 454 billion 740 million yen
R&D ratio: 9.03%
Business Segments: Pharmaceutical business; 79.1%, Others; 20.0%

This company has also adopted the business division systems and consists of two overseas business units and five domestic business units (pharmaceuticals distribution, diagnostic drug business, nutritional products, food and vitamin and the health industry), and overseas business units (the Shaklee Corporation). Drug discovery is divided between the development, clinical and medical center for research and development units. Such medical centers function as research support centers. Among these, drug discovery research centers were reorganized in August 1996 according to fundamental technologies rather than therapeutic categories. These technologies included biotechnology, molecular medicine, microorganisms, chemistry and so on besides a staff organization in the research promotions department. The content of the Tsukuba research center (biotechnology, molecular medicine, microorganisms, the effects of a medicine, the applied effects of a medicine, and chemistry) will now be explored as the heart of the research organization.

The performance evaluation

Three kinds of conference bodies are used in the above company: Search and Research Theme Making Evaluation Conference, Semi-Development Theme Making Evaluation Conference, and General Development Policy Conference. The first-mentioned conference evaluates the project or research theme. The review of projects every six months is executed though the researchers are freely able to set the research themes. Moreover, the result's report at the end of the term is carried out by a research society in the company. It is necessary to give out the latest results of the research after about one and a half years. The Semi-Development Theme Making Evaluation Conference is a conference in the second stage and projects are in the pre-clinical evaluation stage. The General Development Policy Conference is the conference for discussing the project at the pre-clinical or clinical level of the project. The project screening at that conference is decided at both a Research and Development conference and a Management conference. As a result, the discussed project becomes one authorized by the whole company.

According to the individual research stage, each researcher executes Management by Objectives by himself, and his superior reviews the results of his research stage, divided into the first half of the year and the second half of the year, compared to his targets. Each researcher is evaluated taking into consideration the standpoint of differing development efficiency of each project. For instance, drug discovery research is divided into three processes and, in the first process of material search, speed for searching is valued while in the second process of the drug generation process, effectiveness is valued. In the safety process, the element of safety and its effects are considered. However, individual evaluations are not directly reflected in bonuses and promotions. New researchers are basically employed for the drug discovery process stage, and they will then move to the lower part of the research process. In the case of successful product development one of the members of a successful project may sometimes move to the next development process with new drug elements.

Project plan and control

We assume that R&D activities are high-risk, and the above company has succeeded in the research and development of low-risk and high-profit products up to now. For example, they developed digestive medicines, high blood pressure medicines, and asthma control medicines. However, in the future the company will try to develop high-risk and high-return products, for example attempts will be made to advance the development of interferon, bone morpho genetic drugs and septicemia drugs. Project management puts the difference on a systematic activity in three steps so that such a development may succeed. In the discovery research step, a research with the high degree of freedom is done with the bottom–up oriented research style and a lot of research options are discussed. That is, the self-achievement type research is advanced. In the drug delivery and safety research steps, a selection of the research project using the top–down approach is considered, along with the prospective out comes and safety. Moreover, organizational project controls are done consider ing the market base return of new drugs in the clinical development step.

Global research activity

The Shaklee Corporation (1989) of the food industry in the United States was purchased to get the large sales volume. Yamanouchi became involved 'nourishment assistance' food. Yamanouchi USA (1993) was established after this, and the pharmaceutical business was also developed in the United States. Yamanouchi Europe was established in 1991 and drug development (clinical steps) and drug sales in Europe were reinforced. China was established as their Asian sales base in 1994, a sales company was established in South Korea, and the manufacturing company was established in China in 1997.

The company's laboratory was established in Boston in 1996, and this is where the company's research activities are carried out. In Britain, their laboratory was established in Oxford in 1990 and in the United States a new research laboratory in Palo Alto Research Park was established in 1997. To correspond to an increase in research costs, drug sales in foreign countries are aggressively handled. However, because the company's sales networks are not strong enough in foreign countries, research and development activities are carried out in foreign countries to take the development system from a clinical step, with the aim of developing and selling a new drug as soon as possible. Since a drug is strongly affected by a country's culture and ideology, it is a policy for the Shaklee Corporation to achieve the third or higher position in each country's market when selling drugs in each country. Its FTTM project (faster time to market) is executed in order to improve the efficiency of clinical trials in Europe. This aims at the minimization of development time through efficient management of staff, the product and the budget.

Case 3: Takeda Chemical Industries Co., Ltd. (Company C)

Pharmaceutical business 60.0%, health care business 9.9%, food vitamin business 9.4%, chemical goods business 10%, agricultural business 7.5%, and life environment business 3.3%

Research and development organization

The Takeda Chemical Industries Co., Ltd. had adopted division business unit systems in 1960, comparatively early for a Japanese enterprise. In April 1996, the company revised these division business unit systems and adopted Strategic Business Unit Systems instead, which meant large-scale decentralized business units as investment centres. The organization system, which consists of one division business unit and five SBUs, was put in place in 1997, and the division took charge of the pharmaceutical business for medical treatment. Under this division there are three laboratories: Osaka factory district laboratory, a drug safety laboratory and Tsukuba laboratory. There are three laboratories that relate to the SBUs, and their mission is related to synthetic chemical goods, agricultural chemicals and an animal drug laboratory. Here, the first and second pharmaceutical discovery research centres will be examined from the viewpoint of research management.

These laboratories conduct a broad range of projects, including those in cooperation with other public-sector and academic organizations. The development of the drugs of tomorrow requires the application of the latest life sciences know-how. Moreover, recent discoveries in genetic engineering and molecular biology are opening up new medical frontiers. Today basic research is being conducted at genetic and molecular levels, helping to provide a greater understanding of the working of a host of ailments. One new research project is into cell receptor antagonists, such as Endothelin. The second discovery research concentrates on research into enzyme inhibitors and cell function modulators related to diabetes, arteriosclerosis, etc. The entire scales are 150 researchers and 15–20 support stuffs.

About the achievement evaluation

The research section consists of the head, the research manager, the chief researcher, and another researcher. Because research is carried out by a team, two evaluation measures are undertaken according to the project-oriented evaluation for team and individuals. Individual evaluation is carried out once a year. Based on Management by Objectives, a researcher undertakes the result evaluation by his superior with independent targets set by himself before implementation. The evaluation for each team's project is very difficult because of differences in the degree of difficulty within the project. This performance evaluation is totaled with the action evaluation and can influence promotion and post-promotion prospects. Personnel records are kept on leadership, instruction ability, adaptability to change, character, etc. A new pay structure was introduced in April 1997, and a new system reduced the rate of "person pay" which automatically increased every member of staff's salary in April every year from 30% to 60%. The rate of "functional based pay" increased by 70% (July 9, 1997 of a Japanese economic newspaper).

A system was put in place where a bonus of a maximum of 50,000,000 yen would be provided to a researcher who succeeded in the development of a large-scale new medicine. As another incentive, a researcher could retire on a high pension, even if he had only been employed by the company for a short time.

Global research activity

A powerful subsidiary firm in USA is a joint venture, U.S. TAP, between Takeda and the Abbott Laboratories. TAP has succeeded in marketing Lupron Depot (TAP-144SR) and Prevacid (lansoprazol) for the US market. In Europe, Takeda has set up the Takada Europe Research & Development Center GmbH offices in Frankfurt, Germany and London, UK. The center primarily conducts clinical development work for new drug applications.

Case 4: Fujisawa Pharmaceutical Co., Ltd. (Company D)

Pharmaceutical 85.8% others: 14.2%

Research organization and achievement evaluation

The above company's basic laboratory is in Tsukuba. Besides this, there is also a second stage of drug discovery research center and a development research function in the Osaka factory. The company also has a laboratory for research and development for industrialization in the Nagoya factory. Fujisawa concentrates mainly on discovery research, especially in relation to inflammation immunity, metabolic disease, infection related disease and brain infarct. Priority is given to the two following methods — chemical synthesis and fermentation.

Research proposals are divided into one decided through top–down management according to the most important areas, and one biannually as adopted from various proposals from young researchers in the research unit. Projects are decided at a special conference and there is no interference from the company director. Terms of projects are recognized through years of practice and are set for each research project by a special conference. The project decided at the expert conference is basically approved at the management conference. Project budgets are set afterwards.

Management by Objectives is adopted and each superior evaluates their subordinate researcher's results twice a year. Achievement of targets and dates of achievement are evaluated. However, results are not directly related into a personnel record. Moreover, there is so far no plan whereby rewards would be given to a specific person for his own acquired patent. There is not so much difference in compensation systems between researchers and general white-collar workers. However, the 'fellow' system is installed in the research department and big budget discretion is given to research fellows. Moreover, salary increases and increased research support are given to research fellows.

Research and development budget

The expense account codes of all the themes or projects are given to the budgetary cost elements in the laboratory. How much money has been spent and on which research project are all controlled.

Case 5: Mitsubishi Chemical Co. (Company E)

General Data
Founded in 1934
Capital: 140 billion yen (March 1995)
Employees: 14,500 (March 1995)
Sales Volume: 1,000 billion yen
R&D ratio: 6.0%
Business Segments: General chemistry, carbon, inorganic products, oil chemical products and function commodity (function materials, information electronic materials, and medicine)

Research and development organization

The "Kanpany" system (a kind of Japanese investment center) is adopted at Mitsubishi and it is now (as from March 1997) divided into nine "Kanpany" (basic oil chemistry and transformation goods, resin, synthetic raw materials, function chemical goods, medicine, information/electronic, carbon (agriculture), and function materials). Each "Kanpany" is located as an independent unit of the business though each "Kanpany" is a section of the Mitsubishi chemistry in-house company. Therefore, each "Kanpany" has the in-house capital and makes their capital statement for the profit and loss statement and the balance sheet. The main characteristic of this system is a large business bundling according to (1) market-oriented summarized business units' organization; (2) management that has the characteristic of the semi-autonomous intra-business units; and (3) management that responds to the characteristics of each business unit's management.

According to this "Kanpany", research and development, and corporate research and development are composed of staff sections which include an intellectual property section and an environmental safety section, as well as including research and development units which are known as new business development sections for starting up new in-house ventures, R&D department headquarters, and technology headquarters. Also, in 10 factories which are managed under the control of each related "Kanpany", there are 9 development centers. The total number of research staff in these development centers is about 400, and there are around 2,400 research staff in the R&D department headquarters. The headquarters manage five corporate research centers. In this paper, we will mainly explain two of these five corporate laboratories: the Tsukuba laboratory and the Yokohama laboratory.

The Tsukuba laboratory was established as a basic research unit of the Mitsubishi Petrochemical Co., Ltd. before amalgamating. It amalgamated with Mitsubishi Chemical Industries Ltd. in October 1994.

The Tsukuba laboratory is a laboratory organization (synthesis, electronic chemistry, living thing chemistry, new material and physical properties), and it consists of 144 numbers (138 researchers).

The general function of the research and development section is as a research and development headquarters. 50% of all researchers (2,100 persons) belong to three laboratories under the control of the headquarters. 70% of the research and development workers are engaged in mid- or short-term projects (research requested by the capital of the business part) which relates to the business and the remaining 30%, are engaged in mid- to long-term basic technological research. Research and development control are managed by the three steps which mean a system of business domain, business units and research themes. Some research projects, based on each business unit's demand, are managed by annual research planning, manpower requirement planning and a review of expenses for the researchers every month. The main research and development direction is decided by a Management Strategy Conference held every year. According to this guideline, business units' R&D conferences are held to manage the research projects relating to each business. The ideal way for the research and development to be related to the business unit is decided at this conference. On the other hand, the research project of a whole company's mid- and long-term plan is decided by the R&D project conference within the range of the budget which has been decided by top management. The target details and research activity schedules are planned in R&D conferences. The adoption of a new theme, the continuance of an existing theme, and the discontinuance of themes are all decided in the R&D theme examination conference, of which the sponsor is the research and development headquarters. Researchers are able to propose new projects at any time, while some themes are proposed by a company/technology center within Mitsubishi, and the discussion and decision to adopt such proposals or not are carried out in the R&D theme examination conference.

Performance evaluation

The control of research performance is very important. In this company, the results report and the evaluation conference come in succession with the above-mentioned project conference. However, they are carried out by five conference bodies ("Kanpany" theme and results report conference, research and development headquarters results report conference, R&D theme examination conference, whole-company joint research conference, and corporate theme promotion & examination conference).

A researcher's management of his/her laboratory consists of three hierarchies. There is a head researcher a group leader, and a researcher. However, the group leader who is normally promoted to a chief researcher is reviewed once a year, when the group leader system is reexamined. Moreover, the leader assumes a retirement age of 50 years (April 1994) to be a limit. In the activation of the research specialist, the research fellow system and the head special reward systems were introduced. Management by Objectives was also introduced, and this plan and the results were clarified during the year, and the researcher's performance was noted on his personnel record. As a result, the treatment of the researcher became clearer and a positive performance evaluation is reflected by increased pay, bonuses and promotion. However, it is dubious whether management could evaluate the differences in the content of work very fairly, and there are still many problems with the quality evaluation of research and whether it can be made a quantitative evaluation.

Research and development budget

Important business themes (10 through 15 themes for instance) are decided in the strategy section conference under the policy decided at the strategy basic policy conference and short-term and long-term whole company resource allocation plans are decided at the strategy decision conference in October. Based on this plan, a conference on R&D strategy is held in parallel with sales and production planning, and the distribution of investment is decided. The investment distribution decided at this R&D strategy conference is about 70% for corporate laboratories and about 30% for 'company' laboratories. After the amount of resources has been finalized, the R&D expenditure budget for a single term is decided at the budget decision conference. However, the R&D expenditure budget is variable for the execution step.

4. Patterns of Research and Development Management in Pharmaceutical Companies in Japan

Research and development management are said to be of three types (1st generation, 2nd generation, and 3rd generation).[10] R&D management of the third generation is especially necessary for lifecycle management depending on the degree of technology and the degree of linking of technological strategy and management strategy. Because the development of new drugs needs an especially long period, and for knowledge to take place, the typical Japanese management style of simple risk control and uniform management are not the most appropriate for this area. However, the creation of knowledge has been carrying on for a long time in drug manufacturing companies like a lot of Japanese manufacturing enterprises in other sectors. But, as the drug market in Japan opens up and global standards for several stages of medical practices are in demand, Japanese pharmaceutical companies have been thought of as not being able to cope with the competition from European and American companies in their research and development management, disregarding the efficiency of research and development.

However, in Japanese pharmaceutical manufacturing companies, I believe that companies that carry out its R&D activities along the same lines as third generation R&D,[8] still make up a very small number. However, some excellent enterprises are clearly adopting an excellent system in this area. This is likely to separate into three types of research and development management: see the cases explained below.

Type 1: Organization control

This type is one where a strict budgetary control in each project is not done for most R&D cost. However, it tries to raise productivity by decreasing the development time which severely controls the project by subdividing the project into details according to the content of the research and using frequent review processes. The original targets and research activity do not relate much to the new drugs development. The by-product might have some medical effects just as the elements of medicine. Moreover, as the process whereby cost planning has become more important for cost reduction is the upstream of business processes, the degree of validity of the project and planning influences the final result some more. Therefore, to raise the success rate of many research projects we must distinguish the process by which some successful projects are greatly influenced by chance and the process which will be achieved by systematic work. A frequent review process is also needed for decreasing the research and the development risk by applying the knowledge and experience of the individuals who have done basic research. Therefore, project organization should be decided according to the project's purpose when the project control is set, and when time control is central, an immediate review system and functional business units should be used for organizing.

Type 2: Budgetary control

Because the budget is set along the task and is controlled, a research department becomes a so-called cost center although there is no budget set according to a specific project. However, the results reached by a certain project is always traced by its relation to the budget assigned. So, it can be said that the researcher will hold out continuously aiming at project achievement, and very uncertain projects will not be selected. However, there is a tendency of some researchers to make relatively easy project choices and they are inclined to choose a project with a short-term result rather than a bold choice for a project. A research department may have the tendency to avoid risks for a project selection. To prevent researchers from developing a risk-avoidance tendency, a top–down approach is assumed for the project theme selection.

Type 3: Project management

The control target is set according to the project or each research 'seed' and the project is monitored in the management process. The product leader's role is broad and varied. In some cases, the leader takes charge from the development of 'seeds' to, occasionally, marketing the project outputs. Moreover, in drug discovery steps, project-oriented organization is adopted in some cases. In some analysis steps, tests and examinations in the development process, a function-oriented organization is used in order to an improve the research efficiency.

5. Management Accounting for Excellent R&D Activity

Management accounting is an effective technique for manufacturing and distribution management but has no good application for research and development management.[1] A clear framework of management accounting systems in R&D budgeting and performance evaluation cannot be drawn. However, it could be said that setting a foreign-based research laboratory as a cost center in Ezai Pharmaceutical Co., Ltd., and doing individual-oriented management for domestic research laboratory or drug discovery institute in some companies, and furthermore, the setting of satellite laboratory to be done in Otsuka Pharmaceutical Co., Ltd., were a kind of first trial for making the performance of a laboratory to be quantitative.

The measurement and the monitoring of the input in R&D is said to be a step for performance control as long as the output is not clear. Moreover, it is very important that we get the kind of results we can understand, that can be grasped, and the frequency of the feedback interval is also important. Takeda, Yamanouchi, and Eisai Co., Ltd., etc. representing the pharmaceutical manufacturing companies in Japan, believe strongly in such efficiency improvement.

5.1. The characteristics of management by objectives in R&D

How is a researcher's motivation improved? How is the fairness of a researcher's evaluation maintained? The development of the Management by Objectives system is still underway in Japan. However, a movement to try to restructure the evaluation system, based on individuals, has become stronger in Takeda Chemical Industries Co., Ltd. and it could be said that the individual-oriented evaluation reinforcement has become more general with global R&D activity. The chief researcher and a project leader in the movement became the focal-point along this movement.

5.2. Matrix system and project management as organizational control

In research and development activity, there are two types of system, called project leader and product manager. The product manager system is a system that crosses the continuous product development process compared with the project manager system. On the other hand, in the project management, the leaders and the member are changed as the development process advances. However, these two systems have no strict distinction between them and are called by different names with overlapping meanings. In the case discussed here, only Eizai Co., Ltd. aggressively adopted this project manager and leader for their research organization. Efficient management in the pharmaceutical manufacturing industry is still a problem. However, I think that there are management methods in the pharmaceutical manufacturing industry that are different from some development methods which use an active heavy class project manager, as shown in the automobile industry.

The technique in the drug development process must include many things, and research projects and objects become very specific in each project. At the research steps stage 0 or stage 1, the probability of success must be very low. A talent of intuition and the appropriate characteristics as researchers must be demanded by the team leader in such research. On the other hand, the clinical research of stages 4 or 5 need a great deal of capital and cooperation from outside organizations. In addition, a managerial sense is strongly required in clinical development because the amounts of money invested can be very large (up to 10,000,000,000 yen). I believe that different project leaders and project management are demanded at different stages of research or drug creation and at clinical, or non-clinical stages in drug research.

6. The Possibility of Activity-Based Management in R&D in Japan

ABM (activity based management) which had developed in the United States in the 1980s was introduced into Japan, in order for Japanese enterprises to become adaptable in '1990s' and to decrease the indirect costs of their headquarters. Here, let us view the future by examining the company being tried now on the possibility of ABM in order to promote an improvement in efficiency in their research activity and searching for the application in the future.

In activity based management, resources are not consumed in a section or department, but instead resources would be consumed by activities. Management then tries to discriminate whether such activities would produce additional value or not. It is necessary to calculate the research and development process time-basis (as in the following diagrams) and examine activities by their micro and the macro elements (see Fig. 4.3).

In European and American enterprises, as for a big organization, the control target is not set for each year but each day. The reason for this is that sales during a day that correspond to 100 million to 200 million yen would mean that the sales volume during a year would be 30 billion to 60 billion yen. Shortening the development period becomes increasingly important for this reason. Then, increasing the development efficiency has two possibilities: shortening of the delivery date and improving the probability of successful development. It is thought that between these two, it is the shortening of the development time and ABM that have the possibility for the greatest contribution to an enterprise. Management thinks that the activity cost of the research and development section in Fig. 4.3 should be analyzed and each micro-process above would be examined. 35% of costs (other than

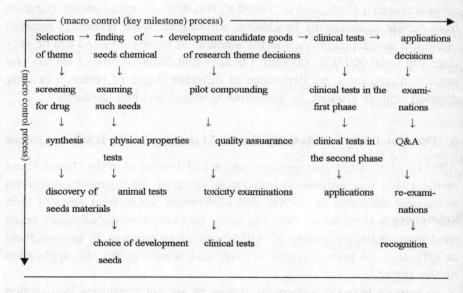

Fig. 4.3. Process seeds diagram of research and development (macro control (key milestone) process).

strategy costs and direct business costs) are reduced. I believe that to decrease the bottleneck and to shorten time is a great contribution towards this reduction, though the cost reduction might also be of great significance. Moreover, when seeing the situation from the point of view of the management of the enterprise, it may be said that for suitable consent from researchers time to be used for a research is not to be discussed directly, but researchers can be persuaded based on the available costs.

7. Conclusion

There are a lot of excellent aspects to the research and development management of a Japanese enterprise when compared with companies in Europe and America. Knowledge creation is done in teams activities and the knowledge is shared by two or more persons of the teams. As a result, even if some person is dropped from the team, the continuity of a project is maintained and the project would produce a kind of synergy which cannot be understood by earnings ratios of an individual project occasionally. However, the creativity of the individual, and the construction of reasonable research process, come to be demanded at the same time as research grows more complex and becomes like everyone's energy war, and synergistic effects between such complex systems and human creativity are requested more and more. R&D management in the future needs the contradicting management that means activation of each individual through incentive systems and project team management. If a balance between the two is difficult, top management should try to find open cooperation between firms for an improved R&D strategy.

References

1. Sakurai, M., Management Accounting (in Japanese), (Doubun Kan), 1997.
2. Kokubo, A., Development Systems for Producing Innovative Products Continuously, R&D MANAGEMENT (in Japanese), (July 1997), 4–12.
3. Kuwajima, K. & Takashi, M., The Strategic Significance of Joint Production Recognition in Pharmaceutical Industry (Iryo and Shakai), *Medical Treatment and Society*, Vol. 7, No. 3, 1997, 134–149.

4. Sakuma, Y., Research and Development Organization has Changed, R&D MANAGEMENT (in Japanese), (August, 1996), 6–15.
5. Yamazaki, M., The Cost Management and Investment of R&D in Pharmaceutical Companies, R&D MANAGEMENT (in Japanese), (October, 1997), 14–20.
6. Hirabayashi, T., The Application of Activity Based Costing for R&D Investment, R&D MANAGEMENT (October, 1997), 22–30.
7. Seki, H., The Evaluation Systems for R&D: Central Laboratry of Daiichi Pharmaceutical Companies, The Practices of Searching and Evaluation of Research and Development Themes, ed. (Kigyo Kenkyu Kai), 1994.
8. Hara, Y., The New Point of View for R&D Management Systems and Investment Effectiveness Evaluation, R&D Planning and Investment Effectivness Evaluation, ed. (Kigyo Kenkyu Kai), 1994.
9. Hamel, G. & Praharad, C. K.. Competing for the Future (Harvard Business School Press), 1994.
10. Rusell, P. A., Third, K. N. & Eriksson, T. J., The Third Generation of R&D (Arthur D. Little, Inc.), 1991.
11. Belcher, A., Hassard, J. & Procter, S. J., R&D Decisions: Strategy, Policy and Innovations (Routlage), New York, 1996.
12. Ellis, Lynn, W., Evaluation of R&D Processes: Effectiveness Through Measurements (Artech House Boston), 1997.
13. Yamanoneh, T., New Technology Management (in Japanese), (Nihon Keizai Sinbun-Pub.), 1992.

Part 3
Cost Management in
New Product Development

Chapter 5

Target Costing and Kaizen Costing in Japanese Automobile Companies*

YASUHIRO MONDEN and KAZUKI HAMADA

1. Introduction

Environmental changes in Japanese automobile companies — for example, the high appreciation of yen currency, the shortening of the product life-cycle, the diversification of demand and keen competition — are severe: With such changes, cost management methods used must be useful for the production of new products which meet customers' demands at lowest cost, as well as cost reduction of existing products by eliminating wastes.

On account of the above, companies have come to need total cost management which includes product development and design activities as well as production activities. This contrasts with traditional cost management which focused on cost control in the production stage. The fact that most of the costs in the production stage are determined in the

*This paper was first published in Journal of Management Accounting Research, Vol. 3, Fall 1991, pp. 16–34. Reprinted with kind permission of the journal.

The authors are grateful to the editor, William L. Ferrara, and anonymous referees for their helpful comments and suggestions to original paper.

stage of new product development and design indicates the need for total cost management.

The purpose of this chapter is to describe the features of the total cost management system in Japanese automobile companies. As the title indicates, the chapter consists of two main pillars. They are "Target costing" (the establishment of a target cost and the method of its attainment) and "Kaizen costing." They can be summarized as follows:

(i) "Target costing" is the system to support the cost reduction process in the developing and designing phase of an entirely new model, a full model change or a minor model change. (Target costing is called "Genkakikaku" in Japanese).

(ii) "Kaizen costing" is the system to support the cost reduction process in the manufacturing phase of the existing model of the product. (Kaizen costing is called "Genkakaizen" in Japanese.) The Japanese word "Kaizen" in Kaizen costing may be a somewhat different concept from the English word "improvement." "Kaizen" refers to continuous accumulations of small betterment activities rather than innovative improvement. Therefore, "Kaizen costing" includes cost reduction in the manufacturing stage of existing products. Innovative improvement based on new technological innovations is usually introduced in the developing and designing stage.[a]

Target costing and Kaizen costing, when linked together, constitute the total cost management system of Japanese companies. The "total" cost management in this context implies cost management in all phases of product

---

[a]See, Ref. 2, Chap. 2. In the glossary of Ref. 2, he defines the meaning of Kaizen as follows: Kaizen means continuing improvement in personal life, home life, social life, and working life. When applied to the workplace Kaizen means continuing improvement involving everyone — managers and workers alike. Further, he says, improvement can be defined as Kaizen and innovation, where a Kaizen strategy maintains and improves the working standard through small, gradual improvements, and innovation calls forth radical improvements as a result of large investments in technology and/or equipment.

life. The concept of total cost management also comes from total involvement of all people in all departments throughout the company.

Since the concept of Kaizen costing is rather new in the U.S.A., we will clarify its concept, procedures, and its relationships with target costing in this chapter. Also, the general idea in the U.S.A. seems to be that floor-level control activities are more useful in modern manufacturing plants as a result of the spread of the JIT (just in time) production system and TQC (total quality control), and that the accounting control system has become useless and unnecessary. We would like to demonstrate in this chapter, however, that the management accounting system is functioning very well in both target costing and Kaizen costing in Japanese automobile companies.

2. Features of Target Costing

Broadly speaking, the step of corporate long-term or middle-term profit planning is included in the process of target costing. Narrowly interpreting target costing would be that it consists of two processes roughly classified as: (a) the process of planning a specific product that satisfies customers' needs and of establishing the target cost from the target profit and targeted sales price of the new product, and (b) the process of realizing the target cost by using "value engineering" (VE) and a comparison of target costs with achieved costs.[b]

At this point it would be appropriate to briefly comment about VE. The basic idea of VE is that products and services have functions to perform and the amount of their value is measured by the ratio of these functions to their costs. By this process, the decision as to whether the product is to be produced is made. For this purpose, it is necessary that the functions of each product, part and service are clarified and that all functions are quantified. For example, VE activities for direct materials can be implemented

---

[b] See, Refs. 9, p. 17, and Ref. 15. Reference 9 is the first paper published in the U.S.A. that described Japanese target costing auld Kaizen costing, which were literally translated from their Japanese terms as "cost planning" and "cost improvement." Reference 18 also covers target costing in many Japanese assembly-type industries and computer software companies.

concerning the material quality or a grade change, the reduction of the number of bolts in a part, the change of a part shape, the common use of an alternative part, the change of painting method, etc.

VE is different from control activities based on traditional standard cost accounting and it encourages the proposal of creative plans designed to reduce cost standards. This contrasts with standard cost accounting which overemphasizes determining and achieving cost performance standards.

The techniques of VE itself were first developed in GE.[5] In the case of GE, however, they were initially aiming at reduction of purchased parts costs, and their VE activities were not linked to corporate target profit and target costs as they are in Japan.

In general, target costing has the following properties.

(i) Target costing is applied in the developing and designing stage and it is different from the standard cost control system which is applied in the production stage.

(ii) Target costing is not a management method for cost control in a traditional sense, but it is one which intends to reduce costs.

(iii) In the target costing process, many methods of management science are used, because the managerial objects of target costing include the techniques of development and product design.

(iv) The cooperation of many departments is needed in the execution of target costing.

(iv) Target costing is more suitable in the multiproduct-small production run firm than in the few product-large production run firm.

In addition to the reasons which we mentioned in the introduction, the reason why target costing has become important is that in Japan the ratio of variable costs to total manufacturing costs has recently increased remarkably (up to 90 percent in the auto industry) and the ratio of direct material costs to total variable costs is about 85 percent in the auto companies as the annual reports show. This means that the management of variable costs has become extremely important. Moreover, as the ratio of direct labor costs to total manufacturing costs is about six percent in the auto companies, the management of direct material costs by target costing has become more important than that of direct labor costs.

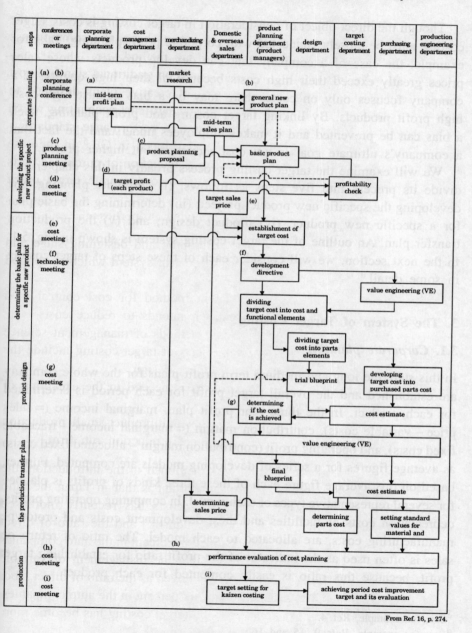

steps	conferences or meetings	corporate planning department	cost management department	merchandizing department	Domestic & overseas sales department	product planning department (product managers)	design department	target costing department	purchasing department	production engineering department
corporate planning	(a) (b) corporate planning conference	(a) mid-term profit plan		market research		(b) general new product plan				
developing the specific new product project	(c) product planning meeting			mid-term sales plan		basic product plan				
	(d) cost meeting	(c) product planning proposal								
		(d) target profit (each product)			target sales price	profitability check				
determining the basic plan for a specific new product	(e) cost meeting				(e) establishment of target cost					
	(f) technology meeting				development directive			value engineering (VE)		
product design	(g) cost meeting				dividing target cost into cost and functional elements					
						dividing target cost into parts elements				
					trial blueprint			developing target cost into purchased parts cost		
				(g) determining if the cost is achieved				cost estimate		
the production transfer plan						value engineering (VE)				
						final blueprint				
			determining sales price					cost estimate		
						determining parts cost		setting standard values for material and		
production	(h) cost meeting		(h) performance evaluation of cost planning							
	(i) cost meeting				(i) target setting for kaizen costing	achieving period cost improvement target and its evaluation				

From Ref. 16, p. 274.

Fig. 5.1. The system of target costing.

Though the direct object of consideration in target costing is costs, target costing must be closely connected with corporate profit planning. Take for example, the case of a company that can develop products whose sales prices greatly exceed their high costs because of their high quality. If a company focuses only on costs, there may be a bias against high cost/high profit products. By linking target costing and profit planning, such a bias can be prevented and it makes employees understand the fact that a company's ultimate goal is not cost reduction but higher profits.[c]

We will examine the target costing process broadly in this chapter and divide its process into five steps as follows: (i) corporate planning; (ii) developing the specific new product project; (iii) determining the basic plan for a specific new product; (iv) product design; and (v) the production transfer plan. An outline of the target costing system is shown in Fig. 5.1. In the next section, we will consider each of these steps of target costing in some detail.[d]

3. The System of Target Costing

3.1. *Corporate planning*

In this step, the long and medium term profit plans for the whole company are established and the overall target profit for each period is determined for each product. In the three-year profit plan, marginal income (= sales price − variable costs), contribution margin (= marginal income − traceable fixed costs), and operating profit (contribution margin − allocated fixed costs) as average figures for a series of developing models are computed. Further, based on this average figure each of these three kinds of profits is planned for several representative types of each model. In computing operating profits, depreciation costs of facilities and dies, development costs and prototype manufacturing costs, are allocated to each model. The ratio of return on sales is often used as the indicator of the profit ratio for establishing target profit, because this ratio is easily computed for each product.

---

[c]See, for example, Ref. 4.

[d]See, for example, Refs. 9, 15 and 16.

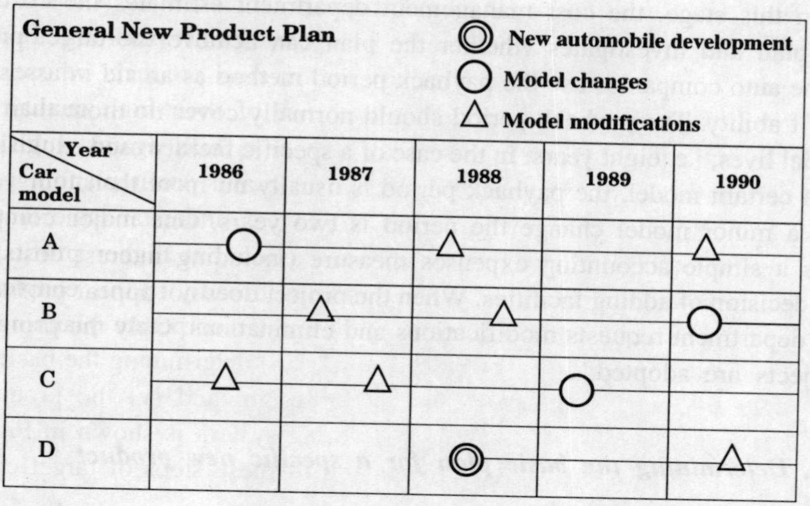

Year / Car model	1986	1987	1988	1989	1990
General New Product Plan		◎ New automobile development			
		○ Model changes			
		△ Model modifications			
A	○		△		△
B		△	△		○
C	△	△		○	
D			◎		△

From Ref. 15, p. 106.

Fig. 5.2. General new product plan.

A corporate plan is drafted by the corporate planing department. As part of the plan, new product development plans are drafted by the engineering planning department and a general new product plan is established. In this plan, the time frame of new product development, model changes and model modifications are established for all cars. This plan is illustrated by the form shown in Fig. 5.2.

3.2. *Developing the specific new product project*

In order to give shape to the general new product plan, the merchandizing department presents the product planning department with its wishes regarding the type of new product to be developed and the content of the model changes based on market research. This is discussed at the top management product planning meeting and the product planning proposal is prepared there. The product manager later gives shape to this plan and establishes the basic product plan.

In this stage, the cost management department estimates the costs of the plan and investigates whether the plan can achieve the target profit. Some auto companies use the payback period method as an aid in assessing profit ability. The payback period should normally cover no more than two model lives; i.e. eight years. In the case of a specific facility used exclusively by a certain model, the payback period is usually no more than four years. For a minor model change the period is two years. One major company uses a simple accounting expenses measure (including interest costs) for the decision of adding facilities. When the project does not appear profitable, the department requests modifications and eliminations. Only the profitable projects are adopted.

3.3. *Determining the basic plan for a specific new product*

In this step, the major cost factors such as design and structure are determined and target costs are established. The product manager requests each department to review material requirements and the manufacturing process, and to estimate costs. According to the reports of the departments, the total "estimated cost" is computed.

At the same time, target price figures are gathered from the domestic auto division and the foreign auto division. From these prices and target profit, "allowable cost" is computed. The method of the computation is as follows:

$$\text{target sales price} - \text{target profit} = \text{allowable cost.}$$

Allowable cost is the cost that top management strongly desires to attain. If this cost is adopted as the target of efforts, the requirement is very severe and not immediately attainable. On the other hand, the estimated cost is not the appropriate target of efforts. Thus it is necessary to establish a "target cost" that is attainable and motivates employees to make efforts to ultimately achieve the "allowable cost." For this reason, studies and positive application of motivational factors regarding employee behavior are needed.

The establishment of the target cost needs to be reviewed on various dimensions regarding the size of the gap between allowable cost and estimated cost. After the target cost is determined, and if that plan is approved, top management orders development based on it. Following that, each department implements VE activities regarding the design method in cooperation with each other in order to identify cost effective products that will fulfill customers' demands.

In addition, the engineering planning department decomposes the target cost into each cost element and functional element with the help of the cost management department.[e] Cost elements are material costs, purchased parts costs, direct labor costs, depreciation costs and so on. Functional elements are engine, transmission system, chassis and so on. Important points are clarified by these detailed classifications. The form of the classification is shown in Fig. 5.3.

Functions \ Cost Elements	Material Costs	Purchased Parts Costs	Direct Labor Costs	•••••	Total
Engine	¥	¥	¥		¥
Transmission System					
Chassis					
• • •					
Total					

The amount should be presented either in the form of the total cost for a single car (in the case of a new model or a model change) or as a deviation from the existing model in the case of model modifications).

From Ref. 15, p. 108.

Fig. 5.3. Target cost broken into cost elements and functions.

---

[e] See Ref. 19 about the method of target development.

Function			Assembly Number							Name		
					Car Model					Direct Labor Cost		
Major Units	Part Number	Part Name	Quantity	Process	A	B	C	Material Cost	Purchased Part Cost	Department	Worker Hours (Minimum)	Amount
									¥	¥		¥

From Ref. 15, p. 109.

Fig. 5.4. Target cost broken into parts elements.

The design department also decomposes the target cost into each part. This classification is made to be followed up by target achievement activities in the production design stage including the purchasing department. For this reason, the classification is detailed. The form of the classification is shown in Fig. 5.4.

3.4. *Product design*

The design department drafts a trial blueprint according to the target cost set for every part. For this draft, information from each department is needed. The design department also actually makes a trial car according to the blueprint and the cost management department estimates the costs of the car.

If there is a gap between the target cost and the estimated cost, the departments execute the VE analysis in cooperation with each other and the trial blueprint is adjusted accordingly. After repeating this process several times, the final blueprint is established.

3.5. *The production transfer plan*

In this step, the preparatory condition of production equipment is checked and the cost management department estimates costs according to the final blueprint. The production engineering department establishes standard values of material consumption, labor hours and so on. Those values are presented to the factory.

Those standard values are used as a data base for computing costs for the purpose of financial accounting and for "material requirements planning" (MRP). Therefore, they are usually fixed for one year. One major firm calls this value the "basic cost." The purchasing department also starts negotiating the prices of purchased parts at this time.

Soon after the target cost is set, production begins. The performance evaluation of target costing is then implemented after new cars have been produced for three months, as abnormal values usually arise during the first three months.

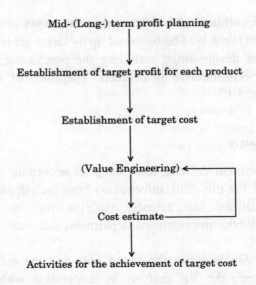

Fig. 5.5. General summary of the target costing process.

The performance evaluation of target costing is implemented to examine the degree to which the target cost is achieved. If the target cost is not achieved, investigations are made to clarify where the responsibility lies and where the gap arises. These investigations also evaluate the effectiveness of the target costing activities.

The above are the features of the target costing process in Japanese automobile companies. In this process which can be summarized in Fig. 5.5 management accounting plays an important role.

As target costing deals with the development and design of new products many technical methods of engineering are needed. However, the management accounting system is important in effectively determining target profits, target costs and estimated costs.

4. Features of Kaizen Costing

When a Japanese accountant hears the words "Kaizen costing," he expects a relation to the cost control system based on standard cost accounting

However, Kaizen costing in Japanese automobile companies has not been implemented according to standard costing. This means that the companies do not implement the traditional cost variance analysis based upon the gap between the standard cost and the actual cost for each period. Kaizen costing is implemented outside the standard cost system as part of the overall budget control system. In essence, the actual cost per car for the latest period is the Kaizen cost budget which must be reduced in each successive period in order to meet the target profit.

The reason why Japanese automobile companies implement Kaizen costing outside the standard cost accounting system is not because cost reduction in the production stage is taken less seriously, but because it is considered to be very important. Standard costing is limited by its financial accounting purpose in Japanese automobile companies and therefore it has many unsuitable features for cost reduction in the manufacturing phase.

Further, the concept of Kaizen costing covers broader meanings than the traditional cost control concept that refers to meeting cost performance standards and to investigating and responding when those standards are not met. Kaizen costing activities include cost reduction activities which requires changes in the way the company manufactures existing products. The inadequacy of standard costs for Kaizen costing purposes is obvious from the viewpoint of "Kaizen" concepts. Also the standard costs are changed only once a year.

Roughly classified, Kaizen costing activities are of two kinds. One consists of activities implemented to *kaizen* actual performance when the difference between actual cost and target cost is large after new products have been in production for three months. The other kind consists of activities implemented continually every period to reduce any difference between target and estimated profit and thus to achieve "allowable cost."

In the former case, a special project team called a "cost Kaizen committee" is organized and the team implements VE activities. The following distinction between VE and "value analysis" (VA) can be made. VE is the cost reduction activity that involves basic functional changes in the new product development stage. VA is the cost reduction activity that involves design changes of existing products.[f] However, the distinction is not made in this case and the term "VE" is used. The establishment of a cost Kaizen committee implies that the car model's Kaizen has a top priority.

The following is a real life example of activities of the cost Kaizen committee. Just after the oil shock in 1973, the profitability of one automobile model showed a marked decrease because of cost increases due to oil. At that time, the plant manager made the following proposals to the top management meeting concerning cost reduction.

  (i) Establishment of a cost Kaizen committee chaired by the plant manager.
 (ii) Promotion of a company-wide cost reduction program for the specific model.
(iii) As substructures to this committee, organization of the following three subcommittees.

    (a) Production and assembly
    (b) Design and engineering
    (c) Purchasing
 (iv) Establishment of a cost reduction goal of 10,000 yen (about $75) per automobile.
 (iv) Expectation that the above goal would be achieved within six months.

Through a concerted effect by all departments based on the decisions of the cost Kaizen committee, the actual result of the plan was 128 percent attainment of goal at the end of six months.

The second category of Kaizen costing means reaching cost reduction targets established for every department as a result of the short term profit plan. Different methods are adopted because of the difference between variable and fixed costs. For example, the variable costs such as direct materials, coating, energy, and direct labor costs are managed by setting the amount of Kaizen cost per unit of each product type. Fixed costs are subjected to "management by objectives" based on the overall amount of Kaizen cost instead of the amount of Kaizen cost per car.

---

[f]Some companies distinguish VA from VE as described above.

Since the purchasing department supervises the purchase prices of parts from outside suppliers, in the factory the most important subject is the use of VE activities to reduce consumption. Usually, the purchasing department is not allocated an amount of Kaizen cost target for its own department expenses, but attempts to reduce costs of parts by promoting VE proposals of vendors as well as by negotiating prices with vendors.

As for direct labor costs, monetary control as well as physical control in terms of labor hours is implemented by using the cost decrease amount as the Kaizen cost target. A similar approach is applied to material costs improvement.

It is much easier for factory workers to understand the Kaizen targets when the amount of cost reduction targets for both fixed and variable costs are presented individually rather than presenting the total cost target. We will consider the method of computation for the second category of Kaizen costing in the next section.

5. Computation of the Target Amout of Kaizen Cost

Japanese automobile companies determine the amount of profit improvement (i.e. Kaizen profit) based on the difference between target profit (planned by a top–down approach) and estimated profit (computed as a bottom–up estimate). They usually intend to achieve half of that amount by sales increases and half by cost reduction.[g] Of course when the industry is in recession such as an oil crisis or a high appreciation of currency greater weight will be imposed on cost reduction.

The reasoning that the increase in sales increases profit is based partly on the notion of profit contribution. This reasoning is also based partly on the idea of ROI from the point of view that the sales increases raise the total asset turnover ratio.

A sales increase can be generated by raising the sales price or increasing sales volume. The former does not cause an increase in variable costs, whereas the latter does.

See, for example, Refs. 12 and 21.

For generating cost savings, reductions of both variable costs and fixed costs are considered. As most of manufacturing fixed costs are needed for maintaining continuous growth, Japanese automobile companies generally think that the amount of Kaizen cost in the plants should be achieved mainly by the reduction of variable costs, especially direct material costs and labor costs.

However, in the non-manufacturing departments, the amount of Kaizen cost (or Kaizen expense) reduction is set for fixed costs. Departments affected include the head office, research and development and sales. The design department is usually not assigned an amount of Kaizen cost and the purchasing department is not assigned one except in special cases such as an oil crisis or a yen appreciation, etc.

The total amount of Kaizen costs in all plants (= (C) in the following formulas) is determined in the cost Kaizen meeting as follows:

amount of actual cost per car in last period (A) = amount of actual cost in last period ÷ actual production in last period

estimated amount of actual cost for all plants in this period (B) = amount of actual cost per car in last period (A) × estimated production in this period

target of Kaizen cost in this period for all plants (C) = estimated amount of actual cost for all plants in this period (B) × target ratio of cost decrease amount to the estimated cost

The target ratio of cost decrease amount to the estimated cost is determined in consideration of attaining the target profit of the year. Usually that ratio is around ten percent. For a new product, the target cost that is determined in the target costing process is expected to be attained within three months from the time production is started on the new product, but after that, the figure can also be reduced further by applying the same technique of Kaizen costing.

The target amount of Kaizen cost assigned to each factory is as follows;

$$\begin{matrix} \text{assignment ratio} \\ \text{(D)} \end{matrix} = \begin{matrix} \text{costs directly} \\ \text{controlled by each} \\ \text{plant} \end{matrix} \div \begin{matrix} \text{total amount of} \\ \text{costs directly} \\ \text{controlled by plants} \end{matrix}$$

$$\begin{matrix} \text{total amount of} \\ \text{Kaizen cost for} \\ \text{each plant} \end{matrix} = \begin{matrix} \text{target of Kaizen} \\ \text{cost in this period} \\ \text{for all plants (C)} \end{matrix} \times \begin{matrix} \text{assignment ratio} \\ \text{(D)} \end{matrix}$$

Costs directly controlled by a plant include direct material costs, direct labor costs, variable overhead costs and so on. Excluded are the fixed costs such as depreciation costs, etc. The amount of Kaizen cost for each plant is decomposed and assigned to each division and that amount is again assigned to smaller units of the organization. Some details about the method of assignment are considered in the next section.

The Kaizen cost target is achieved by daily Kaizen activities. The JIT production system also intends to reduce various wastes in the plant by these daily activities. Therefore, Kaizen costing and the JIT production system are closely related with each other.

5. Kaizen Costing Through "Management by Objectives"

Each manufacturing plant has objectives about efficiency, quality and cost, etc. The concrete targets of physical objectives are determined and evaluated in the production meeting, while Kaizen costs targets are determined and evaluated in the Kaizen cost meeting.

The cost meetings are held at several organizational levels, for example, at the plant, division, department, section and process levels. In the cost meeting for each level, the amount of Kaizen cost — that is, the amount of the reduction target — is assigned through "management by objectives" at that organizational level.[h] That assignment is called "objectives decomposition"

---

[h] For the detail characteristics of Japanese management by objectives, see Refs. 11 and 14, p. 413–423.

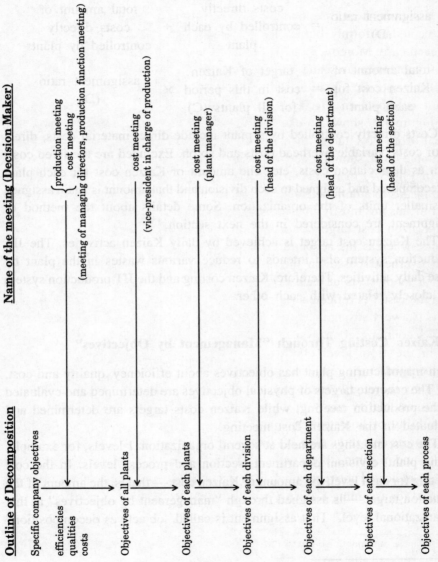

Fig. 5.6. Objectives decomposition in plants

and is implemented according to concrete purposes and policies determined in advance.

However, it is essential that the objectives decomposition not be implemented uniformly, but implemented with the consideration of the specifics of each case. Moreover, the determination of each objective, the evaluation, the countermeasures and so on, must be implemented flexibly depending on each specific situation. The outline of objectives decomposition in the plant is shown in Fig. 5.6.

Figure 5.7,[i] shows an example of objectives decomposition for attaining the Kaizen cost target in a machining department. Figure 5.8, is another example in a stamping department.

In Fig. 5.7, managers at each organizational level determine policies and means to attain the Kaizen cost target in their department. Their policies and means are mostly non-monetary measures, but the purpose is to realize the Kaizen cost target.[j] Managers at each level try to reduce actual labor hours, whereas the accounting department computes the actual labor costs and overhead based on these actual hours. Then actual labor hours and actual labor costs at each organizational level are publicized each month and the result is reflected via incentive pay in the salaries of the employees. This is a very strong incentive for them. Thus, both production management and accounting control are functioning at the same time in the company.

In the floor-level control activities, the JIT production system has contributed to the reduction of costs remarkably. It is a system that reduces costs by thoroughly excluding waste in plants. Reducing inventories makes managers clarify many problems in plants. If inventories are reduced, the possibility of line-stops arising becomes higher in problematic places and this forces cost reductions by investigating causes of line-stops via defective units and machine breakdowns, etc.

As indicated above, through the Kaizen costing process, accounting control is used for assigning Kaizen cost targets to plants, divisions and departments,

---

[i] In Japanese automobile companies each process shown in Fig. 5.7 constitutes the "process" in the process costing system and each process is headed by a foreman.

[j] The managers also have objectives of quality and productivity (efficiency or lead-time reduction) as well as a Kaizen cost target.

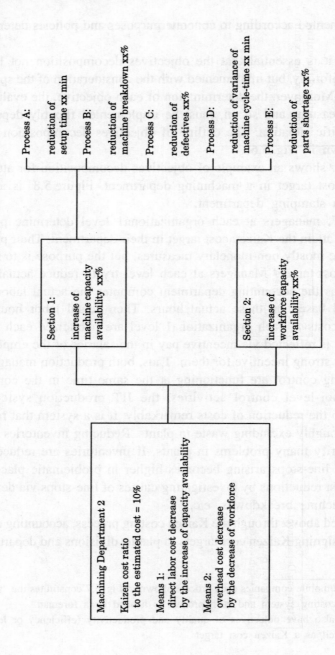

Fig. 5.7. Example of Kaizen cost decomposition in a machining department.

Process A: reduction of setup time xx min

Process B: reduction of machine breakdown xx%

Process C: reduction of defectives xx%

Process D: reduction of variance of machine cycle-time xx min

Process E: reduction of parts shortage xx%

Section 1: increase of machine capacity availability xx%

Section 2: increase of workforce capacity availability xx%

Machining Department 2

Kaizen cost ratio to the estimated cost = 10%

Means 1: direct labor cost decrease by the increase of capacity availability

Means 2: overhead cost decrease by the decrease of workforce

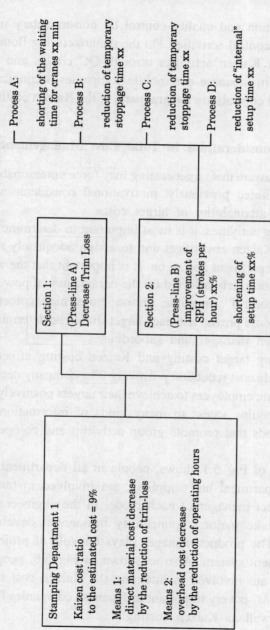

Fig. 5.8. Example of Kaizen cost decomposition in a stamping department.

Stamping Department 1

Kaizen cost ratio
to the estimated cost = 9%

Means 1:
direct material cost decrease
by the reduction of trim-loss

Means 2:
overhead cost decrease
by the reduction of operating hours

Section 1:
(Press-line A)
Decrease Trim Loss

Section 2:
(Press-line B)
improvement of SPH (strokes per hour) xx%

shortening of setup time xx

Process A:
shorting of the waiting time for cranes xx min

Process B:
reduction of temporary stoppage time xx

Process C:
reduction of temporary stoppage time xx

Process D:
reduction of "internal" setup time xx

etc. and the production and quality control by non-monetary measures is used for floor-level control activities. On the manufacturing floor, everyone is involved daily in Kaizen activities through QC circles and suggestion systems, etc. Thus, in Japanese automobile companies accounting controls as well as floor-level controls are integral parts of the Kaizen costing process.

7. Motivational Considerations in Total Cost Management

It is necessary to be aware that target costing may force unreasonable demands on employees. As noted previously, motivational considerations must be considered for the attainability of target costs.

In Kaizen costing activities, it is most important to determine adequately the amount of the Kaizen cost target and to assign adequately that amount for each division, department and so on. It is important that the assignments of the amount are not overly affected by the organizational power structure. Rather, the "self-control" principle (autonomous management by each employee group) should prevail and each target should be determined through consultation between manager and subordinates.

For implementing target costing and Kaizen costing effectively, each employee must tackle cost reduction positively. The company needs to devise methods that motivate employees to achieve their targets positively. Moreover, as VE activities require access to many kinds of information in various departments, methods that promote group activities and co-operation need to be adopted.

As the top row of Fig. 5.1 shows, people in all departments, including the purchasing department and suppliers, are involved in target costing, although the product manager of each model in the engineering planning department must take major responsibility throughout development and designing stages. The product manager plays the role of project leader in a matrix management system. Also as shown in Fig. 5.6, people in every level of the plant are involved in attaining the Kaizen cost target. Thus, "people involvement" is very important in Japanese companies for executing target costing as well as Kaizen costing.

8. Summary

In this chapter, we have considered a total cost management system which includes product development and design activities as well as manufacturing activities. That is, we have considered the features of target costing and Kaizen costing that are the two important pillars in the total cost management system in all phases of the product life cycle of an automobile.

Nowadays, it is certain that the importance of target costing is increasing. However, Kaizen costing should not be slighted. Kaizen costing is entirely different from standard costing in that it aims at continuous reduction of costs in the manufacturing stage, while standard costing aims at achieving and maintaining standard costs. Target costing and Kaizen costing should be inseparably related to each other. If either of them is ignored, total cost management during the whole life of a product cannot be implemented adequately.

References

1. Ban, S. & Kimura, O., Toyota Jidosha Seisanbumon: Kihon no Tettei to Jyunansei no Torikumi, JMA Production Management, October, 1986, 13–22.
2. Imai, M., KAIZEN: The Key to Japan's Competitive Success (Random House Business Division, 1986).
3. Kato, Y., Genkakikaku-katsudo no Shintenkai: Daihatsu Kogyo no Jirei, Kaikei, Vol. 138, No. 4, 1990, 46–62.
4. Makido, T., Recent Trends in Japan's Cost Management Practices, Chapter 1, in Monden and Sakurai [1989], 3–13.
5. Miles, L. D., Techniques of Value Analysis and Engineering (McGraw-Hill, 1961).
6. Monden, Y., Toyota Production System (Industrial Engineering and Management Press, 1983).
7. Monden, Y., Applying Just in Time: The American/Japanese Experience (Industrial Engineering and Management Press, 1986).
8. Monden, Y., JIT Seisan Hoshiki to Genkakeisan, Genkakanri, Kigyokaikei Vol. 40, No. 5, 1988, 24–32.
9. Monden, Y., Total Cost Management System in Japanese Automobile Corporations," Monden [1986], 171–184 and Chapter 2 [1989a] in Monden and Sakurai [1989], 15–33.

10. Monden, Y., Cost Accounting and Control in the Just-in-Time Production System: The Daihatsu Kogyo Experience, Chapter 3 [1989b] in Monden and Sakurai [1989], 35–48.
11. Monden, Y., Characteristics of Performance Control Systems in Japanese Corporations, Chapter 26 [1989c] in Monden and Sakurai [1989], 413–423.
12. Monden, Y., Toyota no Genkakeisan, Genkakanri oyobi Genkakikaku, unpublished.
13. Monden, Y., Cost Management of Japanese Automobile Companies (Productivity Press, 1991).
14. Monden, Y. & Sakurai, M., eds. Japanese Management Accounting (Productivity Press, 1989).
15. Noboru, Y. & Monden, Y., Jidosha Kogyo ni okeru Sogoteki Genkakanri System, Kigyokaikei, Vol. 35, No. 2, 1983, 104–112. (This article was reproduced after partial revisions in Monden [1986], [1989a] and Noboru and Monden [1987].)
16. Noboru, Y. & Monden, Y., Daihatsu Kogyo: Jidosha Kigyo no Genkakanri, Chapter 18, in Okamoto, Miyamoto, Sakurai [1987], 272–289.
17. Okamoto, M., Miyamoto, M. & Sakurai, M., eds. Haitekukaikei (Doyukan, 1987).
18. Sakurai, M., Target Costing and How to Use It, Journal of Cost Management Summer 1989, 39–50.
19. Tanaka, M., Nihon Kigyo no Shinseihin-kaihatu ni Okeru Genkakanri, Kigyokaikei, Vol. 41, No. 2, 1989a, 19–25.
20. Tanaka, T., Cost Planning and Control Systems in the Design Phase of New Product, Chapter 4 [1989b] in Monden and Sakurai [1989], 49–71.
21. Tanaka, T., Toyota no Kaizen Yosan, Kigyokaikei, Vol. 42, No. 3, 1990a, 59–66.
22. Tanaka, T., Jidosha-maker ni Okeru Shinseihin Kaihatsu to Mokuhyo-genka: Toyota no Genkakikaku, Kigyokaikei, Vol. 42, No. 10, 1990b, 46–62.

Chapter 6

Analysis of Variation of Target Costing Practices in the Camera Industry[*]

KENTARO KOGA

1. Introduction

This chapter documents the target costing practices of Japanese camera manufacturers. The purpose of the study is to describe the product development activities, and understand the relationships among them. The documentation covers three aspects of target costing: tables of cost-related information, design reviews and supplier involvement.

Target costing has attracted both academic researchers (e.g. Refs. 1 and 2) and business practitioners (e.g. Refs. 3 and 4). Although past studies have unfolded many aspects of target costing, most have relied on anecdotal evidence, casual observation and firms' description of "standard" practices.[5] Prior research has largely been exploratory and no study has directly documented the details of how the practice is implemented. This chapter explores empirical evidence of how product manufacturing costs are managed during the target costing processes.

[*]I am grateful to the camera manufacturers who participated in this research. I am also indebted to Bob Kaplan, Tony Davila and Partha Mohanram for their helpful comments. The research underlying this chapter was generously funded by Harvard Business School's Division of Research and Arthur Andersen LLP Foundation.

One of the few exceptions of target costing literature which has rarely relied on direct observation is Cooper and Slagmulder's work describing target costing practices of Japanese manufacturers.[2,6] Cooper and Slagmulder, however, study only one firm for a few industries. They do not document intra-industry or intra-firm variation of target costing practices. Moreover, Cooper and Slagmulder's studies lack quantitative data from actual product development projects.

Accordingly, this chapter addresses the following research question:

> *How do target costing practices differ across product development projects and firms in a single industry?*

The present research investigates data of target costing practices of 35 compact camera development projects of seven Japanese manufacturers between 1991 and 1996. A survey of the managers of camera development projects provided information on the product development process; one questionnaire was completed for each development project in the sample.

The major findings of this research are:

1. Product designers used tables of cost-related information more frequently when the tables could be accessed through computers than solely on paper (i.e. hard copies); and when the coverage of the tables contained a larger number of listed parts.
2. The design reviews in the product design stage focused more on the interface among product designers, process engineers and procurement officers than the reviews in the product planning stage.
3. When part suppliers were involved earlier in the process, they made more frequent cost-reduction proposals.
4. Non-Japanese part suppliers made fewer cost reduction proposals.

The rest of this chapter is organized as follows. The second section discusses the research variables chosen for the study. Section 3 outlines the research method. Sections 4–6 report the results for tables of cost-related information, design reviews, and supplier involvement, respectively. The final section concludes the chapter.

2. Research Variables

Target costing consists of two major processes: determining the manufacturing cost target, and achieving the manufacturing cost target.[7,8] This research investigates the latter process in which engineers attempt to achieve the manufacturing cost target.

The premise underlying the selection of research variables is that intensive interactions amongst workers involved in product development contributes to the achievement of the cost target. Iwabuchi[9] and Shimizu[10] argue that target costing is a knowledge creation process[11] in which the cost target triggers interactions among the participants in the process. Likewise, Tani[12] claims that taget costing resembles Simons' interactive control systems[13] of intensive rviews, dialogs and debates. According to Iwabuchi, Shimizu and Tani, frequent monitoring of prospective manufacturing costs, and interactions regarding how to attain the target lead to lower cost product and process designs. In fact, Simons (see Ref. 14) documents that low cost producers in the health care industry use project management systems interactively to develop new products and process improvements that sustain cost advantage.

The intensive interactions in target costing take two forms. First, the interactions occur within the product design function. Second, the interactions occur among the product design, process engineering and procurement functions as well as the material and part suppliers.

The interactions within the product design function involve product designers' activities that enhance, and are driven by, attention to manufacturing costs. An example of those activities is frequent use of tables of cost-related information. Shields and Young[15] find that interactions, in the form of cost-budget participation, create a high degree of cost consciousness among R&D professionals. Cost consciousness motivates them to design a product, with a given functionality, at lower costs. Davila (see Ref. 16) shows that, in the medical devices industry, when cost is the important competitive dimension, managers of product development projects use control systems that provide cost information intensively. The present research measures the use of tables of cost-related information as a variable indicating product designers' attention to manufacturing costs.[a]

The second form of intensive interactions take place among the product design, process engineering and procurement functions as well as material and part suppliers. Product development activities relevant to such interactions include process engineers and procurement officers' participation in design reviews. These interactions are crucial for target costing because they integrate specific knowledge of product designers, process engineers, and procurement officers. Product designers possess expertise in putting together a product from materials and parts. Process engineers and procurement officers are knowledgeable about cost reduction efforts for each material and part as well as the assembly process. Both specific knowledge of putting together a product and reducing costs are critical for target costing. Indeed, Clark and Fujimoto[17] find that, in the auto industry, integrated problem-solving between product design and process engineering significantly improves product development lead time, development productivity and product quality.

This research uses two variables to measure the interactions among the product process engineering and procurement functions and material and part suppliers. The variables are: the participation of process engineers and procurement officers in design reviews; and the supplier involvement.

Although not complete, the three research variables encompass the elements of target costing enumerated by Tani.[18,b] Besides the three variables, this research examines factors that could affect tables of cost-related information, design reviews and supplier involvement. For instance, factors that could be related with the use of part cost table are its form (i.e. database technology underlying the table) and coverage (i.e. number of parts listed in the table).

---

[a]Another activity that reflects product designers' attention to manufacturing costs is frequent cost estimations and revisions. Another study stemming from the present research analyzes cost estimations and revisions.[35]

[b]The elements are: (1) attention to product costs from early stages of product development; (2) setting the cost target and decomposing the target to product components; (3) milestone review meetings; (4) cross-functional participation and concurrent engineering; (5) value engineering; (6) cost tables; and (7) supplier involvement.

3. Research Method

3.1. *Unit of analysis*

The primary unit of analysis of the present research is a completed product development project. The study documents the variation of target costing practices across projects.

Projects in some firms, however, may systematically differ from the projects of other firms, leading to a significant firm effect. Thus, the study also engages in firm-level analysis in order to detect any firm effect. Accordingly, a firm is the secondary unit of analysis.

3.2. *Sample selection*

The present research investigates projects of 35 mm compact cameras developed in Japan between 1991 and 1996. Competition in the compact camera business provides an ideal business environment for the study. The compact camera market is intensively price competitive. Further, the technology of compact cameras is quite mature leaving little room for innovative features. Therefore, manufacturers offer essentially identical product functionality. Since the price points of compacts are well defined in each global region (e.g. in Japan, the price points of compacts are 19,800, 29,800, 39,800, 49,800 and 59,800 yen), firms generally compete over the amount of discount they offer to camera wholesalers and retailers, and eventually to consumers. As a consequence, effective cost management is imperative for survival.

There are several other advantages from studying compact cameras. First, compact cameras are complex enough to require elaborate cost management practices, yet not so complex that the practices cannot be observed and documented.

Second, cameras have been manufactured by stable and similar manufacturing technologies in the industry for the past ten years. Thus, the performance variation stems from how well the cost management practices are employed, and not from innovative manufacturing technologies.

The period between 1991 and 1996 also suits the purpose of the present research because the recession of Japanese economy triggered a domestic price cutting race, which spread to the rest of the world. Between 1991 and 1996, due to the market condition, cost management was an even more crucial strategic concern for Japanese camera manufacturers than other periods.

Seven Japanese camera manufacturers[c] provided data on 49 product development projects. According to the market research by Yano Keizai Kenkyuzyo,[19] the combined Japanese market share of the seven firms was 84.8% in 1994. The target sample included all the projects of the participating firms except for those in which product development was outsourced to a non-subsidiary assembler (i.e. non-*keiretsu* firm).

3.3. Data collection

A survey was administered to collect data on the product development projects. In the survey, the project manager responsible for each camera development project in the sample completed one questionnaire. The survey instrument sought objective information about the product development process, such as the number of days spent for design reviews, and the frequency of table usage. Questions on such objective information reduce the possibility of perceptual biases of responses. In order to decrease recall biases, respondents were encouraged to refer to archival records as much as possible.

The response rate to the survey was 100%. Five responses were not used, however, since they were incomplete due to missing archival records. Furthermore, in order to maintain the homogeneity within the sample, the projects for derivative development were excluded. In contrast with platform development, a derivate development project refines and improves *selected* performance dimensions of an existing product.[20] Specifically, nine projects with newly designed parts of less than 50%,[d] were eliminated from the sample. The resulting sample size is 35.

---

[c]This chapter disguises the names of the participating firms in order to protect their confidentiality.

[d]Percentage is calculated on the basis of product manufacturing costs.

Table 6.1. Profile of cameras in the sample (*n* = 35).

Panel A: Composition by firms

Firm	Frequency (Number of observations in the sample)	Number of responses to the survey
A	5	8
B	3	3
C	5	8
D	7	7
E	5	8
F	3	7
G	7	8
Total	35	49

Firm symbols do not coincide with other tables in order to protect the firms' confidentiality.

Panel B: Composition by market launch years

Year	Frequency
1991	3
1992	4
1993	9
1994	9
1995	9
1996	1
Total	35

Panel C: Summary statistics of major product attributes

	Mean	Standard deviation	Minimum	Median	Maximum
List price (yen)	47,474	10,898	24,800	46,000	66,000
Projected sales volume (1,000 units)	690	490	200	480	2,400
Maximum zoom length (mm)	87	27	32	80	140

3.4. *Profile of products and product development processes in the sample*

Table 6.1 summarizes the profile of the cameras in the sample. Panel A reports the composition of the sample by firms. The numbers of observations of Firms B and F are small. The two firms developed only few cameras by themselves. The rest of their product lines were outsourced to a non-subsidiary firm. Outsourced products are excluded from the sample. Panel B presents the composition by market launch years. There are few observations before 1993 because several development projects of earlier years were excluded from the sample due to missing archival records. Within the sample, only one camera was launched in 1996. In this year the camera manufacturers devoted most of their product development resources to the new photography standard, Advanced Photo System (APS). APS cameras are not included in the study because of its technological novelty. According to Panel C, the mean and median list prices are 47,474 and 46,000 yen, respectively. There is a large standard deviation in the projected sales volume due to observations with extremely high volume. The mean and median maximum 200 m lengths are 87 and 80 mm, respectively.

Figure 6.1 presents the average product development process of the sample. The entire development process, which takes an average of 18.9 months, comprises seven stages. In the *advanced engineering* and *concept study* stages, product designers and marketing personnel examine the technical and commercial feasibility of the prospective camera, respectively. During the *product planning* stage, the product designers plan the major features of product design such as component layout and specifications of important parts. At the end of product planning, the firm holds a meeting called design review to check the product designers' product plan. In *product design*, the product designers work on the engineering drawings of each part. The end of product design is marked by another design review to examine the engineering drawings. The *process engineering* stage includes design of manufacturing tools, part dies and assembly lines. The two *pilot runs* are the final development stages before mass production. During each run, product and process designs are checked to see whether they can withstand the demands of mass production.

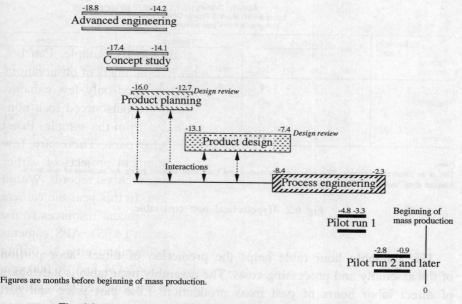

Figures are months before beginning of mass production.

Fig. 6.1. Average product development process of camera firms.

4. Part Price, Part Cost and Assembly Hour Tables

Tables of part price, part cost and assembly hour are tools that product designers use to reduce the product manufacturing costs during product development. Designers can better foresee the cost effect of different design choices by referring to the tables.

Part price and part cost tables assist the prediction of part cost. The part price table records past procurement prices of each part. On the other hand, the part cost table is a database with anticipated cost per part *incurred by the suppliers*. Studies of car manufacturers find that procurement officers negotiate with the suppliers using the part cost tables to infer how much a part should cost to them.[19] Elaborate part price and part cost tables incorporate simulation functions that enable the user to project the price or cost of a unique part depending on its characteristics like material, size and shape. The simulation is structured upon the past experience of part procurement. Figure 6.2 illustrates a hypothetical part cost table.

Activity: Drilling
Equipment: Mark 3 Power Drill
Volume: x units per annum

Type of material	Depth of hole	3 inches				5 inches				7 inches			
		Mat'l	Lab.	OH	Tot.	Mat'l	Lab.	OH	Tot.	Mat'l	Lab.	OH	Tot.
		$	$	$	$	$	$	$	$	$	$	$	$
Plastic		5	2	3	10	7	5	5	17	8	7	8	23
Steel		9	2	2	13	10	2	2	14	12	4	5	21
Aluminium		10	2	2	14	11	3	3	17	12	3	4	19

Note:
This is an illustrative example. The costs are hypothetical and have been selected purely for purposes of this article. Adapted from Yoshikawa *et al.*[23]

Fig. 6.2. Hypothetical part cost table.

The assembly hour table helps the prediction of direct labor portion of the assembly and processing costs. The assembly hour table is a database of direct labor hours of past mass production. Like part price and part cost tables, advanced assembly hour tables allow the user to simulate different design choices in terms of assembly and processing time.

Since the tables relate past manufacturing experience with prospective product design, they are devices to enhance Design for Manufacturing (DFM).[22] The three tables are of interest because how they are used indicates the way cost related information is incorporated in product development.

Yoshikawa *et al.*[23] suggest that having the tables accessible in computer databases are preferable to tables existing solely on paper (i.e. hard copies) because it is easier to construct a simulation function on a database with computers. Moreover, several Japanese researchers maintain that LAN tables are better than databases on personal computers since the product designers will always be working with the most current cost information from the process engineering and procurement functions. These claims imply that product designers will use tables stored in computer databases more often than tables accessible only on paper.

Panel A of Table 6.2 presents the survey responses regarding the forms of the three tables. At the time of each product development, the number of projects without part price, part cost and assembly hour tables were 0, 5 and 4, respectively. A surprisingly small number of each table were available on LAN. The tables with simulation function were limited to 2 cases in part cost tables. Panel B reports the coverage of part price and part cost tables; the coverage represents the proportion of parts listed in the tables relative to the total number of parts of the sample product. Finally, Panel C summarizes the survey responses on one of the research variables, how often an average product designer used any of the tables. The variable is relevant to the product designers' attention to manufacturing costs.

Table 6.2. Summary of responses on form, coverage and usage of tables.

Panel A: Form of tables

	Did not exist	On paper	On personal computer	On LAN	On personal computer with simulation	On LAN with simulation
Part price table (0%)	0 (0%)	12 (34%)	20 (57%)	3 (9%)	0 (0%)	0
Part cost table (14%)	5 (14%)	10 (29%)	12 (34%)	6 (17%)	2 (6%)	0 (0%)
Assembly hour table (11%)	4 (11%)	16 (46%)	10 (29%)	5 (14%)	0 (0%)	0 (0%)

Frequency for each response in upper rows.
Percentage within the sample in lower rows in parentheses.

Panel B: Coverage of tables

	Did not exist	1–25%	26–50%	51–75%	75–100%
Part price table (0%)	0 (0%)	11 (31%)	4 (11%)	3 (9%)	17 (49%)
Part cost table (9%)	3 (9%)	10 (29%)	3 (9%)	3 (9%)	16 (46%)

Frequency for each response in upper rows.
Percentage within the sample in lower rows in parentheses.

Table 6.2 (*Continued*)

Panel C: Frequency of usage

	Not used	0.5/week or less	1–2/week	3–4/week	5–6/week	7/week or more
Product planning						
First half	5 (14%)	25 (71%)	3 (9%)	0 (0%)	2 (6%)	0 (0%)
Second half	2 (6%)	26 (74%)	5 (14%)	0 (0%)	2 (6%)	0 (0%)
Product design						
First half	1 (3%)	21 (60%)	12 (34%)	1 (3%)	0 (0%)	0 (0%)
Second half	3 (9%)	19 (54%)	8 (23%)	5 (14%)	0 (0%)	0 (0%)
Process engineering	4 (11%)	22 (63%)	7 (20%)	1 (3%)	1 (3%)	0 (0%)
Pilot runs	3 (9%)	25 (71%)	6 (17%)	1 (3%)	0 (0%)	0 (0%)

Frequency for each response in upper rows.
Percentage within the sample in lower rows in parentheses.

Table 6.3 presents results from tests on whether more elaborate forms[e] of tables are associated with more frequent use by product designers. In the analyses of variance of Panels A, B and C, the dependent variable is the aggregate frequency of table usage,[f] and the independent variables are forms of the tables. The original six responses on table forms are converted into two categories: non-computer based and computer based. The forms

---

[e]The examination is on association, not causality.
[f]The frequency is calculated as the midpoint of each survey response's range. For example, for the response of "1 to 2/week" the frequency of 1.5/week is used. For the responses of "[Table] did not exist", "0.5/week or less" and "7/week or more", the frequencies of 0/week, 0.5/week and 7.5/week are applied, respectively.

Table 6.3. Analysis of variance of table usage by table form.

Panel A: Part price table

Form	Frequency	Mean of aggregate usage frequency	F statistic	**9.12**
			p value	***0.00***
Computer based	23	7		
Non computer based	12	3		

Panel B: Part cost table

Form	Frequency	Mean of aggregate usage frequency	F statistic	0.64
			p value	*0.43*
Computer based	20	6		
Non computer based	15	5		

Panel C: Assembly hour table

Form	Frequency	Mean of aggregate usage frequency	F statistic	**11.85**
			p value	***0.00***
Computer based	15	8		
Non computer based	20	4		

Table 6.4. Analysis of variance of aggregate table usage frequency by table coverage.

Panel A: Part price table

Coverage	Frequency	Mean of aggregate usage frequency	F statistic	**6.89**
			p value	***0.01***
51–100%	20	7		
1–50%	15	4		

Panel B: Part cost table

Coverage	Frequency	Mean of aggregate usage frequency	F statistic	**8.96**
			p value	***0.01***
51–100%	19	7		
1–50%	16	3		

of part price and assembly hour tables are associated with the frequency of their usage at the significance level of less than 0.01; computer based tables are used more frequently.

Similarly, in Table 6.4, the dependent variable is the aggregate frequency of table usage, and the independent variables are the coverage of part price and part cost tables. The original four classification of table coverage are converted into two groups: 1–50% and 51–100%. The coverage of both part price and part cost tables are associated with the frequency of their usage at the significance of 0.01; tables with coverage broader than 51% are used more frequently (Panels A and B).

In order to investigate whether the table form or coverage is the key factor associated with the table usage, the present research applies the general linear model (GLM). GLM is used instead of analysis of variance because the analysis involves unbalanced data with multiple independent variables,[g] and GLM generates statistics for a marginal effect controlling for the other independent variables. As reported in Panel A of Table 6.5, Spearman rank order correlation of forms among part price, part cost and assembly hour tables is strong. Likewise, the coverage of part price and part cost tables is significantly correlated with each other. In order to avoid multicollinearity, the model includes the form and coverage of only part price table as well as the interaction between the two. The model is:

$$(\text{Table usage}) = (\text{Form}) + (\text{Coverage}) + (\text{Interaction})$$

Panel B shows that the marginal effects of both the form and coverage of part price table as well as the interaction are significant at least at the 0.1 level.

A one-way analysis of variance in Table 6.6 suggests a significant firm effect on the aggregate frequency of table usage at the 0.05 level (F statistic 2.70, p value 0.03). The table also indicates that the effect of part price table's form, coverage and their combination on usage holds at the firm level as well. For instance, in firms with computer based part price tables

---

[g]Analysis of variance does not handle analysis of unbalanced data with more than one independent variable.[24]

Table 6.5. Relationship among table form, coverage and usage.

Panel A: Spearman rank order correlation among table form and coverage

	Form of:			Coverage of:	
	Part price table	Part price table	Assembly hour table	Part price table	Part price table
Form of:					
Part price table	–	**0.71**	**0.63**	0.23	0.30
	–	*0.00*	*0.00*	0.19	0.08
Part cost table	–	–	**0.28**	0.18	0.25
	–	–	*0.10*	0.29	0.15
Assembly hour table	–	–	–	0.40	0.45
	–	–	–	0.01	0.01
Coverage of:					
Part price table	–	–	–	–	**0.94**
	–	–	–	–	*0.00*
Part cost table	–	–	–	–	–
	–	–	–	–	–

Correlation coefficients in upper rows.
Two-tailed p values in lower rows in italic.

Panel B: General linear model of aggregate table usage frequency
by form and coverage of part price table

Marginal effect of:	F statistic	p value
Form	**10.78**	*0.00*
Coverage	**5.05**	*0.03*
Interaction of form and coverage	**2.95**	*0.10*
Entire model	6.26	*0.00*

Table 6.6. General linear model of aggregate table usage frequency by firms.

Firm	Mean of aggregate usage frequency	Frequency for part price table which is:				F statistic **2.70** p value **0.03**
		Non computer based, covering:		Computer based, covering:		
		1–50%	51–100%	1–50%	51–100%	
A	10	0	0	2	3	
B	7	0	0	0	7	
C	6	1	1	2	1	
D	5	3	1	1	2	
E	3	0	0	3	0	
F	3	2	1	0	0	
G	3	1	2	0	2	

Firm symbols do not coincide with other tables in order to protect the firms' confidentiality.

covering more than 50% of the number of the entire product, product designers are likely to use the tables more frequently. Indeed, realizing the importance of the form and coverage, a few firms in the study put high priority within their managerial improvements to upgrade their tables in terms of the technical form and coverage.

The major finding of this section is:

1. Computer based part price tables are used more frequently than the tables solely on paper. Likewise, part price tables with broader coverage are used more often. The interaction between the two has even stronger effect on the use than the aggregation of the two individual effects.

5. Design Reviews

Design reviews are cross-functional meetings held at the end of product planning and product design stages. Design reviews provide opportunities for business functions outside product design, such as cost engineering, marketing and manufacturing, to become informed, review and check the product plans and engineering drawings before the product development activities progress forward. The major participants besides product designers are those related with manufacturing operations, namely, process engineers and procurement officers. When the camera firms outsource the assemblies, employees of the outside assembly firms may join the reviews as well. Process engineers, procurement officers and the outside assembly firm are immediately affected by the outcome of product planning and product design stages.

Process engineers and procurement officers as well as the outside assembly firm translate the product designers' engineering drawings into the actual product through mass production. Process engineers design manufacturing tools and part dies, and lay out assembly lines. Procurement officers identify part suppliers that can meet the specifications of the engineering drawings, and select the proper venders. When the production is outsourced, employees of the assembly firm work together with process engineers to plan the manufacturing process. The three functions not only translate the product designers' ideas into actual manufacturing, but the functions are also responsible for the maintenance and improvement of manufacturing operations once the mass production begins. The present research calls process engineering, procurement, and the outside assembly firm as the "manufacturing functions".[h]

The purposes of design reviews from the standpoint of the manufacturing functions are twofold. First, the reviews are opportunities for the manufacturing functions to understand the product designers' ideas beforehand so that they can prepare for their future responsibilities early. Second, the reviews provide occasions for the manufacturing functions to influence the product designers' ideas. The influencing process includes asking questions, giving approvals, advising or jointly solving problems with product

---

[h]Among the Japanese camera manufacturers, the sites of this research, the procurement function pertains to manufacturing, and is not the corporate staff. Often, procurement is geographically located together with manufacturing operations. This is because the firms perceive that procurement is closely related with the cost management activities at the shop floor.

designers.[i] For example, a process engineer may propose a design change of replacing a screw-in part by a snap-in part in order to reduce the task difficulty of an assembly worker. Product designers are less knowledgeable about the difficulty of different tasks at the manufacturing shop floor.

Consequently, the design reviews are devices for DFM that enhance the interface between product design and the manufacturing functions. Nonetheless, the design reviews are relatively late in accomplishing DFM as they are held at the end of product planning and product design stages. Daily interactions between product designers and process engineers during product planning, for instance, are more timely than the design review at the end of this stage.

While daily interactions are timely interface mechanism, design reviews are more comprehensive covering the overall product plan and engineering drawings. In the reviews of a camera manufacturer participating in the research, for example, product designers explain the engineering drawings of every part. By contrast, daily interactions between product designers and the manufacturing functions focus both parties' attentions on specific issues, but do not necessarily cover every aspect of the product.

Design reviews merit investigation for two reasons. First, it is worth examining the significance of the manufacturing functions in the reviews. This is the second research variable of the present research. The study analyzes how different aspects of the manufacturing functions' participation are related with one another. For instance, one relevant question is whether the representatives from the manufacturing functions played more active roles when more representatives attended. If so, participation modes and the number of representatives are complementary leading to more effective

---

[i]*Approving* refers to the participation mode of giving approval to the product plan and engineering drawings, and opposing only when they have crucial problems. *Advising* refers to the mode of giving advice to the product designers for design changes, although the designers decide afterwards whether to incorporate the advice. *Joint problem-solving* refers to the mode of co-operation between the product designers and the representatives to solve specific problems during the design review. In addition, the response *"attending"* in the questionnaire survey refers to the mode of attending the reviews without any role of approving, advising or joint problem-solving.

Table 6.7. Summary of responses on design reviews.

Panel A: Number of representatives from the manufacturing functions

Design review in:	Mean	Standard deviation	Minimum	Median	Maximum
Product planning	3	3	0	3	8
Product design	6	4	0	5	16

Panel B: Number of days

Design review in:	0	≤ 1	(1,2]	(2,3]	(3,4]	> 4
Product planning	1 (3%)	12 (34%)	12 (34%)	3 (9%)	4 (11%)	3 (9%)
Product design	0 (0%)	13 (37%)	6 (17%)	5 (14%)	5 (14%)	6 (17%)

Frequency for each response in upper rows.
Percentile proportion within the sample in lower rows in parentheses.

Panel C: Percentage of time spent for cost issues

Design review in:	Mean	Standard deviation	Minimum	Median	Maximum
Product planning	19%	16%	0%	20%	50%
Product design	21%	15%	0%	15%	50%

Panel D: Participation mode of the manufacturing functions

Design review in:	No participation	Attending	Approving	Advising	Joint problem-solving
Product planning	5 (14%)	6 (17%)	12 (34%)	12 (34%)	0 (0%)
Product design	1 (3%)	4 (11%)	9 (26%)	11 (31%)	10 (29%)

Frequency for each response in upper rows.
Percentile proportion within the sample in lower rows in parentheses.

DFM activities. The second issue is the relationship between reviews in product planning and reviews in product design.

Table 6.7 summarizes survey responses on the design reviews. A review at the end of *product planning* stage gathered, on average, 3 representatives from the manufacturing functions (Panel A), and typically took 1 to 2 days (Panel B). The mean proportion of the time spent for cost reduction issues was 19% (Panel C). The most frequent modes of participation by the manufacturing functions were approving product designers' product plan and giving advice to them (Panel D). In no camera development project, however, did the manufacturing functions perform active joint problem-solving with product designers.

At the end of *product design*, an average of 6 representatives from the manufacturing functions attended the design review (Panel A). The number of reviews with more than 2 days was greater in product design than in product planning (Panel B). Cost issues occupied 21% of the time (Panel C). The representatives of the manufacturing functions were more active in product design reviews than in product planning reviews; in 10 camera development projects, the representatives jointly solved problems with product designers (Panel D).

There are two major findings about the design reviews. First, longer design reviews had more representatives from the manufacturing functions with more active roles. Table 6.8 reports that Pearson product moment correlation coefficients are 0.31 and 0.57 between the number of days[j] and the number of representatives in product planning and product design reviews respectively, both being significant at least at 0.1 level.[k,l] Moreover, applying

---

[j]In the correlation, the number of days is calculated as the midpoint of each survey response range. For example, for the response of "1 to 2 days" the figure of 1.5 days is used. For the responses of "No design review", "1 day or shorter" and "4 days or longer" the figures of 0 day, 0.5 day and 4.5 days are applied, respectively.

[k]Spearman rank order correlation coefficients are 0.34 and 0.53 for product planning and product design reviews, respectively, both being significant at least at 0.05 level (see Table 6.8).

[l]The positive correlation is more salient for the representatives of procurement; Pearson product moment correlation coefficients are 0.39 and 0.69 for product planning and product design reviews, respectively.

Table 6.8. Correlation between number of days and number of representatives from manufacturing functions in design reviews.

	Number of days (product planning)	Number of days (product design)	Number of representatives (product planning)	Number of representatives (product design)
Number of days (product planning)	– –	0.76 0.00	**0.34** *0.05*	0.28 0.10
Number of days (product design)	0.73 0.00	– –	0.28 0.10	**0.53** *0.00*
Number of representatives (product planning)	**0.31** *0.07*	0.24 0.17	– –	0.52 0.00
Number of representatives (product design)	0.34 0.04	**0.57** *0.00*	0.55 0.00	– –

Pearson product moment correlation on the left of diagonal.
Spearman rank order correlation on the right of diagonal.
Correlation coefficients in upper rows.
Two-tailed p values in lower rows in italic.

one-way analysis of variance, the number of days of the review in which the manufacturing functions undertook active roles (i.e. approving, advising and joint problem-solving) is greater than that of passive roles (i.e. no participation and attending) in both product planning and product design Panels A and B of Table 6.9). Nonetheless, these results are strongly influenced by product development projects of a few firms. The breakdown of the frequency by firms in Panel C suggests that the effects of Firms A and F are strong. When the projects of these two firms are eliminated, most statistical results become insignificant. Firm A seems to emphasize the design reviews as an interface mechanism between product design and the manufacturing functions. On the other hand, Firm F appears to put much less weight on design reviews.

Table 6.9. Relationship between number of days and participation mode of manufacturing functions in design reviews.

Panel A: Analysis of variance of product planning reviews

Participation mode	Frequency	Mean number of days	F statistic	**3.51**
			p value	*0.07*
Active	24	2		
Passive	11	1		

Panel B: Analysis of variance of product design reviews

Participation mode	Frequency	Mean number of days	F statistic	**5.20**
			p value	*0.03*
Active	30	2		
Passive	5	1		

Panel C: Composition by firms

Firm	Number of days	Number of representatives	Participation mode:	
			Active	Passive
A	7	14	14	0
B	5	8	8	2
C	5	10	8	2
D	3	9	6	0
E	2	8	10	0
F	1	3	3	11
G	1	12	5	1

Number of days and number of representatives are sums of the means of product planning and product design reviews.

Participation mode is the total frequencies for product planning and product design reviews.

Firm symbols do not coincide with other tables in order to protect the firms' confidentiality.

Table 6.10. Composition by participation modes of design review.

	Participation mode (product design):				
	No participation	Attending	Approving	Advising	Joint problem-solving
Participation mode (product planning):					
No participation	1	*2*	0	2	0
Attending	0	*2*	3	0	1
Approving	0	0	*6*	6	0
Advising	0	0	0	*3*	9
Joint problem-solving	0	0	0	0	*0*

Frequency for each combination of responses.
Frequencies on the diagonal are in italic.

Second, the role of the manufacturing functions became more important in product design reviews than in product planning reviews. In 23 cases, the representatives undertook more active roles in product design than in product planning, whereas there is no case in which the role lightened (Table 6.10).[m] Applying sign test, the participation modes of product design reviews are significantly more active than the modes of product planning reviews at the 0.01 level (sign statistic 11.5, two-tailed p value 0.00). Also the average number of representatives doubled from 3 in product planning to 6 in product design (see Panel A of Table 6.7). Figure 6.3 presents the box plot of the number of representatives participating in product planning and product design reviews. Wilcoxon signed-ranks test shows that the increasing change is significant at 0.01 level (Wilcoxon statistic 102.5, two-tailed p value 0.00).

In Table 6.10, there are 23 observations above the main diagonal, and none below.

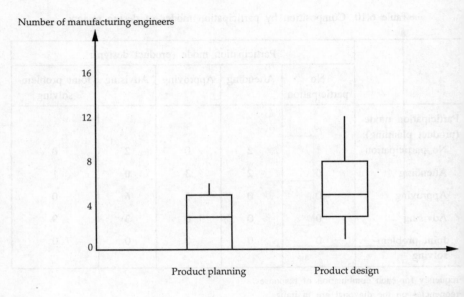

Number of manufacturing engineers

Horizontal line in the box shows the median.
Box shows the inter-quartile range.
Whiskers show the inter-decile range.

Fig. 6.3. Number of manufacturing engineers in design reviews.

In addition, the number of product development projects in which the design reviews in product planning was longer than those of product design is 14; the opposite cases account for only 4 projects (not reported in a table). Figure 6.4 presents the Box plot of the number of days spent for product planning and product design reviews. The difference of the number of days is significant at the 0.1 level (Wilcoxon statistic 42.5, two-tailed p value 0.06).

Overall, the significance of the manufacturing functions was augmented in product design reviews. It can be inferred that the interface between product design and the manufacturing functions became more intense in product design reviews. This finding applies to all firms in the sample

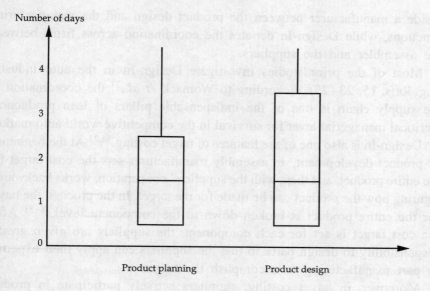

Horizontal line in the box shows the median.
Box shows the inter-quartile range.
Whiskers show the inter-decile range.

Fig. 6.4. Number of days of design reviews.

In summary:

. Length of design reviews, and the number and activeness of the manufacturing functions' representatives are positively related. The results, however, are strongly influenced by the observations of a few firms.
. The manufacturing functions' representatives became more significant in product design reviews than product planning reviews.

. **Supplier Involvement**

Design-In, the heavy involvement of material and part suppliers in product development,[21] is an extension of DFM. DFM refers to the coordination inside a manufacturer between the product design and the manufacturing functions, while Design-In denotes the coordination across firms between the assembler and the suppliers.

Most of the prior studies investigate Design-In in the auto industry (e.g. Refs. 15, 23–25). According to Womack *et al.*,[27] the coordination of the supply chain is one of the indispensable pillars of lean production, a critical managerial lever for survival in the competitive world auto market.

Design-In is also one of the features of target costing.[18,21] At the beginning of product development, an assembly manufacturer sets the cost target for the entire product, and then, with the suppliers' cooperation, works backwards figuring how the product can be made for the target. In the process, the target for the entire product is broken down to the component level.[28–31] After the cost target is set for each component, the suppliers are given greater responsibility to design parts so that the suppliers can apply their expertise in part manufacturing to accomplish the target.

Moreover, in target costing, suppliers actively participate in product development proposing design changes for the overall product design. Even suppliers which only manufacture parts according to the assembler's design make proposals to reduce manufacturing costs. For instance, in camera development a more expensive part made of physically stronger material often can lower overall product manufacturing costs because the part requires less reinforcement. The idea of substituting a physically stronger part for the weaker one is more likely to come up from part suppliers since they know more accurately the trade off between the material's physical strength and its cost.

The number of cost reduction proposals from suppliers, the third research variable of the present research, measures the extent of mutual relationship between the assembly manufacturer and the supplier; more proposals indicate that the supplier's expertise in part manufacturing is leveraged better.

This research focuses on nine parts that are crucial to camera development. They are: shutter, plastic lens,[n] die of back exterior cover, back exterior

---

[n]Among the camera manufacturers, glass lens are mostly manufactured internally.

:over (molding), die of helicoid or cam, helicoid or cam (molding), die
of main body, custom IC and liquid crystal display (LCD). The nine parts
were identified through interviews of a project manager from each camera
manufacturer prior to the questionnaire survey. According to the managers,
these nine parts are mostly custom-made for each camera by the suppliers.
The parts also require elaborate skills to manufacture, and occupy significant
proportion of the entire product manufacturing costs. Thus, reducing costs
during product development requires intensive coordination between the
camera manufacturers and the suppliers of these parts.

Clark *et al.*[32] classify parts in terms of supplier involvement pattern.
Supplier proprietary parts are standard parts taken off from the suppliers'
shelves or catalogs. *Black box* parts are parts the supplier *designs* to meet

Table 6.11. Composition of supplier involvement pattern.

	Internal procurement	Supplier proprietary	Black box	Detail-controlled
Shutter	12 (34%)	0 (0%)	**19 (54%)**	4 (11%)
Plastic lens	22 (63%)	0 (0%)	3 (9%)	10 (29%)
Back exterior cover die	15 (43%)	0 (0%)	5 (14%)	**15 (43%)**
Helicoid/Cam die	8 (23%)	0 (0%)	4 (11%)	**23 (66%)**
Main body die	11 (31%)	0 (0%)	5 (14%)	**19 (54%)**
Custom IC	0 (0%)	2 (6%)	**31 (89%)**	2 (6%)
LCD	1 (3%)	0 (0%)	**28 (80%)**	6 (17%)

Frequency for each response in upper rows.
Percentage within the sample in lower rows in parentheses.

the assembler's specification. The *detail-controlled* parts are parts the supplier only *manufactures* according to the assembler's design. Supplier involvement in product development diminishes in the order of supplier proprietary, black box and detail-controlled parts. Clark *et al.* observe that successful car assemblers rely more on black box parts, for which the suppliers are given heavier responsibility, than detail-controlled parts. In black box parts, there is more room for the suppliers to apply their expertise to the development process.[o]

Table 6.11 presents the supplier involvement pattern of the parts based on Clark *et al.*'s[32] classification. The parts can be divided into three groups: parts that are mainly black box parts; parts that are mainly detail-controlled parts; and parts that are mainly manufactured internally. The present research calls the first group BB parts, which include shutter, custom IC, and LCD. The second group is named DC parts, which comprise dies of back exterior cover, helicoid or cam, and main body. DC parts also encompass molding of back exterior cover and helicoid or cam, which are not reported to be manufactured internally.[p]

Panel A of Table 6.12 reports the composition of the suppliers by whether they proposed design changes to reduce manufacturing costs to the camera manufacturer, and the suppliers' involvement patterns. The cost reduction proposals came from suppliers that provided either black box or detail-controlled parts. Panel B presents the same composition but only for the BB parts (i.e. shutter, custom IC, and LCD). For these parts, the suppliers proposed design changes when they actually manufactured black box parts. Likewise, Panel C shows that for the DC parts (i.e. dies of back exterior cover, helicoid or cam, main body, back exterior cover, and helicoid or cam), suppliers made proposals only for the detail-controlled parts. Consequently, for BB parts, suppliers made cost-reduction proposals when the parts were black box parts, while for DC parts suppliers proposed design changes when the parts were actually detail-controlled parts. Thus, depending on the type

---

[o]Clark *et al.*[32] admit that black box parts require higher capabilities of the suppliers.
[p]Any parts reported to be manufactured internally are excluded from either the BB or DC parts.

Table 6.12. Summary of responses on supplier proposal.

Panel A: Composition of all outsourced parts by supplier involvement pattern

Supplier involvement pattern	Yes	No
Supplier proprietary	2 (100%)	0 (0%)
Black box	22 (23%)	73 (77%)
Detail-controlled	26 (19%)	109 (81%)

Frequency for each response in upper rows.
Percentage within each pattern in lower rows in parentheses.

Panel B: Composition of BB parts by supplier involvement pattern

Supplier involvement pattern	Yes	No
Supplier proprietary	2 (100%)	0 (0%)
Black box	**21** (**27%**)	57 (73%)
Detail-controlled	0 (0%)	12 (100%)

Frequency for each response in upper rows.
Percentage within each pattern in lower rows in parentheses.

Panel C: Composition of DC parts by supplier involvement pattern

Supplier involvement pattern	Yes	No
Supplier proprietary	0 (–)	0 (–)
Black box	0 (0%)	14 (100%)
Detail-controlled	**25** (**22%**)	12 (78%)

Frequency for each response in upper rows.
Percentage within each pattern in lower rows in parentheses.

of the part, there appears to be a supplier involvement pattern that is associated with supplier proposals. For shutter, custom IC and LCD, supplier involvement taking the pattern of black box parts solicits more cost-reduction proposals than the pattern of detailed-controlled parts. Contrarily, for other parts such as dyes of back exterior cover, helicoid and cam, the pattern of detailed-controlled parts better encourages cost reduction proposals than the pattern of black box parts.

Table 6.13. Composition of supplier involvement timing.

Panel A: Timing of first contact to supplier

Part grouping	Before product planning	Product planning	Product desgin	Process engineering	Total
BB parts	21 (23%)	49 (53%)	20 (22%)	2 (2%)	92 (100%)
DC parts	0 (0%)	12 (9%)	52 (41%)	63 (50%)	127 (100%)
Plastic lens	1 (8%)	3 (23%)	8 (62%)	1 (8%)	13 (100%)

Frequency for each response in upper rows.
Percentage within each part grouping in lower rows in parentheses.

Panel B: Timing of supplier selection

Part grouping	Before product planning	Product planning	Product desgin	Process engineering	Total
BB parts	31 (34%)	35 (38%)	20 (22%)	6 (7%)	92 (100%)
DC parts	6 (5%)	10 (8%)	28 (22%)	83 (65%)	127 (100%)
Plastic lens	2 (15%)	3 (23%)	2 (15%)	6 (46%)	13 (100%)

Frequency for each response in upper rows.
Percentage within each part grouping in lower rows in parentheses.

Another factor that could affect cost-reduction proposals from suppliers is the timing when suppliers are brought in the product development process. Earlier involvement will give the supplier a better opportunity to influence the product design because there is broader room for design changes. This effect, however, may differ by the patterns of supplier involvement.

Table 6.13 presents the product development stage when the supplier got involved in the product development. Panel A reports when the supplier was first contacted for the purpose of each camera's development. Applying Mann-Whitney U test, BB part suppliers were first contacted significantly earlier than DC part suppliers at the 0.01 level (U statistic 1245, two-tailed p value 0.00). Panel B reports when the supplier was virtually selected. Similar to the first contacts, the selections of BB part suppliers took place significantly earlier than the selections of DC part suppliers at the 0.01 level (U statistic 1591, two-tailed p value 0.00). Both results suggest that the BB part suppliers joined the development process earlier than the DC part suppliers.

Since both the timing of supplier involvement and the number of parts associated with cost-reduction proposals are ordinal variables, the relationship between the two is analyzed by Kendall tau-b correlation. In Panel A of Table 6.14, the correlation coefficients between the number of BB parts with proposals, and the timing of first contact and selection are −0.32 and −0.15, respectively. When the other timing variable is controlled, the partial correlation coefficients are −0.29 for the first contact, and 0.03 for the selection. Consequently, for the BB parts, earlier first contacts are associated with more proposals. Therefore, early first contact is important to solicit cost-reduction proposals from the suppliers.

Panel B presents the similar analysis for the DC parts. While the correlation coefficient of the timing of first contact is significant, the partial correlation with the control for the timing of selection does not produce a substantial coefficient. The association is weaker than the BB parts.

Table 6.15 presents the composition by firms. The table suggests that the results of the BB parts in the entire sample is driven by Firms A, B and C. By contrast, the results of the DC parts could be dominated by the effect of only Firm A.

Table 6.14. Correlation between number of parts with proposals and supplier involvement timing.

Panel A: BB parts

	Number of parts with proposals	Timing of first contact to supplier	Timing of supplier selection
Number of parts with proposals	– –	-0.29	0.03
Timing of first contact to supplier	-0.32 0.00	– . –	
Timing of supplier selection	-0.15 0.12	0.54 0.00	– –

Kendall tau-b correlation on the left of diagonal.
Kendall partial tau-b correlation controlling for the other timing on the right of diagonal.
Correlation coefficients in upper rows.
Two-tailed p values in lower rows in italic.

Panel B: DC parts

	Number of parts with proposals	Timing of first contact to supplier	Timing of supplier selection
Number of parts with proposals	– –	-0.13	0.01
Timing of first contact to supplier	-0.18 0.04	– –	
Timing of supplier selection	-0.12 0.17	0.69 0.00	– –

Kendall tau-b correlation on the left of diagonal.
Kendall partial tau-b correlation controlling for the other timing on the right of diagonal.
Correlation coefficients in upper rows.
Two-tailed p values in lower rows in italic.

Table 6.15. Composition of supplier proposal by firms.

Firm	Mean number of BB parts with proposals	Proportion of BB parts with proposals when supplier was first contacted during:				Mean number of DC parts with proposals
		Before product planning	Product planning	Product design	Process engineering	
A	1	6/6	1/6	1/2	–	3
B	1	3/6	4/8	0/1	–	1
C	1	2/5	4/6	1/4	0/1	0
D	0	–	1/10	0/4	–	0
E	0	0/4	0/6	0/4	–	0
F	0	–	0/7	0/2	0/1	0
G	0	–	0/6	0/3	–	0

Firm symbols do not coincide with other tables in order to protect the firms' confidentiality.

Finally, the fierce price competition in the compact camera business and the appreciation of yen in the early 1990s pushed Japanese manu facturers' part procurement outside the country, particularly to South East Asia. It is worthwhile to examine whether this phenomenon had any effect on cost-reduction proposals from suppliers. Procurement outside Japan could be accompanied by less proposals because non-Japanese suppliers have less experience in working with the camera manufacturers. Also, the geographical distance between overseas suppliers and the Japanese manufacturers makes timely proposals difficult. According to Panel A of Table 6.16, the correlation[q] between the number of DC parts with proposals and the proportion of overseas part procurement is negative and significant; higher overseas procurement is associated with less proposals. No effect on the BB parts is understandable because the camera manufacturers rarely acquire those parts overseas. The BB parts require higher capabilities of the suppliers than the DC parts. In sum, the Japanese camera manufacturers might have reduced part cost

---

[q]Correlation after controlling for the number of parts manufactured internally.

Table 6.16. Relationship between supplier proposal and non-Japanese parts.

Panel A: Partial correlation

	Number of BB parts with proposals	Number of DC parts with proposals	Percentage of non-Japanese parts at 3rd month of mass production	Percentage of non-Japanese parts at 12th month of mass production
Number of BB parts with proposals	– –	0.48 0.00	−0.20 0.26	−0.27 0.13
Number of DC parts with proposals	0.34 0.05	– –	**−0.54** *0.00*	**−0.52** *0.00*
Percentage of non-Japanese parts at 3rd month of mass production	−0.17 0.33	**−0.40** *0.02*	– –	0.90 0.00
Percentage of non-Japanese parts at 12th month of mass production	−0.10 0.57	**−0.42** *0.01*	0.93 0.00	– –

Pearson partial product moment correlation controlling for number of internally produced parts on the left of diagonal.
Spearman partial rank order correlation controlling for number of internally produced parts on the right of diagonal.
Correlation coefficients in upper rows.
Two-tailed p values in lower rows in italic.

Panel B: Composition by firms

Firm	Mean number of DC parts with proposals	Mean percentage of non-Japanese parts at:	
		3rd month of mass production	12th month of mass production
A	3	0%	6%
B	1	17%	32%
C	0	7%	13%
D	0	20%	20%
E	0	28%	29%
F	0	45%	53%
G	0	98%	98%

Firm symbols do not coincide with other tables in order to protect the firms' confidentiality.

by purchasing non-Japanese parts but, as a consequence, the overseas suppliers made fewer proposals. This result, however, is dominated by the effects of Firms A and G in Panel B.

The major findings regarding part supplier involvement are as follows:

1. The relationship between the supplier involvement pattern and the supplier proposals depends on the characteristic of the part; for the BB part, black box involvement is accompanied with more proposals; and likewise for the DC parts.
2. For the BB parts, the earlier the part supplier is contacted, the more frequent it proposed design change.
3. Recent increase in non-Japanese part procurement has been accompanied by less cost-reduction proposals from suppliers.

7. Conclusion

This chapter documents the target costing practices of Japanese camera manufacturers. The study focuses on three research variables: frequency of use of tables of cost-related information; the manufacturing functions' participation in design reviews; and supplier proposals of cost-reduction. Furthermore, the study examines the factors that are likely to affect the three variables. The analysis is primarily at the product development project level, but additional investigation is conducted at the firm level.

The present research is the first cross-sectional study to document the variation of target costing practices in a single industry. The findings have several implications to the research and practice of target costing.

First, there is significant variation in the target costing practices across camera development projects, and, in particular, across firms. The results suggest that managers can use different levers to achieve the cost target. For instance, the interface between product design and the manufacturing functions could be augmented either by increased presence of the manufacturing functions at design reviews or dense daily communication between the two parties. Of course, each lever encompasses different degrees of effectiveness and costs. Thus, the project manager, or the firm, must select the alternative with the greatest net benefit to achieve the purpose.

Second, the discrepancy between the findings of the present research and the extant literature may be due to industry characteristics. Past investigation of target costing has mainly focused on the auto industry, especially the practice of Toyota (e.g. Refs. 28, 33 and 34). It is not clear whether the past findings can be generalized to other industries. This research demonstrates that camera manufacturers' approach to target costing is different from car makers. For instance, part suppliers appear to be much less significant for the camera manufacturers than the car makers. Thus, there can be more than one way to carry out target costing. If this is the case, the past description of target costing, such as Tani's seven elements,[18] may be misleading to firms outside the auto industry. It is important to identify the core target costing practices by separating out those practices that are peripheral in certain businesses.

References

1. Kato, Y., Genka-kikaku: Senryakuteki Kosuto Manejimento, Target Costing: Strategic Cost Management (Nihon Keizai Shinbun, Tokyo, Japan, 1993).
2. Cooper, R., When Lean Enterprises Collide: Competing Through Confrontation (Harvard Business School Press, Boston, MA, 1995).
3. Society of Management Accountants of Canada (Society of Management Accountants of Canada, Hamilton, Ontario, Canada, 1994).
4. Economist 1996, 59–60.
5. McMann, P. J. & Nanni, A. J. Jr., Management Accounting Research, Vol. 6, 1995, 313–346.
6. Cooper, R. & Slagmulder, R., Target Costing and Value Engineering (Productivity Press, Portland, OR, 1997).
7. Fisher, J., Journal of Cost Management, Vol. 9, 1995, 50–59.
8. Gaiser, B., Journal of Cost Management, Vol. 11, 1997, 41–45.
9. Iwabuchi, Y., Kigyo-kaikei, Vol. 44, 1992, 41–47.
10. Shimizu, N., Kigyo-kaikei, Vol. 44, 1992, 91–96.
11. Nonaka, I. & Takeuchi, H., The Knowledge-Creating Company: How Japanese Companies Create the Dynamics of Innovation (Oxford University Press, Oxford UK, 1995).
12. Tani, T., Management Accounting Journal, Vol. 6, 1995, 399–414.

13. Simons, R., Levers of Control: How Managers Use Innovative Control Systems to Drive Strategic Renewal (Harvard Business School Press, Boston, MA, 1995).
14. Simons, R., Strategic Management Journal 12, 1991, 49–62.
15. Shields, M. D. & Young, S. M., Journal of Management Accounting Research, Vol. 6, 1994, 175–196.
16. Davila, A., The Information and Control Functions of Management Control Systems in Product Development: Empirical and Analytical Perspectives, Unpublished doctoral dissertation (Harvard Business School, Boston, MA, 1998).
17. Clark, K. B. & Fujimoto, T., Product Development Performance: Strategy, Organization, and Management in the World Auto Industry (Harvard Business School Press, Boston, MA, 1991).
18. Tani, T., Kaikei, Vol. 150, 1996, 521–534.
19. Yano Keizai Kenkyuzyo., Nihon Maketto Shea Jiten (Japanese Market Share Directory) (Yano Keizai Kenkyuzyo, Tokyo, Japan, 1995).
20. Clark, K. B. & Wheelwright, S. C., Managing New Product Development and Process Development (Free Press, New York, NY, 1993).
21. Okano, H., Nihonteki Kanri-kaikeino Tenkai: Genka-kikakueno Rekishiteki Shiza (Japanese Management Accounting: A Historical & Institutional Perspective) (Chuo Keizaisya, Tokyo, Japan, 1995).
22. Ulrich, K. T. & Eppinger, S. D., Product Design and Development (McGraw Hill, New York, NY, 1995).
23. Yoshikawa, T., Innes, J. & Mitchell, F., Journal of Cost Management, Vol. 4, 1990, 30–36.
24. Cody, R. P. & Smith, J. K., Applied Statistics and the SAS Programming Language (Prentice Hall, Englewood Cliffs, NJ, 1991).
25. Cusumano, M. A. & Takeishi, A., Strategic Management Journal, Vol. 12, 1991, 563–588.
26. Nishiguchi, T., Strategic Dualism: An Alternative in Industrial Society, Unpublished Ph.D. Dissertation (Oxford University, Oxford, UK, 1989).
27. Womack, J. P., Jones, D. T. & Roos, D., The Machine That Changed the World: The Story of Lean Production (Rawson Associates, New York, NY, 1990).
28. Monden, Y., In Japanese Management Accounting: A World Class Approach to Profit Management, Monden, Y. & Sakurai, M., eds. (Productivity Press, Cambridge, MA, 1989).
29. Cooper, R., Tokyo Motor Works, Ltd.: Target Costing System, Unpublished Case Study (Claremont Graduate School, Claremont, CA, 1994).

30. Cooper, R., Komatsu, Ltd. (A): Target Costing System, Case Study 9-194-037 (Harvard Business School, Boston, MA, 1994).
31. Cooper, R., Nissan Motor Company, Ltd.: Target Costing System, Case Study 9-194-040 (Harvard Business School, Boston, MA, 1994).
32. Clark, K. B., Chew, W. B. & Fujimoto, T., Brookings Papers on Economic Activity, Vol. 3, 1987, 729–781.
33. Tanaka, T., In Firudo Sutadi: Gendaino Kanri-kaikei Shisutemu (Field Studies of Contemporary Management Accounting Systems), Tanaka, T., ed. (Chuo Keizaisya, Tokyo, Japan, 1991).
34. Tanaka, T., Kaikei, Vol. 145, 1994, 771–789.
35. Koga, K. & Davila, A., Dynamic Strategic Resources: Development, Diffusion and Integration, Hitt, M.A., Clifford, P. G., Nixon, R. D. & Coyne, K. P. eds. (John Wiley & Sons, 1999).

Chapter 7

A Method for Simultaneously Achieving Cost Reduction and Quality Improvement

KAZUKI HAMADA

1. Introduction

As target costing is executed at the beginning, managers do not think only about cost reduction, but also need to investigate the possibility of cost reduction while letting products correspond to customers' needs. In other words, managers need to consider quality and cost at the same time. The purpose of this chapter is to consider this subject from the view of management accounting.

This chapter will discuss the method of QFD (quality function deployment) which has been studied in the field of quality control. The method of QFD is the method that makes clear the first qualities which should be considered when relating customers' needs to technological quality characteristics, and then deploys them by making contact with functions, mechanisms, parts, reliability and costs.

QFD regards functions as one of the most important keys, just as with VE (value engineering). However, it is assumed that the functions of QFD join customers' needs together with technology. From this, it is thought that it is more customer-intensive than VE. In contrast to QFD, VE mainly places stresses on the technological approach, though it considers both

161

functions and costs. It also seems that VE has not always considered whether functions are led by customers' needs.

Over recent years Hitachi Co. Ltd. changed the name of VE to VEC (value engineering for customers) in order to reflect the customers' intentions. The company also points out that their goals are to raise customer satisfaction and to implement cost reduction. If we interpret VE in this way, the meaning of function in QFD becomes the same as that in VE.

The necessity of the simultaneous attainment of quality improvement and cost reduction will be described in the next section, and after that the management method by using QFD will be presented.

2. The Necessity of Simultaneously Examining Quality and Cost

Figure 7.1 illustrates serial flows from the setting of product strategy to mass production in a company. The characteristics of quality improvement and cost reduction are also shown in this figure.

Michael E. Porter enumerates the cost leadership strategy, the differentiation strategy and the concentration strategy as a product strategy, but it is the former two points that are regarded as a fundamental form.

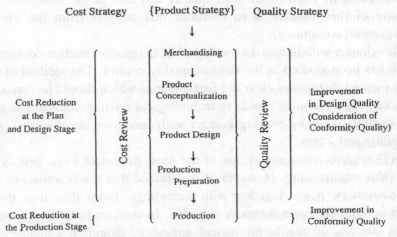

Fig. 7.1. Cost reduction and quality improvement.

Whichever of these two types of strategy managers select, the need to consider both quality and cost is clear even if there is a difference in their degree of importance.

A quality review is carried out to investigate the current level of operation quality, and a cost review is carried out for costs throughout all stages, as shown in Fig. 7.1, based on the product strategy. Ways of dealing with quality and cost, however, are different at the pre-production stage and at the production stage. With regard to cost reduction, it is important to investigate the possibilities of cost reduction at the pre-production stage, and it is important to deal with cost reduction in manufacturing processes at the production stage.

There are two kinds of important quality concepts to consider when we think about quality improvements. One type is design quality, which is a quality concept concerning to what degree market needs or customer expectations are reflected in the design specification. The other type is conformity quality, which is a quality concept concerning to what degree the design specification and the real result are equal. Design quality mainly relates to the pre-production stage, and conformity quality relates to the production stage. Even at the pre-production stage, however, managers need to examine the selection of parts and the technology required for an improvement in conformity quality.

Information acquired from customer questionnaires, information from sole agents and stores, business information, information from rivals and social economic information, to name but a few sources, all becomes necessary to improve design quality. In particular, the positive discussions within market infrastructures are necessary in the development of a product for which customers cannot understand the characteristics or merits of use. "Market infrastructures" are persons, companies and parties that influence the purchasing decision of customers, such as advanced users, tie-up companies and business experts. These persons and groups know the potential customers' needs well. Therefore it is important to create a system which can work with them from the plan and design stage.

There is a high probability that the improvement of conformity quality ties in with cost reduction, but there are many cases where the improvement of design quality increases costs. Besides, when design quality improves, conformity quality often lowers. Therefore the relationships between quality and cost become more complicated and the company needs to examine the relationships between design quality, conformity quality and cost, at the plan and design stage. Since quality and cost are almost fully decided upon at the plan and design stage of a product, this becomes particularly necessary. At every turning point of each stage in Fig. 7.1 managers must thoroughly check the quality and cost (and the appointed date of delivery) of a product. The relationships between quality and cost become clear through this check and the company can prevent cost reduction by lowering quality forcibly. This total check is often called the design review.

The next section will examine QFD, which· is an important method by which managers can consider quality and cost, both totally and theoretically.

3. The Characteristics of QFD

When QFD is executed, the quality chart plays an important role. Professor Yoji Akao has defined the quality chart as follows.[1] "The quality chart is one which describes the true qualities that customers need by language expressions, and indicates the relationships between them and quality characteristics, and converts customers' needs into substitutive characteristics and design qualities." There are several types of quality chart, but Fig. 7.2 shows a fundamental type. The triangular parts are deployed as the first parts but the second and the third parts become a detailed deployment chart (distribution chart).

The relationships between the required qualities and the technological quality characteristics are described in a matrix chart in Fig. 7.2. The matrix chart is convenient in the case of relating between many different elements. Managers can better understand the total constitution of a business if they use this chart, as it is easy to search problems and get ideas from the two-dimensional relationship. This quality chart can be described as the conversion chart which converts customers' needs into different technological levels.

The planned qualities and the design policy of quality that shows which levels of qualities are required for customers should be aimed for on the

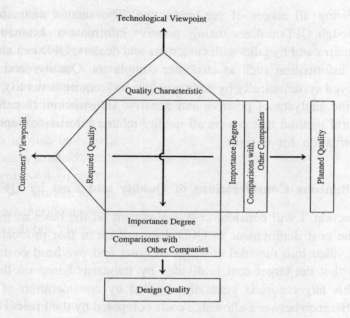

Fig. 7.2. Quality chart. From Ref. 4, p. 21.

basis of the degree of importance and sales points through comparison with other companies, as shown in the chart. Qualities that become necessary from the technological level must also be added to the items of required qualities of customers, since there is a possibility that common qualities and basic qualities are not included in the list of customers' required qualities.

The quality chart described in Fig. 7.2 should be used by functions, mechanisms and parts. All relationships between quality characteristics and functions, functions and mechanisms, functions and parts, etc. can be easily related by using matrix charts. Because functions, mechanisms and parts consist of several factors, by using matrix charts, relating between various factors, and relating between one matrix chart and another become easy.

I will now mention the important characteristics of QFD. The first characteristic is that QFD can clarify customers' needs and covers the problems of all stages from the product plan stage to the design stage, thus covering all stages of pre-production. The second characteristic is that, although QFD utilizes mainly positive information obtained through questionnaires and by talks with customers and dealers, QFD can also utilize negative information such as customer complaints. Quality enhancements are deployed systematically by adding engineers' requirements to the results through the analyses of positive and negative information; therefore QFD is a general method that covers all quality-related information and utilizes this information for designs.

4. Simultaneous Considerations of Quality and Cost by QFD

In this section, I will consider cost deployment on the basis of the quality chart. The cost deployment in QFD does not mean that production costs are subdivided into material costs, labor costs and overhead costs; instead it means that the target cost is divided by standards based on the quality chart. This target cost is generally decided by consideration of the size of the difference between allowable costs computed by the inverse operation and estimated costs in the present situation. The function weight which indicates the degree of importance of a function is used as a division standard for checking the balance between costs and functions, because customers expect the "attainments of functions" and customers decide the amount of money that they will pay according to the importance they place on various functions. Sometimes function weights are estimated from customers' needs and sometimes they are estimated from a technological viewpoint; however managers need to consider both cases, because there is a possibility that the weights of important basic functions may become very low if weights are only estimated through customers' needs.

Two methods to determine the balance between costs and functions are as follows:

1. *Comparison between functional target costs and functional actual costs*
   Functional target costs are computed by dividing the overall target cost using function weights. Functional actual costs are computed as follows. First, the contribution degree of each part to each function is estimated

parts costs are divided by this degree, and then the divided amount is added up for each function. The computed amount is the functional actual cost. If each functional target cost and each functional actual cost are approximately equal, the situation is well-balanced, but if the latter is larger than the former, a remedy will become necessary.

2. *Comparison between target parts costs and actual parts costs*

Target parts costs are computed as follows. Functional target costs are divided by the contribution degree of each function to each part, and the results are then added up for each part. The computed amount is the target parts cost. If each target parts cost and each actual parts cost are approximately equal, the situation is well-balanced, but if the latter is larger than the former, a remedy will become necessary.

Regarding the above two methods, the overall target cost is composed of the total function cost in all cases. This function cost is in turn composed of the total parts cost. Each function is allocated costs according to its importance. Generally speaking, it is necessary to consider the target function cost before considering the target parts cost. If a manager does not do this he/she is likely to be limited in his/her ability to create and visualize new ideas. Managers will be able to consider quality and cost simultaneously by executing the aforementioned cost deployment method based on the quality chart.

I will now try to examine how this is enforced in a real Japanese company. First, I will describe AGS (Ambitious Goal Seeking) activities in The Japan Steel Works Co. Ltd.[2] AGS activity is the planning and control activity at the source stage to develop unique products in time in order to meet customers' needs. This activity is the one that fixes strategic goals and enforces the attainment of these goals by gaining information from the SBU (strategic business unit). This is called Precedence Integration Development activity and the company uses the quality/cost-technology chart to support this activity. This deployment chart is QFD, and it is used to consider the relationship between quality/cost and technology on the basis of the quality chart. I will consider the details of this in the following section.

At Toyota Auto Body Co. Ltd., QFD is also used at the new product plan stage and at the product design stage in the development of a new product. At both stages, the relationship between qualities and costs is considered. In particular, QFD is examined in relation to the technology development effects at the former stage and the detailed examination is executed at the latter stage. Companies using QFD use this method as a central technique in quality improvement and cost reduction.

4.1. *An example of simultaneous consideration of quality and cost*

The example of the Yokohama factory of the Japan Steel Works Co. Ltd.[2] will be considered in this section. This company uses QFD to clarify NE (neck engineering). The method is as follows.

(1) NE is clarified by the difference between planned quality and actual quality. Planned quality is set by the quality required by customers
(2) NE is also clarified by the difference between target parts costs and actual parts costs. Target parts costs are computed by converting the target cost into functional costs, and functional costs are further divided into parts.

These methods are shown in Fig. 7.3. The first route in Fig. 7.3 converts the degree of importance of quality required into the degree of importance of each quality characteristic in the consideration of the sales points. Next planned quality and the actual quality are compared, and NE is extracted (the extraction of the first NE). Managers also search for the mechanism and the parts that are related to the characteristics judged as NE (the extraction of NE), and plans are put in place to improve these.

The second route in Fig. 7.3 is begun by dividing the overall target cost in consideration of the degree of importance of required quality and computing required quality costs. This required quality cost is computed because it is generally thought that it is good to spend a high proportion of cost on aspects which customers think are important qualities. Next, required qualities are converted into functions, and by relating to this correspondence the required quality costs are divided into each function and functional costs are calculated. These functional costs are divided into each mechanism by the function-mechanism conversion chart, and mechanism costs are

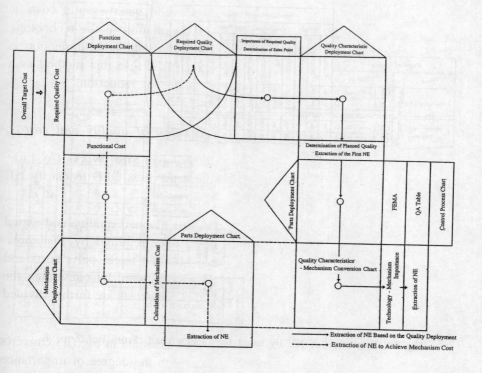

Fig. 7.3. Quality/cost — Technological deployment chart. From Ref. 2, p. 95.

calculated. These mechanism costs are further divided into parts by the
mechanism-part conversion chart, and parts costs are then calculated. These
parts costs are the targeted parts costs which the overall target cost is divided
into by stages, and by the comparisons between these costs and actual parts
costs, the extraction of NE is completed.

These procedures will now be shown using an application example, an
example of a small hydraulic pump.[2] Figure 7.4 shows an extraction example
of NE by the second route. Managers must first execute customers' evaluation,
company evaluation and future needs evaluation to decide the importance
of the required qualities. Then absolute importance (or "weights") is calculated
by considering these factors, along with the comparison with other companies

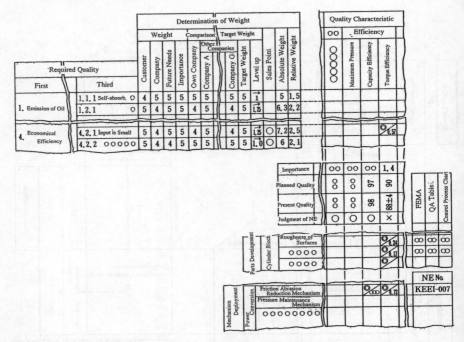

Fig. 7.4. Extraction of NE by using the quality chart. From Ref. 2, p. 96.

and sales points. For example, the relative weight of one quality shown, "input is small" is calculated as follows:

[{(importance degree) × (level up) × (sales point)} ÷ Σ (absolute weight)] × 100 = {(5 × 1.25 × 1.2)/300} × 100 = 2.5

In Fig. 7.4, "sales points" are multiplied by 1.2. Next, the quality characteristics related to required quality are searched, and the degrees of relationship are evaluated by three grades (◎ = 3 points, ○ = 2 points, △ = 1 point). For example, as the required quality of "input is small" is related to the torque efficiency, the relative weight of the required quality is divided by the relation degree. By this calculation, the importance degree of the torque efficiency becomes 0.57, and the total degree of torque efficiency becomes 1.4. If managers consider this degree of importance and compare

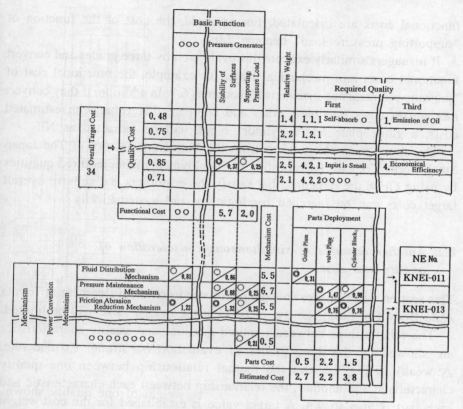

Fig. 7.5. Extraction of NE to achieve overall target cost. From Ref. 2, p. 97.

the required qualities with existing qualities they will judge the torque efficiency to be NE. As the torque efficiency relates to the friction abrasion reduction mechanism, it becomes necessary to improve the cylinder block.

Figure 7.5 shows an extraction example of NE by the second route. First, the required quality costs are calculated by dividing the overall target costs by the relative weights of the required qualities. Next, the relations between required qualities and functions are evaluated by three grades (◎ = 3 points, ○ = 2 points, △ = 1 point) and the required quality costs are divided into each function. Next they are added up according to each function and the functional costs are calculated. For example, the cost of the function of "supporting pressure load" become 2.0.

If managers similarly execute this evaluation by three grades and convert functional costs into mechanical costs, for example, the functional cost of "pressure maintenance mechanism" becomes 6.7. In addition, if they convert mechanism costs into parts costs and compare this value with estimated costs, a guide plate and a cylinder block will be extracted as NE.

The above example is taken from the Yokohama factory of The Japan Steel Works Co. Ltd. By repeating the deployments from required qualities by using QFD, the remedies that satisfy the customers and achieve overall target costs can be searched for logically and systematically.

4.2. Another example of simultaneous consideration of quality and cost

This section will consider an example of windscreen development in Toyota Auto Body Co. Ltd.[3] The use of QFD at the design stage will be limited.

The relationships between required qualities and quality characteristics are showed by the three grades of evaluation (◎: strong, ○: moderate, △: weak) in Fig. 7.6 and the mutual relationship between one quality characteristic and another; the relationship between each characteristic and each part is also shown. A target value is established for the cost/weight of a part and a comparison is made with the present value. On the other hand, aims and means for planned goals are made clear, and proposals to attain them are shown. If the execution of one proposal is completed it is shown by ○ in the chart, which it contributes to quality, cost or weight. Through the chart, it becomes easy for the company to select the best proposals in order to balance their improvements in power, cost reduction and weight reduction.

At the Toyota Auto Body Co. Ltd., as above, their reasons for using QFD were different from the example in the previous section. It was not to decide the degree of importance and the distribution amount of costs but to clarify the relationships between required qualities and quality characteristics, and the relationships between those and the parts. It was

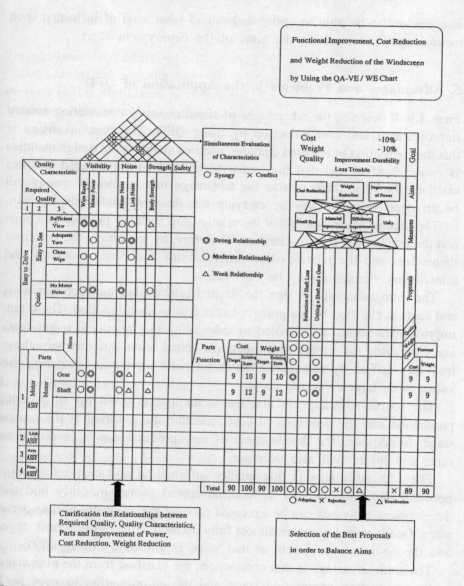

Fig. 7.6. Cost reduction and quality improvement by using the QA-VE/WE chart. From Ref. 3, p. 27.

also devised to be able to easily understand what kind of influence each measure gave to attaining the aims of the deployment chart.

5. Advantages and Problems in the Application of QFD

First, I will describe the advantages of simultaneously considering quality improvements and cost reduction by using QFD. The first advantage is that the connection of required qualities, planned qualities and design qualities is easily clarified and that the items that should be emphasized are also clarified. Besides, there is also the advantage that customers' needs can be arranged systematically by carrying out required quality deployment.

The second advantage is that the relationship between product functions and the functioning parts is clarified. Therefore, by examining the functions themselves and the relations between functions and parts, necessary and unnecessary functions may be clarified.

The third advantage is that the desired relationship between functions and costs is clarified by assigning a target cost to each function. Therefore, improvement points are clarified by calculating the functional target costs and comparing the values with functional actual costs. Alternatively, these may be clarified by calculating the target parts costs and comparing the values with targeted actual costs.

The fourth advantage is that the technological problems of product production and the problems of cost reduction are clarified at the source stage. In addition, the development of new products can be executed in time, and losses will also decrease.

The fifth advantage is that quality information and cost information between departments will be communicated more smoothly and the development activities can be executed all over the company at the source stage. Qualities and costs are almost fully decided at the development stage and the co-operation system at that stage is gained by using QFD.

The sixth advantage is that connections are clarified from the plan stage to the production preparation stage and the co-ordination to cope with complicated and diversified development themes will be prepared. Therefore each stage flows smoothly to the next stage.

The seventh advantage is that when the plan and the proposal of a new product become concrete, it is easy to build up a consensus within the company. Because this method, and its plans and proposals, are logical, the mutual influence relations also become clear.

The eighth advantage is that QFD is useful in creating a situation where group decisions are easily executed because the processes of deployment are shown. In particular, this method is useful for making product development decisions because that is of most importance and there are many cases where the decision is not made by an individual but rather by a group.

However, there are also problems in using QFD. The first problem is that if managers are going to thoroughly perform quality deployment and cost deployment, much time is lost through the data handling procedures and in drawing up the chart. There are also problems that occur when the chart becomes overcomplicated, or if managers demand too much rigidity.

The second problem is that the required qualities and function weights differ greatly between objective customers. Therefore it is important to consider to what level of customers the product is oriented.

The third problem is that, as QFD deploys more and more processes, its reliability decreases by degrees. Therefore it is necessary to decide the degree of deployment.

The fourth problem is that, even if there are big differences between functional target costs and functional actual costs, or between targeted parts costs and actual parts costs, managers cannot always reduce costs. If managers cannot ascertain this at the planning stage, they will over-examine the need, even if improvements are impossible and large losses will thus be accrued.

The fifth problem is that as QFD is not carried out through statistical reasoning but instead by intuition, the idea is that managers should handle cases where rigid reasoning is necessary, very simply and in a straightforward way.

The above are the advantages and problems in simultaneously considering qualities and costs by using QFD. When managers use QFD, they must utilize these advantages and pay a great deal of attention to potential problems.

6. Summary and Remaining Problems

This chapter focused on the problems of qualities and costs that occur as target costing is carried out. The necessity of simultaneously looking at product quality and cost, and methods of doing this, were discussed. There are various methods that consider qualities and costs simultaneously but here I adopted QFD and examined two examples in this chapter. However, as I only focused on the development of a product that attains its required quality and cost, there are other important problems that were not discussed here. Therefore, this chapter will conclude by presenting two remaining problems.

First, an appointed delivery date problem. As market competition becomes more intense, the development competition of new products intensifies and the life-cycle of a product shortens. Therefore, the company raises the speed of developing new products and needs to offer a product quickly to the market. It is also now known that a big difference in profit is caused by the length of time from the development stage to offering the product to the market. Therefore, in Professor Yasuhiro Monden's definition,[4] the appointed date of delivery is considered to be as important a topic as cost and quality. "Target costing means a company-wide profit management in the new product development stage. This is a company-wide activity, first planning a product that will meet the required qualities of customers; then deciding on the target cost of the new product (or the target amount of investment) in order to achieve a target profit over the medium-term or long-term, subject to market environment conditions. Target costs are planned around the design of the product, as long as the required qualities and the appointed date of delivery are met." A management accounting laboratory in Kobe University analyzed this and demonstrated that while market competition is intense or innovation is rapid or sales means are various, the development of new products which fit in with customers' needs, and the introduction of new products in time, is utilized to the maximum.

The second problem is that, since I focused only on customer satisfaction, I have not considered employee satisfaction here, but a rise in employee satisfaction is important from a long-term point of view. Therefore, in addition to offering products that fit in with customers' needs, cost reduction and shortening the appointed date of delivery, the rise of employee satisfaction should also be considered at the same time. I will consider in detail, in a later chapter, Total Productivity management that aims at customer satisfaction and employee satisfaction.

In addition to the above, there are many other factors which managers must consider, but the problems that have been described in this chapter are especially important.

References

1. Akao, Y., Introduction of Quality Function Deployment (Nikka-Giren Shuppansha, 1991).
2. Hasegawa, A., Maekawa, Y. & Aizawa, K., Quality/Cost — Technological Development Chart for Developing a New Product: Extraction of NE to Achieve Planned Quality and Target Cost by Using the Quality Chart, Hinshitu, D13–3, 1983, 92–97.
3. Kawai, T., Standardization by Considering the Balance of Quality and Cost, Hyojunka to Hinshitu-Kanri, D38, 1985. 2, 23–32.
4. Monden, Y., Target Costing and Kaizen Costing to Gain Competitive Advantages (Toyo-Keizai Shuppansha, 1994).

Chapter 8

How QFD and VE should be Combined for Achieving Quality & Cost in Product Development

MAHFUZUL HOQUE, MAHMUDA AKTER
SACHIE YAMADA and YASUHIRO MONDEN

1. Introduction

Japanese companies plan and control quality and cost (QC) simultaneously during the product development process, as these are controllable cross functional goals to achieve the ultimate customer satisfaction and profit ability. Among all the system tools that are being used in a target-costing environment, value engineering (VE) and quality function deployment (QFD) have caught the attention of the practitioners since their introduction. Recently, there are many instances of using these subsystem simultaneously, independently, alternatively or complementarily. When used independently, it is obvious that both QFD and VE are effective in their own ways with their inherent limitations. However, in an environment where they co-exist and are used in a mixed form, the results maybe interesting.

In exploring the relationship between VE and QFD, it is found that each needs the other to maximize their respective success. Both are generally perceived incorrectly by the population at large and both are relatively under-used, and in many cases even unknown. It is known that functions are basic to successful VE and are an essential control used in QFD.[11] The way of handling functions differs between VE and QFD. A review of current literature reveals that no study has so far been conducted on finding particularly which way of conducting VE and QFD will provide best possible QC performance in product development. This paper will report on which method between VE and QFD provides quality and cost performance relatively at the highest level both for model change and entirely new products. Again, a combination derived from the functional relationship between VE and QFD that will provide the simultaneous achievement of quality and cost will be identified.

Findings are based on a questionnaire survey which was administered to collect data from the product development managers of eight hundred and seventy eight Japanese manufacturing companies listed in Tokyo Stock Exchange Part I. Two hundred and twenty five companies answered by the deadline (7 November 1997), among them eighteen responses could not be used due to their incompleteness. The response rate is about 26.54% and the effective response rate is 23.58%.

. Quality Function Deployment (QFD)

The concept of quality function deployment (QFD) was first introduced in Japan in 1966 by Yoji Akao. Its first successful implementation was made in 1972 at Mitsubishi Kobe shipyard site. Since then QFD has been successfully used by Japanese manufacturers of consumer electronics, home appliances, clothing, integrated circuits, synthetic rubber, construction equipment and agricultural engine. Japanese designers use it for services like swimming schools and retail outlets and even for planning apartment layouts.[10,13]

QFD is a structured and disciplined process that provides a means to identify and carry the voice of customer through each stage of development and implementation. QFD focuses on planning and problem prevention in the early development phase, thereby reducing design errors, which results in fewer problems in production.[11] It is a language, communicated through a group of charts which is viewed by Don Clausing as the "house of quality

(HOQ)." The house of quality is a kind of conceptual map that provides the means for inter-functional planning and communications.[10] It should be noted however that, in reality there is no sequential way of doing QFD. It is a concurrent activity where the cross-functional team is formed by the participation of individuals, both from the down stream (finished product) and up stream (designing), and they do their respective jobs from the initial stage. The basic foundation of QFD is the belief that products should be designed to reflect customers' desires and tastes, so marketing people, design engineers, and manufacturing staff must work closely together from the time a product is conceived.[10] The overall QFD process can be summarized in the following way.

Market survey: A consumer market survey of the target market is conducted by the merchandising department to get the expressed and the latent demand of the consumers. A competitive market analysis is done simultaneously to find out the company's own position in the market place. Thus, the company can decide the products or services it has to produce and their respective selling features (sales points).

Demanded quality deployment: On the basis of the information collected from the market, demanded quality as well as the degree of importance of each demanded quality are determined. This degree of importance is then converted into weight of each demanded quality. The demanded quality deployment chart incorporates the customers' demanded qualities and weight of each demanded quality. To prepare demanded quality deployment chart usually the KJ method (an affinity diagram system named for its Japanese inventor, Jiro Kawakita) is used.

Quality characteristic deployment: The product development department transforms the demanded qualities into quality characteristics, that is, the voice of the customers is translated into designers' language. The competitive performance standing of the company in relation to each quality characteristic or element is defined here. Quality characteristic deployment chart incorporates the counterpart quality characteristics of each demanded quality. From the weight of each demanded quality, the weight of each quality characteristic is determined. By converting each demanded quality into quality characteristic, and analyzing the customers' complaints, different weights of demanded qualities and quality characteristics, the *design quality* of the concerned product or service is established.

Function deployment: Even after the design qualities are determined, it is still difficult to create immediately a link with the technology needed to achieve these qualities. Therefore, it is necessary to determine the functions that express the quality characteristics, and the mechanisms that are required to realize those functions. The function deployment chart converts the quality characteristics into functions that the product should contain. Here, based on the weights of the demanded qualities, the weights are assigned to functions. At this point it is also important to determine the priority of functions among themselves from the technical standpoint. Analytical hierarchy process (AHP) is an effective tool for doing it.

Mechanism deployment: In mechanism deployment chart, the functions are converted into mechanisms and the functional priority is converted into mechanism priority, that is, the mechanism weights. This phase analyses whether the required functions can be realized with the company's special technology or not. If not, then the particular issue becomes an engineering bottleneck (BNE) and methods like process decision program chart (PDPC) and reviewed dendrogram (RD) can be used to handle such a BNE situation.[1]

Parts deployment: The mechanisms that are required for realizing the functions demanded by the customers are further devised into parts. The weights of parts are also converted from mechanism weights. In the part deployment chart, the relationships among parts, mechanisms and functions are displayed in a matrix form. When the function, mechanism and part deployments are combined, it is called the technology deployment. The combined chart is called the technology deployment chart that helps to detect technological bottlenecks. Technological bottlenecks can also be called the bottlenecks from quality perspective. These bottlenecks arise when the current technology of the company becomes inadequate to realize the functionality of the product required by the customers.

Cost deployment: The purpose of the cost deployment is to build into the engineering process a systematic way to reduce product cost while maintaining a balance with quality. Cost deployment refers to the allocation of target cost to demanded qualities, quality characteristics, functions, mechanisms and finally to the parts of the product. There are different practices among the companies regarding this allocation process. For example, some companies start allocation from demanded qualities, some start from the quality characteristics. Usually target cost is assigned by their relevant weights of the respective stages. Cost deployment touches all the phases of the QFD and incorporates the overall cost impacts of the development process. The objective of cost deployment is to screen out the cost bottlenecks from the development process. Generally, after assigning the mechanism target cost to the parts based on weight, a comparison is made between the part's estimated cost and the assigned target cost. If the estimated cost is higher than the target cost of the part, that becomes an object for cost improvement, thus a candidate for bottleneck engineering. A detail revision or study of function and mechanism level deployment is essential to solve the problem. The chart showing cost deployment is called the cost engineering deployment chart.[1] The overall QFD process can be presented in Fig. 8.1

3. Value Engineering (VE)

The concept of value engineering originated in the West in late 40s and was introduced in Japan in 50s. At the initial stage, value engineering was the domain of the engineering discipline, but the concept has been modified and broadened by the Japanese management accountants. At present, it is one of the most effective tool used by the Japanese management accountants for the purpose of controlling cost and achieving quality of the existing as well as the new products in the development stage. In recent years most of the Japanese manufacturing and service industries are using value engineering concept for product and service development. Though the concept of VE was introduced in Japan in 50s but its formal introduction was made in 1976, during the first oil shock.[17] Since then Japanese experts are deploying VE more effectively with significant modifications.

The Society of Japanese Value Engineering[14] defines value engineering as "a systematic approach to study the functions of products or services

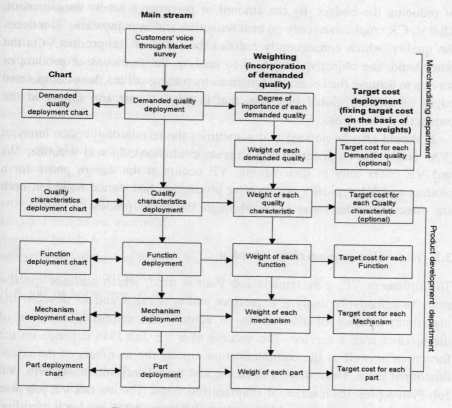

Fig. 8.1. Overall quality function deployment.

in order to achieve their necessary functions with minimum costs". The Japan Value Engineering Association defines VE as "organized efforts to implement functional analysis of products and/or services to reliably achieve all required functions at the lowest possible life cycle cost."

There is a great deal of misunderstanding and confusion among managers in the workplace about the distinction between VE and Cost Reduction (CR), especially in an environment where VE is newly introduced. Cost reduction can be defined as a cost cutting technique that focuses on parts, which might result in quality or performance reduction to meet the goal of reducing the budget, by the amount or percentage set by management. That is, CR emphasizes only on cost reduction and in many cases, it reduces the quality, which consequently reduces the value of the product.[2] On the other hand, the objective of VE is to analyze the functions of product or service to achieve the necessary functions by trading-off the three competitive edges of modern global business, that is quality, cost and timing of the products or services.

It should also be noticed that sometimes the terminology value analysis (VA) and value engineering (VE) create confusions. In real practice, VA and VE differ only in their timing. VE occurs at the design phase for a product and VA typically occurs after production has started however, both are directed to the same goals, through the same process.[3,4]

3.1. *The value engineering job plan*

To implement VE, a systematic Job Plan is used, which outlines specific steps to effectively analyze a product and/or service and to develop the maximum number of alternatives to achieve the required functions of the product and/or service. The success of a VE Job Plan depends on the formation as well as the communication among the members of the cross-functional team, flexibility of thinking and sound information system. VE Job Plan represents a series of standardized steps. The overall VE job plan consists of three basic steps: (A) Function Definition, (B) Function Evaluation and (C) Selection of Improvement Plan.

(A) **Function Definition:** This is the first basic step of VE activities where the understandings of the targeted functions are made. Here the VE cross-functional team clarifies the purpose and characteristic of the target functions. For this purpose the team has to go through three more steps as stated below.

(i) Collection of data related to VE object: This is the preparatory task for the VE project that involves collection of information about principal areas like user or customer wants and needs (customer's voice), sales requirements (sales points), design, manufacturing, distribution, cost and finally rules and regulations. Complete data set should be available to the cross-functional team before going any further.

(ii) Function definition: The target object is visualized through a product configuration drawing and then the particular functions of the product are identified and defined by using active verbs and measurable nouns. This is often referred to as *Random function definition*. Following are two examples of random function definition:

Product	Active verb	Noun
Clock	(i) indicate (ii) decorate	(i) time (ii) wrist
Tie	decorate	chest

(iii) Systematize the function: At this phase the VE cross-functional team tries to distinguish between necessary and unnecessary or less important functions and to draw a border line between the fundamental (basic) and secondary (supporting) functions of the products or services. It is usually a strenuous process. The function analysis system technique (FAST) or the function family trees are the most effective tools that may help to systematize the relationships among functions.

(B) **Function Evaluation:** The function evaluation phase provides a proportional value of each function to identify the functions having high or low value involvement to determine the value improvement targets. This basic phase consists of three steps as stated below.

(i) Function-specific estimated cost: In case of a model change product, the function specific estimated cost implies the function-specific actual cost, while for an entirely new product, it is determined by adjusting the function-specific cost fluctuation components, based on new product conceptualization drawing, with the actual cost of the existing similar products of the company.

(ii) Function evaluation: An estimation of relative value of each function to the customer is to be made here, to assign the product's target cost to each of the functions. The function evaluation is done through a comparison between the function-specific target cost and estimated cost

(iii) Selection of functions needing improvement: A detailed comparison between the estimated and target cost of the end-functions leads to the detection of end-functions needing improvements. The functional areas with the lowest proportional values are the prime candidates for value improvement. The cross-functional team calculates the "proportional value" for each function using the following formula

   Value = Function's target cost/Function's estimated or actual cost.

(C) Selection of Improvement Plan: As the first two basic steps are completed, the functional areas that require the most value improvement efforts are identified and at this phase the effort should be on problem solving. This basic phase includes the following steps.

  (i) Idea generation: The objective of the idea generation phase (sometimes referred to as the "Speculation phase") is to develop a large number of ideas for performing each function selected for study. Free flow of thoughts and ideas without criticism is encouraged here.[18]

 (ii) Summary evaluation: The objectives of the summary evaluation are to gather and analyze data concerning ideas generated and presented in the "idea generation" phase and select the feasible ideas or recommendation for specific value improvement. Using the criteria established in the function systematization phase, the newly generated ideas are sorted out and rated as to how well they meet those criteria.

(iii) Detail evaluation: Finally, a careful evaluation of the few selective proposals is to be made by the VE cross-functional team, to select the best proposal by applying appropriate tools like, technical test and cost estimations. If none of the final proposal appear to satisfactorily meet the criteria, the team has to return to the "idea generation" phase

(iv) Presentation: The objective of the presentation phase is to obtain concurrence and a commitment from the designers, project leaders and other management to proceed with implementation of the recommendations. This involves an initial oral presentation followed by a complete written report.

The usual practice of VE Job plan is summarized in Fig. 8.2.

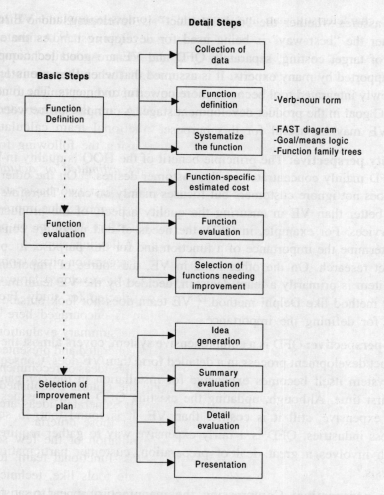

Fig. 8.2. Overall VE activities through a VE job plan.

4. Comparison Between QFD and VE

The theoretical discussion on QFD and VE shows that they have many similarities, dissimilarities and in some aspects have good functional relationships. If they are thought together, the relationship can be seen as,

QFD assures whether the "right product" is developing and VE assures whether the "best way" is being used for developing it.[15] As the system tools of target costing, separately QFD and VE are good techniques and are supported by many experts. It is assumed that when they are integrated, the newly integrated tool becomes more powerful and convenient to achieve the QC goal in the product development stage. A comparison between QFD and VE may be useful for this purpose.

Quality perspective: The principle benefit of the HOQ is quality in-house, as QFD mainly concentrates on the customer desires.[10] On the other hand, VE does not ignore customers but focuses mainly on cost. Therefore, QFD suits better than VE in ensuring the quality aspects of the products and/ or services. For example, in QFD, the needs of end users are considered to determine the importance of a function and for this purpose, it conducts market research. On the other hand in VE, the source of importance for each item is primarily a team decision, decided by the VE team members, using method like Delphi method.[12] VE team does not look outside of the team for defining the importance.

Cost perspective: QFD is a comprehensive system, covers almost the whole product development process in a detailed form than VE does. Consequently, the system itself becomes expensive for installation in the companies for the first time. Although, updating the existing QFD for new issues is not very expensive, still it is costlier than VE. It is found that, in software process industries, QFD is a fairly expensive way to gather requirements, which involves a great deal of preparation, customer participation, and analysis.[9]

Time perspective: Compressing the manufacturing and new product development cycles will lead to better financial performance. If cycle time is reduced, cost will go down and quality up.[7] QFD requires a significant amount of time to establish as well as for problem solving than VE. VE projects are usually measured in days or weeks, while, QFD projects are usually measured in weeks or months.[11] Therefore, to have a quick solution to any problem and to save time VE may be considered as the ideal substitute for QFD.

Comprehensiveness: VE addresses different scopes of the issues separately, whereas QFD looks at different scopes in an integrated fashion, all at once.

Measuring customers' satisfaction: QFD establishes a complete set of company measures (such as, quality, cost and timing) and controls to identify when the customers' needs are met. By contrast, VE concentrates exclusively on cost to measure customers' satisfaction.

Communication: VE uses functions as an aid to smooth the technical communication within the team, but this technical language is not easy to understand by the people outside the team. On the other hand, QFD uses lists and matrices to make methodical communication within the entire team and with all who need it outside of the team. The QFD chart is extremely efficient at communicating an immense amount of information.[11]

Documentation: VE uses FAST diagram to organize the information and provide a framework for perspective, discussion, and documentation, which is not that much communicative because of its technicality as mentioned before. QFD provides a detailed view of all the issues and considerations that went into any process. This also provides long term documentation that radically improves future similar decisions.

Methodologies: VE tends to have many customizations to its methodology, but seldom couples with other existing methodologies. Whereas, QFD couples with and makes use of a multitude of these additional methodologies, including VE.[1]

Sequencing: VE uses a logical sequence but the sequencing abilities within QFD are severely limited since QFD works in different directions simultaneously.[11] On the contrary, logical sequencing may distort all other activities which could be done concurrently. Therefore, from the view point of simultaneous engineering QFD is preferable to VE.

QFD and VE address certain areas differently, however, there are some fundamental areas where they can be integrated. The issues are: both of them work with functions of the product and use cost deployment; a cross-functional team is required in either systems; both the processes start with defining the product and/or service, where VE is guided by a Job plan and QFD uses the QFD matrices; both the systems focus on the customers, where QFD considers the voice of the customers and VE considers team members decision; and finally, QFD is a problem identification process while VE is for solving the problem.

5. Issues to be Addressed

5.1. *Trade-off relationship between quality and cost (P)*

Quality and cost targets are set simultaneously using a variety of information-based methods that encompass customer needs, field failures, competitor performance and trends, regulatory trends and technology availability. The processes to set and allocate quality and cost targets from the end-product level to subsystems and components occur simultaneously, with reconciliation between cost and quality taking place during the basic product planning stage. In studying the automotive industries of Japan, U.S. and German companies, it is found that the best practice companies do not have a hierarchy of rules that prioritizes quality over cost, or vice-versa, nor do they think in terms of trading off one set of targets over another. Instead, they try to determine an optimal set of component target parameters during product planning that do not compromise the end-product's quality and cost targets.[5] In a case study of Yaskawa Electric, Akao[1] encountered that in the trade-off between quality and cost, greater priority was given to quality results in the failure of cost target attainment. On the other hand, if the product loses its quality, it implies that the cost will be increased in a geometric rate after the product is shipped.[16] Therefore, it may be concluded that over-emphasis on quality will hinder the cost target achievement and vice-versa. In the product planning and detailed design phase, usually QFD and VE put emphasis on both quality and cost issues. However, the method of dealing with quality issues by QFD is more representative of actual customer desire than VE. From this perspective it may be asserted that when the companies provide equal priority to quality or both quality and cost in determining their targets, they are more inclined to use QFD. On the other hand, companies focusing mainly on cost elements prefer to use VE.

5.2. *Cost improvement objects (C)*

The major objective of target-costing systems is to achieve the target cost without sacrificing the quality of the product and still remain profitable and competitive in the market. Therefore, it becomes necessary to check whether the assigned target costs in different levels of the product development are achieved or not. If in any situation target cost is not achieved, the system conducts analysis on that particular location and tries to determine the required improvement object for cost reconciliation. Sometimes, the improvement activities with the existing resources of the company may not be sufficient to achieve the target cost. That is, if the gap between the estimated and target costs cannot be reconciled by extending the existing capabilities of the company, it is called a bottleneck situation. To identify the cost improvement objects as well as bottlenecks, target-costing system deploys both QFD and VE system tools. The ways of ascertaining cost improvement objects and bottlenecks by these two subsystems are significantly different. In the case where QFD is used, the cost improvement objects as well as the bottlenecks are identified based on parts level deployment while VE identifies the same based on end-functions. The processes are stated below.

5.2.1. *QFD approach to identify the cost improvement objects (C_{QFD})*

In QFD, a comprehensive process is followed to discover the cost improvement objects. First, part target cost is calculated from mechanism target cost and then it is compared to the part estimated cost in order to identify the cost improvement object. In this process, after identifying the demanded qualities based on market survey, weights are assigned to each demanded quality on the basis of its priority. The voice-of-the-customer (VOC) is emphasized and integrated in assigning the weights of each demanded quality. Besides VOC, the competitive products in the market, market trend and sale points are also considered. Based on the assigned weights of the demanded quality, target cost of the product is apportioned among the various demanded qualities. At this point the weight of each demanded quality becomes a unit of cost. The demanded quality target costs are further divided into the relevant quality characteristics and functions

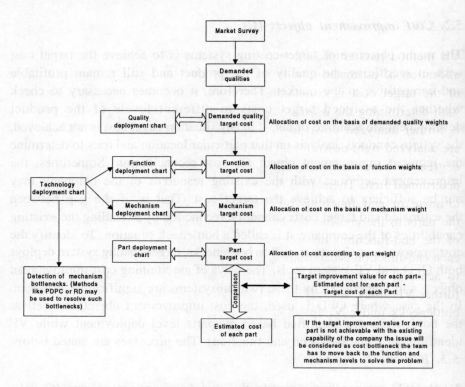

Fig. 8.3. QFD approach to identify the cost improvement objects and bottlenecks.

on the basis of their respective weights. The method used for function target cost determination is also used to determine mechanism target cost. The mechanism target cost is further broken down to determine the part level target cost and the target cost of each part is analyzed from the mechanism viewpoint. At this stage, the target and estimated cost for each part are compared and the cost improvement objects are identified. If the improvement object seems to be difficult to achieve by the existing capabilities of the company, the particular object becomes a bottleneck issue. To have an appropriate solution to the problem, QFD activity moves back to the function and mechanism deployments for further analyses and re-examinations.

The process of identifying the cost improvement object as well as the bottlenecks in QFD method can be presented in Fig. 8.3.

5.2.2. *VE approach to identify the cost improvement objects (C_{VE})*

VE method puts emphasis on function and cost of the product. Here, the allocation of estimated cost is somewhat complicated while the allocation of the target cost is comparatively easier. The identifying process starts with determining the estimated cost of each function and the function cost is further analyzed down to the part level. The functions of the products are analyzed right down to the ultimate functions or the end-functions. The degree to which each of the parts contributes to the end-functions is determined first. Thereafter, the part's estimated cost is apportioned to the ultimate or end functions on the basis of the degree of contribution of the parts to the end-functions. Subsequently, the target and estimated cost of the end-functions are compared and the cost improvement object for each end-function is determined. If the improvement object becomes difficult to achieve, then it is considered as a bottleneck issue and extended for further VE study. Identifying process of the cost improvement objects and bottlenecks under VE method are presented in Fig. 8.4.

5.3. *Bottleneck engineering (B)*

Bottleneck engineering is defined as an engineering practice applied to technical problems, that must be solved in order to implement quality and cost targets, but that cannot be resolved with the current technology of the company.[1] In case of QFD, the bottlenecks are identified mainly in two phases, first from the technology deployment phase, where the existing technological capability (mechanism) of the company fails to realize the required functions demanded by the customers. Here, *the bottleneck issues are mainly related to the mechanism and in turn, related to quality*. Second, in the cost engineering deployment phase where to have an appropriate solution to the problem, QFD activity moves back to the function and mechanism deployments for further analyses and re-examinations. That is, *QFD method emphasizes mainly on mechanism deployment rather than cost deployment for solving bottlenecks* (Fig. 8.3).

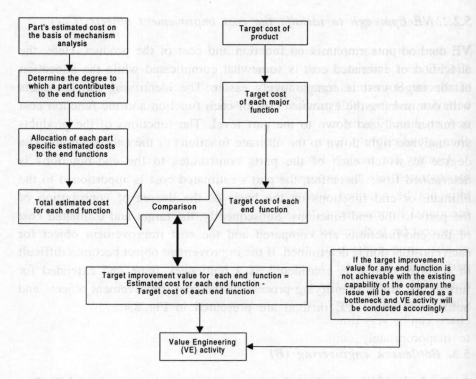

Fig. 8.4. VE approach to identify the cost improvement objects and bottlenecks.

On the other hand, in case of VE, the end-functions that are less important for the product get higher priority for improvement. The identified improvement objects become bottleneck issues, if the targets seem to be difficult to achieve with the current capabilities of the company (Fig. 8.4). At this stage the issue is extended for VE study. The VE study team comes up with different ideas to solve the problems by using the brainstorming techniques and summarizes them in a systematic way. The summarized ideas are evaluated by comparing the quality and cost perspectives of the product. Finally, the VE team appears with the best possible solutions for the concerned bottleneck issues. The cross-functional team focuses mainly on cost deployment. In this case, the technological as well as the cost bottlenecks are merged together and cost deployment gets higher priority.

5.4. *Model change versus entirely new products*

VE does not integrate the customers' voices into the product design directly as QFD does, instead, the VE team conducts it indirectly from the customer's standpoint. Sometimes team context may not properly represent the customers' behavior and thus, this practice may not be effective for developing entirely new product.[1] Therefore, for measuring quality performance of both model change and entirely new products, QFD method is better than VE method.

Usually for model change products, the customer verbatim is already incorporated into the product and detailed inquires on customers' choices may not be required. Instead these products may require emphasis on functional improvements. In addition, the installation of QFD set-up will incur cost for both model change and entirely new products and the process is also time consuming that again raises cost. Thus, for higher cost performance of model change product, VE method may be a better choice than QFD. Both QFD and VE system charts are prepared for both model change and entirely new products. Japanese companies cautioned that quality charts can be very time-consuming to develop and can cause an organization to inappropriately emphasize quality over cost.[5]

6. Analysis of the Results

The variables to be analysed are trade-off relationship between quality and cost ($P = P_C$, P_{QC} and P_Q) methods of determining cost improvement object ($C = C_{VE}$ and C_{QFD}), and methods of detecting bottleneck engineering ($B = B_C$, B_{MC} and B_M). The effects of the eighteen combinations (consisting of variables P, C, and B, having categories three, two and three respectively) have been tested to find a desirable combination that maximizes QC performance for both model change and entirely new products.

6.1. *Quality performance*

It is observed that for model change product, the quality performance improves the most when a company employs QFD method for determining cost improvement objects (C_{QFD}), emphasizes more on cost deployments (B_C)

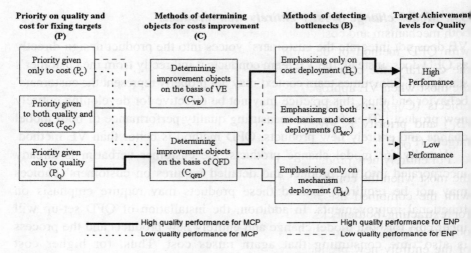

Fig. 8.5. Quality performance for both model change and entirely new products.

for detecting bottlenecks and gives priority only to quality (P_Q). On the other hand, the quality performance of the model change product approaches the lowest level when a company gives priority only to cost (P_C) and uses both mechanism and cost deployments for detecting bottlenecks (B_{MC}) along with the use of QFD for determining cost improvement objects (C_{QFD}).

For entirely new product, the quality performance, $QTAL_{ENP}$, reaches the highest level when the companies emphasize only on mechanism deployment (B_M) together with QFD method of determining cost improvement objects (C_{QFD}), and gives equal priority to both quality and cost (P_{QC}). Conversely, it reaches nearly the lowest level when the companies emphasize both on mechanism and cost deployments (B_{MC}), gives priority only on cost (P_C) and use VE method for determining cost improvement objects (C_{VE}). The quality performance for both model change and entirely new products is depicted in Fig. 8.5.

6.2. Cost performance

In case of model change product, relative to all other possibilities, the companies will be able to improve their cost performance at the highest level if they give equal priority to both quality and cost (P_{QC}), uses both mechanism and cost deployments for detecting bottlenecks (B_{MC}) along with QFD method of determining cost improvement objects (C_{QFD}). On the contrary, the cost performance of the model change product declines the most when VE approach is followed to determine the cost improvement objects (C_{VE}), cost deployment is emphasized for bottleneck detection (B_C) and priority is given both to quality and cost while setting their targets (P_{QC}).

For entirely new product, the cost performance of the companies improves the most when the companies prioritize both quality and cost together (P_{QC}) with the combined use of both mechanism and cost deployments (B_{MC}) for extracting bottlenecks and QFD method for fixing cost improvement objects (C_{QFD}). On the other hand, it also found that the cost performance of the entirely new products declines the most, when the priority is given only to quality (P_Q) while determining the quality-cost targets, along with the use of VE for determining the cost improvement objects (C_{VE}) and both mechanism and cost deployments are emphasized for detecting the bottlenecks. The cost performance for both model change and entirely new products is presented in Fig. 8.6.

6.3. *Simultaneous achievement of quality and cost*

To identify the combination providing the attainment of quality and cost simultaneously, the effects of the first-four best combinations of different categories of the independent variables on each of the quality and cost performance are summarized in Table 8.1.

6.3.1. *Model change product*

When an individual company emphasizes mainly on quality, to achieve it at the highest level it uses (P_Q,C_{QFD},B_C). On the other hand, when a company focuses on cost issues, the use of (P_{QC},C_{QFD},B_{MC}) provides the highest cost performance. The only combination that improves both quality and cost performance of a model change product is (P_{QC},C_{QFD},B_{MC});

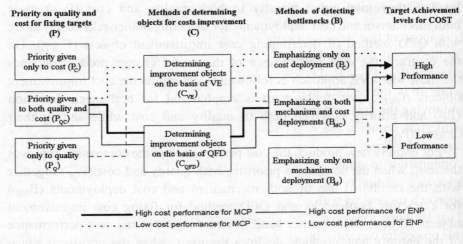

Fig. 8.6. Cost performance for both model change and entirely new products.

Table 8.1. Effects of the first four combinations of different categories of the independent variables on QC performance.

Target Achievements	Ranking of the Combinations			
	1	2	3	4
Model change product:				
Quality	(P_Q, C_{QFD}, B_C)	(P_Q, C_{VE}, B_{MC})	$(P_{QC}, C_{QFD}, B_{MC})$	(P_{QC}, C_{QFD}, B_M)
Cost	$(P_{QC}, C_{QFD}, B_{MC})$	(P_{QC}, C_{VE}, B_{MC})	(P_C, C_{VE}, B_C)	(P_C, C_{QFD}, B_C)
Entirely new product:				
Quality	(P_{QC}, C_{QFD}, B_M)	(P_Q, C_{VE}, B_{MC})	$(P_{QC}, C_{QFD}, B_{MC})$	(P_Q, C_{QFD}, B_C)
Cost	$(P_{QC}, C_{QFD}, B_{MC})$	(P_{QC}, C_{QFD}, B_M)	(P_Q, C_{VE}, B_M)	(P_C, C_{QFD}, B_C)

however, this is the first-best performer for cost and the third-best for the quality. If the objective is to achieve these goals simultaneously, there is no alternative other than $(P_{QC}, C_{QFD}, B_{MC})$ that satisfies both together. Thus for simultaneous attainment of QC of model change product, the only solution is $(P_{QC}, C_{QFD}, B_{MC})$.

6.3.2. *Entirely new product*

It is apparent that the simultaneous attainment of quality and cost is possible by the use of two combinations, (P_{QC}, C_{QFD}, B_M) and $(P_{QC}, C_{QFD}, B_{MC})$. The effect of (P_{QC}, C_{QFD}, B_M) is the highest in improving the quality performance while it is the second-best combination for cost performance. Again, in improving the cost performance, the effect of $(P_{QC}, C_{QFD}, B_{MC})$ is the highest while this combination is the third-best performer in attaining the quality targets. Between these two, it is rather difficult to choose a particular combination to attain the quality and cost goal simultaneously. To have a suitable solution to this dilemma, the multi-attribute value (cost) function, an approach for dealing with multiple criteria decision problems can be applied.[6,7] That is, when a company has multiple goals to be achieved simultaneously, this procedure can solve this, if it is possible to define a preference relationship among all the goals.

It is observed that the general notion among the Japanese companies is to give more priority to quality than cost. Thus for entirely new products, when both quality and cost targets are to be achieved concurrently, the combination (P_{QC}, C_{QFD}, B_M) should be chosen since as a goal, quality is preferred to cost. However, it should satisfy the minimum cost requirements of the company. Figure 8.7 represents the combinations providing the simultaneous achievement of QC for model change and entirely new products.

7. Conclusions

In this paper the problem of combining QFD and VE for achieving quality and cost in product development in the Japanese manufacturing industries is addressed. The main aspect considered here is related to find out which ways the companies are adopting to improve their quality and cost performance either individually or simultaneously, and also whether the results vary between model change and entirely new products. Two subsystems, VE and QFD, in a target-costing environment are compared to identify their effects on quality and cost performance.

It is found that QFD method is suitable to attain the highest quality performance for both the products. However, emphasizing cost deployment

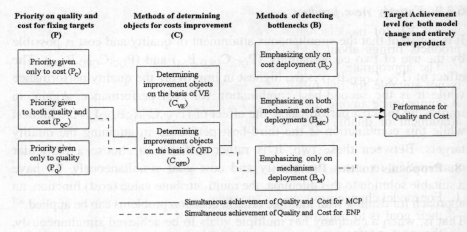

Priority on quality and cost for fixing targets (P)	Methods of determining objects for costs improvement (C)	Methods of detecting bottlenecks (B)	Target Achievement level for both model change and entirely new products

Fig. 8.7. Simultaneous achievement of quality and cost for both model change and entirely new products.

and prioritizing quality for model change product and highlighting mechanism deployments along with preferring both quality and cost aspects for entirely new product offer the best way of attaining quality performance.

Again, QFD method also provides the highest cost reduction performance both for model change and entirely new products when equal priority is given to quality and cost aspects along with the uses of both mechanism and cost deployment methods.

Comparison of the effects of all possible combinations reveals that both for model change and entirely new products, the ways to attain QC simultaneously are very similar. Both of them use QFD method for determining cost improvement objects (C_{QFD}) and give equal priority to both quality and cost aspects in the product planning stage (P_{QC}). However, for detecting bottlenecks, entirely new products require emphasis only on mechanism deployments (B_M) while model change products emphasize both mechanism and cost deployments (B_{MC}). From the overall findings it is also observed that QFD method is relatively more effective than VE method.

Survey of previous literature[1] shows the tendency to use VE for model change and QFD for entirely new products. This tendency is also observed in this study. However, no consistent evidence is found on whether the use of VE for model change products and that of QFD for entirely new products brings about highest QC performance.

The appropriate way to attain a particular objective at a higher level is not suitable for the fulfillment of other objectives at the same degree. A compromise among the goals can show the avenue for the simultaneous attainment of quality and cost.

8. Proposals to the Practitioners

1. For model change products, the companies should use (P_Q, C_{QFD}, B_C) when their goal is to improve only the quality performance, while to improve the cost performance alone, they should use $(P_{QC}, C_{QFD}, B_{MC})$. The simultaneous achievement of quality-cost is possible by the use of $(P_{QC}, C_{QFD}, B_{MC})$.

2. In case of entirely new products, the companies should use (P_{QC}, C_{QFD}, B_M) when quality is their only goal to improve, while for improving only the cost performance they should employ $(P_{QC}, C_{QFD}, B_{MC})$. Since the general notion of the Japanese companies is to prefer quality to cost, to achieve quality and cost simultaneously, they should choose the combination giving the highest quality performance, that is (P_{QC}, C_{QFD}, B_M). However, an individual company may select the combination $(P_{QC}, C_{QFD}, B_{MC})$ for simultaneous attainment of QC, if it fulfills *the minimum quality requirements* of the company by making a compromise with quality.

3. Japanese companies should avoid $(P_{QC} \rightarrow C_{VE} \rightarrow B_C)$, the popular way, for attaining quality and cost objective either individually or simultaneously for both model change and entirely new products.

References

1. Akao, Y., Quality Function Deployment (QFD): Integrating Customer Requirements into Product Design (Productivity Press, Portland, Oregon, 1988).
2. Alasheash, S., Why Some Managers Think of Value Engineering as Cost Reduction (SAVE Proceeding, 1993).

3. Ansari, S. L. & Bell, J. E., Target Costing (Irwin Professional Publishing, Chicago, 1997).
4. Cooper, R. & Slagmulder, R., Target Cost and Value Engineering (Productivity Press, Portland, Oregon, 1995).
5. Arthur Andersen and Co, QCT Product Development Report, 1993.
6. Chankong, V. & Haimes, Y., Multi-objective Decision Making: Theory and Methodology (Elsevier Science, New York, North Holland Series, 1983).
7. Curtis, C. C., Nonfinancial Performance Measures in New Product Development, J. Cost Management, Fall 1994, 18–26.
8. Goiceochea, A., Hansen, D. & Dunkstein, L., Multi Objective Decision Analysis with Engineering and Business Applications (John Wiley, New York, 1982).
9. Guerrieri, E. & Taylor, B. J., DEC TP WORK center: A Software Process Case Study, Digital Technical J., Vol. 5, No. 4, Fall 1993, 47–58.
10. Hauser, J. R. & Clausing, D., The House of Quality, Harvard Business Review May–June, 1988, 63–73.
11. Lyman, D., The Functional Relationship Between QFD and VE (SAVE Proceedings, 1992), 76–79.
12. Monden, Y., Target Costing and Kaizen Costing: Cost Reduction System (Productivity Press, Portland, Oregon, 1995).
13. Quevedo, R., Quality Function Deployment in Manufacturing and Service Organizations, Proceedings of the 3rd Annual Management Accounting Symposium (San Diego, California, March, 1989), 33–52.
14. Society of Japanese Value Engineering, A Guide Book of Value Engineering Terms (in Japanese), (Tokyo, Society of Japanese Value Engineering, 1992).
15. Syverson, R., Quality Function Deployment and Value Analysis (SAVE Proceedings, 1992).
16. Taguchi, G. & Clausing, D., Robust Quality, Harvard Business Review January–February, 1990, 65–75.
17. Yoshikawa, T., Innes, J. & Mitchell, F., A Japanese Case Study of Functional Cost Analysis, Management Accounting Research 6, 1995, 415–432.
18. Value Methodology Standard (SAVE International, The Value Society, 1997).

Part 4
Cost Management of
Manufacturing Activities

Chapter 9

Just-In-Time and Its Cost Reduction Framework

1. Introduction

More than ever before, manufacturing companies are faced with greater challenges, this being largely due to increasing globalization of the market — a consequence of the growing emphasis on free trade. The recent phenomenal growth in information technology, with such new elements as Internet trade, is playing a significant role in bringing about this scenario. On the one hand, this is a very welcome development for the consumer, who now has ample opportunity to maximize utility of his resources. On the other, however, stiffer competition faced by the manufacturer makes it more difficult for it to increase or maintain market shares. This then compels it to seek ways to be innovative in all spheres of its operations. The areas of concern relate not only to product development, but also to others, such as: production technology, marketing and purchasing strategy, etc. Also of importance is the manufacturer's vigorous pursuit of the key elements of competitiveness including: product functionality, quality, cost, lead time for product delivery, product differentiation. Within the limits of performance expectation of a product, cost plays a very important role in the consumer's behaviour. This is a reflection of the basic psychology of the consumer, which dictates that he (she) purchases a product only if its perceived worth is not less than its price.

The Just-In-Time manufacturing paradigm was developed by Toyota Motor Corporation in Japan, and it aims at eliminating all forms of wastes in manufacturing, and consequently reducing costs. This makes it possible to offer products to the consumers at a very competitive price. The JIT concept grew out of the challenges of the global oil crises in 1973, and it has become widely adopted, particularly in the repetitive manufacturing industry.

Although much of the cost reduction that is achievable for a product hinges on improvements at the product development stage, in a number of cases, costs reduction during manufacturing can be quite significant as well. Therefore actions taken in this respect play a very important role in the firm's continuous drive towards higher levels of competitiveness. In this chapter, we examine the broad framework of the JIT concept, and in particular, the mechanisms by which it achieves cost reduction.

2. The Just-In-Time System

The literature is replete with various definitions of the meaning and scope of Just-In-Time. In a narrow sense, it relates to the mechanism by which products and their component parts are produced and distributed within a manufacturing system, with a view to reducing parts and finished products inventory. Simply put, JIT means to produce the necessary units, in the necessary quantities at the necessary times. A JIT production system exhibits a "pull" phenomenon, whereby units are produced by a subsequent process to make up for those used up by a preceding process. This is unlike the conventional "push" system, where a preceding process makes and stocks units for the subsequent process, without particular consideration of the needs of this process. Thus, JIT production primarily addresses the problem of inventory in the entire system. Indeed, the ideal of JIT is single piece production and conveyance of all items in the multi-echelon manufacturing system. It therefore makes the entire system somewhat linked by an invisible conveyor line. It is important to emphasize, though, that JIT production is not a zero-inventory or stockless production system per se, but it maintains only the necessary inventory between adjoining processes. The maintenance of more-than-necessary inventory creates a chain effect on entire system performance. This has in recent times, particularly, drawn the attention of practitioners and academia alike, to the study and analysis of issues relating to the implementation of JIT production.

The JIT concept started out primarily with production and related operational areas in manufacturing, such as distribution and purchasing, and it is finding increasing application in non-manufacturing areas as well. Feather and Cross[1] discuss the similarities between production and administrative operations, and report how a Contracts Management Organization improved its operations by applying JIT principles and workflow analysis. One of the major accomplishments of the firm was the reduction in throughput time by 60% and reduction in backlog by more than 80%. Whitson[9] notes that most hospitals have until now, focused their cost containment efforts on lowering acquisition price of supplies, instead of lowering total delivered costs, which includes transaction, storage, handling and transportation. (This is in spite of the fact that approximately 70 cents to $1 is spent in logistics for every dollar of supplies.) He therefore discusses opportunities whereby JIT principles can improve performance and reduce costs in a hospital setting. Within a narrow framework, JIT production, *Autonomation* and Total Quality Management (TQM), form the bedrock of the famous Toyota Production System.

The term, JIT, is also used in a much broader perspective — that is, as a new management philosophy that concerns the total system, and that is geared towards making the firm competitive in the market. Within this broader framework, it comprises two main management thrusts, namely Effective Production Management, and Total Quality Management (TQM). Using production as the base, and in recognition of its wastes' elimination capability (which leads to smaller consumption of resources as compared to conventional production), it is sometimes referred to as "lean" production system.[10] Furthermore, a firm that applies JIT principles to all its operations is referred to as the lean enterprise. In the ensuing discussions, we adopt the broader definition of JIT, while the term, *JIT production* is used in a more restrictive sense to describe the production aspects.

3. Foundations for Implementing JIT

Preparations based on the fundamental concepts that support JIT are necessary for its successful implementation. These core concepts: production smoothing, work standardization, setup time reduction, multifunction and flexible workforce are described below. (This section is based mainly on the discussions in Monden.[5])

3.1. *Production smoothing philosophy*

One of the most important and fundamental elements for JIT implementation is production smoothing. Broadly speaking, smoothing is necessitated by the uneven nature of demand for the final product. For example, there are certain periods in a year or month when demand for a given product is high, whereas at other periods it is low. As was mentioned earlier, the ideal of JIT production is single piece production and conveyance. However, the nature of consumers' demand as well as prohibitive setup costs would generally make it difficult to implement this directly. Nevertheless, the adoption of appropriate actions can make for effective production in response to demand, with resultant cost reduction. While the smoothing we refer to in the foregoing primarily relates to the final products, there is the need to also smooth the consumption of subassemblies and parts used for making the products. This is necessary because it bears on the amount of in-process inventories in the factory. This latter point is of particular significance in large-variety-small-volume type of repetitive manufacturing systems, as exemplified by those for the manufacture of automobiles, electronics, and telecommunication equipment. There are various dimensions to the smoothing concept:

- Smoothing of total production quantity
  This aims at minimizing the variance in total product output between two sequential time periods, for example, every day. (The daily production requirement is the estimated total monthly demand divided by the number of operating days in a month.)

- Smoothing of each model's production quantity
This ensures that each of the models is represented for a given day, in proportion to the needs. It forestalls the scenario where a large number of units of some models are scheduled for manufacture for a certain day, whereas none or too few units of other models are scheduled.
- Mixed-model production
This mode of production is particularly useful for large-variety-small-volume type production, necessitated by the vastness of consumers needs for these types of products. For example, one consumer may want a car model of a particular series, with a sun-roof and 4-wheel drive transmission system, while another one may want a hardtop with a front wheel drive. The other specifications and parts may be common for both. Since these varieties are essentially similar, switch-over cost between models is small. Therefore, it is more desirable economically to have them introduced intermittently into the assembly line, than to have each of them produced in batches. (Figure 9.1 illustrates mixed-model production in contrast to batch production.) This format of production ensures continuous flow of each model, and it reduces in-process and finished goods' inventory. The benefits of mixed-model production are however not limited to the final assembly lines, as it can, and is sometimes applied to fabrication of subassemblies.

3.2. Work standardization

This is geared towards making all the operations that are performed at the various processes within the manufacturing system as standard as possible. Since an operator is made to master his process or activities, work time variability is largely eliminated. In other words, this standardization of activities results in the elimination of wasteful motions, which are generally non-value-adding activities. The pursuit of non-defective production and incorporation of means for elimination of accidents, are also helpful in achieving this. In reverse, this also helps to facilitate quality production.

The standardization of the work involves many aspects, such as the determination of: the cycle time, the completion time per unit, the standard operations routine, and the standard quantity of work-in-process. All these

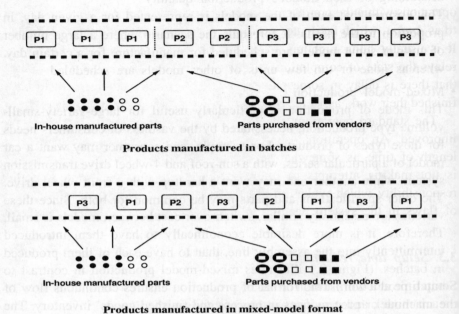

In-house manufactured parts   Parts purchased from vendors

Products manufactured in batches

In-house manufactured parts   Parts purchased from vendors

Products manufactured in mixed-model format

Fig. 9.1. Comparison of batch and mixed-model production.

culminate in the preparation of *the standard operations sheet*, which primarily serves as a guideline for each worker to keep to his standardized operations routine.

The determination of the cycle time is very essential in the standardization procedure. It is important to note that the total daily operation time is not designed to account for allowances due to machine breakdowns, miscellaneous idle time, such as time for awaiting materials. In the same vein, the daily output does not take defective items into account. These mechanisms are intentionally built into the system to help expose any problems, which readily become visible under these circumstances. These elicit efforts at their elimination, which in turn eliminates wastes, improves performance and increases productivity. One element that facilitates this is synchronization, whereby all processes contributing to the final output are designed to finish all their operations within the pre-determined cycle time. An electronic device, referred to as *Andon*, which facilitates visibility, is particularly useful in this respect. It is usually hung high up in the factory for all workers to see, and it relays the state of completion, or otherwise, of the processes. In the event that there is delay in some process, workers in other processes, who have finished their work, assist the concerned process to resolve problems promptly.

The standard operations sheet is revised regularly as the processes are improved. An operations' sheet which is not revised for a considerable length of time, is somewhat an indication that the Supervisor in charge is not making attempts to improve. This therefore creates a sense of responsibility, which evokes efforts towards the identification and elimination of flaws in the system, leading to improved operations and productivity.

3.3. *Setup time reduction*

Setup time at a workstation or process is the time interval required to prepare the machine or process for another production run after a given run. This is one of the core elements in the efforts at lead time reduction, since it impacts greatly on the suitable lot size for production. One of the main reasons for lot production is to enable the firm to derive cost benefits arising from the lack of need for frequent setups. This concept which forms the basis of the conventional Economic Order Quantity (EOQ) model, seeks the lot size that minimizes total cost, comprising inventory carrying cost and setup cost. However, this model is inadequate for world-class production, particularly in view of the fact that it does not take into account a number of factors such as: quality issues, continuous improvement, and worker motivation. By virtue of small lot production, which is characteristic of a JIT system, setup costs would tend to be prohibitive if appropriate measures are not taken to reduce setup times. Therefore, efforts at setup time reduction become a very important foundation on which successful implementation of JIT is built.

For a given system capacity, the reduction of setup time by n times would make it possible to reduce the lot size by a factor of n without increasing the total time span for production. This consequently reduces the lead time of the units. In other words, since lot size is smaller, the time interval required for a given unit to be released from the process would be shortened — the unit in question would not need to be held down until others in the larger batch are completely processed. It is not uncommon in conventional systems, to have setup for a given operation requiring as much as 4 hours or sometimes 1 working day. As early as the 1970s, Toyota embarked on a positive drive to reduce setup time in a bid to achieve its JIT goals. It has succeeded in reducing setup time to as small as 1 minute in some cases. Four basic principles that govern setup elimination and reduction are as follows:

- Do away with the setup, if possible
  In some cases, it is possible to completely do away with the setup action. This can be achieved for a punch press, for example, by appropriate product design, whereby the various part types are incorporated in the same die, enabling them to be produced at the same time. Another way to do away with setup is to use multiple less expensive machines to facilitate parallel production of parts.

- Separate internal setups from external setups
  This entails identification and separation of the two types of setup, namely internal setup and external setup. External setups are aspects of the setup action that are performed outside the machine; that is, those for which the machine could be running while being performed. Internal setups are actions whose performances require that the machine stop operation. It is quite common to have a number of avoidable operations, such as tool search due to cluttering, included in the setup procedure. Proper arrangement of tools, standardization of the setup procedures, and identification-assisting procedures can significantly reduce setup time.

- Convert internal setups to external setups as much as possible
  Since the external setup actions are carried out simultaneously with the machine operation time, this conversion does a lot in keeping to a minimum the amount of time the machine is idle.

• Eliminate unnecessary adjustments
It is possible by appropriate design of the setup action to avoid unnecessary adjustments (of nuts for example). These types of adjustments account for a substantial part of the overall setup time. This can be achieved, for example, by appropriate design of the processes to use minimum number of fasteners, or use of hydraulic clamping devices.

3.4. *Appropriate machine layout*

The nature of production system output serves as a basis for classifying repetitive manufacturing industries into Process industries and Discrete-item industries. By their very nature, the output of the former, which are either gases, pellets or liquids, can be automatically made to flow continuously, in which case, lotless production results. In the latter, however, the nature of the products as well as the human inconsistencies associated with their handling, make it somewhat difficult to have continuous flow. Since flexibility and derivable productivity gains make it desirable to have continuous production, the ultimate for discrete manufacturing, therefore, is to have the production process approach continuous flow as much as possible. The form of layout adopted is useful in facilitating this.

Assembly lines are designed for continuous flow. However, the attainment of the JIT objective entails the incorporation of this concept, not only in assembly lines, but in components fabrication as well.

Various types of machine layouts are used in industry. Traditional machine layouts include the Bird cage layout and the Isolated island layout. In the first type of layout, several machines of a given type are arranged at a particular location, so that the operator can sequentially perform tasks on different units. This eliminates operator waiting time while a given unit is being processed. Completed units are then stacked after the process as an input to the next process, with another type of machine (say Milling machine) arranged in a similar format. This generally results in very large in-process inventories. The isolated island layout is designed such that each cell consists of all types of machines required to complete the product. This is an improvement over the bird cage layout by virtue of smooth flow of units, and easy and prompt accessibility of the operator to the machines. Since problems still exist with respect to imbalance of production among the various processes, as well as unnecessary inventory, restructuring is essential to improving efficiency.

Two kinds of layout structures that have been used to address these are the Linear layout and the U-form layout. In the linear layout, all the different machines are arranged sequentially in a straight line, according to their processing order. The operator moves from one machine to the next while performing the desired operations. Problems do exist with this layout as well because of the inability to effectively reallocate operations to workers in response to demand changes. The U-form layout, as the name indicates, is one in which all the machines are arranged in a U format, with the entrance of units at about the same position as the exit. This layout generally incorporates the cellular manufacturing paradigm of group technology, characterized by close location of dissimilar machines or processes, dedicated to a set of similar parts or products. The U-form layout represents the ultimate in performance of the production process. This is because it allows for

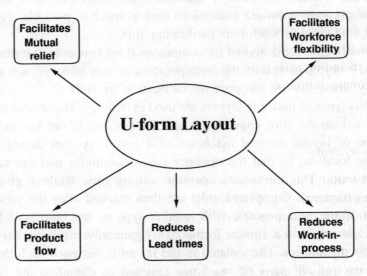

Fig. 9.2. Advantages of U-form machine layout.

smooth flow of the units, permits flexible and effective allocation of tasks to operators, and makes it possible for mutual assistance among operators. (Figure 9.2 illustrates major advantages of the U-form layout.) In order to enhance this flexibility and performance efficiency, it is common to have several of these lines combined to form an integrated system of processes. This aggregation of U-form lines is particularly useful, in view of the savings in workforce created from resolving the problem of "fractional workers." This problem arises from the difficulty in load balancing for workers on a single U-form line. The aggregation of several of these lines facilitates the removal and addition of workers to the line in response to demand changes.

4. Components of JIT

4.1. *JIT "pull" production*

The "pull" phenomenon of which JIT production is characterized, involves the manufacture of units by a preceding process, only in response to the needs of its corresponding subsequent process. In other words, the subsequent process pulls its requirements from the preceding processes in question. This generally applies to every level in the multi-echelon production system, including parts produced inhouse and those purchased from vendors. The ultimate source of the initiation of the pull is the consumers of the product.

Kanban system

One very useful and effective mechanism by which JIT pull production has been implemented is the Kanban system, which is a signaling system for controlling the movement of parts among processes. What this system does is essentially to facilitate the transmission of information among processes. In order words, it tells a preceding process to manufacture and replace the units of parts that have been used up by a subsequent process. Usually, a Kanban contains the following information:

- Item name
- Item identification number
- Container type and capacity
- Name of preceding and/or subsequent process

Due to the cascading format of manufacturing systems, the final assembly line serves as the initiator of the pull within the system, and this is passed down to the other processes at the various levels. The system of Kanbans ensures that they circulate between all pairs of processes, resulting in a scenario whereby all processes of the manufacturing system are somewhat chained together. Therefore, when there is a change in demand for the final products, the system makes for this to be uniformly implemented across the various levels.

There are a wide variety of types of Kanban, whose specific uses are well suited to particular manufacturing conditions. However, the *Production-ordering* kanban and the *Withdrawal (Move)* Kanban — the two main types of Kanban used — can be considered representative.

This pair of Kanbans are utilized in the following way. (See illustration in Fig. 9.3.) An operator takes the number of withdrawal kanbans in the post where they are stored, along with an equivalent number of empty containers or pallets to its immediate preceding process. He withdraws the desired units there, and detaches the production-ordering Kanbans attached to each of these containers, replacing each with a withdrawal Kanban. The detached production-ordering Kanban, which is then placed in its post in the preceding process, now becomes an order for this process to produce what has been withdrawn. The operator takes the withdrawn physical units to the subsequent process where the units are to be used. As the units are consumed in the subsequent process and the containers become empty, the attached withdrawal Kanbans are placed in its post. This remains here pending when they are again collected for withdrawing units from the preceding process. An increase (decrease) in demand in the subsequent process, for example, will mean more (less) withdrawals, which will automatically elicit more (less) production at the preceding process. Some very important rules guiding the use of Kanban are:

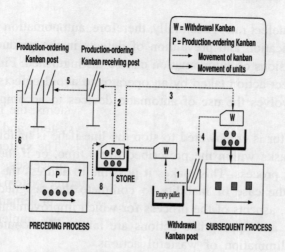

Fig. 9.3. An illustration of the Kanban system.

- Defective units must never be conveyed to the subsequent stage
- No withdrawal should be made without Kanbans
- The number of Kanbans must be minimized

Since every full container carries a Kanban, Managers can be assured that the build-up of inventory does not exceed specified limits. Usually, the total number of Kanbans circulating between any two processes is kept constant, except there is Management intervention to either drain the system of Kanbans or inject some more if necessary.

4.2. *Autonomation and total quality management*

Autonomation, a term used to refer to autonomous defects control, encompasses all aspects of the production process, and serves as an important element in the overall quality control drive of the firm. We recall that JIT production aims at single unit production and conveyance. Thus, if disruption in the flow of the units is to be avoided, the units moved from one process to another should be defect free. The concept of a permissible defect rate used in conventional quality control is not adopted here; rather, the system aims at a zero defect rate. Essentially, therefore, autonomation is a technique for the identification and prevention of defects in the production process.

Two dimensions of autonomation can be distinguished. First, that which involves a direct action taken by an operator to avoid defects; and second, that which involves the use of automatic devices to accomplish the same goal.

Each operator is empowered to stop the line if he is unable to complete his assigned tasks within the prescribed cycle time, or if there is a defect in a preceding process. This makes it possible to address the problem very promptly. In the case of inability to complete the assigned tasks within the cycle time, aspects of the process for which improvements are possible are identified, and appropriate actions are taken. This could for example involve the elimination of wasteful actions.

Two types of automatic devices used are Mechanical Checks and Foolproof Devices. The first one are devices set to prevent the operator from moving into the next workstation to complete his assigned tasks. The operator's motion which indicates this, automatically activates a trigger causing the line to stop. This helps to forestall the situation where the operator is unwilling to stop the line, even though he is unable to complete his assigned task within the prescribed cycle time. The second one is a Foolproof system consisting of a signaling device and a restricting device. It is set to eliminate defects arising from an oversight on the part of the operator; for example, it detects when a part has not been installed into the product. Also, various installed visual controls play a very significant role in the monitoring of the state of the system — one of these is the Andon described earlier. It is equipped with lights of different colours, which help to indicate whether there is machine trouble, there is need for setup, or line stop due to shortage of materials. The importance of avoiding the production of defective items in the attainment of the overall company objective cannot be over-emphasized. (Figure 9.4 indicates the chain effect of the manufacture of defective products.) The defect may or may not be identified in the factory. In case of the latter, apart from the image damage — which is not quantifiable, costs may result from reclaims, and in extreme cases, from litigation. It may be possible to effect corrections, in which case rework cost would

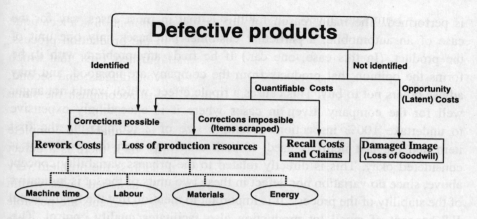

Fig. 9.4. The results of defective production.

be incurred. Otherwise, if the items are completely scrapped, complete loss of production resources (Machine time, Labour, Materials and Energy) would result.

Quality control — which serves as a support for the JIT ideology — relies very much on the autonomation concept discussed above. Although the term "Total Quality Control (TQC)" is well known, and is a part of conventional Western practice, in most cases, the responsibility for quality tends to be confined to quality control departments. True quality control that supports JIT involves the development of strategies and procedures to ascertain high quality in all processes. In other words, quality is seen as a company-wide responsibility, involving all persons concerned with production, and this also elicits a high level of consciousness about its need.

The control of processes to track variability, particularly as it relates to machine performance (sometimes referred to as process control) and eliminate them, is very fundamental to the quality assurance drive. Consistent with the JIT philosophy of delivering high quality products, this activity does not apply only to selected processes, but involves all processes. In a similar vein, unlike Western practice that utilizes random sampling from a lot for inspection, in a number of cases, 100% inspection of all parts is performed. The main reason for this is that in most cases, say for the case of an automobile, a particular customer purchases only one unit of the product. (In this case, one car.) If he finds any problem with it, he forms the opinion that products from the company are no good, and may advise others not to buy. This causes a ripple effect, which would not augur well for the company. Even in cases where it is exceedingly expensive to undertake 100% inspection, a sample size of 2 (comprising the first item and the last item) is used. If both are okay, then the whole lot is considered okay. This is directly related to the process variability concept above, since no variation nor defect in these two units of the lot is indicative of the stability of the process. It is important to mention that the fundamental JIT concept of small lot production also facilitates quality control. This is so because, under this scenario, problems are quickly identified and nipped in the bud, before they cause significant damages.

4.3. *Multifunction and flexible workforce*

The concept of a flexible workforce is closely linked with work standardization, appropriate machine layout, and job rotation, all of which provide a foundation for facilitating its implementation. It is quite common in Western industry to have tasks performed by specialists. For example, a lathe machinist does nothing else, but to work on the lathe, and welding is performed only by those who specialize in welding. In some cases, trade union policies within these firms make it extremely difficult to have a single person perform multiple types of tasks. While this idea of specialization has its benefits from the viewpoint of mastery of tasks, it is very unsuitable for a JIT environment.

There are various facets of the concept of flexible workforce. One of these is the mutual relief concept, where other workers in adjoining processes come to the aid of a particular worker who, due to problems being encountered, is unable to complete his assigned tasks. Sometimes, Management deliberately removes some workers from the processes or lines, as a way of identifying shortcomings in the system, and with a view to improving the processes. In other cases, change in demand for certain items may require the movement of workers to other dedicated lines where demand is needed. This is consistent with the JIT ideology of stopping production of any product type that is not immediately in need. Producing only as a way of keeping the workers busy is considered a waste.

4.4. *Focused supply chain*

Effective management of the supply chain for the parts that go into making the product plays a significant role in the overall profitability of the company. There are a number of elements that characterize the JIT supply strategy, and which help to maximize the effectiveness of the whole supply network. The key point about this is that the plants of the Parts Supplier (PS) are somewhat seen as extensions or workcenters of the Parent Manufacturer (PM). The main characteristics of JIT supply are as follows:

• Few suppliers
• Long-term relationship between Parent manufacturer and its parts' suppliers
• Just in time delivery of parts by suppliers to Parent manufacturer's plants.

The traditional supply policies of a number of manufacturers involve outsourcing from very many suppliers. For a very complex product as the automobile, the number of suppliers are sometimes as many as 2,000. In some cases, a particular part is outsourced from too many suppliers. Although this has the advantage of preventing stockouts in case one supplier has problems in its plants, outsourcing from too many suppliers raises concerns about product uniformity and quality, and also impacts on effective coordination.

JIT supply policy involves far less suppliers than traditional systems, and a given part is usually supplied by one or a few number of suppliers. This focused nature of the supply chain makes it possible for the PM to develop a long-term, cordial relationship with its suppliers. Too many suppliers of a given part has been known to hamper mutual trust between the parties. This is particularly so when suppliers' price bids become the overriding factor in their selection. This lack of trust between the PM and a supplier is exhibited in various ways. For example, the supplier may be wary of giving details about its production operations for fear of losing out, or the PM on the other hand might be always suspicious of the supplier. This spurs the PM to engage in a constant search for a better deal. Although JIT supply policy may seem to have the disadvantage that better price deals are lost, immense benefits are derived from quality, openness and mutual commitment to success. This would generally more than pay for the seeming losses on the long run. Therefore, adopting a policy of mutual cost-analysis, price determination, and profit sharing between the PM and part suppliers creates a relaxed atmosphere, which fosters benefit for both parties.

Just-In-Time delivery is not limited to items produced in the factory, but also extends to the suppliers, who are sometimes required to supply the units several times in a day. This requirement is sometimes erroneously seen as an unfair means by which the PM transfers the inventory burden to the supplier. On the contrary, it helps the supplier to improve its processes on a continuous basis leading to its ability to derive among others, the quality and cost reduction benefits of JIT. Furthermore, since the relationship between them is cordial and long lasting, the supplier is able to locate its factory very close to the plant, making it possible to respond quickly to demand.

5. Kaizen Activities — Engine for Advancing JIT

What is good for today is not good enough for tomorrow, is the principle behind the Kaizen philosophy, which spans all aspects of the activities of the firm. In other words, every member of the entire system is imbued with the understanding that there is always room for improvement. It is not uncommon in production, for example, to remove (reduce) safety stocks between adjoining processes, with a view to "straining" the system, expose its flaws, and consequently creating an opportunity for improvements. One aspect that provides vast opportunity for improvements in production is the unearthing of non-value-added activities, such as double transfers, unnecessary transportation distances, etc. The conception of the production system as a laboratory (Ref. 6, p. 65) provides interesting insights on the usefulness of Kaizen activities. Usually, engineers and production workers tend to seek the causes of problems in the system only when a problem that poses a great threat to continuance of production occurs. However, from the laboratory viewpoint, this is not sufficient. Rather, there is the need to introduce systematic ways for occasionally altering the environment and observing the results. This management strategy helps to continuously increase and refine knowledge both about the process and the product, even when there is no immediate problem. The following are useful elements for implementing Kaizen activities:

- Always trace all problems to their sources
  It is quite possible in a number of cases to find temporary solutions to problems as a way of saving time or relieving emotional stress arising from them. There is a likelihood that a problem may reoccur, resulting in greater damage. Therefore, a better approach is to trace the problem to its source. Use of Cause-effect (Fishbone or Ishikawa) diagrams prove quite useful.

- Adopt a systematic way for documenting problems and observing results.
  Whenever either a problem occurs during operation of the system, or the environment is altered to expose them, methods adopted to resolve them, as well as the problems themselves should be well documented. This is particularly necessary because there might be a reoccurrence of the problem after a considerable length of time in the future, and workers in a process change from time to time.

- Flow of information regarding the state of the system
  It is not sufficient to just gather information, say about quality or general problems about the system. There is the need to disseminate this information to all those concerned. Apart from the fact that this approach has a positive effect as a morale booster, knowledge derived thereby might be useful in tackling related problems in the future.

6. Wastes Elimination and Cost Reduction Framework of JIT

Results from studies of the operation of repetitive manufacturing firms that have implemented JIT, indicate that, successful implementation leads to wastes elimination and consequently, cost reduction.[5] The framework for this is based on the inter-relationships of the fundamental elements for its implementation described in the previous sections. Waste here is defined as any action or activity which does not improve the performance of the system, or those which do not add-value. Since elimination of these wastes provides a great deal of opportunities for the system's improvement, the importance of their continuous identification cannot be over-emphasized.

The major elements that constitute wastes in a manufacturing system are outlined as follows:

- Excessive production resources
- Inefficient material handling
- Excess inventory
- Superfluous product design
- Poor quality
- Excessive capital investment

Strictly speaking, the waste related cost elements for a product can be broadly classified into two, namely: opportunity (latent) cost, and quantifiable cost elements. Opportunity costs are those resulting from loss in market share due to shortcomings in the performance of the product. This is the loss to the firm when potential buyers go elsewhere to obtain the product, or change their minds entirely. This may be termed latent costs because they are somewhat difficult to quantify. On the other hand, quantifiable costs are those that can be directly measured. A discussion regarding the cost reduction framework of JIT encompasses these two aspects and they are as detailed in Fig. 9.5 below.

As was noted in a previous section, for certain types of products such as an automobile, a given consumer only purchases one unit. So, if that product is defective, from this consumer's viewpoint, the defective rate is not 1 in say 100,000 manufactured cars, but 100%. This creates a bad image, which, depending on the consumer in question, can result in a very great damage. A greater dimension to this is the case, where, due to some unidentified problems during manufacture — which were also not tracked during final testing — are delivered directly to the dealers. Consequently,

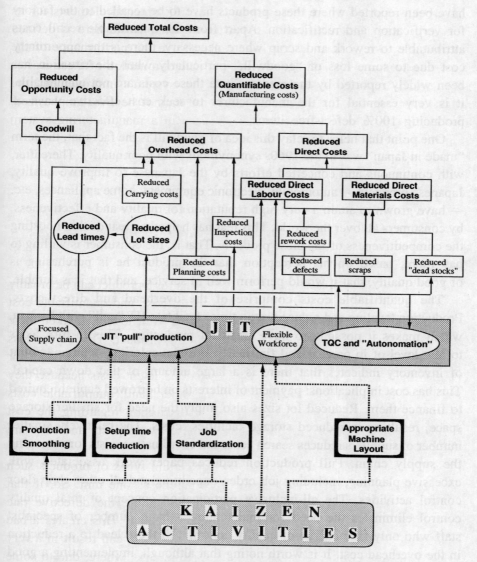

Fig. 9.5. A conceptual model of the cost reduction framework of JIT.

a bunch of defective products are passed on to the consumers. Cases have been reported where these products have to be recalled to the factory for verification and rectification. Apart from the quantifiable recall costs attributable to rework and scrap where necessary, there is the opportunity cost due to some loss of "goodwill," particularly when the situation has been widely reported by the media. Since these costs are not quantifiable, it is very essential for the manufacturer to seek cost effective ways of producing 100% defect-free items.

One point that helps to relay this idea of goodwill is the fact that, the term "made in Japan" was in the 1960s synonymous with poor quality. Thereafter, with continuous and concerted efforts by the Japanese to improve quality, Japanese products — automobile, electronic equipment, home appliances, etc. — have grown to attain a very high reputation for quality and effectiveness, by consumers all over the world. This feat has helped a great deal in boosting the competitiveness of Japanese products. That is, the consumer is willing to pay more, based on his perception that the product he is purchasing is of good quality, that it would perform well in service, and that it is durable.

The quantifiable costs comprise of the overhead and direct costs. Production leveling and reduced setup times facilitate JIT "pull" with kanban, which makes it possible to have small lot production. This in turn leads to low level of in-process and finished goods' inventories. A large amount of inventory indicates that there is a large amount of tied down capital. This has cost implications: payment of interests on borrowed capital required to finance them. Reduced lot sizes also imply the need for smaller storage space, resulting in reduced storage facilities' costs. The relatively smaller number of suppliers reduces search costs and coordination costs for managing the supply chain. Pull production reduces paper work associated with excessive planning, including job order, expediting and all other shop floor control activities. The all-inclusive participation concept of total quality control eliminates the need for maintaining a large number of specialist staff who only take charge of quality control. All these lead to a reduction in the overhead cost. It is worth noting that although, implementing a good quality control program involves some costs, these are in general, far less than costs arising from an improper quality control program.

Small lot production results in reduced lead times. First, this facilitates quality due to prompt feedback. This in turn leads to reduced defects and hence reduced rework costs, and reduced scrap, which both reduce unnecessary labour and material costs associated with production anomalies. (See also Fig. 9.4 above.) Second, reduced lead times result in reduced costs associated with "dead" stocks — "dead" stocks are items that can either not be sold or used, due to model changes or some new technological innovations. This issue is of particular importance in this age of rapid technological innovations and model changes.

TQC and Autonomation boost the image (goodwill) of the manufacturer and thus reduces the opportunity costs to the firm. Another aspect of the opportunity cost is loss of goodwill when the manufacturer cannot respond promptly to consumers' demand. Therefore, shortening the lead time, which JIT production ensures, improves goodwill and reduces the risk of loss in sales arising from records of unmet due dates.

Flexible workforce is facilitated by an appropriate machine layout, and this, coupled with the multifunction capabilities of the workers reduces direct labour costs. This is because it makes for effective utilization of available workforce in response to demand.

The application of Kaizen activities, supported by small group discussions, the suggestion system and quality control circles lead in general to the improvement of all processes. This in turn leads to reductions in overhead and direct costs. For example, one aspect of these improvements relate to processing methods. This would eliminate unnecessary motions, reduce processing time, and consequently reduce direct labour costs, as well as machining overhead costs.

7. Conclusion

The JIT paradigm when successfully implemented leads to many benefits to the firm, all summed up in the fact that it boosts its competitiveness. Indeed many firms, including its founder, Toyota Motor Corporation, have reported substantial improvements in their operations by its implementation.

Although some of the principles encompassed in JIT are not necessarily unique to the system, the key element in its power to produce significant cost reductions, with resultant high productivity lies in the issue of synergy of the various elements of which it is comprised. In other words, the whole operation is far greater than the mere sum of all the elements. It is important to note that successful implementation would require proper preparations by introducing the elements that constitute the foundation. Some companies that have attempted to adopt JIT, abandoned it midway due to the lack of adequate preparation.

JIT, supported by Kaizen activities is a powerful, constantly evolving philosophy, that places a very high premium on the workforce. By virtue of this and its flexibility, it will continue to play a significant role in making the implementing firm competitive into the 21st century and beyond.

References

1. Feather, J. & Cross, K., Workflow Analysis, Just-In-Time Techniques Simplify Administrative Process in Paperwork Operation, IIE Solutions, Vol. 88, 1997, 32–40.
2. Funk, J., A Comparison of Inventory Cost Reduction Strategies in a JIT Manufacturing System, Int. J. Production Research, Vol. 27, 1989, 1065–1080.
3. Gilbert, J., The State of JIT Implementation and Development in the USA, Int. J. Production Research, Vol. 28, 1990, 1099–1109.
4. Miltenburg, J., A Theoretical Framework for Understanding How JIT Reduces Cost and Cycle Time and Improves Quality, Int. J. Production Economics, Vol. 30–31, 1993, 195–204.
5. Monden, Y., Toyota Production System: An Integrated Approach to Just-In-Time (Engineering and Management Press, Georgia, 1998), Third Edition.
6. Hall, R., Zero Inventories (Dow Jones Erwin, 1983).
7. Schonberger, R., Japanese Manufacturing Techniques: Nine Hidden Lessons in Simplicity (The Free Press, 1982).
8. Harrison, A., Just-In-Time Manufacturing in Perspective (Prentice Hall, 1992).
9. Whitson, D., Applying Just-In-Time Systems in Health Care, IIE Solutions, Vol. 88, 1997, 33–37.
10. Womack, J., Jones, D. & Roos, D., The Machine that Changed the World: The Story of Lean Production (Harper Perrenial, 1990).

Chapter 10

Kaizen Costing: Its Function and Structure Compared to Standard Costing*

YASUHIRO MONDEN and JOHN Y. LEE

The usefulness of standard cost systems, which have been used as the primary cost control vehicle by U.S. firms for the last several decades, recently has been questioned by many practitioners and academicians.

Activity-based cost management has gained a prominent status in cost management by clearly depicting the demands a firm's various activities, production as well as other corporate functions, place on the firm's resources. On another front, target costing has emerged as the system that is effective in managing costs in the new product design and development stage.[a]

---

*This chapter is a slightly revised version of the paper first published in *Management Accounting* (Institute of Management Accountants), August 1993, entitled as: "How a Japanese Auto Maker Reduces Costs: Kaizen costing drives continuous improvement at Daihatsu". pp. 22–26. Reprinted with kind permission of the journal.
[a]Please refer to Y. Monden and K Hamada, "Target Costing and Kaizen Costing in Japanese Automobile Companies," *J. Management Accounting Research*, Fall 1991, pp. 16–34, for an overall perspective of the total cost management approach used by Japanese automakers. (This paper is reprinted as Chap. 5 of this book.)

229

Kaizen costing, a critical means of ensuring continuous improvement activities used by Japanese automakers, supports the cost reduction process in the manufacturing phase. Employed together with target costing, Kaizen costing helps Japanese manufacturers achieve their goal of cost reduction in the entire product design development production cycle.

To illustrate this process, we look at the Kaizen costing practice used by Daihatsu Motor Company of Osaka, Japan. Daihatsu, a mini-car manufacturer owned in part by Toyota, ranks seventh of the nine Japanese automakers in terms of their domestic sales volume. In Japan, Daihatsu's mini-car sales out number Isuzu, Mazda, and Subaru. It has established mini-car markets in more than 120 counties. In the United States, Daihatsu began marketing Charade, its only U.S. passenger car, and Rocky, a sports truck, in 1988 from its subsidiary, Daihatsu America Inc. of Los Alamitos, California. In early 1992, Daihatsu announced its plan to withdraw from the U.S. market due to its strategy change. As a partner of Daihatsu, Toyota uses a similar system of Kaizen costing discussed here.

1. The Aim of Kaizen Costing is Different

Kaizen costing, functions in a similar fashion as a budgetary control system, operates outside the standard cost system. It aims at reducing the actual costs below the standard costs — in distinct contrast to the focus of a standard cost system, which emphasizes meeting the cost standards. Daihatsu's Kaizen costing calls for the establishment of a cost reduction target amount, and its accomplishment through Kaizen activities — continuous improvement in operations.

Daihatsu defines Kaizen costing activities as those activities that "sustain the current level of the existing car production costs, and further reduce it to the expected level based on the company plan." These cost-improvement activities are very specific with respect to each department and each accounting period.

The periodic cost-improvement process is preceded by the annual budgeting process, or short-term profit planning process, which represents the first-year segment of Daihatsu's five-year long-range plan. In the short-term profit planning process, each department prepares the following:

Plan 1. Production, Distribution, and Sales Plan (which includes projections of contribution margins from sales).

Plan 2. Projected Parts and Materials Costs.

Plan 3. Plant Rationalization Plan (projected reductions in manufacturing variable costs).

Plan 4. Personnel Plan (for direct labor work force and service department personnel).

Plan 5. Facility Investment Plan (capital budget and depreciation).

Plan 6. Fixed Expense Plan (for prototype design costs, maintenance costs, advertising and sales promotion expenses, and general and administrative expenses).

These six projections and plans, when their costs and profits are incorporated together in the current period planning process, become the annual profit budget.

The production, distribution, and sales plan is the nucleus of the current period planning process. The plan establishes the planned profit contributions using a variable costing approach, based on the actual cost performance for the previous year, and the estimated volumes and prices of car models in the coming year.

In a formula,

$$\begin{matrix} \text{Total planned} \\ \text{profit contribution} \end{matrix} = \begin{matrix} \text{the sum of} \\ \text{contribution margin per} \\ \text{unit of each car} \\ \text{model } i \text{ of the} \\ \text{previous year} \end{matrix} \times \begin{matrix} \text{estimated sales} \\ \text{volume of the car} \\ \text{model } i \end{matrix}$$

The actual cost performance of the previous year is used as cost standards for the coming year.

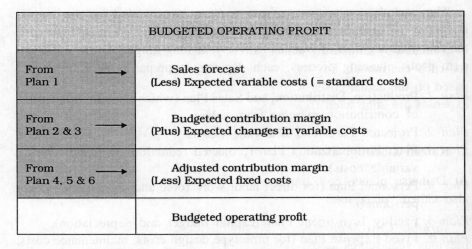

Fig. 10.1. From sales forecast to budgeted operating profit.

Projected parts and materials costs provide the targets to attain for the purchasing department. The plant rationalization plan, which represents projections for reductions in manufacturing variable costs, is the core component of Kaizen costing practice in a plant. It provides variable manufacturing cost reduction targets. The personnel plan provides cost reduction targets for direct and indirect labor.

The sales forecast for the year turns into budgeted operating profit through the following process, as illustrated in Fig. 10.1. Expected variable costs, which represent standard costs, are subtracted from budgeted sales to yield budgeted contribution margin in Plan 1. Plans 2 and 3 provide expected changes in variable costs, which are used to adjust the contribution margin. Expected fixed costs from Plans 4–6 are deducted from the adjusted contribution margin to produce budgeted operating profit. Labor costs are treated as fixed costs because labor transfers within the company do not change the total labor cost used in the profit plan for the company as a whole. At Daihatsu, the cost improvement plans (Plans 3 and 4) are integrated with the profit plan. Plans 2, 5 and 6 also influence costs.

The annual budgeted profit for the company is broken down to budgeted profits of the sales departments. The performance of each sales department is evaluated by comparing actual profits to budgeted profits, which is done for each car model. For this purpose, standard costs of sales (computed based on the actual costs of the previous year) and general administrative expenses are subtracted from actual sales revenues to yield actual profits.

2. Kaizen Costing: Plant Cost Improvement System

At Daihatsu plants, cost improvement through Kaizen costing, which is also called "plant total expense management," is practised as follows:

Variable Cost Improvement. The actual production cost per car of the previous year serves as the cost base of the current year. Cost reductions will be determined from this base figure. The ratio of the target reduction amount to the cost base is called the target reduction rate. Figure 10.2

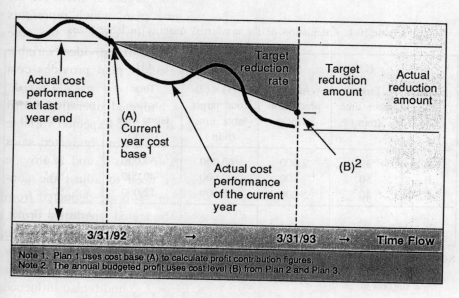

Fig. 10.2. The cost base and the target reduction amount.

illustrates the relationships among them. The horizontal axis represents monthly measurements. The vertical axis denotes amounts.

Total cost base of the current month is calculated as follows:

$$\begin{matrix} \text{Total cost base} \\ \text{of the current} \\ \text{month} \end{matrix} = \begin{matrix} \text{Current cost} \\ \text{base per car} \end{matrix} \times \begin{matrix} \text{Actual production} \\ \text{quantity of the month} \end{matrix}$$

The production quantity of the month, which is used in the above formula, represents the "converted quantity" for a typical car model. The converted quantity, which is measured based on labor hours, is used to determine what grade of performance has been achieved as explained below.

Let us assume we want to measure department performance using the production quantity converted in a car model A. As presented in Table 10.1, target labor times of all the models — A, B, and C — are multiplied by

Table 10.1. Calculation of the converted quantity in labor hours.

Models	(1) Target labor time (min.)	(2) Actual production quantity	(3) = (1) × (2) Total target labor time (min.)	(4) Total actual labor time (min.)	(5) = (4)/(2) Actual performance per car (min./car)
A	30	2,000	60,000	57,000	28.5
B	50	800	40,000	40,000	50.5
C	40	200	8,000	12,000	60.5
		3,000	108,000	109,000	Achieved Grade 99.1%

NOTE: "Converted quantity" for car model
= Total target labor time/target labor time per car of model A
= 108,000/30
= 3,600

the respective production quantities to yield total target time, which is calculated as 108,000 minutes. Total target time (108,000 minutes) divided by the cost base per car of model A (30 minutes) produces the converted quantity of 3,600 units. [108,000/30 = 3,600] The actual performance per a converted model A, 30.3 minutes, is computed by dividing total actual time (109,000 minutes) by the converted quantity of 3,600 units. [109,000/3,600 = 30.3] The achieved grade of 99.1% is calculated by dividing the target labor time for model A (30 minutes) by the actual performance per converted model (30.3 minutes). [30/30.3 = 99.1%]

In order to evaluate the performance of each department, actual cost reduction, called actually rationalized amount, is first computed. This amount is compared to the target reduction amount, and the variance is calculated as follows:

$$\text{Actually rationalized amount (A)} = \text{total cost base of the current month} - \text{total actual cost of the current month}$$

$$\text{Variance} = \text{actually rationalized amount (A)} - \text{target cost reduction amount}$$

The variance calculated here is the real performance indicator for a specific department. It indicates whether an actual cost reduction that has been achieved is satisfactory compared to the target. Even a positive actually rationalized amount (A) is evaluated as "unfavorable" if the variance from the target is negative (Table 10.2).

In Table 10.2, Plant A, as a whole, has exceeded the Kaizen target by +5 although the actually rationalized amount of indirect labor cost was −5. Plant B, with an unfavorable variance of 3, has not attained the Kaizen cost target.

Fixed Cost Improvement. The target cost reduction amount is not prepared for fixed costs in the same manner as it is done for variable costs, with the exception of energy cost. For fixed costs, the total budgeted amount of each cost element is considered a target. If the actual performance is better than the budgeted, the rationalization objective is regarded as achieved.

Table 10.2. Kaizen costing performance evaluation.

	Current month			Cumulative		
	Target	Actual	Variance	Target	Actual	Variance
Plant A costs						
Direct labor	40	35	(5)	160	165	5
Indirect labor	0	(5)	(5)	0	(35)	(35)
Material	15	25	10	60	75	15
Energy	10	15	5	40	50	10
Transportation	5	5	0	20	35	15
Total	70	75	5	280	290	10
Plant B costs						
Direct labor	20	25	5	80	75	(5)
Indirect labor	0	5	5	0	10	10
Material	10	5	(5)	40	25	(15)
Energy	5	0	(5)	20	15	(5)
Transportation	5	2	(3)	20	15	(5)
Total	40	37	(3)	160	140	(20)

Note: Target: Target cost reduction amount
Actual: Actually realized amount
( ): Loss or unattained amount

3. Determination of Cost Reduction Targets

Daihatsu establishes the target cost reduction rate for each cost element,
relating to the cost base per car, at each year-end for the following year
as shown in Table 10.3. The company-wide target reduction amount is
computed as follows:

Company-wide target reduction amount

$$= \text{Sum of} \begin{pmatrix} \text{Cost base per} & \text{Converted production} & \text{Target reduction} \\ \text{car for each} \times & \text{quantity of the} \times & \text{rate for each} \\ \text{cost element j} & \text{current year} & \text{cost element j} \end{pmatrix}$$

Table 10.3. Target reduction rate for each cost element.

Cost elements	Evaluation measures	Annual target Reduction ratio
Direct materials costs		
Raw material (casting material sheet metals, etc.)	Monetary amount per unit of car	2%
Purchased parts	Monetary amount per unit of car	4%
Other direct materials (paints, thinner, etc.)	Monetary amount per unit of car	8%
Conversion costs		
Variable:		
Variable indirect materials (supplies, etc.)	Monetary amount per unit of car	8%
Parts transportation	Total monetary amount	10%
Variable overhead (utilities)	Monetary amount per unit of car	4%
Direct labor	Labor hours per unit of car	6%
Fixed:		
Indirect labor	Number of workers and overtime	Note 1
Other fixed costs:		
Office utilities	Total monetary amount	4%
Service department	Total monetary amount	Note 1
Depreciation	Total monetary amount	Note 1

Note 1: The target reduction rate is not established for these cost elements. The difference between the budgeted and actual total amounts is used to evaluate the rationalization (cost reduction) efforts. The target reduction rate shown here are examples only.)

Variations in prices and wage rates are not reflected in performance evaluation. Reductions in labor hours, resource usage, and expense figures are scrutinized. The target reduction rate for each cost element is almost fixed each year. Only small changes are made, with the exception of transportation and energy costs, which undergo changes on a larger scale. The assigned target reduction rate in each plant may be higher or lower than the company wide rate.

The company-wide cost reduction target amount is allocated to each plant based on the proportion of the following cost (C) of each plant to the combined total cost of all plants:

$$(C) = \begin{matrix} \text{Total cost base of a} \\ \text{plant per car at the end} \\ \text{of the previous year} \end{matrix} \times \begin{matrix} \text{Actual converted} \\ \text{production quantity of the} \\ \text{plant in the previous year} \end{matrix}$$

While the calculation formula is established, the allocation process is not rigidly set. The director in charge of all plants incorporates other factors which are unique for each plant, into consideration also before allocations are finalized.

The decision to decompose the cost reduction target into various cost elements and departments is delegated to each plant. Within each plant the objective decomposition process proceeds downward through the hierarchical organization line:

$$\begin{matrix} \text{Plant top management} \rightarrow \text{Department} \rightarrow \\ \text{Section} \rightarrow \text{Subsection} \rightarrow \text{Process} \end{matrix}$$

During the decomposition process, multiple meetings are held at each hierarchical level within the plant. In such meetings the target reduction rate will be determined on the basis of how successful each unit was in the previous year in achieving the assigned Kaizen cost target. The decomposition process helps section managers to become more cost conscious.

4. Changes in Target Rates

The target reduction rate in Kaizen costing sometimes represents the integration of (a) the target reduction rate of the cost improvement system that functions within the annual profit planning process and (b) the target reduction rate of a cost improvement project or a cost improvement committee, which is initiated on an *ad hoc* basis.

The *ad hoc* cost improvement project or committee is established (1) when the company faces serious external challenges, such as an oil crisis, yen currency's sudden appreciation, etc.; and/or (2) when the company faces a specific need to reduce the costs of certain car models.

Accordingly, the integrated target reduction rate of a cost element represents the combination of the rate (a) and the rate (b). The total Kaizen cost target, therefore, should reflect the integrated target reduction rates of all cost elements.

The target reduction rates shown in Table 10.3 are yearly rates. For actual implementation of Kaizen activities, however, the yearly rates must be translated into monthly rates. This is usually done by dividing the yearly target reduction rates by 12 months. Based on the monthly rates, the monthly Kaizen costs, target direct labor hours, and so on, are established.

Although target reduction rates are applied in a linear fashion, the rates are often revised in mid-year for the following reasons:

4.1. *A design change in the middle of the year*

A design change may be caused by:

- Specification change from the viewpoint of the quality reliability countermeasures against customer claims;
- value analysis (value engineering) based on continuous improvement (Kaizen) activities; and
- certain demands of customers for additional options of a car.

Among all the factors that cause a mid-year design change, the first factor would certainly increase costs. This would lead to an upward revision of the cost base of direct labor hours and the target Kaizen cost. The revisions would support a fair evaluation of cost improvement activities of a plant. Such revisions are made on a monthly basis.

Currently value engineering is performed most thoroughly in the development and design phase, and target costing is applied to this phase. The role of value engineering is rather limited in the Kaizen costing process that is employed in the manufacturing phase. The coordination of target costing and Kaizen costing is done to ensure a proper implementation of the total cost management goal for the company. This is necessary because, when safety as a quality is emphasized in the development phase, the sheet metal, for example, could be made very thick. This could satisfy the safety criterion at the expense of other improvement activities when work-pieces flow in the line.

4.2. *The alteration of mixed model production*

The second reason for the change in target reduction rate is the alteration of the models in an assembly line in any month. When models change, the average assembly labor hours will change. This leads to the subsequent change in the converted quantity of a representative model. The monthly cost base G (standard) will be

$$G = \frac{\text{Cost base of all cost elements}}{\text{per a representative car}} \times \frac{\text{Monthly converted}}{\text{quantity}}$$

Therefore, when the car models that flow in a line change in the middle of the year, the monthly reduction target for direct labor hours should be revised accordingly.

5. Kaizen Costing: Strengths and Weaknesses

When related to the stages of product development, design, and manufacturing, Kaizen costing follows target costing when time flow is considered, as illustrated in Fig. 10.3. A substantial part of many Japanese auto makers' successful cost control is realized in the product development and design stage employing target costing.

Kaizen costing as compared to standard costing aims at reducing costs in a very aggressive manner. See Table 10.4. As a result, it may be overly stressful and taxing to the employees and managers. In order not to overwhelm

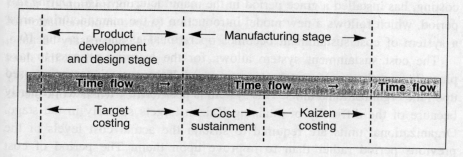

Fig. 10.3. Time flow and Kaizen costing.

Table 10.4. Standard versus Kaizen costing.

Standard costing concepts	Kaizen costing concepts
Cost control system concept	Cost reduction system concept
Assume current manufacturing conditions	Assume continuous improvement in manufacturing
Meet cost performance standards	Achieve cost reduction targets

Standard costing techniques	Kaizen costing techniques
Standards are set annually or semiannually	Cost reduction targets are set and applied monthly
	Continuous improvement (Kaizen) is implemented during the year to attain target profit or to reduce the gap between target profit and estimated profit.
Cost variance analysis involving standard costs and actual costs	Cost variance analysis involving target Kaizen costs and actual costs reduction amounts
Investigate and respond when when standards are not met	Investigate and respond when target Kaizen amounts are not attained

them, Daihatsu, as well as those other Japanese automakers who use Kaizen costing, has installed a grace period in the manufacturing stage. During this period, which follows a new model introduction to the manufacturing area, a system of cost sustainment becomes operational as shown in Fig. 10.3.

The cost sustainment system allows for the learning process to take place before the goals of target costing and Kaizen costing are imposed upon the organizational units. This system is positioned where it is primarily because of the difficulty of attaining Kaizen targets so early in the stage. Organizational units are required to sustain the actual cost levels of the previous period rather than to improve upon them. The period of cost sustainment lasts about three months from the date of a new model introduction.

As we discussed earlier, Kaizen costing is implemented outside the standard cost accounting system and is not limited by the financial accounting focus of the standard costing system in Japanese automakers. The strength of Kaizen costing comes from its close link with the profit planning process of the whole company. This consistent connection with the overall planning and budgeting process ensures that the company can monitor its progress toward the long-term goals without being confined to the tasks of meeting cost standards and investigating variances in conventional cost control systems.

Chapter 11

Cost Management System Integrated into TPM

SHUFUKU HIRAOKA

TPM (Total Productive Maintenance) is one of the management techniques to have been typically used in Japanese companies. However, some relations between TPM and cost systems have not yet been clarified. We consulted some leading studies about them,[14,15] which will be developed in this chapter. First, we emphasize that TPM improves the business constitution of a company as a whole, and explain the aspects of cost management needed to implement TPM. Also, when preparing the introduction of TPM, the role of cost management is described. Next, we illustrate the cost management related to autonomous maintenance and individual improvement in the production department. Moreover, the costs about maintenance department activities and evaluating the efficiency of maintenance activities are made clear. Lastly, we describe some problems with costs of quality maintenance, safety, sanitation and environments ("the respect of human nature" is the most important).

1. TPM and Cost Management

The origin and definition of TPM, and the contents of cost management which is necessary for implementing it, are made clear. We describe the importance of gathering costs according to types of PM (productive maintenance) and the cost concepts dealt with TPM.

243

1.1. *The origin and definition of TPM*

PM was proposed by GE (General Electric) Inc. in the United States. In Japan, it was introduced into Toa-nenryo Industry Inc. for the first time. It has spread to the main Japanese companies since then, however, it seemed to have started in the maintenance department in the United States. While machines were repaired, wastes in waiting time had occurred. Also, operators had only scarce knowledge about maintenance. Because of operating by mistake, machines stopped and damage losses occurred. Perishing losses occurred with them, too. To solve these problems, in Japanese companies, "autonomous maintenance" has been thoroughly educated in small-group activities, and people think that all employees should relate to plant maintenance, and they have thus established the consciousness and the improvement activities for it. As a result, PM has been performed as company-wide activities (i.e. TPM) which improves one production system synthetically rather than one machine (Fig. 11.1).

According to Japan Institute of Plant Maintenance, TPM is defined as follows.

1. Making the business constitution to pursue the synthetic improvement of one production system boundlessly.
2. With actual articles in each field for the whole life cycle of the production system, building the mechanism is to prevent all losses such as disaster, defect and failure, and to make those losses zero.
3. Including not only the production department but also development, sales, management front line employees, and so on.
4. From top management to front-line employees, making all members participate.
5. With overlapping small-group activities, achieving to make losses zero.

1.2. *Cost management in TPM*

Ultimately, the synthetic improvement of a production system is to produce the maximum output with the minimum input and to improve value-added productivity in a company as a whole. Cost management becomes one means

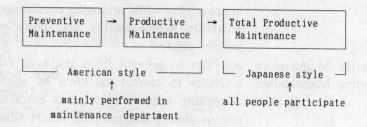

Fig. 11.1. From PM to TPM.

Source: Japan Institute of Plant Maintenance., Our TPM (Japan Institute of Efficiency, Tokyo, 1991), 9.

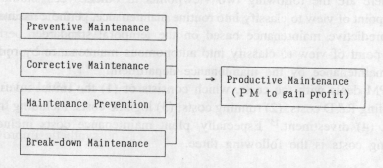

Fig. 11.2. The four elements of productive maintenance.

Source: Japan Institute of Plant Maintenance., Our TPM (Japan Institute of Efficiency, Tokyo, 1991), 10.

to the purpose. In this case, two viewpoints are necessary. One is the viewpoint of cost control to assume that each machine is a cost center. The other is the viewpoint of cost management which aims to minimize the life cycle cost which concerns the production system in a company as a whole while considering some structural changes. PM is classified as follows according to some purposes of maintenance (Fig. 11.2). While corresponding to them, cost data must be classified, totaled, reported and managed.

Maintenance Prevention: achieving the design of production system which can prevent all losses which obstruct the synthetic improvement while arranging conditions such as reliability, maintainability, operability, resource-saving, safety.

Preventive Maintenance: activities to prevent from stop-type failure.

Corrective Maintenance: activities to correct machines by aggressively consulting improvement plans extracted from routine checks and grasping failure situation by operators.

Breakdown Maintenance: activities to repair after machines stop by breaking down and their efficiencies decline.

There are the following two viewpoints in others.

A point of view to classify into routine maintenance, periodic maintenance and predictive maintenance based on the temporal standard.

A point of view to classify into autonomous maintenance by operators and maintenance by the maintenance department.

TPM deals with the costs, which consists of (1) the initial investment, including R&D costs; (2) running costs; (3) logistic costs, including training costs; (4) divestment.[15] Especially, plant maintenance costs included in running costs is the following three.

(a) Maintenance expense: this expense is maintenance material, maintenance labor, maintenance expense disbursed to other companies. These are measured as outlay costs.

(b) Downtime losses from equipment stoppages: these are calculated as opportunity costs by multiplying either of the following values by the total of scheduled downtime and sudden failure downtime.

Fixed costs spent to operate a process for 1 hour.
Contribution margin which the line invents per hour.

(c) Other losses: these are defect, rework and disaster losses directly caused by machines. Maintenance expense is managed by the budget and is decided on by the following procedure.[15]

1. Top management decides a maintenance budget policy in the next term.

2. According to a profit plan, each cost center decides a gross limit of maintenance costs in the next term.
3. Considering some experiences and budget policies in the past, maintenance works are made clear. Each department estimates the costs spent on them.
4. Maintenance department makes the total departmental budget requirement harmonize with the gross limits recommended by each cost center.
5. A formal maintenance budget is decided in the director's meeting.

When performing the above procedure, the following four must be judged about each maintenance cost.

Is it a capital expenditure or a revenue expenditure?
Is it a long-range cost or a short-range cost?
Is it a variable cost or a fixed cost?
Should entrust maintenance to outside companies or should perform it personally?

Two types of costs related to the 4th judgement described above are as follows.

A: costs paid when a maintenance was entrusted to outside companies
B: costs spent when maintenance was personally performed

If A is higher than B, the maintenance should be personally performed. A and B are computed as follows.

A = outlay repair costs + additional ordering inspection costs + downtime losses from equipment stoppages when entrusting outside companies with the maintenance

B = variable maintenance costs + downtime losses from equipment stoppages when performing the maintenance personally

As computed above, fixed maintenance costs are not related costs (that is, sunk costs), which are originally excluded.

1.3. *Cost management in preparing the introduction of TPM*

Cost management is related to setting basic policies and goals of TPM. Especially, Japanese cost management systems such as Target costing and Kaizen costing include a profit plan and budgeting to achieve the goal profit. Also, they are connected with management by objectives.

Therefore, they are indispensable when TPM and management plans are coordinated. Besides, attention must be paid for costs in preparing the introduction of TPM including Kickoff rally (refer to Chap. 14).

2. Measuring Maintenance Activities to Manage in the Production Department

At first, we explain the contents of autonomous maintenance activities. They are routine maintenance works of people who operate facilities directly. Then, we describe some points of the effect measurement needed to manage them. Next, the way of managing costs for individual improvement is illustrated. Then, we utilize the synthetic index called *overall equipment efficiency*. There are some losses which obstruct from making it 100 percent. We can define some improvement points by a cost variance analysis that computes those losses in terms of the amount of costs. Also, the relationship between the individual improvement and Kaizen costing is described. Moreover, I explain the point to measure the maintenance department's activities and to manage them. I introduce some indexes used to evaluate maintenance activities as described above as a whole.

2.1. *Measuring autonomous maintenance activities to manage*

Autonomous maintenance is performed as follows by seven steps.[11]

1. Housekeeping (with everybody participating in keeping the Works clean).
2. Identifying problem causes and hard-to-clean places and taking the necessary countermeasures.
3. Drawing up standards for cleaning and oiling.
4. Reviewing the total system.

5. Setting standards for voluntary checking procedure.
6. Making sure everything is in order and in place.
7. Policy deployment.

At first, factory workers perform the 5-S movement (refer to Chap. 14), arrange some basic conditions to cut off the causes that raise losses and conform to some useful conditions defined. When these are insufficiently done, machines cannot draw out some functions equipped with them originally. Rather, artificial machine deterioration occurs, and it shortens their lifetimes remarkably. Before those troubles actually occur, some potential defects (of garbage, dirt, raw material adhesion, abrasion, looseness, leakage, corrosion, transformation, flaw, temperature, vibration, sound and so on) often occur. It is desirable to remove those cost drivers before they cause failures. When operators discover some malfunctions, they restore them if possible. When they cannot do, the maintenance engineers do so. It is important to measure costs spent on autonomous maintenance activities. Operators must perform improvement activities which bring out the effect of maintenance with shorter time and fewer resources for controlling autonomous maintenance costs. Also, they standardize the field control items steadily, perform visual control, and attempt to make maintenance management a perfect system. In spreading company-wide goals, their circle goals are decided finally. Then, they select some improvement themes and make the basis which continues autonomous management to improve production.

2.2. Cost management for individual improvement

In TPM, individual improvement is to exclude all losses thoroughly by improvement activities in production fields to bring out the maximum efficiency each machine has. Those losses obstruct from pursuing the equipment efficiency to the utmost. Before starting cost management to eradicate the losses, the following two points must be made clear.

What are losses obstructing equipment efficiency at present?
Therefore, how much waste has occurred?

Overall equipment efficiency expresses the equipment operating ratio contributed to the manufacture of non-defective parts (or products).

If

> R1 ... time utilization ratio
> R2 ... net operating ratio
> R3 ... speed operating ratio
> R4 ... non-defective parts (or products) ratio
> R5 ... capacity utilization ratio
> R6 ... contact time ratio

Then

$$\text{overall equipment efficiency} = R1*R2*R3*R4$$
$$= R1*R5*R4$$
$$= R6*R3*R4$$

However, on condition that:

> H1 ... loading time
> H2 ... actual operating time
> H3 ... contact time
> H4 ... net operating time
> H5 ... total standard operating time
> H6 ... net standard operating time

Then

$$R1 = H2/H1$$
$$R2 = H3/H2$$
$$R3 = H4/H3$$
$$R4 = H6/H4$$
$$R5 = H5/H2$$
$$R6 = H3/H1$$

H1–H6 are defined as follows.

H1: This is a plan operating time, too. It is the monthly normal capacity when computing pre-determined (standard) application rate.

H2: This is the time that the facilities operated actually. It is the monthly actual capacity in computing actual cost by pre-determined application.

H3: This is the value which is the actual cycle time multiplied by the quantity of material invested (or processed). Actual cycle time is the time taken actually to manufacture per part with an equipment.

H4: This is the value which is the ideal cycle time multiplied by the quantity of material invested (or processed). Ideal cycle time is the time that should be taken to manufacture per part with an equipment.

H5: This is the value which deducted the loss time spent on abnormal defective work from H4.

H6: This is the time that should be taken to produce non-defective parts (products). It becomes the basis which computes appreciated standard conversion costs to products.

In this case,

R1 is the index consisting of (1) breakdown losses, (2) set-up & adjustment losses, and (3) start-up & yield losses.

R2 is the index of (4) idling & minor stoppage losses.

R3 is the index of (5) speed losses.

R4 is the index of (6) defect & rework losses.

R5 is the index of (7) capacity utilization losses.

R6 is the index of (8) contact time losses.

Those losses can be shown with the amount of cost variance as the occurrence cause of operation variance and efficiency variance in standard conversion cost variance analysis. For example, operation variance consists of (1)–(3).

If

T1 ... breakdown overtime
T2 ... set-up & adjustment overtime
T3 ... start-up & yield overtime
α ... fixed conversion cost ratio

Then, each of the losses is shown with the amount of cost variance by the following formulas.

(1) Breakdown losses variance = $\alpha*T1$
(2) Set-up & adjustment losses variance = $\alpha*T2$
(3) Start-up & yield losses variance = $\alpha*T3$

Because a condition is $H1-H2 = (T1 + T2 + T3)$
operation variance = $\alpha*(T1 + T2 + T3)$

Also, the efficiency variance consists of (4)–(6). If

β ... standard application rate

Then, each of the losses is shown with the amount of cost variance by the following formulas.

(4) Idling & minor stoppage losses variance = $\beta*(H2-H3)$
(5) Speed losses variance = $\beta*(H3-H4)$
(6) Defect & rework losses variance = $\beta*(H4-H6)$

Defect & rework losses variance can be divided into abnormal defective work losses variance $(= \beta*[H4-H5])$ and normal defective work losses variance $(= \beta*[H5-H6])$, too.

Also, (7) capacity utilization losses variance is the total of (4) and (5). (8) Contact time losses variance is the total of operation variance and (4). If we establish the system which can always provide cost data about those losses variances continuously, it can support TPM powerfully from the viewpoint of cost control.

As mentioned above, Ratio–Losses–Cost variance relationship is shown Fig. 11.3.

An example of overall equipment efficiency and standard conversion cost variance analysis

①–④, ⑥–⑧, ⑩, ⑪, ⑭, ⑮, ⑰, ⑳, ㉑ are given as the conditions.

① Monthly operating time = 15,000 min.
② Scheduled downtime = 500 min.
③ Admissible set-up & adjustment time = 350 min.
④ Admissible start-up time = 100 min.

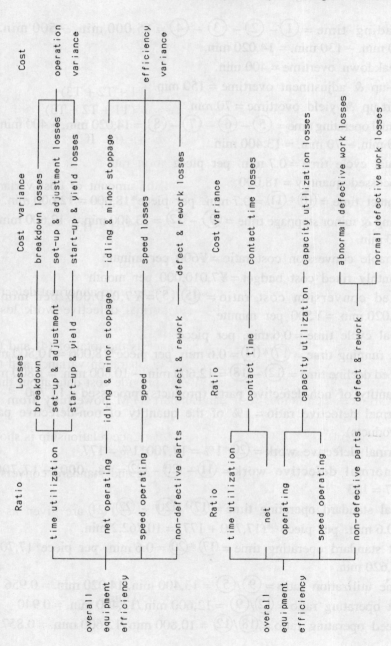

Fig. 11.3. Ratio-Losses-Cost variance relationship.

⑤ Loading time = ① − ② − ③ − ④ = 15,000 min. − 500 min. − 350 min. − 130 min. = 14,020 min.

⑥ Breakdown overtime = 400 min.

⑦ Set-up & adjustment overtime = 150 min.

⑧ Start-up & yield overtime = 70 min.

⑨ Actual operating time = ⑤ − ⑥ − ⑦ − ⑧ = 14,020 min. − 400 min. − 150 min. − 70 min. = 13,400 min.

⑩ actual cycle time = 0.7 min. per piece

⑪ processed quantity = 18,000

⑫ contact time = ⑩ * ⑪ = 0.7 min. per piece*18,000 = 12,600 min.

⑬ idling & minor stoppage time = ⑨ − ⑫ = 13,400 min. − 12,600 min. = 800 min.

⑭ variable conversion cost ratio = ¥600 per minute

⑮ monthly fixed cost budget = ¥7,010,000 per month

⑯ fixed conversion cost ratio = ⑮/⑤ = ¥7,010,000 per month/ 14,020 min. = ¥500 per minute

⑰ ideal cycle time = 0.6 min. per piece

⑱ net running time = ⑰ * ⑪ = 0.6 min. per piece*18,000 = 10,800 min.

⑲ speed decline time = ⑫ − ⑱ = 12,600 min. − 10,800 min. = 1,800 min.

⑳ quantity of non-defective parts (products) processed = 17,700

㉑ normal defective ratio = 1% of the quantity of non-defective parts (products)

㉒ normal defective work = ⑳*1% = 17,700*1% = 177

㉓ abnormal defective work = ⑪ − ⑳ − ㉒ = 18, 000, − 17,700 − 177 = 123

㉔ total standard operating time = ⑰*{⑳ + ㉒} = 0.6 min. per piece *(17,700 + 177) = 10,762.2 min.

㉕ net standard operating time = ⑰ * ⑳ = 0.6 min. per piece*17,700 = 10,620 min.

㉖ time utilization ratio = ⑨/⑤ = 13,400 min./14,020 min. = 0.956

㉗ net operating ratio = ⑫/⑨ = 12,600 min./13,400 min. = 0.940

㉘ speed operating ratio = ⑱/⑫ = 10,800 min./12,600 min. = 0.857

㉙ non-defective parts (or products) ratio = ㉕/⑱ = 10620 min. 10,800 min. = 0.983

㉚ capacity utilization ratio = ⑱/⑨ = 10,800 min./13,400 min. = 0.806

㉛ contact time ratio = ⑫/⑤ = 12,600 min./600 min. = 0.899

㉜ overall equipment efficiency = ㉕/⑤ = 10,620 min./14,020 min. = 0.757

$\quad$ = ㉖*㉗*㉘*㉙ = 0.956*0.940*0.857*0.983 = 0.757

$\quad$ = ㉖*㉚*㉙ = 0.956*0.806*0.983 = 0.757

$\quad$ = ㉛*㉘*㉙ = 0.899*0.857*0.983 = 0.757

㉝ breakdown losses variance = ⑯*⑥ = ¥500 per minute*400 min. = ¥200,000

㉞ set-up & adjustment losses variance = ⑯*⑦ = ¥500 per minute* 150 min. = ¥75,000

㉟ start-up & yield losses variance = ⑯*⑧ = ¥500 per minute*70 min. = ¥35,000

㊱ idling & minor stoppage losses variance = {⑭ + ⑯}*⑬
$\quad$ = ¥1,100 per minute*800 min. = ¥880,000

㊲ speed losses variance = {⑭ + ⑯}*⑲ = ¥1,100 per minute* 800 min. = ¥1,980,000

㊳ normal defective work losses variance = {⑭ + ⑯}*⑰*㉒
$\quad$ = ¥1,100 per min.*106.2 min. = ¥116,820

㊴ abnormal defective losses variance = {⑭ + ⑯}*⑰*㉓
$\quad$ = ¥1,100 per minute*73.8 min. = ¥81,180

㊵ capacity utilization losses variance = ㊱ + ㊲ = ¥2,860,000

㊶ contact time losses variance = ㉝ + ㉞ + ㉟ + ㊱ = ¥1,190,000

㊷ operation variance = ㉝ + ㉞ + ㉟ = ¥200,000 + ¥75,000 + ¥35,000
$\quad$ = ¥310,000 = ⑯*{⑤ − ⑨}
$\quad$ = ¥500 per minute *(14,020 min. − 13,400 min.) = ¥310,000

㊸ efficiency variance = ㊱ + ㊲ + ㊳ + ㊴
$\quad$ = ¥880,000 + ¥1,980,000 + ¥116,820 + ¥81,180 = ¥3,058,000
$\quad$ = {⑭ + ⑯}*{⑨ − ㉕}
$\quad$ = ¥1,100 per minute*(13,400 min. − 10,620 min.) = ¥3,058,000

2.3. *Individual improvement and Kaizen costing*

In TPM, the standard cost applied for individual improvement seems to be more severe than "the standard cost" used in Japanese automobile companies. Because, as for the former, the overall equipment efficiency reaches 100%. Then, without causing all losses with the equipment, the standard conversion cost is distributed to non-defective products. On the other hand, the latter is no more than the standard cost achieved by the end of the previous term as a result. It is only the standard value which the actual cost should not exceed at least in the current period. Therefore, the former seems to be lower than the latter. Especially, in some processes or machine centers which have machine operating time as the main cost driver, the factory workers must perform some improvement activities which make up for the difference with those two standard costs. They are none other than cost reduction activities performed in the Kaizen costing system. Actually, there are some means related to overall equipment efficiency in many policies to achieve the target amount of Kaizen (or the target amount of Kaizen profit) in Japanese Kaizen costing system as follows.

(a) Reducing minor stoppage time
(b) Improving strokes per hour (SPH)
(c) Shortening lead time
(d) Shortening set-up time
(e) Reducing defective ratio

These means eradicate losses which obstruct the overall equipment efficiency from reaching 100%.

There are various processes in automobile factories where Kaizen costing is well established, and each process's cost driver is different subtly. As described above, the standard conversion cost variance analysis can be utilized in the machine manufacture process and the heat-treatment process which have machine operating time as a main cost driver. However, it supposes that those present manufacturing conditions are invariable. If people who perform the improvement activities change them, then they change the condition in computing standard application rate, too. For example, when set-up time is reduced by VA (value analysis), set-up actions are sometimes achieved within 9 minutes 59 seconds. Also, if a corrective maintenance is performed, admissible set-up & adjustment time, scheduled downtime, admissible start-up time may be shortened. Therefore, when making the monthly operating time constant, the loading time becomes long. Then, the standard application rate itself is set lower and the standard cost is more severe than the previous one. Shortened set-up time is a result of work improvement invented by VA. Corrective maintenance is contained in equipment improvement.

2.4. *Measuring and managing activities in maintenance department*

For the maintenance department, it is necessary to make the system to perform "PM to gain profit", and it is necessary to make the system to perform "Life-cycle management of equipment". Especially, they examine natural machine deteriorations, restore them, and perform corrective maintenance, teach maintenance skills, plan maintenance. When distinguishing the cost spent on these maintenance activities from autonomous maintenance cost and measuring it to manage, each of the results can be easily evaluated. When an equipment deteriorates naturally because of insufficient autonomous maintenance, even if it was checked, satisfied data cannot be obtained. As a result, maintenance department has loads which are more than necessary. In this case, maintenance costs must be classified so as to be clear of where and who has responsibilities for them. When condition diagnosis equipment are used and predictive maintenance is implemented, if they are introduced after the artificial machine deterioration is excluded, reliable data is obtained, and the maintenance activities can be more effectively implemented from the view of cost management, too.

As mentioned above, it seems to be difficult to measure the effects of maintenance activities and costs. However, in some companies that implement TPM, it said that they observe not only some indexes described above but also the following indexes by the time series.[15]

(a) Variable maintenance costs/current production volume
(b) Fixed maintenance costs/average number of machines
(c) The number of times of sudden equipment failure per month

(d) Sudden failure downtime/loading time
(e) Maintenance costs/acquisition costs of equipment
(f) Maintenance costs/production costs
(g) Total maintenance costs
(h) (Preventive Maintenance time + Corrective Maintenance time)/(Preventive Maintenance time + Corrective Maintenance time + Breakdown Maintenance time)
(i) Equipment downtime/loading time

In future, these must be more systematized. As for the TPM project, we must solve some problems for the economic analysis, the analysis of variance from budget, combining decision accounting with measure of performance.

3. The Cost Management for Quality Maintenance, Safety, Hygiene and Environments

Quality maintenance activities have to guarantee quality in each process and equipment so as to secure product quality without defects. Those points are as follows.

(1) Making the equipment without defective works.
(2) Establishing the conditions for (1)
(3) Managing the conditions established for (1)

(1) means MP (maintenance prevention) designs. (2) means PM analysis, autonomous maintenance and the application of CDT (condition diagnosis techniques). PM analysis means neither productive maintenance analysis nor a preventive maintenance one. It is for analyzing physically some chronic defective phenomena according to the principle and making those mechanisms clear. (3) is to neatly observe the conditions.

Mainly, target costing and quality costing relate to quality maintenance. As for target costing, when manufacturing new products with the existing equipment, the target cost is related to the cost of maintenance (containing corrective maintenance) and autonomous maintenance consults former maintenance information. When manufacturing new products with new equipment, the following two should be implemented in the framework of "new equipment target costing" at least.

Estimating the costs which relate to the maintenance aimed to eradicate defective works.

Planning for the capital investments into which the life-cycle costs and MP designs of some machines are incorporated.

New equipment target costing means the activities to achieve the target cost of the products produced by some new machines from the planning phase to the operating phase.

As for quality costing, prevention costs are input factors to measure the effect of quality maintenance activities. Each prevention cost is included in the cost of conformance. Then, output factors consist of the reduced amount of appraisal costs, the reduced amount of cost of non-conformance and the reduced amount of opportunity cost which would have occurred if defective products had be sold.

At least, the following four are contained in management for safety, hygiene and environments.

> The maintenance activities which eradicate all disasters for "the respect of human nature".
> Managing employee's health.
> Securing hygiene facilities.
> The maintenance activities to prevent from pollution.

It is most important for TPM to secure the safe offices which does not have all labor disasters. Some safety activities are incorporated into the autonomous maintenance, and it is effective to perform them as routine works in the view of cost management, too. The points to aim at zero disaster is as follows.

(1) Making machines that do not make disasters occur.
(2) Establishing the conditions for (1).
(3) Managing the conditions established for (1).

Dirty, tight and dangerous works must be diminished as much as possible, and three safety principles (the 5-S movement, standardization, check & arrangement) must be thoroughly kept. Also, it is efficient and effective to utilize some leeway spaces as hygiene facilities. Moreover, most companies take the responsibility for preventing pollution to society. However, it is not always possible to measure all efforts only in terms of the amount of pollution control equipment. Actually, it is important not to pollute the atmosphere, water, environments and so on. Then, employees should be willing to make their local community beautiful.

4. Summary

Some Japanese companies have established TPM activities as excellent practices. Then, they have pursued the synthetic improvement of the production system fully. In this chapter, I tried to make the relation between TPM and cost management as much clear as possible. But, I mainly described cost control and Kaizen costing, because these are directly related with production activities. Also, I stated maintenance budget management, measuring maintenance activities to manage, quality maintenance and safety, hygiene and environments, too. Besides, TPM contains some important activities which were not described in this chapter. They are as follows.

(1) Establishing systems for initial phase product and equipment check.
(2) Establishing efficiency improvement systems for administrative and indirect departments.
(3) The activities to establish TPM.

   (1) is related to PART 1 and PART 3 in this book. (2) is related to PART 5, and (3) is related to PART 7. In future, those relations should be made clear and would be some important problems in TPM.

References

1. Imai, M., KAIZEN: The Key to Japan's Competitive Success (McGraw-Hill, New York, 1986), 189.
2. Kobayasi, T., Gendai-genkakeisanron: Senryakuteki-Cost Management eno Approach (Chuokeizaisya, Tokyo, 1993), 143–170.

3. Makido, T., Nihonteki GenbaKaizen giho, Kigyokaikei, Vol. 45, No. 12, 1993, 54–59.

4. Monden, Y., Toyota Production System: An Integrated Approach to Just-In-Time, 2nd edition (Industrial Engineering and Management Press, Institute of Industrial Engineers, Norcross, Geogia, 1993).

5. Monden, Y., Total Cost Management System in Japanese Automobile Corporations, Monden, Y. & Sakurai, M., eds. Japanese Management Accounting a World Class Approach to Profit Management (Productivity Press, Cambridge, Massachusetts, 1989), 15–33.

6. Monden, Y. & Hamada, K., Target Costing and Kaizen Costing in Japanese Automobile Companies, Journal of Management Accounting Research, Vol. 3, Fall 1991, 16–34.

7. Monden, Y., Toyota Management System: Linking the Seven Key Functional Areas (Productivity Press, 1993).

8. Monden, Y., Genkakaizen no Mechanism: Hyojungenkakeisan to no Taihi, Kaikei, Vol. 143, No. 2, 1993, 63–75.

9. Monden, Y. & Lee, J., How to a Japanese Auto Maker Reduce Costs, Management Accounting, August 1993, 22–26.

10. Monden, Y., Genkakikaku Genkakaizen Genkaiji no Kigen to Hatten, Kigyokaikei, Vol. 45, No. 12, 1993, 42–46.

11. Monden, Y., Kakakukyosoryoku o tukeru Genkakikaku to Genkakaizen no Giho (Toyo keizai sinposya, Tokyo, 1994).

12. Monden, Y., ed., Kanrikaikeigaku text (Zeimukeiri Kyokai, Tokyo, 1995).

13. Nakajima, S., Seisankakusin no Tameno Sin TPM Nyumon (Nihon Noritu Kyokai Management Center, Tokyo, 1993).

14. Okamoto, K., Genkakeisan, 5th edition (Kunimoto syobo, Tokyo, 1994), 829–870.

15. Okamoto, K., Planning and Control of Maintenance Costs for Total Productive Maintenance, Monden, Y. & Sakurai, M., eds. Japanese Management Accounting a World Class Approach to Profit Management (Productivity Press, Cambridge, Massachusetts, 1989), 97–113.

16. Sakurai, M., Kigyokankyo no Henka to Kanrikaikei (Dobunkan, Tokyo, 1991), 39–41.

17. Tanaka, T., Toyota no Kaizen Yosan, Kigyokaikei, Vol. 42, No. 3, 1990, 59–66.

Chapter 12

How Japanese Companies are Using the "Standard Cost" for Managing Costs

GUN-YUNG LEE

1. Introduction

It is acknowledged that the role of today's standard costing has been declining due to the change in the manufacturing environment, such as factory automation/computer-integrated manufacturing (FA/CIM), product variety and the shortening of product life-cycles. However, with the criticism that standard costing is no longer useful for productivity improvement, activity-based costing (ABC) systems based mainly on overhead costs have become more prominent.

In spite of these tendencies, in the investigation by Schiff,[14] ABC was used in 36% of the investigated companies; of this 36%, companies using ABC instead of standard cost accounting systems made up 25%. In other words, only 9% of the investigated companies were using ABC. 91% of companies had used standard cost accounting systems as the only system or alongside ABC. In another investigation for Japanese companies, standard cost accounting systems were used by 64% in 1994.[16] This rate had not decreased compared to a previous investigation. It has to be pointed out that many companies use standard cost accounting as it is easier to prepare

262

financial statements. However, this is not the case for cost control on the shop-floor.[7]

Today, there are two viewpoints about how the tightness of standard costs has been influenced by a change in customer needs and the manufacturing environment. These viewpoints insist on a shift to tight standard costs or a shift to actual costs. The former viewpoint supports perfection standards as standard costs. Perfection standards are an aim of continuous improvement that measures waste, and then remove that waste based on the best level of performance. The "currently attainable" standard costs generally used permit waste and inefficiency that cannot be avoided.[1,4] The latter viewpoint supports the past rolling average of actual costs as standard costs. Since today's information technology can keep track of the actual costs with cost effects, the standard costs estimated by engineering are not necessarily useful. The benchmark of continuous improvement as the criterion of performance evaluation or cost target is employed.[2,10] While the two viewpoints insist on a shift from the currently attainable standard costs to ideal standard costs as the final goal, the former viewpoint emphasises the adoption of perfection standards and the latter the adoption of the past rolling average actual cost as current standards.

Looking at Japanese companies, there is the example of TDK, the manufacturer of electric materials, who has fixed ideal standard costs as its long term achievement target, and improves current standards in every period. As another example, there are automobile companies adopting the Kaizen costing, where the cost reduction results achieved during the precedent period are used as the new standard costs of the current period. As a result, the long-term final goals are equal, in the different viewpoints of standard costs today, but the tightness of current standards is different and can vary.

Thus, in this chapter, based on the survey results regarding standard costing, the features of standard cost management in Japanese companies will be analysed and clarified. Firstly, this chapter will summarise the influence of environmental change on standard costing and several characteristics of today's standard cost management in Japanese companies from the precedent studies. This chapter will then examine a number of other themes and draw conclusions from the survey.

2. Positioning of Standard Costing

Standard costing is used to manage occurring costs toward cost standards. The main objective is to control the occurring costs within a standard range while keeping constant quality and the required manufacturing conditions. For example, manufacturing conditions include a variety of materials, purchasing methods, storage methods, working conditions and methods and classes of workers. Therefore, standard costs must be established based on these various conditions. Standard costs need to be set under the following conditions.[8]

- The operation can be repeated or it may be planned as a combination of repeated operations.
- A manufacturing structure exists where manufacturing facilities, methods, materials used, etc. are fixed.
- A functional relationship exists between production volume and cost elements, such as costs, materials used or operating time, which can be measured to show efficiency.
- The cost of setting standard costs can be fully compensated by cost savings achieved when standard costs are applied.

Such standard costs have been used as an effective means for the efficiency management of physical standards applied mainly under the stable manufacturing conditions of mass production. Since price is determined in the market and wage rates by negotiations with labour unions, so an efficiency evaluation only by physical standards has become possible in today's manufacturing environment.

3. Influence of Environment Change on Standard Costing

3.1. *A change of market and manufacturing environment*

The role of today's standard costing has been altered due to changes in the environment such as FA/CIM, product variety and the shortening of product life cycles. A change in customer needs, called individualisation, has resulted in short product life cycles and a greater product variety. Due to this individualisation, companies have had to produce various kinds of products to match consumer needs. Also, due to technical innovation, a change in labour circumstances has become a factor promoting FA. Among Japanese companies, it is said that the necessity of automation was increased by a labour shortage, an increased reluctance among young workers to carry out hard, dirty and dangerous jobs, the rapid fluctuations in the exchange rate and the rise of Newly Industrialising Economies (NIES).[13] In particular, the shift to FA/CIM due to an improvement in information processing ability, with cost effects, has brought about a big change in the manufacturing environment. The individualisation of customers and development of FA has modified the role of traditional standard costing.

3.2. *Factors reducing the importance of standard costing due to a change in the manufacturing environment*

The reconsideration of today's standard costing has been brought about by the environmental change. Due to the following reasons, the role of standard costing has declined.[9,12,13]

- In a CIM environment where industrial robots have become the main tools of operations, the necessity of managing workers by standard costs based on efficiency has declined. Furthermore, because of large decreases in direct labour costs, the setting of standard direct labour costs may lose its meaning. On the other hand, in a CIM environment, if manufacturing processes and methods are established for direct materials costs once, the waste of materials by using hands does not occur and the setting of standard direct materials costs may lose its meaning.
- Due to increased product variety and the shortening of product life cycles, the stabilisation of manufacturing processes as the most important condition of standard costing, is lost. Therefore, the setting of standard costs may not only be difficult but may also lose its meaning. Furthermore, deciding on the level of stabilised normal capacity becomes difficult, hence the standard fixed manufacturing overhead costs rate, (which is established on the basis of normal capacity), becomes vague.

- Because of increased product variety, the shortening of product life cycles and the increased use of industrial robots, the significance of cost control at the manufacturing stage is declining. Conversely, the focus of cost management has shifted from the production and assembly stages to the planning and design stages.
- Because of the removal of repeated operations and normal products, the standardisation of manufacturing conditions has become an unnecessary concept. However, the standardisation of manufacturing conditions based on kinds of products has become necessary.

4. The Opposite Results of Automation and Human-Centered Manufacturing System

In Japanese factories, the move away from FA (although FA has been thought to be desirable until now), has occurred mainly in assembly-orientated industries. This is the opposite function of automatic manufacturing systems managed with computers, such as automatic warehouses, material conveyance robots and numerical control (NC) machines. Problems, such as flexible manufacturing adjustment, the collection of invested funds, the use of skilled workers and alienation of workers, cannot be solved by the automatic manufacturing system alone. Thus, the flexible production structure, a method allowing diversification of manufacturing levels as well as solving these problems, has become necessary.

A manufacturing system using multi-skilled workers called the "cell system", has come into use. This is the multi-work process system developed from the "U-shaped line", and can be seen as a return to human-centered manufacturing after the limits of automation have been reached. The problems of an automatic manufacturing system can be summarised as follows:[6,15]

- Since an automatic manufacturing system under a specific condition must be adjusted when rearranging manufacturing processes, enormous costs and time are incurred.
- As automatic manufacturing systems become complicated and computerised, they often cause trouble. Therefore, automatic manufacturing

systems increase overtime work to supplement low output and the number of maintenance workers due to the trouble, but total productivity does not rise.

- Workers, apart from specified repair persons, cannot repair automatic manufacturing systems so they are deprived of their role in operations. Thus, the sense of demoralisation caused by the alienation of workers is increasing.
- In periods of low growth, the increase of production volume becomes impossible to anticipate, and the collection of funds invested in automatic facilities becomes difficult.
- Break-even outputs of automatic facilities cannot be met due to the shortening of product life cycles. Therefore, handicraft by multi-skilled workers, called the "cell system", becomes more important than automation, and productivity also rises.

This shift to human-centered production motivates workers, and highlights the possibility of returning to standard costing for efficiency management as before.

5. The Japanese Standard Cost Management System

Due to today's environmental changes, such as the individualisation of customers and increased automation, the formation of a new manufacturing system to respond to these changes has influenced the style of standard cost management. The "production orientated" or "technology orientated" traditional method for the setting of cost standards has taken the place of the "market orientated" or "strategy orientated" method. This change of management direction influences the managerial target of traditional standard costing. Traditional standard costs have been used as an effective means for cost control mainly in the stable manufacturing environment of mass production. However, this new management direction directly influences standard cost management in a keen competitive environment as well as the setting of standard costs. In Japanese companies, where process improvements are frequent, the control of the occurring costs by standard costs management methods becomes difficult. Costs are reduced by the source management in upstream manufacturing processes instead of the control of occurring costs.

Due to market and/or strategy-orientated thought, the necessity of "make-to-cost" in upstream manufacturing processes has increased, so that the main activities have shifted to cost reduction by the change of production conditions. Cost reduction activities at the planning and design stage are called "target costing". Cost reduction activities by the change of production conditions are known as "Kaizen costing". Kaizen costing reduces product costs at the manufacturing stage.

In general, Japanese automobile companies use the term "cost maintaining" instead of "standard costing". With "cost maintaining", the cost level achieved at the end of the precedent period becomes the standard cost for the current period. The actual costs of this period must not exceed this standard level. Additionally, the new standard level tightens due to Kaizen costing. However, Kaizen costing activities to systematically improve the standard level for achieving the expected costs, are carried out at the manufacturing stage. The aim of such Kaizen costing is to continually reduce costs in the manufacturing stage in order to bridge the gap between the target profit (budget profit) and the expected profit of any fiscal period.[11] Today's Japanese cost management includes both aspects of cost maintaining (standard cost) and Kaizen costing. The differences between the concepts of standard costing and Kaizen costing are shown in Table 12.1.[11]

Table 12.1. The comparison between standard costing and Kaizen costing.

Standard costing	Kaizen costing
1. Control to reconcile occurring costs with standard costs	1. Cost reduction system to generate the actual costs under the standard level
2. Assumes stability in current manufacturing processes	2. Control to achieve the amount of reduction target
	3. Cost reduction is carried out by the continuous improvement of existing manufacturing processes

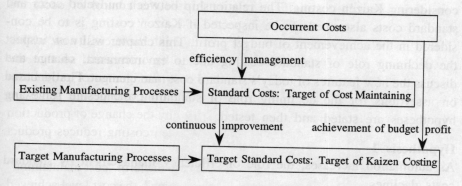

Fig. 12.1. Standard cost management including Kaizen costing.

Therefore, Japanese standard cost management today is used for the purpose of improving the cost standard itself at the manufacturing stage. As discussed above, unless Kaizen costing is included within standard cost management, we cannot fully understand the Japanese style of standard costing. Standard cost management including Kaizen costing is summarised in Fig. 12.1.

6. Setting Hypotheses for Standard Costing

As previously discussed, it has been acknowledged that the role of standard costing has declined with an increasingly automated manufacturing environment. However, an opposite result of automation has also been seen. As the role of flexible, multi-skilled workers has increased with product variety, human-centered production within the assembly process has been observed. This may be the outcome of the search for a balanced role for humans and machines.

The change of market and manufacturing environments as well as improvements to existing manufacturing processes influences standard cost management. The main target of standard cost management has shifted to the improvement of manufacturing processes, called Kaizen costing. Therefore, today's standard cost management needs to analyse standard costing while considering Kaizen costing. The relationship between budgeted costs and standard costs also needs to be inspected if Kaizen costing is to be considered in the achievement of budget profit. This chapter will now inspect the declining role of standard costing due to environmental change and discuss the new features of today's standard cost management. Firstly, based on assertions for the declining role of standard costing, the following hypotheses are stated and then tested.

Hypothesis 1
As automation increases, the role of efficiency management by standard costs declines.

Hypothesis 2
Due to product variety and low-volume production, the setting of cost standards becomes more difficult.

Hypothesis 3
Due to the shortening of product life cycles, the setting of cost standards becomes more difficult.

7. Analysis of Survey Results

7.1. *Survey introduction*

Survey data for this research was collected in May 1997, and looks at standard costing practices in Japanese companies. For this survey, questionnaires were sent to section chiefs or department managers of accounting or finance departments of 500 head offices of companies in the manufacturing industry. Answers were received from 109 companies, of which 104 were valid replies. The breakdown of replies by industry is as follows — iron and steel or non-ferrous metal, 11; chemical, 12; machinery for transport, 16; machine, 22; metal products, 4; electronics, 26; others, 20. Among the above, the number of companies involved in several industries numbered 6.

In the survey, it was assumed that the managerial costs were used for cost management, cost control or the making of financial statements.

Questionnaires were prepared and answers expected under this assumption. Among the managerial costs used in business practices, there are costs of various tightness related to this purpose. Japanese companies generally use managerial costs, such as target costs and pre-determined costs, as well as standard costs. Since standard costs are also used at several levels of tightness, cost levels near to an ideal cost or an actual cost, target cost and pre-determined cost can also be included within standard costs. Therefore, this survey also asked what were the terms used as managerial costs. Companies using only actual costs were outside this investigation.

7.2. *The tightness and purpose of standard costs*

As previously discussed, Japanese companies use standard costing based on Kaizen costing. Therefore, the terms for standard costing vary and may be different from the traditional concept of standard costs. The cause of such change may be the shift from efficiency management to an improvement of the manufacturing processes. As shown in the survey mentioned above,[16] the tightness of standard costs was *"the cost that is expected to realize in the next period"* (45%) and *"the cost that the past results were averaged and added a prospective trend"* (41%), and the two types occupied 96% together. *That is, the tightness of standard costs in Japanese companies is not extreme.* This result may indicate that the use of only one term, "standard cost", is insufficient.

A standard cost is, essentially, a cost calculated scientifically. "Scientific" in this context, means the "objective method by which anyone can understand". Therefore, theoretically, pre-determined costs are distinguished from standard costs established scientifically. However, pre-determined costs regarded as only estimates are often called, and used as, "standard costs" in business practices. In particular, when standard costs are used as the realistic expected costs, the distinction between standard costs and pre-determined costs is not clear.[3] This tendency was also found in the survey. As shown in Table 12.2, nearly 30% of companies use the term, "pre-determined costs" for managerial costs. In Table 12.2, duplicate answers are included. Valid replies totalled 104.

Table 12.2. Terms used for managerial costs.

Managerial costs	Standard costs	Target costs	Pre-determined costs	Planning costs	Cost target	Others
Number	58	19	31	5	3	2
%	55.77	18.27	29.81	4.81	2.88	1.92

Table 12.3. The relationship between terms for managerial costs and their tightness in materials usage standard (number of companies).

	Theoretical performance	Theoretical performance reflecting reality	Average past performance added a trend	Average past performance	Row total
Standard costs	13	23	9	4	49
Target costs	0	4	4	1	9
Pre-determined costs	3	5	11	5	24
Column total	16	32	24	10	82

T value = 13.57, P value = 0.035
When target costs were categorised with pre-determined costs
T value = 11.59, P value = 0.009

In order to examine the difference of tightness by terms, the relationship between terms for managerial costs and their tightness based on the physical criterion was examined. In general, we can expect the trend that the term, "pre-determined cost" will be used as the level near to the past performance value and the term, "standard cost" as the level near to the theoretical performance value. So it is expected that the business will use the term pre-determined cost, instead of the term standard cost, when the standard cost is not tight. In order to inspect such a relationship, for each item of physical standard for materials, labour and manufacturing overhead, χ^2 tests were performed. The results are shown in Tables 12.3–12.5. In each

Table 12.4. The relationship between terms for managerial costs and their tightness in labour time standard (number of companies).

	Theoretical performance	Theoretical performance reflecting reality	Average past performance added a trend	Average past performance	Row total
Standard costs	9	20	12	5	46
Target costs	1	3	6	0	10
Pre-determined costs	1	8	15	2	26
Column total	11	31	33	7	82

T value = 10.45, P value = 0.107
When target costs were categorised with pre-determined costs
T value = 9.73, P value = 0.021

Table 12.5. The relationship between terms for managerial costs and their tightness in capacity standard (number of companies).

	Theoretical performance	Theoretical performance reflecting reality	Average past performance added a trend	Average past performance	Row total
Standard costs	6	22	14	3	45
Target costs	0	3	5	0	8
Pre-determined costs	0	7	13	3	23
Column total	6	32	32	6	76

T value = 10.12, P value = 0.120
When target costs were categorised with pre-determined costs
T value = 8.72, P value = 0.033

table, there are a few companies using terms besides standard cost, target cost and pre-determined cost, however, they were removed from the analysis because they were rare, compared with the other terms shown in Table 12.2 Furthermore, the change of the sample number is due to the fact that duplicate answers were removed.

As a result of χ^2 testing, the relationship between terms of managerial costs and their tightness for materials usage was statistically significant as shown in Table 12.3. This result agreed with the above expectation. How ever, a meaningful difference was not found for labour time and capacity As a result, besides materials usage, there was no special relationship between terms and tightness of managerial costs.

Interestingly, there were statistically significant results for all cost type when target costs were categorised with pre-determined costs. *That is, there was a trend that the terms, "pre-determined cost" or "target cost" were used at the level near to the past performance value and the term, "standard cost" as the level near to the theoretical performance value.*

7.3. *Automation and efficiency management of standard costing*

Three hypotheses were abstracted from preceding studies about the declining role of standard costs due to the result of a change in the manufacturing environment. The first hypothesis was that "as automation progresses, the role of efficiency management by standard costs declines". Thus, the degree of automation and tightness of managerial costs were studied in this survey in order to confirm this hypothesis, and χ^2 testing was carried out to examine the relationship between the two. But a meaningful difference was not found between the degree of automation and tightness of managerial costs i materials usage standard (see Table 12.6). The assertion discussed previously that, "in the automation environment, once manufacturing processes an methods are established for direct materials costs, the waste of material by using hand, does not occur, so that the setting of standard direct material costs may lose its meaning" was thus not supported.

However, as shown in Tables 12.7 and 12.8, meaningful differences wer obtained between the degree of automation and tightness of managerial

Table 12.6. The relationship between degree of automation and tightness of managerial costs in materials usage standard (number of companies).

	Theoretical performance	Theoretical performance reflecting reality	Average past performance added a trend	Average past performance	No setting	Row total
Partial automation of each machine	6	7	8	1	1	23
All automation of each machine	2	8	3	1	0	14
Automation of production line	8	16	11	4	3	42
FMS or CIM	1	5	1	4	0	11
Column total	17	36	23	10	4	90

value = 14.41, P value = 0.275

Table 12.7. The relationship between degree of automation and tightness of managerial costs in labour time standard (number of companies).

	Theoretical performance	Theoretical performance reflecting reality	Average past performance added a trend	Average past performance	No setting	Row total
Partial automation of each machine	6	6	9	3	0	24
All automation of each machine	2	9	2	1	0	14
Automation of production line	2	19	19	0	2	42
FMS or CIM	0	5	3	3	0	11
Column total	10	39	33	7	2	91

value = 25.30, P value = 0.013

Table 12.8. The relationship between degree of automation and tightness of managerial costs in capacity standard (number of companies).

	Theoretical performance	Theoretical performance reflecting reality	Average past performance added a trend	Average past performance	No setting	Row total
Partial automation of each machine	3	6	10	3	1	23
All automation of each machine	1	8	5	0	0	14
Automation of production line	3	15	20	0	3	41
FMS or CIM	0	4	1	3	2	10
Column total	7	33	36	6	6	88

T value = 23.59, P value = 0.023

costs with regard to labour time and capacity. The assertion discussed previously that in a CIM environment where industrial robots became the main tools of operations, the necessity of managing workers by the standard costs based on efficiency declined was supported. In other words, for labour time and capacity, the tightness of managerial costs shifts to the past performance level from the theoretical level due to the progress of automation.

7.4. *The relationship between high-variety/low-volume production and standard costs*

The second hypothesis obtained from previous survey results for the cause of the declining role of standard costs due to a change in the manufacturing environment, was that "due to product-variety and low-volume production the setting of cost standards becomes more difficult". Firstly, the reality about the variety of products and production volume was investigated before this hypothesis was tested. The results in Table 12.9 shows that 7 companies (82.3%) produced products with a high-variety/low-volume

Table 12.9. The reality of high-variety/low-volume production.

	Low-variety	Medium-variety	High-variety	Row total (= n)
Low-volume	8.33%	8.33%	83.33%	100% (36)
Medium-volume	0%	23.33%	76.67%	100% (30)
High-volume	3.33%	10%	86.67%	100% (30)
Column total (= n)	4	13	79	96

Table 12.10. High-variety/low-volume production and tightness of managerial costs at materials usage (number of companies).

	Theoretical performance	Theoretical performance reflecting reality	Average past performance added a trend	Average past performance	No setting	Row total
Low-volume/ High-variety	6	10	9	3	2	30
Medium-volume/ High-variety	7	8	6	1	0	22
High-volume/ High-variety	1	10	9	5	0	25
Column total	14	28	24	9	2	77

T value = 11.19, P value = 0.191

However, the comparison of product variety and tightness of managerial costs is difficult, due to the low occurrence of companies in the low and medium variety sections of this sample. Since production varies from low to high volume even if a company is producing a high-variety of products, the relationship between production volume with high-variety production and tightness of managerial costs was investigated.

In order to test this relationship, χ^2 testing was carried out. The results are displayed in Tables 12.10–12.12. As shown in each table, meaningful

Table 12.11. High-variety/low-volume production and tightness of managerial costs at labour time (number of companies).

	Theoretical performance	Theoretical performance reflecting reality	Average past performance added a trend	Average past performance	No setting	Row total
Low-volume/ High-variety	5	10	11	3	0	29
Medium-volume/ High-variety	4	11	7	1	0	23
High-volume/ High-variety	0	9	15	1	1	26
Column total	9	30	33	5	1	78

T value = 10.72, P value = 0.218

Table 12.12. High-variety/low-volume production and tightness of managerial costs at capacity (number of companies).

	Theoretical performance	Theoretical performance reflecting reality	Average past performance added a trend	Average past performance	No setting	Row total
Low-volume/ High-variety	2	9	10	5	1	27
Medium-volume/ High-variety	3	10	9	1	0	23
High-volume/ High-variety	1	10	13	0	1	25
Column total	6	29	32	6	2	75

T value = 9.38, P value = 0.312

differences were not found between varying degrees of production volume with high-variety production and tightness of managerial costs. Without differences in production volume, the tightness of managerial costs was "the value that reflected reality to theoretical performance value" or "the value that added a trend to the average past performance". Each ratio was 68% at materials usage, 81% at labour time and 81% at capacity. Therefore, the assertion, that "due to product variety and low-volume production, the setting of cost standards becomes more difficult", was not accepted. Such results may mean that "attainable good performance" standards can be established and are necessary as an effort target regardless of production volume.

7.5. *The relationship between product life cycles and standard costs*

Earlier in this chapter it was stated that the declining role of standard costs is due to increased automation and high-variety/low-volume production. Therefore, the final hypothesis to be presented is that "due to the shortening of product life cycles, the setting of cost standards becomes more difficult". To test this hypothesis, a ratio of products produced for less than 3 years in each company was investigated. In order to inspect the relationship between a new product ratio and the degree of production volume with high-variety production, χ^2 testing was used, and the results are shown in Table 12.13. As a result, a meaningful difference was not found between a ratio of new products and varying degrees of high-variety production volume. This shows that a meaningful difference does not exist between product life cycles and various levels of high-variety production.

In order to test the last hypothesis, the relationship between the ratio of new products and the tightness of managerial costs was tested. As shown in Tables 12.14–12.16, meaningful differences were not found between the two. The assertion discussed previously, "due to the shortening of product life cycles, 'stabilisation' of the manufacturing process as the most important condition of standard cost management, is lost. Therefore, the setting of cost standards may not only be difficult but also lose its meaning" was not supported.

Table 12.13. The relationship between a ratio of new products and degree of production volume with high-variety (number of companies).

Ratios of products produced for less than 3 years	Low-volume/ High-variety production	Medium-volume/ High-variety production	High-volume/ High-variety production	Row total
Less than 25%	12	9	7	28
26% ~ 50%	2	8	5	15
51% ~ 75%	3	0	1	4
75% ~ 100%	6	5	5	16
Column total	23	22	18	63

T value = 7.42, P value = 0.284

Table 12.14. The relationship between a new products ratio and tightness of managerial costs at materials usage (number of companies).

Ratios of products produced for less than 3 years	Theoretical performance	Theoretical performance reflecting reality	Average past performance added a trend	Average past performance	No setting	Row total
Less than 25%	5	11	11	4	2	33
25% ~ 50%	2	10	3	4	1	20
51% ~ 75%	2	2	1	0	0	5
76% ~ 100%	4	9	6	2	1	22
Column total	13	32	21	10	4	80

T value = 6.91, P value = 0.864

Table 12.15. The relationship between a new products ratio and tightness of managerial costs at labour time (number of companies).

Ratios of products produced for less than 3 years	Theoretical performance	Theoretical performance reflecting reality	Average past performance added a trend	Average past performance	No setting	Row total
Less than 25%	3	13	15	2	1	34
25% ~ 50%	1	12	4	3	0	20
51% ~ 75%	0	4	1	2	0	5
76% ~ 100%	2	8	9	2	1	22
Column total	6	37	29	7	2	81

T value = 8.99, P value = 0.704

Table 12.16. The relationship between a new products ratio and tightness of managerial costs at capacity (number of companies).

Ratios of products produced for less than 3 years	Theoretical performance	Theoretical performance reflecting reality	Average past performance added a trend	Average past performance	No setting	Row total
Less than 25%	2	14	14	1	1	32
25% ~ 50%	1	9	6	2	2	20
51% ~ 75%	0	2	1	0	2	5
76% ~ 100%	0	8	9	3	1	21
Column total	3	33	30	6	6	78

T value = 13.45, P value = 0.337

8. Standard Costs and Budgeted Costs

There are two disputed points regarding standard costs and budgeted costs. The first is the difference of tightness in both costs and the second is whether or not budgets can be established by the accumulation of standard costs.[3]

A difference of tightness in both costs is disputed according to whether or not budgeted costs are as tight as standard costs. The viewpoint that budgeted costs have tightness emphasises the following point: budgeted costs have a control function, such as tightness, so that they can carry out the function of plan setting. However, the viewpoint that budgeted costs have no tightness emphasises the following point: budgeted costs are the costs at which zero cost variance is anticipated because the costs are expected realistically, so that budgeted costs cannot have tightness.

A debate exists about whether or not budgets can be established by the accumulation of standard costs. Consequently, there is also debate about whether or not budgeted costs must be prepared separately from standard costs. One viewpoint is that the realistic standard costs thought to be most suitable for cost management are the costs that can be achieved by good performance. Unfavourable variances occur in many cases. A contrasting viewpoint is that the realistic standard cost can also be achieved by a company's standard performance and unfavourable variances are not expected. When the former standard cost is used, budgeted costs must be prepared to cover the unfavourable variance that occurs if only a 'standard' effort is made by the company. Therefore, in this case, a difference of tightness exists between standard costs and budgeted costs. With the latter viewpoint, budgeting can be prepared by using standard costs only.

These viewpoints can change in response to environmental change. As mentioned in the introduction to this chapter, many companies use standard costing systems as it is easier to prepare financial statements. However, in today's keen competitive environment, it is also acknowledged that the relationship between budgeted costs and allowable costs is very close, i.e. budgeted costs become similar to tight standard costs and the allowable costs because profit targets must be achieved.[5]

These two business practices are directly opposing. *The former involves the use of standard costs to be not as tight as the budgeted cost.* This is based on the traditional viewpoint as discussed above. *The latter involves the use of standard costs to be as tight as the budgeted cost.* Therefore, the relationship between the tightness of standard costs and budgeted costs needs to be investigated. As shown in Fig. 12.1, because the budget target is achieved by Kaizen costing, the confirmation of this relationship is also important.

In order to inspect this relationship for all cost types, χ^2 testing was carried out. The results are shown in Tables 12.17–12.19. Meaningful differences were not observed between direct materials costs and manufacturing overhead costs. However, a meaningful difference was found with

Table 12.17. The relationship between tightness of standard costs and budgeted costs at materials usage (number of companies).

	Very tight	Tight	Loose	Very loose	Row total
Budgeted costs equal to standard costs	11	21	14	8	54
Add allowance to standard costs as budgeted costs	2	9	3	0	14
Budgeted costs separate with standard costs	5	6	6	2	19
Column total	18	36	23	10	87

T value = 5.34, P value = 0.501

Table 12.18. The relationship between tightness of standard costs and budgeted costs at labour time (number of companies).

	Very tight	Tight	Loose	Very loose	Row total
Budgeted costs equal to standard costs	3	18	21	3	45
Add allowance to standard costs as budgeted costs	1	14	3	0	14
Budgeted costs separate with standard costs	5	7	11	3	26
Column total	9	39	35	6	89

T value = 14.74, P value = 0.022

Table 12.19. The relationship between tightness of standard costs and budgeted costs at capacity (number of companies).

	Very tight	Tight	Loose	Very loose	Row total
Budgeted costs equal to standard costs	2	18	18	3	41
Add allowance to standard costs as budgeted costs	0	8	7	0	15
Budgeted costs separate with standard costs	4	10	10	3	27
Column total	6	36	35	6	83

T value = 6.06, P value = 0.416

direct labour costs. Thus, when standard costs are tight, budgeted costs are prepared by adding allowance to the standard costs. However, with direct materials costs and manufacturing overhead costs, this tendency was not found; and for direct labour costs, the test result does not agree that tight budgeted costs must become similar to tight standard costs to achieve budget profit.

9. Conclusions

It is acknowledged that the role of today's standard costing has been declining due to the changing manufacturing environment, such as FA/CIM, product variety and the shortening of product life cycles. These viewpoints have been summarised as three hypotheses and discussed. However, in contrast, reflecting excessive automation, a shift to human-centered production to increase the motivation of workers has also occurred.

Today's standard cost management in Japanese companies is different from traditional standard costing. In Japanese automobile companies, standard cost management is divided into cost maintaining and Kaizen costing. Unless Kaizen costing is included within standard cost management, we cannot understand Japanese cost management.

Thus, in order to confirm the declining role of standard costing and discuss the features of Japanese cost management today, three hypotheses and the role of budgeted costs have been researched and tested.

References

1. Horngren, C. T., Foster, G. & Datar, S. M., Cost Accounting — A Managerial Emphasis, 8th ed. (Prentice Hall, 1994), 233–234.
2. Huruta, T., Gendai Kanri-kaikeiron (Chuo-keizaisya, 1997), 31–34.
3. Itagaki, T., Hyojyungenka-keisan (Dobunkan, 1979), 16–34, 185–196.
4. Ito, K., Kaikei, Vol. 152, No. 4, 1997, 90–107.
5. Ito, H., Kigyokaikei, Vol. 44, No. 8, 1992, 17–24.
6. Japan Economy Newspaper, Feb. 2, Dec. 24, 1992; Feb. 6, Feb. 7, 1996; Dec. 11, 1997.
7. Kawano, K., Kigyokaikei, Vol. 48, No. 10, 1996, 84–93.
8. Kobayashi, K., Haiteku-kaikei, *Chap. 3*, Okamoto. K. *et al.*, ed. (Doyukan, 1988), 40–52.
9. Kobayashi, T., Gendai Genka-keisanron (Chuo-keizaisya, 1993), 53–67.
10. McNair, C. J., Mosconi, W. & Norris, T., Beyond in the Bottom Line: Measuring World Class Performance (Dow Jones-Irwin, 1989), 84–89.
11. Monden. Y., Kagaku-kyosoryoku wo Tsukeru Genka-kikaku to Genka-kaizen no Giho (Toyokeizai-shinbosya, 1994), 5, 220–221.
12. Nakane, T., Kanrigenka-keisan no Shiteki-kenkyu (Dobunkan, 1996), 284–285.
13. Sakurai, M. & Scarbrough, D. P., Japanese Cost Management (Crisp Management Library, 1997), 26–27.
14. Schiff, J., Cost Accounting: A Managerial Emphasis, cited by Horngren, C. T., Foster, G. & Datar, S. M. (Prentice Hall, 1994), 161.
15. Syukan-daiamondo (Jun. 18, 1994), 88–98.
16. Takahashi, H., Kaikeigaku-kenkyu, Vol. 8 (The Accounting Research Institute, College of Commerce, Nihon University, 1996), 53–66.

Part 5
Cost Management in Administrative and Factory Indirect Departments

Chapter 13

Management Accounting System for Productivity Improvement in Administrative Departments: Monden's Kaizen System

YASUHIRO MONDEN

1. Introduction

Recently, there have been many sorts of cost reduction systems that try to improve productivity in manufacturing departments. These systems include (1) cost control activity by use of traditional "standard costing", (2) cost improvement activity based on Just-in-Time production system and "Kaizen costing", and (3) cost innovation activity in a product development phase through the "target costing" system and VE or QFD.

It is very hard, however, to build up a system for productivity improvement activities in administrative or service departments.

The reason for such difficulty lies in the following facts:

1. it is difficult to establish performance targets for administrative or service departments,
2. it is difficult to make a link between the company-wide goal and individual departmental goals, and therefore
3. it is difficult to measure actual performance in the light of the goal, and as a result

4. it is hard to determine an appropriate reward based on the performance evaluation.

However, the above problems can be solved if the managerial accounting system is connected to *"Management-by-Objectives"* (*MBO*) system i.e. the docking of systems between managerial accounting (mid-term profit planning, budgeting and budgetary control) and *"Management-by-Objectives."*

For this to work, managers in the accounting department or managerial accountants must play a greater role in preparing and executing systems of productivity improvement in administrative departments.

Thus this paper will explain how to introduce and establish productivity improvement schemes into administrative or service departments, by combining management accounting system, *management-by-objectives* and many other systems developed in Japan.

The following sections will explain how the company-wide profit target may be broken down into various targets at different organization levels, and finally how the performance of target achievement will be evaluated. The whole system will be called "Monden's Kaizen System" (abreviated MKS), because the writer's contribution lies in combining many systems to form a total system. His originality exists especially in the introduction of managerial accounting system to a total system. The total system has been successfully implemented in many Japanese companies.

Section 2 will explain the relationships between Management-By-Objectives and the management accounting system. Section 3 will conduct the methods of preparing the corporate profit target and the divisional profit target. Section 4 will describe how the divisional target will be decomposed into the departmental and/or individual's targets. Sections 5 and 6 will explain how the topics or objects to be improved at various organizational levels and/or group or individual levels will be found out. In these sections the main topic is how to investigate the operation (or activity) whose share of human resources should be reduced or eliminated, or whose way of operation should be changed to increase efficiency. Section 7 conducts a performance evaluation method under the MBO system. Finally, Sec. 8 will discuss how to cultivate human resources to be able to conduct improvements in administrative departments.

2. Management-by-Objectives Linked to Management Accounting System

First let us consider a typical manufacturing company which has many profit-center based divisions. Such a company usually has both mid-term (or long-term) and short-term profit-planning as well as budgetary control systems. The main purpose of these systems is profit management.

Such profit management goals should not be given only to divisional managers who are at the top-management level, but the profit originated goals should be broken down to much lower levels, where "Policy Deployment" or "Goal Deployment" linked to the Management-By-Objectives will be used as a means of goal allocation.

In other words, Management-by-Objectives can be regarded as a system that motivates people to achieve budgets. However, Management-by-Objectives is different from the budget system of managerial accounting in the following ways:

(1) A budget will be given to each department as a whole, but the target (of Management-by-Objectives) will be broken down to targets for the individual member of each department.
(2) A budget is a target of a comprehensive financial performance expressed mainly by means of a monetary amount, by which top management tries to control departmental managers. MBO, on the other hand, takes the part of deciding the concrete policy and methods to achieve budgetary targets.

3. Establishing the Corporate Target and Divisional Target

Let us consider how the MBO will be launched in a multi-divisional company, where the corporate target profit and each divisional target profit are to be determined as a first step of MBO. Such decisions will take the following three steps and must be confirmed by the top-management meeting.

Step 1. Decide on the ideal financial state of the company three years in the future.

Decide on the financial performance of the company as a whole for three years in future. The targeted operating profit must be determined by considering the dividend ratio (= dividend/paid-in capital) and the dividend propensity (= dividend/operating profit) of the rival companies in the same industry and the company's actual figures. These two measures are important from the viewpoint of owners of the company.

Step 2. *Measure the division's attainable profit.*

For measuring the realistic ability of attaining the profit of each division, some rational and fair allocation bases (cost drivers) of common resources must be applied. In other words, for the costs of supplementary service departments located within the company, such as the information system (mainframe computer) department, the transportation department, the purchasing department, etc., some utilization-based cost drivers should be used. Also, for the central headquarter cost drivers should be used for allocation, investment, total labor costs, or a combination of these factors, exactly following the guide by conventional management accounting text.

Step 3. *Establish the target amount of profit improvement.*

The gap between the target operating profit (determined in Step 1 above) and the estimated achievable profit of each division (measured in Step 2 above) will be the target amount of profit improvement; the target Kaizen amount of profit. That is:

The target amount of profit improvement = Target operating profit of the company − Total of all divisional estimated profits.

This profit improvement target of the company as a whole must be assigned to each division by considering the specific characteristics of each industry of the individual division. For example, suppose that the corporate target level of dividend ratio of a certain iron and steel company was determined as 15%, but the dividend ratio of the steel industry (to which the steel division belongs) is 20–30% and the ratio of the automobile industry (to which the stamping division belongs) is at most 10%. In such a case the relatively higher amount of profit improvement target must be allocated to the steel division, and the lower profit improvement target must be assigned to the stamping division.

Next, the following points are important in setting the Kaizen amount (improvement target) in general:

1. Establish the target as high as possible.

   It is much better to establish the highest possible target, which seems hard to achieve and which is considered as an ideal figure or image of the company. A target that only slightly improves the current state cannot induce any innovative idea or plan that is different from the previous or current convention.

2. The target should be quantitative rather than qualitative.

   Qualitative targets such as moral improvement or notability improvement are hard to measure and cannot give people any feeling of accomplishment, unlike Kaizen. Therefore, it is desirable to set some quantitative target, that is "by when (by what day) who will make x amount of Kaizen". Also the target measure itself should not necessarily be a monetary amount, but is good enough if it is merely quantitative. For instance, it is right to set a target of 30% rationalization (reduction) of the workforce in existing operation fields in order to introduce 30% manpower to the new strategic business field."

4. Target Decomposition and Topics Registration

4.1. *Target assignment*

The corporate target should be broken down sequentially into various hierarchical levels, from the top through departmental, sectional and sub-sectional targets down to the target of each small group of individual employees. The basic idea of such target breakdown is shown in Fig. 13.1 (Diagram of objectives system), and the image of Kaizen (continuous improvement) along such objectives system is shown in Fig. 13.2.

When the target of each small group is achieved, then the corporate target can also be attained accordingly. The understanding of such a causal

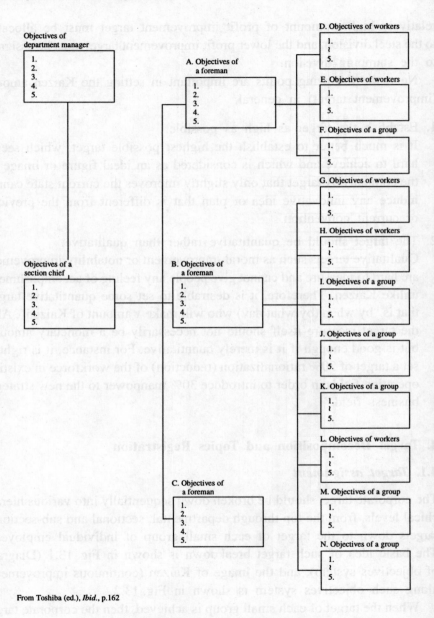

From Toshiba (ed.), *Ibid.*, p.162

Fig. 13.1. Diagram of a one-year objectives system.

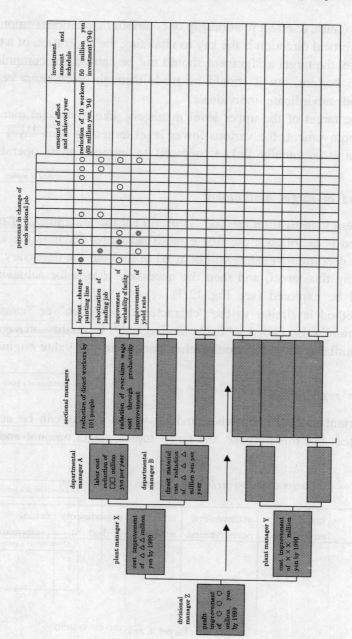

Fig. 13.2. Image of Kaizen along objectives system.

relationship (cause & effect relationship or contributing relations) among employees in vertical direction is the key to vitalizing the realization of a target.

Therefore, the target assignment should not be carried out compulsively from top to bottom, but it should be made through discussions between superior and subordinate individuals.

Since the target of the upper level managers, like divisional managers, is profit improvement, the various lower level targets at each layer in the organization is eventually linked to profit to improve their operations.

4.2. *Method of target assignment*

The "problem investigation method" is useful for the assignment of targets. This method is as follows: the first established target (such as the amount of profit or cost improvement) will be used to find out the necessary policy for achieving this target, and then the necessary means for achieving the policy will be explored (see Fig. 13.3).

This method is similar to the "characteristic diagram" or "cause-and-effect diagram" (also called a "fishbone diagram") in quality management, and also similar to the "functional schematics chart" of value engineering.

4.3. *Topics registration*

It is important to clarify by when and by whom targets can be achieved or completed. For this purpose, the target topics, target amount and target

Target Card (xxyear/xxterm : person or group name)

topics titles	target contribution	achievement policy/means	time schedule	departments to deal	actual performance
topic A topic B					

Fig. 13.3. Target Card.

	Nth term of the year		Objective card			Contracting parties (with whom)		Section chief of the administration department		
Field	Weight (from which)	Objectives (what)	Standards of Accomplishment (how much)	Policies for accomplishment (how)	Schedule (deadline)	Individuals	Groups	Self-evaluation	Result evaluation (what is the result?)	Evaluating supervisors
	30	Drafting the plan of the system modification	10/1 Present to a meeting of top management	Primary focus is on the issue of revising the divisionalized system	Research → Drafting → Presentation to top meeting		Top group	A Ⓑ C Research was insufficient	A Ⓑ C Submitted data was insufficient	
	25	Promotion of the facsimile network plan	The first term: Tokyo-Osaka	To compose a project team with the operational division	Establishing the → Preparation → Construction master schedule		Telecommunication operation division	Ⓐ B C Success	Ⓐ B C Although successful, cost exceeded budget by 20%	
Business Objectives	20	Transfer of stock affairs to dealers	Complete the transfer by the end of the term	Total transfer Transfer of volunteer	Drafting → Negotiation → Preparation → Execution		X Trust Inc.	Ⓐ B C Finished successfully	Ⓐ B C You did a good job	
	15	Revising rules on division duties	A trial will be made at the operational branch in Osaka	Establishing a revision committee whose primary concern is performance fields	Research meeting → Drafting a tentative plan → Discussion and revision → Execution		Operational branch in Osaka	A B Ⓒ Unsatisfactory because of poor results	A B Ⓒ Use this time's experience to redo it	
	10	Rationalizing the service section	15% personnel reduction	Concentrate on passenger cars and telephone	Drafting → Negotiation → Execution			A Ⓑ C Reduce personnel by 10%	A Ⓑ C Fortunately, there was no trouble	

Fig. 13.4. An example of the administration department's target card.

Objectives	Weight	Measures	Person / Frequency	Method	Schedule	Responsible section	Self-evaluation	Supervisor evaluation
Self-improvement and development objectives	50	Dispatching staff section members to foreign law schools	Mr. Aoyama	Replacements must be graduates of next year's group	Leave Japan → Matriculation (Execution)	The education section	Ⓐ B C Everything proceeded according to the plan	Ⓐ B C The vacancy needs to be filled until next spring.
	50	Conducting study meetings concerning environmental relations	Once every other month	Lectures by specialists Discussion	Execution Execution Execution	The group outside the company	A B Ⓒ It was held only once due to difficulties in getting lecturers	A B C

Modification of objectives: None

State of progress: lack of efforts by the business division revision committee study meetings concerning environmental relations not yet held

Advisory item: contact between staff section and service section was encouraged

The process is midterm follow-up

First term objectives

Notes

From Toshiba (ed.), *Ibid*, pp. 179-180

Fig. 13.4 *(Continued)*

schedule, etc. should be registered on the "Target Card" (See Fig. 13.3) per person or per workgroup.

This Target Card has a matrix form where the topic's title will be described in rows and all the other items will be positioned in columns.

An example of a Target Card is shown in Fig. 13.4.

5. Methods of Investigating the Topics for Improvement: Inventorization of Operations and VV Analysis

In order to find out which topics are objects for improvement in administrative departments, Japanese companies often take the following steps:

(1) Inventorization of Operations; in other words an inventory (list) is made of the operations.
(2) Determination of the topics for improvement through VV Analysis (or Value and Volume Analysis), etc.

5.1. *Inventorying the operations*

5.1.1. *Preparation of the "Operations Item List"*

As the first step for making an inventory of current operations, an Operations Item List (see Fig. 13.5) must first be made.

The main purpose of improvement of indirect or administrative departments is to increase efficiency (or reduce the lead-time) of each department's operations and to reduce the number of employees in the department. For this purpose, the function of each operation should be reconsidered taking into account its necessity (value) and costs (man hours spent).

Thus the "operations item list" is first prepared, to classify the operations hierarchically into the following three classes:

(1) Large class: Jobs which should be essentially done in the department in question.
(2) Middle class: Each job in the large class will be divided into the middle class jobs.

classification of operations			appearance	classification	class code		
large class	middle class	small class	note 1	note 2	large	middle	small
purchasing			daily		01		
	ordering		daily			01	
		check of order slip	daily	R			01
		ordering (customer, volume, date), Tel, Fax	daily	R			02
		posting in the inventory sheet	daily	R			03
		filing the order slips	daily	R			04
	inspection of delivered goods		daily			02	
		stamping on the receipt	daily				01
		classification of delivery slips	daily				02
		inspection of delivered goods	daily				03

Not 1 : operation's appearance cycle (daily or monthly, etc.)

Fig. 13.5. Operations item list.

(3) Small class: Each job in the middle class will be divided into the small class jobs.

Examples of large class jobs are the purchasing of materials, sales support, market research, etc. Examples of middle class jobs that belong to the large class of "purchasing of materials", for instance, are negotiation, ordering, report preparation, inspection of the delivered goods, inventory control, voucher preparation, etc. Small class jobs are the ones into which the above middle class job is divided, so that each small class job usually corresponds to one employee who is in charge of this job. However, several small class jobs are often assigned to a single member of staff.

The classification could further be made as four classes rather than three classes: large, upper middle, lower middle, and small classes.

The total number of small class job items that belong to one department should be approximately 200. Various related events such as committee or working group meetings, presentations of group improvement activities, and so on should also be included.

The additional reference rows in the Operations Item List (Fig. 13.5) will show the following. This point also implies the need for further division of small class jobs.

(1) division of routine and non-routine jobs
(2) difference in processing cycle (or processing frequency)

Moreover, any job that takes especially long hours (over 300 hours) in total over the year should be separated. On the other hand, if plural jobs are effectively processed by a single number of staff, those jobs should together be classified as a single job.

5.1.2. *Preparation of the "Operations Inventory Table" (Necessary-Time Matrix)*

This is the second step for the inventorization of operations. The "Operations Inventory Table (or Necessary-Time Matrix)" is the table on which the operations items (or jobs) specified by the operation item list (Fig. 13.5)

class code		large class: 01								
	middle class	**01**					**02**			
	small class	(total)	01	02	03	04	(total)	01	02	03
time of processing per day, processing time	actual time per one time operation — A		0.08	0.17	0.08	0.1		0.17	0.08	0.08
	times of processing per day — B		10	10	15	2		3	4	4
	processing time — C=A*B		0.8	1.7	1.2	0.2		0.5	0.3	0.3
	occurring cycle (yearly, monthly, daily)		day	day	day	day		day	day	day
	times of processing per year — D		244	244	244	244		12	244	244
	total necessary processing hours — C*D	951.6	195.2	414.8	292.8	48.8	152.4	6	73.2	73.2
types of processing	consideration		10	30						
	document reading — routine		40	70						
	document reading — non-routine		30		10					
	report preparation — routine — use of word-processor		10		85					
	report preparation — routine — manual writing		52		208					
	report preparation — non-routine — use of word-processor									
	report preparation — non-routine — manual writing			50						
	other transmitting tools		53	265						
	telephone use									
	meeting or training — in house — move								30	
	meeting or training — in house — actual operation								35	
	meeting or training — out office — move									
	meeting or training — out office — actual operation									
	waiting, etc.					48.8	65	2		

Fig. 13.6. Operations Inventory Table (or Necessary-Time Matrix).

are shown in columns and the characteristics of each job (especially the necessary-time) are shown in rows (see Fig. 13.6).

The procedure for preparation of the Operations Inventory Table is as follows:

(1) The processing type must be examined for each job item in the small class, where the processing type stands for routine or non-routine, telephone use or other transmitting instruments, etc.
(2) The actual time spent on each job per operation must be measured for each individual staff, together with the times of processing per day, the occurring cycle, times of processing per year, and finally the total necessary processing hours (see the right side of Fig. 13.6).
(3) The total annual processing hours will be summarized for each department.

How to measure the actual necessary time will be the key point in making the Operation Inventory Table. For this measurement there are two approaches:

1. Industrial Engineering approach
   (a) Stopwatch Method
   (b) Work-Sampling Method
2. Experience-based estimation approach

A clerical operation is the combination of various simple operating elements such as classification, writing, computation and judgment, etc. Therefore, anyone can determine the necessary time of his/her job or operation by summing up the elemental processing time which he/she estimated. Then each individual person will write his/her processing time individually on the Operations Inventory Table as a self-proposal.

When the above two approaches are compared, the industrial engineering approach takes much more time to collect the data and the experience-based approach is much easier, so I therefore recommend the second approach.

The experience-based estimation method may induce people to overestimate the necessary processing time so that the workforce in their department will not be reduced. However, their proposed processing times could be verified by comparing them with the time-data of similar jobs in other departments, or by running some sample tests.

5.2. Determination of the topics for improvement

Next is the step of investigating and determining the topics or operations which need improvement. For this purpose there are the following three methods:

(1) VV analysis
(2) Satisfaction Deployment (a type of QFD)
(3) Comparison between the ideal or correct workforce and the actual workforce in each department.

5.2.1. VV analysis (Value and Volume Analysis)

After preparation of the Operations Inventory table, the VV analysis will be conducted. As shown in Fig. 13.7, the VV analysis displays various job items according to the priority of the job's Value on the horizontal axis, and shows the histogram of the necessary time of each job as Volume on the vertical axis.

By using this figure, those jobs that have lower Values and nevertheless have higher Volumes will be taken as problematic jobs, or as topics to be improved.

Taking the example shown in Fig. 13.7, the reader can apparently find out that the Volume (= time) of the "general affairs (miscellaneous) operation" which is priority 8 exceeds that of the "ordering operation" which is priority 2. Therefore, it follows that the "general affairs operation" is actually a problem to be improved. Similar problems can be found in the sixth priority job.

In general, the procedure for streamlining the current operation and creating surplus manpower is as follows:

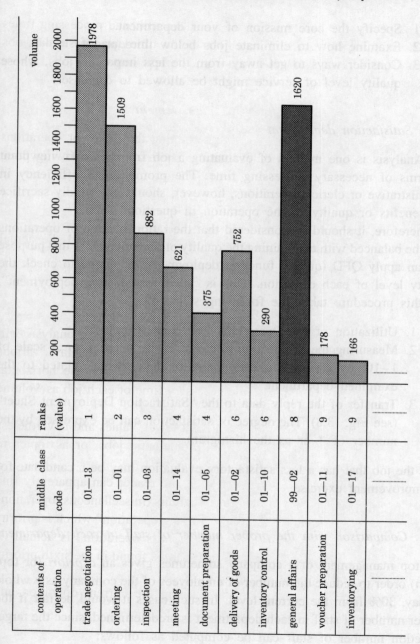

Fig. 13.7. "VV Analysis" applied to the purchasing department in the middle class.

Step 1. Specify the core mission of your department.
Step 2. Examine how to eliminate jobs below third priority.
Step 3. Consider ways to get away from the less important jobs, whose quality level of service might be allowed to decrease.

5.2.2. *Satisfaction deployment*

VV Analysis is one method of evaluating a job from a Costs viewpoint in terms of necessary processing time. The promotion of efficiency in administrative or clerical operations, however, should not blindly sacrifice the benefits or quality of the operation in question.

Therefore, it should be considered that the rationalization of operations must be balanced with maintaining the quality of operations. For this purpose we can apply QFD (quality function deployment) technique to check the quality level of each operation. This is called "satisfaction deployment", and this procedure takes the following steps:

Step 1. Utilization of the Operations Item List (Fig. 13.5)
Step 2. Measuring the satisfaction grade of each operation on a scale of 1–10, by giving a questionnaire to departments related to the examined department.
Step 3. Transfer of the reply data to the "Satisfaction Deployment Sheet" (see Fig. 13.8). The degree of satisfaction can be expressed by the number of * or as the histogram.

Thus the job that has a less satisfactory evaluation may be a candidate for an improvement exercise.

5.2.3. *Comparison with the proper number of staff in each department*

The top management of a company sometimes gives an *a priori* (or top-down) order to reduce the number of employees of the company as a whole by, say, 30% from the current level. In such cases it would be fair if the proper number of staff in each department is predetermined, since the target reduction number of staff can be computed as follows:

classification of operations			degree of satisfaction
large class	middle class	small class	
purchasing	ordering	check of order slip	*****
		selection of suppliers	*****
		volume of order size at a time	**
		delivery timing	*****
		posting in the inventory sheet	*****
		filing the order slips	******
	inspection of delivered goods	stamping on the receipt	***
		classification of delivery slips	****
		inspection of delivered goods	***

Fig. 13.8. Satisfaction development table: An example.

Target reduction number of workforce at each department = current number of employees in the department − proper number of employees of the same department.

How the proper workforce number can be determined will be explained in Sec. 6.

6. Estimation of the Correct Number of Employees and Evaluation of Actual Workforce

When it comes to the productivity improvement in administrative or service departments, the ultimate purpose of this is to reduce the operation lead-time for the customers and/or cost reduction by reducing the size of the workforce.

Therefore, it is useful to predetermine the proper number of employees in each department. That number is utilized to determine the target employee reduction and also to motivate people to reach that workforce number.

Thus let us consider in this section the formula to determine the proper workforce and to evaluate the actual performance of work-force reduction. The author's proposal here is the utilization of a single regression analysis or a multiple regression analysis.

6.1. *The corporate-wide (or departmental) proper number of administrative employees (CNE)*

This will be estimated and determined by using the following formula:

$$CNE = A \times [annual \; sales] + B \qquad (1)$$

Equation (1) is a single regression equation estimated by use of the data of the past ten years or so. Here the data of actual workforce number of the corporate or departmental level will be used on the left-hand side. The data of actual annual sales will be introduced on the right-hand side. Since this formula may be too approximate for use in each individual department, the formula below is an alternative.

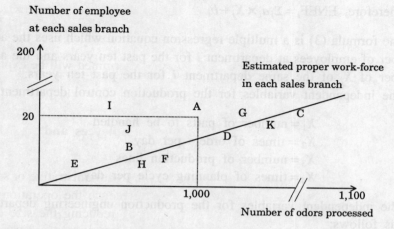

Fig. 13.9. Estimation of proper number of employee for each sales branch.

6.2. *The departmental proper number of employee (DNE)*

This will be estimated and determined by the formula below. Suppose that there are many sections or branches that belong to department i (e.g. many sales branches that belong to a sales department). Then,

DNE of each section of department $i = a_i$ [annual number of operation of each section in the department i] $+ b$ (2)

where the "annual number of operations" is, for instance, the number of orders processed, the total amount of sales, and the total number of training days, etc. (see Fig. 13.9). For estimation of the above Eq. (2) the number of employees of sales branches A through K and the number of orders processed at these branches must be utilized as data.

6.3. *The estimation of the proper number of employees in each factory's administrative department (ENEF)*

ENEF may be dependent on the various factors which are peculiar to each department. Thus I will use the independent variables X_i at each factory's administrative department i.

Therefore, $\text{ENEF}_i = \Sigma_j a_i \times X_j + b_i$ (3)

The formula (3) is a multiple regression equation which uses the actual number of employees at department i for the past ten years and the actual number of X_j of the same department i for the past ten years.

The independent variables for the production control department are:

$X_1 =$ number of parts to be handled
$X_2 =$ times of orders per day
$X_3 =$ number of production lines
$X_4 =$ times of planning cycle per day

The independent variables for the production engineering department are as follows:

$X_1 =$ annual amount of facility orders
$X_2 =$ annual amount of tooling and dies orders
$X_3 =$ annual amount of productivity improvement in terms of costs
$X_4 =$ number of designers
$X_5 =$ number of prototypes

The independent variables at the quality assurance department are:

$X_1 =$ number of customer's claims
$X_2 =$ amount of improvement in terms of costs
$X_3 = \Sigma a_i \times$ (inspection time per inspection item i)

For the manufacturing departments the following formula can be applied:

Number of indirect staff in the manufacturing
department $= a \times$ number of direct workers $+ b$.

7. Performance Evaluation in the Management-by-Objectives system

The performance of each manager at various hierarchical levels and/or each work-group at the bottom level must be evaluated periodically; that is, either twice a year, quarterly or monthly.

Such evaluation also links up with the "productivity" measurement of the administrative or white-collar departments. The "productivity" implies an actual reduction in the number of workforce hours described in the Sec. 5.1.2.

Since the evaluation of performance will later be reflected on the merit rating of each employee for their bonus and/or promotion, it should be as fair as possible. Thus the evaluation process conducted in Japanese companies is as follows:

Step 1. First the subordinate employee will evaluate his/her performance and discuss how he/she achieved the target in the preceding period.

Step 2. He will report his evaluation to the superior manager, and both of them will discuss the employee's performance and his evaluation.

Step 3. When agreement has been reached through their discussion, the superior manager will finally decide the evaluation and write it on the "Target Card" mentioned above (see Figs. 13.3 and 13.4).

Step 4. Sometimes presentations of MBO results by small-groups or individuals will be made to each department.

As mentioned above, the results of evaluations will be linked to the merit rating of each employee, but the result of this MBO system should be reflected on the short-term bonus amount which is additional to the basic salary that corresponds to the amount of minimum living standards. This is the conventional, merit-rating system used in Japanese companies.

8. Career Development Program

For productivity improvement in administrative departments, it is very important to cultivate individual ability. Important examples are the various capabilities of using information technology, such as the use of office-computers for word-processing, intranet and internet utilization and the introduction of ERP (Enterprise Resource Planning) information systems for rationalizing main business operations.

Such human ability should be cultivated through CDP (Career Development Program), which should be geared to the MBO system. Thus the MBO

CDP card			CDP plan					Name					Development program (from the time of joining the company to 10 years after)
Date of plan	Position at time of plan	1st year	2nd year	3rd year	4th year	5th year	6th year	7th year	8th year	9th year	10th year		
1975 Nov.	Department of X		Magnetron examination experiment	The same as left negative pole design	The same as left positive pole design	Magnetron department of output design	Magnetron magnetism design					Magnetron general engineer
	In charge of X											
1976 Nov.	The same as above			The same as above	The same as above	The same as above						
1977 Nov.	The same as above			The same as above	The same as above							

From Toshiba (ed.), *Mokuhyo Kanri shinko*, pp. 58-59

Fig. 3.10. An example of the CDP Card.

needs to establish the "career development target" as one of its objectives beside the ordinary operations' targets.

It will be desirable that CDP has the following three phased targets (these points are also written on the CDP Card; see Fig. 13.10):

(1) Establishing a "career cultivation vision" for each employee which covers the next ten years.
(2) Preparation of "three year career development plan tasks" or yearly skills improvement plans.

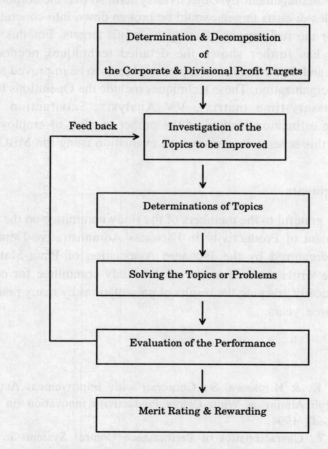

Fig. 13.11. Total framework of the Monden's Kaizen system.

(3) Yearly evaluation of the achievement level of the plan, which is examined between the person in question and his/her supervisor, and then revision of the three year plan on a rolling basis.

9. Conclusion

This conclusion will briefly summarize the outline of Monden's Kaizen System (see Fig. 13.11). The author proposed to link a managerial accounting system to the Management-by-Objectives system, so that the corporate-wide profit and sales & costs targets would be broken down into concrete targets for action for the realizations of company profit targets. For this purpose, this chapter has further shown the detailed techniques needed in the investigation and determination of topics or objects to be improved at various levels in the organization. These techniques include the Operations Inventory Table (necessary-time matrix), VV Analysis, Satisfaction Deployment, and an estimation method of the proper number of employees. The final step of this scheme is performance evaluation using the MBO system.

Acknowledgments

The writer is grateful to the members of the study committee on the Methods of Improvement of Productivity in Factories Administrative Departments, which was organized by the Japanese Association of Plant-Maintenance (JAPM). The writer was Chairman of this study committee for compiling and systematically grasping the results of presentations by many practitioners for about three years.

References

1. Ishikawa, K. & Hirokawa, S., Corporate-wide Improvement Activities of Topy Kogyo Aiming at White-Colors Productivity Innovation (in Japanese) (unpublished), 1994.
2. Monden, Y., Characteristics of Performance Control Systems in Japanese Corporations (in English) Monden, Y. & Sakurai, M., eds. Japanese Management

Accounting: A World Class Approach to Profit Management (Productivity Press, 1989), 413–423.

3. Monden, Y., Management Accounting System for Productivity Improvement in the Administrative Departments (in Japanese), Kigyo-Kaikei, Vol. 47, No. 4, 1995, 31–38.

4. Monden, Y. & JAPM(ed.), Practical Methods of Improvement on Productivity in Factory's Administrative Departments, Japan Association of Plant-Maintenance. (in Japanese), 1995.

5. Nakamori, K., Computation Method of the Standard Number of Staff in the Indirect Departments for Use of Re-engineering (in Japanese), Management 21 (May, 1994), 74–78.

6. Nakamori, K. & Ozawa, I., Effective Utilization of the Standard Number of Staff for Re-engineering (in Japanese), Management 21 (June, 1994), 76–80.

7. Toshiba Electric Co. (ed.), Cultivation of Management-By-Objectives, Aoba Publ. Co. (in Japanese), 1977.

Chapter 14

Reform Works in Administrative and Indirect Departments: The Case Study of Z Company

SHUFUKU HIRAOKA

Japanese companies have almost excluded their production waste by using JIT, TQC and TPM. As a result, companies have achieved high productivity in quality, quantity (time) and cost. However, in administrative and indirect departments, they have not sufficiently improved their productivity. Therefore, in the prosperous period of the second half of the 1980s, Japanese businesses had a high cost structure. In many Japanese companies, this problem was often solved by making staff redundant, which some Japanese called 'restructuring'.

On the other hand, some companies which have achieved high performance levels have successfully utilized 'Kaizen', not only in their production departments but also in their administrative and indirect departments. In these companies, top management set high goals for the company and its employees improved various working procedures to achieve these goals. The surplus manpower that occurred with those improvements has been shifted to new businesses and creative works. As a result, companies could hold layoff to a minimum.

We participated in a committee which studied practical methods in improving productivity in a factory's administrative department,[a] the

[a]It was organized by the Japan Institute of Plant Maintenance.

chief examiner of which was Yasuhiro Monden.[b] Then, I heard some cases of productivity improvement activities in indirect departments in Japanese companies. In this chapter, one of those success cases is discussed.

1. The Outline of ZPM

One company is introduced in this chapter, which will be called Z company. It has performed TPM activities in both its production and indirect departments. Its reform activities were called ZPM, since they contained both productive maintenance and productivity management, in Z company. The outline of ZPM's goals is shown in Fig. 14.1.

In indirect departments especially, the importance of management was emphasized. ZPM's promotion headquarters were organized as a project team, playing the role of the promotion secretariat. ZPM also practised innovation in working practices in indirect departments, that consisted of various activities to manage productivity.

First, top management decided on long-range company goals. Next, all employees improved their organisational climate and working procedures to achieve those goals. ZPM activities were redivided into the following three blocks.[c]

1. Development block: improving works in R&D department.
2. Production block: improving works in the production department.
3. Indirect block: improving works in sales and marketing, planning, and general affairs, the accounting department, and the design and study experiment of each block except the development block.

---

[b]Professor of Management Accounting and Production Management, University of Tsukuba.

[c]The number of employees on 31st March 1993 was 6,606. The number of people in indirect departments was approximately 3,000. There were about 1,000 people who belonged to the R&D teams. 2,000 people or less are members of the 'indirect' block.

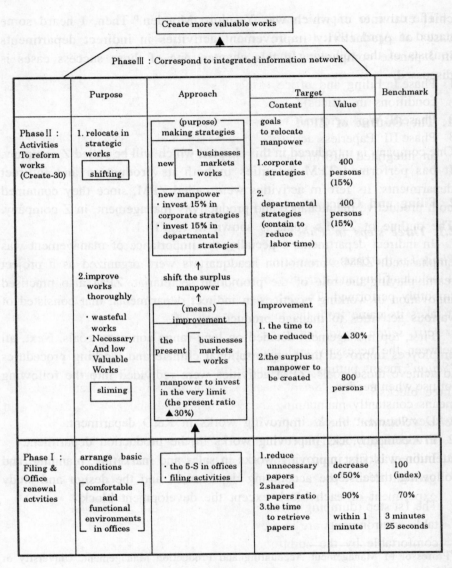

Fig. 14.1. The outline of ZPM's goals.

Source: Japan Institute of Plant Maintenance (the editorial representative is Monden, Y.), Practical Methods Improvement Productivity Factory's Administrative Department (Japan Institute of Plant Maintenance, Tokyo, 1995), 80.

The drive to improve work in administrative and indirect departments started in April 1991. It is placed as one of eight activities[d] in ZPM, and consists of the following three phases:

1. Phase I: Filing and office renewal activities (arranging basic working conditions in offices)
2. Phase II: Work reform (Create-30) activities (scraping and building works)
3. Phase III: Paperless activities (that is, those which do not use paper but an integrated information network)

2. Filing and Office Renewal Activities: Phase I

2.1. *Three steps in Phase I*

Phase I is the basis of work improvement implemented in most companies. It includes filing and *Kaizen* in offices. *Phase I* activities were comparatively smoothly performed. The 5-S movement was implemented in this phase. It takes its name from the initials of five Japanese words that start with s: *seiri, seiton, seiso, seiketsu, and shitsuke.* "*Seiri*" means differentiating between the necessary and unnecessary and discarding the unnecessary. "*Seiton*" means putting and keeping things in order so that they are ready for use when needed. "*Seiso*" means keeping the workplace clean. "*Seiketsu*" means constantly maintaining the 3-S mentioned above, *seiri, seiton,* and *seiso.* "*Shitsuke*" means following procedures in the workshop.[1,2]

In Z company, used papers had been almost unified to A4 size. Therefore, attention was first paid to filing. *Phase I* was further redivided into the following three steps.

1. The 1st step (dumping): Unnecessary papers are removed and uncomfortable environments are improved. Moreover, this step makes the offices comfortable by the addition of plants.

---

[d]Besides this, there are activities which improve production and product development, job training, initial phase equipment stage checks, planned maintenance and so on.

2. The 2nd step (filing): Papers are functionally classified again. Unnecessary papers are thrown away again. In principle, private files should be abolished. The system for classifying individual 'know-how' files is clarified. All papers are presented for common use, with some files, exceptionally, being for private or confidential use (for example, performance-related files on staff, which the chief of a section holds).

3. The 3rd step (implementing the mechanism): This step is in order to implement the mechanism and rules to establish the activities of the first and second steps.

Small-group activities were performed throughout Z Company and ZPM promotion headquarters gathered 20 people from various places to act as the examination members. Then they looked over each office and checked whether or not there were any unnecessary papers according to the checklist. If there were no problems, the qualification of the first step pass was given and an adhesive label was pasted to the office. Next, an inspection was made for second step filing. The examination members were told to go around each office again one month later and encourage people in the office. Thus, the second step was begun.

2.2. *The results of activities*

The height of papers after activities: the piled height of papers was measured in file meters (fm).

1. The piled height of papers thrown away was 4,535 fm. Before *Phase I* was done, the average height of paper per person was 2.9 fm. After throwing away unnecessary papers, it became about 1.7 fm (Fig. 14.2). There were few private files whose contents could not be understood.

2. Reducing the time taken to retrieve papers: Before *Phase I* was done, when the person who was not engaged in certain paperwork answered or took a query, the time taken was about 4 minutes. After Phase I, this became about 40 seconds (Fig. 14.3). The response time to inquiring by telephone from the customer became about one minute. Before *Phase I* was completed, the number of departments that could find the required

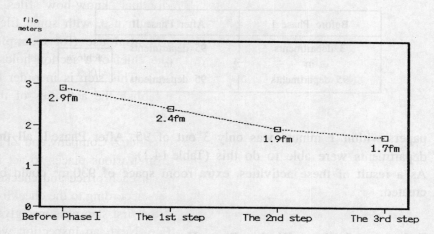

Fig. 14.2. How high papers were piled up? (the average one person had).

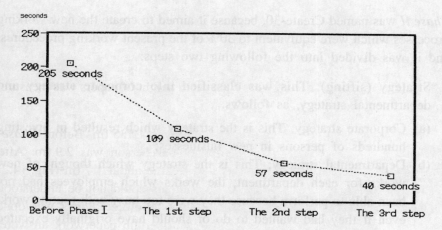

Fig. 14.3. The change of time taken to retrieve papers.

Table 14.1. The number of departments that can take out
required papers within 1 minute.

Before Phase I		After Phase II	
3 departments in 95 departments	→	95 departments in 95 departments	achieve 100%

papers within 1 minute was only 3 out of 95. After Phase I, all the
departments were able to do this (Table 14.1).
3. As a result of these activities, extra room space of 930 m^2 could be
created.

3. Reforming Indirect Works: Phase II

3.1. *Two steps in Phase II*

Phase II was named Create-30, because it aimed to create the new working
processes which were equivalent to 30% of the present working procedures,
and it was divided into the following two steps:

1. Strategy (sifting): This was classified into corporate strategy and
   departmental strategy, as follows:
   (a) Corporate strategy: This is the strategy which resulted in investing
       hundreds of persons in new businesses;
   (b) Departmental strategy: This is the strategy which thought of new
       works for each department; the works which employees had not
       been able to perform because they were too busy with routine work,
       even if they had wanted to do or should have originally executed
       these tasks to improve the performance of each department.
       Departmental strategy is rather different from general strategy. It
       means aggressively creating new works which seem to be necessary.

2. Improvement: This improved the working processes which are carried out at present to create the surplus manpower which was necessary for this strategy to be realized. Z Company repeated the cycle to steadily shift the surplus manpower created in the process of these activities to new works. The two points of improvement activities in Z Company are as follows:

   (a) Overall: This means improving works related to some or all departments.
   (b) Departmental level: This means improving works within each department unit.

The theme of re-engineering is of overall importance. This must be accomplished at the same time as arranging information infrastructures. It occurred as a new problem during Create-30's process.

3.2. *The characteristics of Create-30*

The characteristics of Create-30 are as follows:

1. It is at one with Z company's strategy;
2. The aim is to achieve "improvement" at the same time as employing the strategy;
3. Its aim is to thoroughly improve 30% of the working processes which are carried out at present.

Create-30 invents new works that were equivalent to 30% of the present working procedures. However, it was necessary that 30% of the present works were improved in order for new works to be done in future and for the surplus manpower to occur. Firstly, this included a long-range management vision. Next, a long-range plan was settled on and management created a new policy. Create-30 was thus placed in management by their new policy, and was executed.

In Create-30, one main aim is 'to improve indirect works' and its purpose is 'to create surplus manpower for strategic relocation'. In other words, it does not improve a company's indirect works in order to lay off employees.

Its aim is to strengthen employees and to invest the surplus manpower gained into both strategies and new works. "To improve indirect works" with regard to improvements in productivity in indirect departments is also a means of securing people as necessary to perform strategies and new works.

The number of people in indirect departments was computed as 2,800.

$$2,800 \text{ persons} \times 30\% = 840 \text{ persons}$$

Here, we take 800 as an average.

The surplus manpower of 800 people was created by the improvements in present works. These personnel are then invested in strategies and new works. Since 400 of these were invested in corporate strategy, these people left their departments. Another 400 are left to carry out new works in each department. An active unit is composed of 20–30 people per department. Each department forms an execution 'corps' and each chief director becomes each department's leader. This way of executing ZPM includes creating organisational leadership in offices and performing small-group activities. Here, each department becomes an execution unit. For promoting these activities throughout Z Company as a whole, ZPM promotion headquarters included top management, which became its secretariat. The planning headquarters settled on new management strategies. ZPM promotion headquarters, the personnel department and the planning headquarters all therefore helped to promote ZPM.

3.3. *An overview of Create-30*

The overview of Create-30 is shown in Fig. 14.4.

First, a top-management seminar was held to motivate executives and chief directors. Next, a "kickoff rally" was held. This was divided according to the departments from the 1st spread to the 4th and each was held step-by-step. The 1st spread was done as a trial in only 10 departments. Since the 2nd spread, each spread has been executed in about 20 departments. All the people concerned were gathered and the future of Z Company was discussed with them. They were clearly told that all employees must reform

```
          Top management seminar
                    ↓
              Kickoff rally
                    ↓
       Departmental strategic conference
                    ↓
      Departmental improvement conference
                    ↓
          Reports to top management
                    ↓
         Implementation and following
```

Fig. 14.4. The overview of Create-30.

the works of the whole company. After the executives and consultants talked, the chief directors expressed their opinions and motivated their staff.

After "the kickoff rally" ended, a departmental strategic planning conference was held. Here, employees planned new works that, up until now, could not have been done. They organized several teams with about 12 people per team. They shut themselves up in their meeting room for four days to argue. This led to some small meetings being held after this. As a result, people created new jobs. There was no longer any negotiation in this step and they rapidly thought of some new jobs which should be done. Then, they argued how to improve the current jobs to carry out new jobs. This was called a departmental improvement conference. Members of different teams participated in this conference for four days.

After the results of the two conferences were examined, reports were made to top management. In these, each chief director showed all the other executives the strategy and purpose behind his own department, its expected output, the ways found to allot new jobs, manpower and the time it had taken to achieve this. At the same time, the following matters were also discussed:

• How many hours will be reduced within 1 year?
• Where does the surplus manpower occur?

- When will the surplus manpower be assigned?
- Where is the surplus manpower assigned?
- How many people are assigned there?

After these reports had been made to the top management, which took about 40 minutes per department, and the reports had been approved, these plans were implemented by ZPM. Finally, the contents of the two conferences were incorporated into the company management by the creation of new policies. At the same time, each of the chief directors performed "following" and "interim review of performance" in the management by policy. Also, improvement cases were heard every month. The executive team, and various people who belonged to different departments, visited all offices. A consulting activities bulletin board was installed, introducing and explaining the present situation and future company and office activities. ZPM's secretariat also implemented an activity called "the monthly progress following". Those activities were all implemented according to plan. 400 people required for corporate strategy left each department and were almost all better invested in new positions.

However, there were still some company-wide problems to be solved. These extended to involving some or all departments in re-engineering. For example, one problem consisted of improving processes to manage agreed delivery dates, making new man-day systems and new accounting systems. In Z Company, each of these projects was developed and they were performed concurrently. At present, both the improvement activities and other projects in each department have been progressing simultaneously.

3.4. *Departmental strategic planning conference*

This conference consisted of about ten steps in the four-day schedule. All the members argued on various matters and finally completed their departmental strategy. First, they decided on "the mission statement" of their department and "the domain" of this mission (i.e. the area of activities within their department). Then they tried to clarify what they should accomplish within their mission. Of course, the elements of customer satisfaction (CS), employee satisfaction (ES) and competitive advantage were considered in this process. As a result of this, what should be done in each department was gradually clarified and discussed. Here, the change in external environment, the strengths and weaknesses of Z Company and the strengths and weaknesses of their competitors were discussed, along with related business opportunities and threats. Finally, the impact of these factors on department performances was analyzed, and the unimportant factors were ignored.

This process is similar to that of traditional strategic planning. However, this must be reformed according to the situation in each department. In the case of corporate strategy, it is mainly businesses that are evaluated. On the other hand, in departmental strategy, each department's works are evaluated. The theory is to reform poor aspects of departments and, in order to do this, techniques like PPM (product portfolio management) are introduced as tools, and strategies are thus settled on. Departments decided when to invest, who to invest and how many people to invest in for their new works within each department. But, all departments did not make it clear who to invest in concretely in this process.

3.5. *Departmental improvement conference*

This conference consisted of eight steps in a 4-day schedule. After each mission was made clear for each department, the department's present function was investigated according to this mission. Then, these functions were ranked into three classes of importance (high, medium, low).

First, the mission of the core function of each department, i.e. department output, was made clear. For example, in the sales department, this was expressed by aims such as "earning a billion yen of sales". Therefore, salespeople visited their customers, made written estimates and performed various works. It is important for them to achieve their goals. In short, they had to decide what to achieve as their core mission.

Next, departments prioritised each of their functions into three classes. At the 'least important' level, there were 200–300 types of work per department. A number was given to each work according to its importance.

Z Company needed to regard 30% of its present processes as unimportant and think out ways of cutting these out.

It was quite difficult to cut out 30% of the present processes from the beginning but it was possible to cut out 10%. After 10% of the processes had been cut out, they considered improving the 20% that had been left behind. However, they were restricted in making office automation (OA) or information systems, because wasteful working processes are wasteful even if they are automated.

Departments first discussed stopping wasteful working processes. If there were some processes that could not be stopped, ways were considered to decrease these. Automation was still severely restricted. Instead of this, they thought of another way of doing things. Finally, departments were obligated to create the surplus manpower that was equivalent to 30% of the present work.

There are various options for implementing the above-mentioned improvement. One is to look at work-flow. There are some work-flows in one department that are related to or cross over with other departments. After the characteristics of each department had been understood, each department examined ways to improve workflow. One way is to integrate some organizations and abolish others. Because there were several departments in Z Company, it had various organizations. Several functions overlapped between departments. These were gathered and integrated into one department.

3.6. *The results of these activities*

One index to show the results of *Phase* activities is the reduced working hours that were achieved. This was considered to be more important than the total hours spent on works in Z Company. Many works within the company change every month, so the time spent on each work was not measured too strictly: even if this had been done, working practices can always change in future. Therefore, unnecessary works were made clear and the time spent on them was measured accurately. This was the target time to reduce, and was estimated at 137, 000 hours. In June 1993, 71, 000 hours had been reduced. By March 1994, this fell a little below the planned

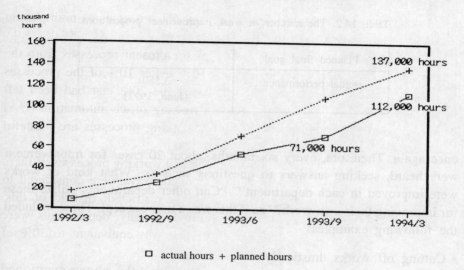

Fig. 14.5. The change of working hours to be reduced.

time. However, 112, 000 hours had still been reduced (Fig. 14.5). The planned number of improvement propositions was 6, 100. In June 1993, 3, 580 had already been performed (see Table 14.2).

Finally, 400 people had left each department. Most of these people were invested in one of the following corporate strategies:

1. The strategy of new products and businesses to encourage future sales growth.
2. The strategy of information systems and accounting in order to strengthen management function.
3. The strategy of the project team for cost reduction which is connected with profit, merchandising etc.

There were also some shifts, such as the transference to strategic subsidiaries and retirement. Also, another 400 people were moved to new functions within each department. After the promotion headquarters inspected each department every six months, the workforce needed to be stirred up

Table 14.2. The number of work improvement propositions.

Planned final goal	6,100
actual performance	3,580 (June, 1993)

once again. Therefore, every six months, about 20 cases for improvement were heard, seeking answers to questions such as "What kind of works were improved in each department?" "Can other departments utilize these for improving their own work?" as if this was a new concept. These included the following examples:

- Cutting off works drastically.
- Improving workflow.
- Reconsidering and improving flow of the procedures for bookkeeping and slips.
- Integrating organizations or abolishing them.
- Making OA.
- Preparing a practice manual.

3.7. *Create-30 collection and actual performance monthly reports*

Departments held an 'announcement' meeting about some improvement cases, which was called the "Create-30 collection" like a fashion-show so that it remained informal. Actual performance monthly reports were also issued and distributed to all employees each month.

3.8. *Investigating the possibility of achieving goals*

At first, each department investigated the possibility of achieving the goal of reducing 30% of the present works in each department in the planning stage from the 1st to the 4th spread. For example, it was reported that the accounting department and the quality control department had already reached 30% and the service department had not reached 30%. Also, departments looked at what manpower had been created from each department for corporate strategies.

3.9. *Managing input and output of persons*

People were rated as S (super) class, A, B and C. Only people in the S and A categories left each department to work on corporate strategy. The ousting of lower ranks from each department was not permitted in Z company in order to raise each department's performance. The personnel department led this input and output of staff, and people in S and A classes were compulsorily selected for corporate strategies.

3.10. *Some future problems*

In Create-30, the basic unit of activity was each department. Therefore, each department had improved their working processes and functions, since the original problems occurred among departments and their functions. These problems have been solved by some projects. However, not all problems have yet been solved.

In Z Company, the way of solving these problems is by re-engineering. For re-engineering to be implemented, an information network and sharing database must be built. Therefore, a network was made and an infrastructure was set up. However, departments must know what is arranged and utilized as a database and they need to know whether they can operate it efficiently. This must be linked with some problems in workflow to be improved in Z Company as a whole. Z Company tried to restructure their organization, because it had been much too subdivided. It consisted of 75 departments and the numbers of sections were about 3 times as much as their departments. Therefore, part of them had to be integrated or abolished.

The cycle of ZPM ended in April 1994. How should re-engineering be promoted in future? It would be important to seek an answer to this.

4. Conclusion

In the past, the 5-S movement has acted as the basis of "Kaizen" in many Japanese companies, and it has already penetrated indirect departments. In Z company, this belonged to the activities grouped as "Filing & office renewal activities". Basically, all unnecessary activities were scrapped, and methods of filing were thoroughly reconsidered. It was emphasized that anyone should be able to retrieve the necessary papers immediately.

Strategy and improvement comprised the activities to reform indirect works in Z company. The former meant thinking of corporate strategies and new works for each department. The latter meant creating the surplus manpower needed to perform strategies and new works. They called these activities together *Create-30*. This consisted of the following steps: "top management seminar", "kickoff rally", "departmental strategic planning conference", "departmental improvement conference", "reports to top management", and "implementation and following".

The *top management seminar* and *kickoff rally* were the activities to motivate all staff of Z company. The *departmental strategic planning conference* included planning strategies, defining the mission and domain in each department, and determining the number of people needed to perform new works and corporate strategies. The *departmental improvement conference* was the step to perform improvements equivalent to the manpower needed to perform strategies and new works in each department. Z company came up with solutions such as stopping unnecessary work, improving working methods and workflow, and integrating organizations and abolishing unnecessary ones, etc. *Reports to top management* was the step where the executives approved the results of two conferences reported to them. Lastly, in the step of *implementation and following*, such activities were performed such as "interim review of performance", "hearing of improvement cases" and "the monthly progress following". Finally, means of communication such as the "Create-30 collection" and "actual performance monthly reports" were effectively utilised.

In Create-30, the company-wide goal was decided by the ZPM promotion team, including top management. This goal was primarily to create new works equivalent to 30% of all the works. Therefore, employees needed to cut 30% of their present works. However, each department was entrusted with thinking and discussing the contents of new works, deciding on works to omit, and improving the remaining works. This is rather similar to the Kaizen costing process. In Kaizen costing, top management leads in deciding target costs in order to achieve the target profit. However, each department is entrusted with thinking out means of filling the gaps between the target costs and the estimated costs, and performing them. The reformation of indirect departments described in this chapter can be interpreted as having a similar concept to the Kaizen costing system, since Z company has been simultaneously aiming at floor-level improvement activities by employees and management improvements based on the long term goals set by top management. Japanese Cost Management seems to involve a common sense that exceeds some differences between the production department and indirect departments.

As important work functions change according to changing needs, unnecessary works can be stopped rapidly. Instead of these, new necessary works are begun within companies, which also changes the allocation of manpower. This is similar to the change in product functions in Target costing. As the functions of important products change according to changing needs, the target costs allocation ratio changes according to these functions in the Target costing process.

In future in Z Company, re-engineering will be emphasized, because this was a problem that surfaced naturally in the activities based on department units. In this chapter, I have not discussed Phase III (paperless activities, that is, an integrated information network). However, basically this emphasizes the setting up of an information infrastructure to promote re-engineering. In future, if people perform activities in order to utilize electronic information such as CALS, EC, and EDI to a higher level, depending on the utilization of Information Technology, the cost structure of indirect departments would improve much more dramatically.

References

1. Imai, M., KAIZEN: The Key to Japan's Competitive Success (McGraw-Hill, New York, 1986), 233–234.

2. Monden, Y., Toyota Production System: An Integrated Approach to Just-In-Time, 2nd edition (Industrial Engineering and Management Press, Institute of Industrial Engineers, Norcross, Geogia, 1993), 199–219.

3. Monden, Y., An Approach to Innovation, Improvement and Maintenance to Improve Productivity of Administrative Department, IE Review, Vol. 35, No. 2, 1994, 73–75.

4. Japan Institute of Efficiency Consulting, The Secret of TPM Success: Cases of Success Companies 21 (Japan Institute of Plant Maintenance, Tokyo, 1996), 244–294.

5. Japan Institute of Plant Maintenance (the Editorial Representative is Monden, Y.), Practical Methods Improvement Productivity in Factory's Administrative Department (Japan Institute of Plant Maintenance, Tokyo, 1995).

Chapter 15

A Case-Study of Operational Restructuring Using ABM

KAZUHITO MIURA, NORIKA IKEDA
and YOSHIO MATSUSHITA

1. Application of ABM to Operational Restructuring

1.1. *The relationship between business process innovation and ABM*

Cost has been one of the important indexes for measuring the utilisation of corporate resources. Cost index has been introduced because this index can be readily shared for decision making in the entire corporation. In addition, the quantitative index is highly valued because cost objectives are directly related to, and mirror, corporate objectives and performance. Diversification, however, of customers' needs and the consequent variation of products and services is imposing new tasks of cost management on corporations. First of all, one corporate section is facing difficulty in calculating the cost of a product because product line-ups, which the section deals in, are diversifying. In particular, indirect expenses of production are increasing, including charges of material procurement and inventory management, which are not easily distributed to particular products. As a result, the total cost management of respective products is becoming more challenging.

Besides production costs, the other expenses of distribution and after-care services in order to meet a broad range of services to customers are increasing. In the meantime, personnel costs occupy most of these expenses, and an effective way to measure the costs of each product and service have not yet been established.

Now a new concept has appeared to solve these issues: the concentration on "activity" for cost management. There are two kinds of application here to improve costs in terms of "activity". One is to focus on streamlining each "activity", which organises operations inside the corporation. This is based on an idea that an increase in productivity of individual "activity" will lead to the improvement of productivity of overall operations in the corporation. Another alternative is to improve business processes, which connect one "activity" to another. This results in improving the productivity of a single "activity" and, in doing so, by making joint activities more efficient.

In both cases, the investigation of operational restructuring must follow an analysis of the following factors.

- How much each operation costs and to what extent is the operation improved?
- Does each business operation create values-added inside the corporation (inside and outside the section where the operation occurs) and in the organisation of customers?
- Do indirect divisions and administrative departments of the headquarters create correspondent values to costs?
- What are the determinants that impact on operational performance and cost?

The objective of Activity Based Management (ABM) is to effect key successful factors by improving "activities", which include corporate enterprises. This is the right answer for the above questions. ABM is based on the concept of "activity cost", instead of the traditional idea of financial cost. Figure 15.1 shows major business operations in the corporation. The principle of ABM is the breakdown of business operations into smaller particles of "activities" and the distribution of diverse costs through corporate operations, including payrolls, bonuses, fringe benefits, leases, supplies charges, communication fees and depreciation expenses, in proportion to the quantity of each "activity". Because the combination of "activities" comprises corporate operations, the identification, integration, and analysis of "activity cost"

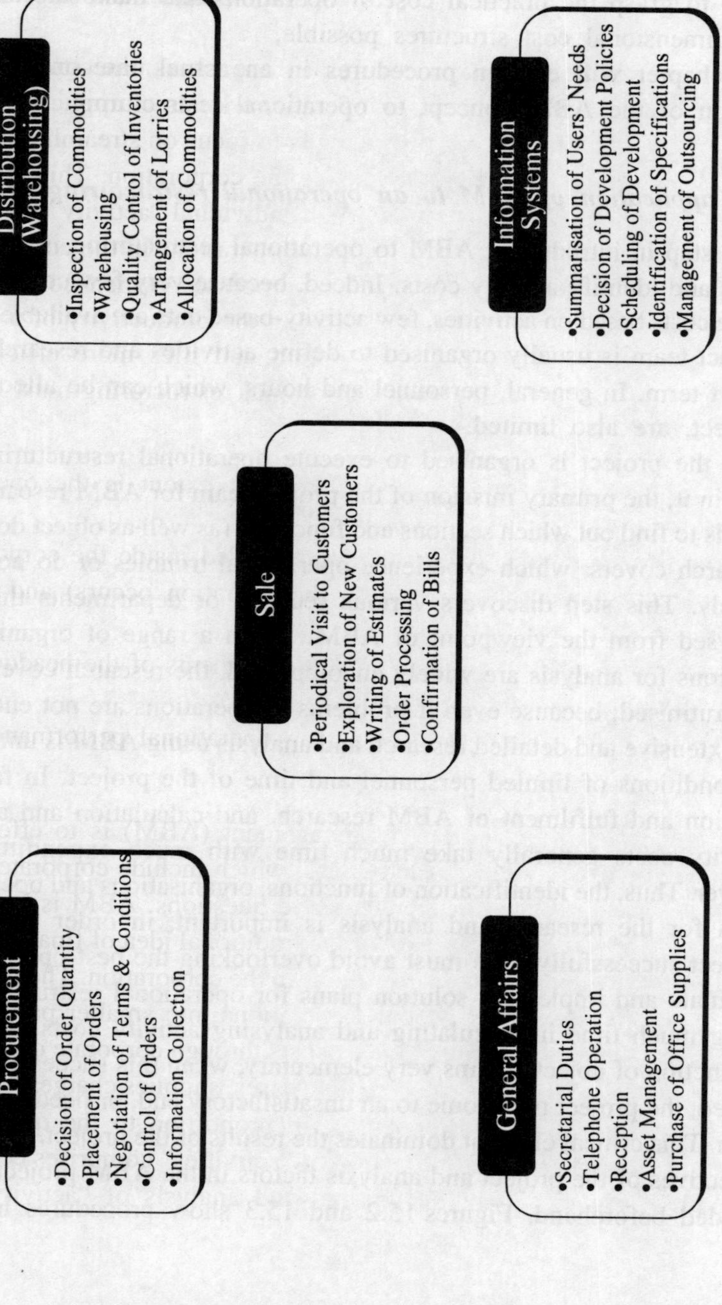

Distribution (Warehousing)
- Inspection of Commodities
- Warehousing
- Quality Control of Inventories
- Arrangement of Lorries
- Allocation of Commodities

Information Systems
- Summarisation of Users' Needs
- Decision of Development Policies
- Scheduling of Development
- Identification of Specifications
- Management of Outsourcing

Sale
- Periodical Visit to Customers
- Exploration of New Customers
- Writing of Estimates
- Order Processing
- Confirmation of Bills

Procurement
- Decision of Order Quantity
- Placement of Orders
- Negotiation of Terms & Conditions
- Control of Orders
- Information Collection

General Affairs
- Secretarial Duties
- Telephone Operation
- Reception
- Asset Management
- Purchase of Office Supplies

Fig. 15.1. Example of activities in corporation.

will help to grasp the practical cost of operations and make the analysis of multidimensional cost structures possible.

This chapter will explain procedures in an actual case-study of the application of the ABM concept to operational restructuring.

1.2. *The application of ABM to an operational restructuring project*

The first step in introducing ABM to operational restructuring is to define activities and identify activity costs. Indeed, because very few corporations recognise costs based on activities, few activity-based data are available. Thus, the project team is usually organised to define activities and research costs in a short term. In general, personnel and hours, which can be allocated to the project, are also limited.

Once the project is organised to execute operational restructuring and succeed in it, the primary mission of the project team for ABM research and analysis is to find out which sections and functions (as well as object domains) the research covers; which experience operational troubles or do not work effectively. This step discovers various sections or departments that may be analysed from the viewpoint of ABM. When a range of organisations or functions for analysis are widely encompassed, the research coverage is again scrutinised; because even if problems in operations are not enough to locate, extensive and detailed research and analysis using ABM is unrealistic under conditions of limited personnel and time of the project. In fact, the preparation and fulfilment of ABM research, and calculation and analysis of activity costs generally take much time with much expenditure and manpower. Thus, the identification of functions, organisations and operational domains for the research and analysis is important, in order to execute the project successfully. One must avoid overlooking the best opportunities to formulate and implement solution plans for operational restructuring by spending much time in calculating and analysing activity costs. Although the distinction of objects seems very elementary, when this successful factor is ignored, the project may come to an unsatisfactory end, or need additional research. This critical element dominates the results of the project. Therefore, the objectives of the project and analysis factors in the ABM project should be decided beforehand. Figures 15.2 and 15.3 show procedures in ABM

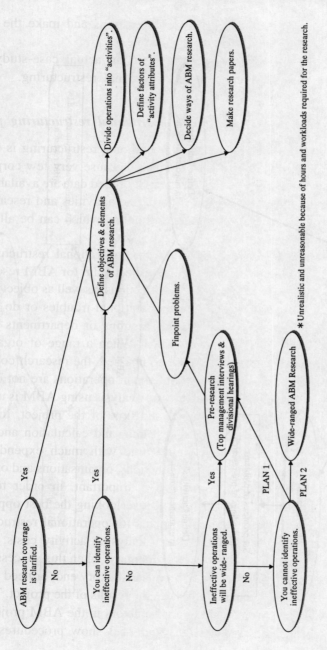

Fig. 15.2. Design of ABM research.

* Unrealistic and unreasonable because of hours and workloads required for the research.

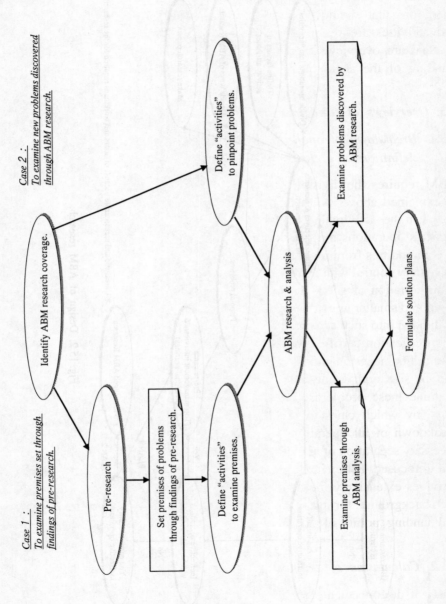

Fig. 15.3. Application of ABM.

research and analysis. Pre-research is imperative for selecting specific operations that should be refined, in order that problems can be solved, and activities are set in a unit, by which premises can be testified.

Next are overviews of the five basic steps of ABM, to deepen understanding of the above principles.

1.3. *Overviews of fundamental ABM analysis*

1.3.1. *Breakdown of operations into activities and definition of activities*

ABM requires the division of various corporate operations into activities, as explained above. After this step, individual activity should be defined; i.e. what the activity indicates or means among operations. For instance, logistics operations may be separated into activities, including "inspection of commodities from manufacturers", "stocking (or warehousing) of items", "inventory control with quality management", "allocation of goods to lorries", "transportation of goods to customers", etc. These activities can be broken down into smaller units: "Inspection of commodities from manufactures" may be divided into such activities as "confirmation of receiving slips", "collation of specification certificates with order slips", and "opening packages with check of damages on goods". Activities must be separated into an appropriate unit or size and delineated so that the unit may pinpoint problems and examine these problems. In addition, activities should be separated into parts, by which clues to problem solving can be discovered. A uniform breakdown of all operations in the corporation is unsuitable because unnecessary separation of activities makes the analysis of problems complicated and unfocused. Efficient and precise analysis requires discussing operations activities extensively; nevertheless, a certain level of activities depends on each background: for instance, the crucial factors of operational restructuring and landing points of ABM research.

1.3.2. *Calculation of activity cost*

Costs of disconnected activities are calculated by tracing general financial data to the activities. First, categorise the costs based on account title into

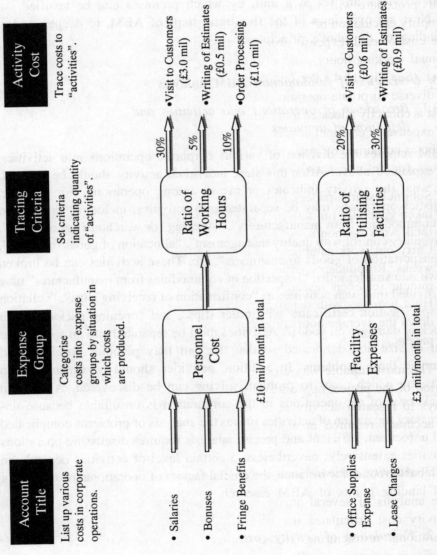

Fig. 15.4. Example of calculation of activity cost.

groups according to the conditions which these costs will bring about. Payrolls and fringe benefits are sorted into the expense group of personnel cost. This procedure will illuminate the relations between activity and cost, and simplify calculation of activity costs. Secondly, decide the criteria of tracing the cost of each expense group to a given activity (e.g. the percentage of annual working hours, ratio of utilising facilities) and calculate the activity cost. (See Fig. 15.4.) Personnel cost is one of the major parts of total costs in diverse corporate operations. Consequently, it is important that personnel cost is correctly allocated to a particular activity, without uncertain distribution of expenses. Personnel cost is usually apportioned to activities in proportion to hours consumed by given activities. Typical ways to measure and determine hours for definite activities are as follows:

1. Submit research papers. Respondents estimate and write down total hours taken generally for activities or put down percentage of activities out of total working hours.
2. Carry out work sampling for a certain period, for instance, one or two weeks. Respondents write down an actual record of activities in a 10-minute scale on research papers.
3. Hold hearings with departmental managers. Managers estimate and put down the average hours or percentage of particular activities on research papers.

The most suitable way among these three options depends on the total period of the project or workload allowed for data processing and analysis. Ways to research activity costs should be devised according to the level of accuracy required in analysis.

1.3.3. *Activity attribute analysis*

The analysis of several attributes of activities as well as the analysis of activity cost articulates the nature of tasks that should be attained for operational restructuring. If the quality of customer service in a certain activity is maintained in the course of business process redesign, the analysis of attributes can be one of the determinants used to investigate the tasks;

for example, whether the workforce shifts from full-time to part-time employees or whether the outsourcing of parts of operations is feasible, in terms of the skills required for each activity.

One of the typical analyses of activity attributes is value-added analysis, which measures what achievements (such as values for customers or other organisation inside the corporation) have been built by each activity. Value-added here can be quantified by estimating to what extent level of services, which should be improved in the corporation or organisation, will increase after adjusting the quantity of activities or improving the quality of activities.

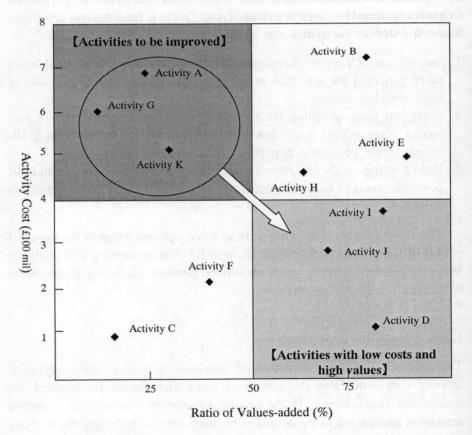

Fig. 15.5. Example of distributed range of activity costs and values.

Services of the corporation or organisation are often assessed by the speed at which information is provided and by the quality and accuracy of information provided. For instance, information includes lead-time for replying inventory level to customers, the estimated hours to deliver shipped goods to customers, or the current location of lorries transporting commodities. Cross-sectional analysis between activities and values-added makes it possible to distinguish which activities should be refined in quality or quantity. Figure 15.5 is a four-grid matrix, which suggests a correlation between costs and values of activities. Activities in the left upper corner are obviously high-cost and low-value activities; undoubtedly they should be improved or eliminated. Considering measures which move activities to the right lower corner on the grid helps to formulate solutions.

Other measures are the analysis of the experience or skills required, and the analysis of activity constituents, etc. The latter figures out which smaller particles of activities compose activities; or what categories of activities constitute activities, such as negotiations with other sections, co-ordination, clerical processing, and jobs which transfer from one site to another. By effecting an activity attribute analysis, the feasibility of shifting to a part-time workforce and outsourcing operations, and the economic value of education for employees is evaluated.

1.3.4. *Cost driver analysis*

Cost driver analysis is the analysis of identifying factors (or drivers), which have an influence on deciding activity costs and values-added, and to measure to what extent the drivers impact on activity costs and values. In cost driver analysis, it is significant to observe the results of activity costs and values by changing the common drivers of many activities. This is the case, for instance, when the driver of "change of ordering factors", such as number of items or delivery due date, impacts immensely on a series of operations, as listed below. Cost driver analysis can pinpoint the objects of restructuring to be focused on in order to reduce and improve cost.

- Receipt of order from customers
- Inventory confirmation

- Order processing to manufacturers
- Notice of estimated delivery date to customers
- Make-up of order slips
- Input of account receivables
- Revision or suspension of orders
- Planning of transportation

1.3.5. *Cost segment analysis*

Cost segment analysis is the analysis of cost structures, segment by segment. By combining activity costs, several segments are established to analyse cost structures for operational improvement, including business processes, types of products, customer sectors, marketing channels and market areas. Cost segment analysis makes it possible to simulate practical profitability in various segments. The simulation can locate where corporate resources should be intensively concentrated.

The next section is an example of an actual case of application of ABM to operational restructuring.

2. Case of Business Process Innovation by Application of ABM

2.1. *Background of client corporation and project*

Company A is one of the largest interior material wholesalers that has a 10 to 15 percent market share. The number of employees is about 500. The wholesaler does not produce their own commodities, but purchases products from some 750 manufacturers, selling items to the second wholesalers or directly to customers. Revenue is composed from two main segments of products. One segment is "regular" items, which consists of products of a certain size, colour, and materials. This category accounts for 50%. The other 50% of products are "customised" items, which are manufactured according to customers' requirements of dimension and specifications.

While the market for interior materials was still developing, competition between companies was becoming more intense. In this industrial climate,

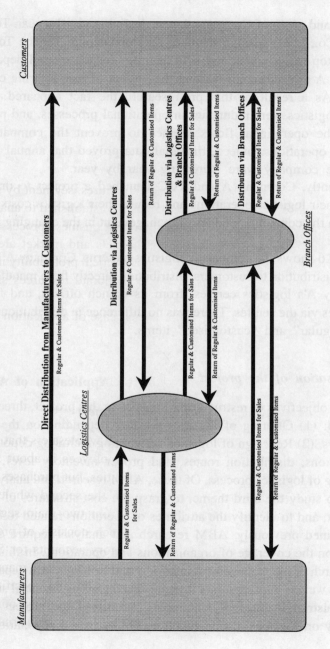

Fig. 15.6. Company A's logistics networking.

the turnover and profit of Company A was declining year by year. Tohmatsu Consulting Co., Ltd. (TCC), a member firm of Deloitte Touche Tohmatsu, interviewed top management and held hearings for the overall departments of Company A to prepare for starting the project of restructuring company operations. As a result of this pre-research, the fact appeared that the company's logistics were redundant in operational processes, and problems caused by the operational flows seemed to prevent the company from streamlining operations. Indeed, financial data proved that annual logistics costs for the company were increasing year by year.

Consequently, Company A and TCC launched a project to drastically restructure their logistics operations and reduce their logistics costs, as well as strengthen the competitive edges of management in the changing business environment.

Figure 15.6 shows the company's logistics patterns. Company A had four methods of distribution to customers: distribution directly from manufacturers; via Company A's logistics centres; from its branch offices; and from the branch offices via the centres. There was no difference in distribution patterns between "regular" and "customised" items.

2.2. *Organisation of the project*

To attain the objectives of restructuring logistics in this project, three options were offered: (1) Offering of logistics services depending on the rank of the customers, (2) Redesign of logistics networking including depot (branch office) locations, distribution routes, and proper inventory level, and (3) Restructuring of logistics process. Of these, ABM research and analysis were performed to study the third theme, to grasp the cost structures of the total logistics cost, and to identify the attributes of operations related to logistics.

As explained previously, ABM research and analysis require decisions to be made on the coverage of organisations and operations. In this project, the pre-research of top management interview and hearings with departmental managers, as well as information of internal data regarding financial situations, and the industrial features of wholesalers prompted the project team to focus mainly on logistics-related functions. Moreover, a correlation of the

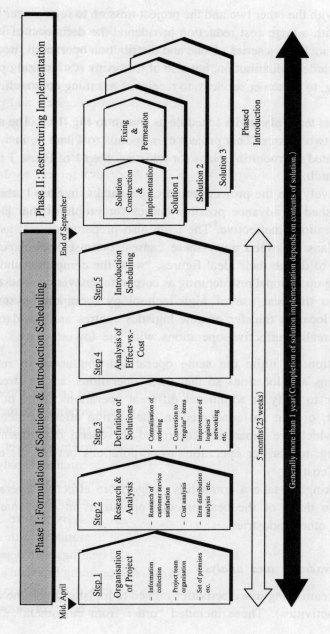

Fig. 15.7. Schedule of logistics operation restructuring project in Company A.

third theme with the other two and the project mission to re-engineer logistics operations with a huge cost reduction broadened the definition of logistics. This mission includes a series of sale and distribution operations, not only of external forwarders' distribution, but also of Company A's internal operations from ordering, to customer services, to receipt of returning commodities from customers.

The project team planned a schedule as shown in Fig. 15.7. The schedule consisted of two phases. This project corresponds to Phase 1, in which the team formulated restructuring plans for logistics. Step 1 of Phase 1 involved the pre-research.

To effectively use the project period of 23 weeks, in Step 1, the project team established in advance possible causes for problems that had made logistics operations ineffective. The team also prepared several aspects of resolution plans to sweep away these causes; because such aspects help corporations to define their ideal figures, "what the companies should be", after realising operational restructuring as corporate innovation. These aspects are based on the best use of high technology (computer systems and equipment), location transfer or new logistics centres and standardisation, in order to realise effective operations with the lowest costs.

- Centralisation: to unite the same operations conducted in respective organisations and locations so that these operations can be streamlined.
- Integration: to unify or administer different operations either in a single department; or that are conducted in one section after another section, or those which are separately controlled in several departments.
- Outsourcing: to transfer operations to corporations outside the company to reduce cost.
- Benchmarking: to take a competitive edge from effective operations by referring to those of the best practice operations in companies in the same and other industries.

2.3. *ABM research and analysis*

The project team categorised activities related to logistics into nine activities (first-level activities). These included "order from customers", "order to manufacturers", "receipt of commodities from manufacturers", "stocking (warehousing) of commodities", "arrangement of transportation", "shipping from warehouse", "transportation", "return of commodities from customers", and "others"... These activity groups were divided further into smaller activities (the second-level activities). Afterwards, the team presented research papers including these set activities and submitted these to all employees in the branch offices, the distribution centres, and the Department of Commodity Administration and Promotion of the Headquarters.

As activity tracing criteria, which also means operational quantity of activity out of all the workloads, the team used the percentage of activity among annual working hours of employees including working overtime. The objective of using the tracing criteria is to evaluate the feasibility of re-structuring plans; not to calculate exact activity cost.

The project team adopted Company A's practical wages and bonus of its employees in a certain year, as personnel costs, including overtime wages. These cost data were decisive factors in evaluating plans of distribution of employees, the outsourcing of partial operations, and employees' responsibilities at the stage of formulating solutions in the project.

To trace corporate and divisional expenses in organisations, the team made a rule. According to this rule, respondents to this research broke down, by percentage, such expenses as repair fees and fuel, transportation, communication, and meetings to each activity.

ABM research and analysis identified the following issues:

- Activity cost structure analysis of the logistics operations found that the aggregated cost of "order from customers" and "order to manufacturers" was very high, compared to cost of "transportation". Figure 15.8 demonstrates that the ratio of "order from customers" and "order to manufactures" account for 37% of the total cost. The combined cost was higher than that of "transportation".
- Driver analysis of these costs identified the activities relating to "customised" items attributed more to an increase in cost and quantity of operation rather than those of "regular" items, especially in those relating to ordering activities.

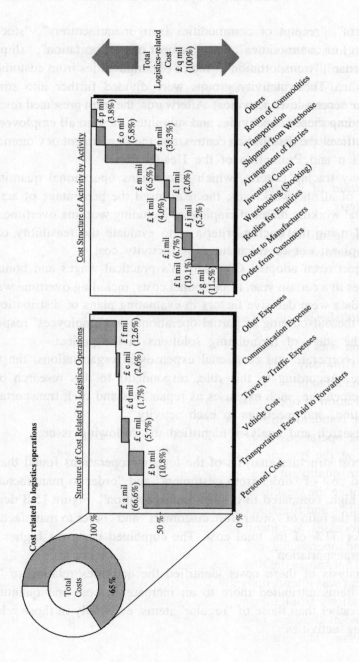

Fig. 15.8. Example of cost structure analysis of logistics operations.

Cost Structure of Activity by Activity

- Return of Commodities — £ p mil (3.8%)
- Transportation from Warehouse — £ o mil (5.8%)
- Shipment from Warehouse — £ n mil (35.3%)
- Arrangement of Lorries — £ m mil (6.5%)
- Inventory Control — £ l mil (2.0%)
- Warehousing (Stocking) — £ k mil (4.0%)
- Replies for Enquiries — £ j mil (5.2%)
- Order to Manufacturers — £ i mil (6.7%)
- Order from Customers — £ h mil (19.1%)
- Others — £ g mil (11.5%)

Total Logistics-related Cost £ q mil (100%)

Structure of Cost Related to Logistics Operations

- Other Expenses — £ f mil (12.6%)
- Communication Expense — £ e mil (2.6%)
- Travel & Traffic Expenses — £ d mil (1.7%)
- Vehicle Cost — £ c mil (5.7%)
- Transportation Fees Paid to Forwarders — £ b mil (10.8%)
- Personnel Cost — £ a mil (66.6%)

Cost related to logistics operations

Total Costs — 65%

- Analysis of operations relating to "customised" items found that these operations took a longer time and produced complicated processes, whilst their profitability was low.
- Attribute analysis explained that activities of "order from customers" and "orders to manufacturers" required employees to have high-ranking skills and long experience, and it seemed that such features might deter the business development of Company A in the future.

2.4. *Definition of solutions and analysis of effect-vs.-cost based on ABM analysis*

To solve the identified problems, the project team introduced the following plans of "establishment of ordering centre" and "conversion to 'regular' items".

2.4.1. *Establishment of ordering centre*

One solution was to reorganise business processes. Previously, the branch offices of Company A had received orders from customers and placed orders to manufacturers. The establishment of the ordering centre intended the centralisation of operations relating to ordering in one location. Simultaneously, the standardisation of ordering procedures at the centre was aimed to make the operations more effective, that is, to decrease the number of employees at the branch offices who were engaged in ordering, and to improve the quality of the operation.

To facilitate the establishment of the centre, the project team defined the responsibilities and function of the new centre, redesigned the activities and business processes, and identified the support systems including information systems and operational rules.

Figure 15.9 shows the main processes of the new operation. Productivity improvement was intended, by integrating ordering operations and separating these operations from transportation operations.

To redesign the new operational process, the team took advantage of ABM analysis. The benefit of this analysis is real-life simulation. ABM

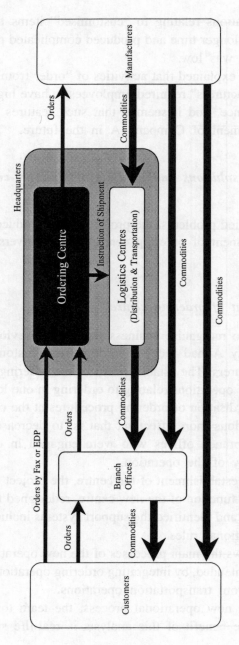

Fig. 15.9. New business process after establishment of ordering centre.

Operational Function	First Level Activity	Second Level Activity	Current Activity Cost	[Case 1] Effect by Introducing Solutions	[Case 2] Effect by Introducing Solutions
Placement of Order	Inventory Control for Placing Orders	Confirmation of Orders and Prediction of Demands	£ mil	+ 10%	+ 20%
		Comparison of Current Inventory by Items and Standard Inventory	£ mil	▲ 20%	▲ 20%
Receipt of Order	Order from Customers	Receipt of Phone & Fax Orders	£ mil	▲ 30%	▲ 40%
		Print-out of Order Forms	£ mil	▲ 10%	▲ 30%
Logistics	Warehousing	Inspection	£ mil	± 0%	± 0%
		Stocking to Flow Rack	£ mil	± 0%	± 0%
	Inventory Control	Quality Control of Inventory	£ mil	± 0%	± 0%
		Confirmation and Processing of Dead Stock	£ mil	± 0%	± 0%
		Total Cost Reduction	£ mil	£ mil	£ mil

Fig. 15.10. Simulation image using ABM analysis.

analysis can articulate the cost, attributes and values-added of individual activity, as well as the required skills, experience, frequency, constituents of the activity, etc. Thus, the analysis made a quantitative simulation of effects (cost and operational hours) after introduction to new business process possible. Procedures of simulation are to:

1. Select activities which will be decreased or discontinued after the introduction of new business processes.
2. Estimate the decrease ratio of each activity according to the effects of the new business processes. The ratio can be set case by case, such as maximum, minimum, and the most feasible one.
3. Study a combination case, a case integrated with distinct cases of decreased or discontinued activities; the case will be investigated on the basis of each ratio of activities.

Figure 15.10 shows a simulation image. If the current cost of each activity is identified, the amount of decreases in these activities would reach an accurate estimate of the total cost reduction after the introduction of new business processes.

Several risks have been predicted from the attributes of these activities, for instance, "Whether new business process retains current functions and values for customers, when investigated from the point of view of required skills and operational frequency of activities?"

In simulations, the influence of new activities and new effects, including cost reduction in procurement and increase in profits, by new business processes, must be taken into consideration and quantitative estimation.

2.4.2. Conversion to "regular" items

This was the solution that focused on the cost driver, a factor that increases activity. By replacing "customised" items, which accounted for 60% of total revenue, with "regular" items, the reduction of ordering activities and the simplification of these activities should be achieved. The solution was intended to lower the required skills and level of experience for activities because skills and experience relating to "customised" items were higher than those relating to "regular" ones. (See Fig. 15.11.)

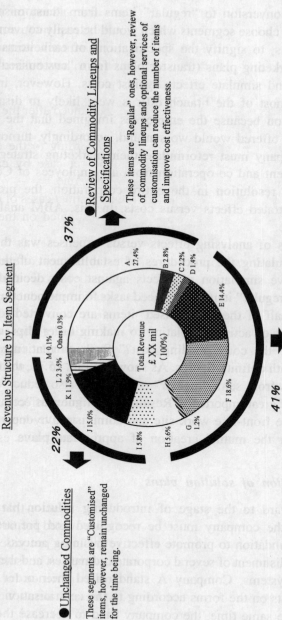

● Review of Commodity Lineups and Specifications

These items are "Regular" ones, however, review of commodity lineups and optional services of customisation can reduce the number of items and improve cost effectiveness.

● Promotion of Conversion to "Regular" Items

● Unchanged Commodities

These segments are "Customised" items, however, remain unchanged for the time being.

Revenue Structure by Item Segment

Total Revenue
£ XX mil
(100%)

A 27.4%
B 2.8%
C 2.2%
D 1.4%
E 14.4%
F 18.6%
G 1.2%
H 5.6%
15.8%
J 15.0%
K 11.9%
L 2 3.5%
M 0.1%
Others 0.3%

37%

41%

22%

Fig. 15.11. Revenue by item segment and conversion to "regular" items.

To affect the conversion to "regular" items from "customised" items, it was important to choose segments which would be easily converted among "customised" items, to signify the specifications of each items again, as well as renew marketing plans (transfer plans from "customised" items to "regular" ones), and simulate effects against costs. However, in the case of Company A, most of the branch offices were likely to disagree with the planned solution because the employees imagined that the quality of customer services offered would worsen and, accordingly, turnover would decline. The company must reformulate their marketing strategies. Thus, to receive agreement and co-operation from all employees of Company A and promote this resolution in the entire corporation, the project team explicitly demonstrated effects versus costs. In this, ABM analysis again played a key role.

The procedures of analysing effects versus expenses was the same as that taken in simulating the procedures of establishment of the ordering centre. Quantitative simulation of effects against costs decided the level of conversion to "regular" items and placed tasks to implement the solutions. For example, if half of the 'customised' items are converted to "regular" ones, what percent of activities relating to making order slips will reduce and also decrease the corresponding cost?" Such simulation verifies the effects of plans with definite figures. As shown in Fig. 15.11, the conversion to "regular" items from semi-"regular" ones would also reduce cost. Thus, quantification is of great importance. Results using figures as "communication tools" between the front-line work site and administrative departments can be favourable for the mutual creation of appropriate plans.

2.5. Implementation of solution plans

In stepping forward to the stage of introducing solution plans, several prerequisites in the company must be recognised and prepared: a solid organisational foundation to promote effective business process innovation, reviews and establishment of several corporate ordinances, and the prevalence of information systems. Company A standardised their order forms and examined elements on the forms according to the centralisation of ordering operations. At the same time, the company tried to decrease the skills and experience required for ordering activities. The project team attempted to phase in the new organisational system of the ordering centre. Through the transition period, the project team took care of maintaining the quality of customer services in response to this organisational change.

The following five factors must be generally considered when implementing resolutions:

2.5.1. *Adequate set-up of organisational foundation to promote resolutions*

A team should be organised that consists of high-calibre members who are skilful and have enough experience to implement solution plans. Regardless of constituting the implementation team, human networking across the corporation is necessary to solve issues inside the company.

2.5.2. *Empowerment across corporations enable plans to proceed*

Implementation of solution plans must be empowered to the team members. In addition, ongoing plans must be acknowledged by the entire company. Prolonged decision-making is one of the worst examples. Even though the redesign of new business operations is sometimes accompanied by uncertainty, it is important to decide first of all "Who should make a final decision".

2.5.3. *Sharing of plan directions and motivation of employees*

Share directions of solution plans among employees of the corporation. Moreover, inspire motivation amongst employees to change the organisation themselves. When taking mid- to long-term resolutions, or resolutions whose effects take a certain period to be seen, provoke continuous innovations. Do not lose employees' involvement in plans.

2.5.4. *Cooperation across divisions*

Operational restructuring is a corporate-wide project. Integrate employees together and encourage them to cooperate with each other beyond the company divisions. People who are able to exercise leadership in each corporate department should participate in the implementation team.

2.5.5. *Reviews of implementation plans*

Watch carefully the progress of the implementation of solution plans. To prepare for and respond appropriately to several sorts of contingency, add or decrease task elements. Distribute opportunely management resources to the implementation team. Reschedule plans. Establish milestones to evaluate the progress of the implementation of each plan. It is hoped that contingency plans will be prepared in advance for influential factors over the overall progress of plans.

2.6. *ABM development at solution implementation stage*

In logistics operational restructuring, the project team defines concrete plans for innovations and the scheduled implementation of resolutions. At the second stage, it is important to measure the effects after introduction and to respond properly to these results. Repeating ABM research monthly to measure effects is unpractical and unreasonable; because such frequent research would use too many man-hours. Meanwhile, simplified and biannual or annual ABM research on a specific part of operations is of great value.

At Company A, a year after the establishment of the ordering centre, the activity cost of personnel except facility expenses was researched again in the area of ordering operations only. The effects of the solution were measured.

Although full ABM research makes multi-dimensional analyses, it is time-consuming and demanding to process data. Therefore, simple and focused ABM research should be in force to review the effects at the stage of implementing and fixing resolutions to the corporation.

3. Features of ABM Concept and Remarks about ABM Research

Finally, the application of ABM concept to the operational restructuring project, including overviews of fundamental ABM analysis, is summarised as follows:

3.1. *Identification of issue domains and presentation of solution directions*

ABM is the methodology used to pinpoint problem areas with quantitative evidence and to provide a guide to problem solving in a relatively short term and involving least workload. The average period of ABM research and analysis takes, though it depends on perspectives, scales and ways of research, 4–6 weeks. ABM is, in a sense, comprehensive research. ABM helps management to make decisions. Thus, it must be understood that if the detailed design of business operations is anticipated through ABM analysis, it will be necessary to examine the project in detail including the allocation of personnel resources.

3.2. *Balance between multi-dimensional analysis and analysis workload*

Consider the multiple aspects of ABM analysis and the extent of its scrutiny. One of the key features of ABM is its grasp of "activities" and of several attributes such as drivers and values to customers. These aspects create a multi-dimensional analysis. In turn, excessive pursuit of these features creates a heavy workloads of analysis. The relations between efficiency and the level of preciseness in ABM analysis should be examined case by case according to the objectives of the project and premises of issues. ABM should be used with the understanding that by its nature, this is not the methodology pursuing high accuracy of cost accounting. As is often the case, there are complex arguments like, "What is its 'true' cost?" Companies should always remember what their objectives are and what information is necessary.

3.3. *Prevalence of motivation and innovation at worksite and continuous advancement*

It is rare that employees at the front-line work site are aware of their "activity", and sometimes difficult for them to understand a concept of "activity cost".

ABM is based on the concept of activity costing, from the analysis of current situations, identification of problems, formulation of solution plans, through the evaluation of effects after the introduction of plans. Therefore, procedures of ABM enable employees at the worksite to realise the concept of "activity costing", motivate them to transform their practical operations, and encourage them to promote these innovations. "Activities" should be defined so that employees at the worksite can understand this term, communicate with each other in the "common language" of "activity cost", and have the concept of "activity costing" known at the site through the project; this will maximise the effects of ABM.

Activities that constitute corporate business operations still exist even if forms of the operations change. For instance, activity of notice of delivery to customers still remains whether it is manual or automatic, through a computer network, or by the forwarder outside the company. This is the reason why concentrating on "activity cost" can build foundations on which several solution plans are investigated. In reality, the defining of activities and the cost calculation at the beginning of the project are painstaking; however, after these duties are completed, the simulation of solution feasibility will be boosted in quality.

Chapter 16

The Cost Reduction Approach to the Manufacturing Administrative Departments in a Japanese Industrial Machinery Manufacturing Company

YOSHIYUKI NAGASAKA

"Reengineering The Corporation" by M. Hammer and J. Champy[4] also became a major topic in Japan where many Japanese corporations started to examine Business Process Reengineering (BPR). Although the methodology proposed by M. Hammer and J. Champy to reinvent business processes can be anticipated to induce a big effect, it has been pointed out that there are risks that BPR will not be successful and will not be readily accepted by Japanese employees who are familiar with bottom–up procedures.[1,2,11–13] Moreover, the Activity Based Costing approach (ABC) and the Activity Based Management approach (ABM) have been enthusiastically studied for BPR recently in Japan. However, case studies have not yet provided enough evidence of this. It is only mentioned that there are many methods of BPR being practised in Japan. The Japanese manufacturing industry now faces stiff competition where productivity improvements in the indirect section of the company are seen as an important problem that needs to be addressed. Conventionally, many industrial robots and automatic machines were in use and have actually reduced direct costs by a considerable amount. However, it is hard to say if there has been a sufficient improvement in indirect works such as the production preparation process. For this reason, it is recognised by many people that there is a possibility that cost reductions in the indirect section can be realised if advanced information technology (IT) is correctly applied. Considering this background mentioned, the method for "cost reduction of an indirect section through IT" used in Japanese manufacturing companies is discussed in this chapter. Also, a case study performed in Komatsu Ltd., a famous Japanese industrial machinery manufacturer will be reported.

1. The Pre-production Process in an Industrial Machinery Manufacturing Company

A case study was performed in Komatsu Ltd. in Japan. Construction machinery such as excavators and bulldozers as well as industrial machinery such as press machines and numerically controlled machining centers are manufactured by Komatsu Ltd. which is said to be the second biggest company in this field in the world.

In Komatsu Ltd., operations from product design to mass production, are carried out in the following stages. A rough investigation into mass production is carried out after a concept drawing of a new product has been proposed by the design division. Next, detailed-drawings are released and various pre-production procedures are started in each manufacturing section before mass production is started. At the same time, information about new goods are communicated to the business department and the customer support section, and a business strategy and a sales promotion plan are considered. A flow of the information is schematically shown in Fig. 16.1.

All the information in the drawing is communicated to several business sections and transformed into different data such as "parts book", "NC data for machining" and "documents of the manufacturing process plan". These data conversions are said to be pre-production processes. The relationship between several pre-production processes is shown in Fig. 16.2. For example, in the casting production section, drawings of cast designs and mould designs are prepared, the product cost is estimated and a job operation manual is written out. In the metal plate welding section, a drawing of the cutting layout, a plan of the manufacturing process and the teaching operation of

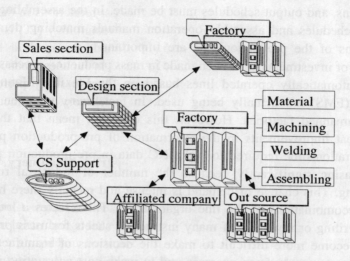

Fig. 16.1. A schematic drawing of a flow of the information.

Labels: Sales section — Design section — Factory — CS Support — Factory — Material — Machining — Welding — Assembling — Affiliated company — Out source

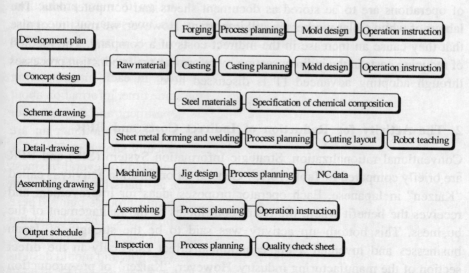

Fig. 16.2. Pre-production processes in an industrial machinery manufacturing company.

Development plan — Concept design — Scheme drawing — Detail-drawing — Assembling drawing — Output schedule

Raw material:
- Forging — Process planning — Mold design — Operation instruction
- Casting — Casting planning — Mold design — Operation instruction
- Steel materials — Specification of chemical composition

Sheet metal forming and welding — Process planning — Cutting layout — Robot teaching

Machining — Jig design — Process planning — NC data

Assembling — Process planning — Operation instruction

Inspection — Process planning — Quality check sheet

industrial robots are necessary. In the machining section, process planning, jig designs, and output schedules must be made. In the assembling section, output schedules and assembly operation manuals matching demand and conditions of the production line are important.

A lot of investments have been made in mass production processes where many automatically operated lines based on the Flexible Manufacturing System (FMS) are actually being used. In fact, there are even plans to build unmanned factories. However, this does not mean that there have been great improvements in the reformation of pre-production processes. The operation time required to make NC data in pre-production processes is increasing significantly because the number of industrial robots are increasing. This change of demand is intense and recently there have been many recombinations of the line organization. This creates a lot of work in the writing or rewriting of many instruction sheets for mass production. It has become more difficult to make the decisions of manufacturing, to arrange parts supply from overseas and to make cost accounting in a short time. Pre-production processes are very complicated, because the results of operations are to be stored as document sheets and computer data. The labour of white collar workers is still important. However, we must recognise that they cause an increase in the indirect costs of a company. The method of reducing costs in the indirect section by reforming pre-production processes through adopting advanced IT is discussed here.

2. The Activity for Reduction of Indirect Costs and BPR

Conventional rationalization, Strategic Information System (SIS) and BPR are briefly compared in Table 16.1.[13] General rationalization activity is called "Kaizen" in Japanese. Each operator proposes ideas for improvement and receives the benefit where the result contributes to the management of the business. This bottom–up activity was said to be the strength of Japan businesses and invented a big economical effect especially in the direct section of the manufacturing industry. However, "Kaizen" of pre-production processes has not progressed very much because it is difficult to handle various kinds of data in a flexible manner.

Table 16.1. Comparison between conventional rationalization, SIS and BPR.

	BPR	SIS	Rationalization
Expected effect	Labor reduction	Profit enhancement	Cost reduction
Beneficiary	Executive	Executive	The person in charge
Direction	Top–down	Top–down	Bottom–up
Object	Business process	Management project	Each enterprise function
Risk	large	Middle	Small

In the indirect section, IT was regarded, particularly up until the 1980's, as a tool to replace the troublesome operations of humans with the more effective computer. Relatively simple clerical work were reformed by using IT. However, the application of IT to pre-production processes in which various kinds of data must be flexibly handled was still restricted at that time. Instead, SIS was developed to collect and analyze information for management decision making. This was very useful for executives but not for pre-production engineers.

BPR is a method to entirely redesign business processes by focusing only on these business processes and not on business sections. BPR requires all past measures and schemes to be disregarded and original figures are to be drawn up afresh.[4] The prospective result of BPR is attractive to executives, but there is also a high risk that it will not be successful. A few reliable methodologies for indirect work based on the concept of BPR have been reported,[6,11] but these methods are insufficient to be applicable to pre-production processes, which is the objective here. In fact, some papers about BPR say that these methods are not mature enough to be compatible with so-called Japanese management[2] and that making a large leap from the origin is not rational.[1,14]

In the Japanese manufacturing industry, there is the general belief that it is most important to manufacture products and that the company should consist of manufacturing. People tend to stick to manufacturing because they recognise that current business procedures have been built up and are based on the accumulation of improved activities and know-how over many years. It is not easy for them to suddenly disregard all the current procedures and build up new ones. Even if somebody designs a plan for reinventing business processes, it is not certain who should execute it and how it should be carried out. Therefore, it is necessary to consider the custom of employment in Japanese businesses. There are many barriers in the application of BPR in Japanese companies such as the corporate culture. Ideas to reinvent business processes should be based on techniques that can actually be realised. In addition, the technical level of the company must be considered. The idea for cost reduction should be matched with the company level. There are said to be four conditions to the success of BPR in Japanese businesses.

(1) The strong leadership of executives with indomitable resolve
(2) The presentation of clear management vision on the basis of customer satisfaction
(3) Appropriate "surplus personnel countermeasures" such as the re-education of middle-ranking managerial officers.
(4) Effective exploitation of information technology mainly on an open network system.

Creating work for those white-collar workers who are made redundant as a result of BPR is absolutely necessary. It must be noticed that the range of responsibility and power of middle-ranking managerial officers in Japan is different from any other country. In Japan, it is usual for the work flow to be dependent on the personal resources of middle-ranking managerial officers. By all means, middle-ranking managerial officers should recognise the necessity of BPR.

How can we find a solution through the use of IT must be considered. In order to do so, a deductive method is necessary. A deductive approach is similar to the "drastic reinvent" concept of the original BPR. However, of course, because it is also important to analyse the problems of the conventional business processes, find solutions and evaluate them, both deductive and inductive methods are necessary. The guideline that pre-production processes must be completely reformed if recent advanced information technologies are to be applied correctly must be established for each company. Here, a middle–up and gradual approach is recommended rather than the top–down, drastic approach suggested by Hammer *et al.* The leadership of understanding executives is also a necessary requirement.

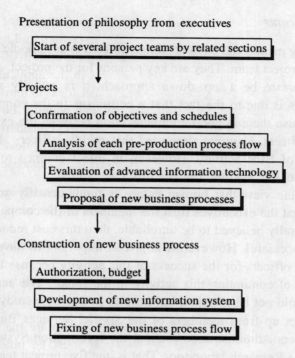

Fig. 16.3. Cost reduction activity by IT.

3. The Method of Enforcing "Cost Reduction Activity by IT"

The procedures of "Cost reduction activity by IT" performed in the case study in Komatsu Ltd. is described as follows (see the summary in Fig. 16.3).

3.1. *A director of the "cost reduction activity"*

As Hammer *et al.* point out in their original BPR, the activity should be started with an address by the executive or the director concerned to those responsible for carrying out the reform. Therefore, it can be seen that an address by an executive to the leader who is responsible for the reform is absolutely necessary. As the activity is started with an address by top management, it appears to be a top–down approach. However, this is not the case as the following paragraph will explain.

3.2. *Project teams*

Middle-ranking managerial officers (simply refered to as "Middle") must participate in the project team. They are key persons for the project. Although the activity appears to be a top–down approach, it is actually a middle–up approach. This is due to the fact that a consensus in the company can be obtained because there is good communication between the executives and the middle officers. Hammer suggested that middle officers should not be at the centre of BPR activity. However, in direct contrast to this middle officers played the leading role in this case study.

Based on the view that human nature is fundamentally good, it is indispensable that the executives trust the members of the company. If human nature is generally believed to be unreliable, then this cost reduction activity will not be successful. However, it is just as important to have the support of the middle officers for the success of this activity because they have the responsibility of continuing this activity in the future. The activity of cost reduction should not be transient but lasting. In this case study, five project teams were set up from members of the Special Services Bureau section, the headquarters Administration section, the Information Systems Division section and the Research laboratory. That is, the five project teams consisted of the staff of cross-functional sections.[11]

3.3. *Setting the objectives of the "cost reduction activity by IT"*

It is important to make clear that the objective of the cost reduction activity is just a "cost reduction" and not a "layoff". However, although the main objective is to reduce costs, the final goal should be planned to also include a complete change of business processes. The reform should progress gradually with difficult but achievable targets in every short term period. Hammer said in his book that, to accumulate small improvements would not be good and would make the company weak. However, in the Japanese business management style, even small improvements are approved if they lead to the final goal. Of course, clear objectives and schedules must be recognized quantitatively by all the members and explained to the executives.

3.4. *Analysis of the enterprise function*

There are three approaches to analysing the enterprise function, which keeps in mind business processes. These approaches are either inductive or deductive and are adopted to thoroughly analyse the enterprise function of pre-production processes. In the descriptions of the flow of the enterprise function, Data Flow Diagrams (DFD) or recent IDEF0 in CALS are often used. IDEF is a generic term for the various tools used in enterprise function analysis, data flow descriptions and work flow analysis for the development of an information system. IDEF was proposed by the U.S. Air Force through the research and development project ICAM in 1977. IDEF0 is a tool to describe with detailed figures the strata of business processes such as decision, action and activity. In another example, a bird's-eye view was introduced to describe the work flow.[3] In this case study, the business flow chart as shown in Fig. 16.4 was described. The business process flow chart has no set form and it focuses on business processes and not on the enterprise functions of each section. It describes in precise detail the average clock time of each operation, the stoppage clock time and the output of each process (documents and computer input data).

The flow chart must be analyzed so that a reform bill can be derived at a later stage. In recent years Activity Based Management (ABM) has attracted attention as being a method for BPR. An ABM reform bill consists of the following.

(1) Business process analysis
(2) Definition of process activity
(3) Cost totalization of each process activity
(4) Process value analysis
(5) Improvement planning

In an analysis of this "ABM", the cost of each activity is quantitatively presented and the processing time of each activity is subdivided in detail. That is, it examines whether or not a value is produced in each process. The value (V) is calculated by the equation of F(Function)/C(Cost) compared with the allowance for cost reduction, (C–F). The activities are examined

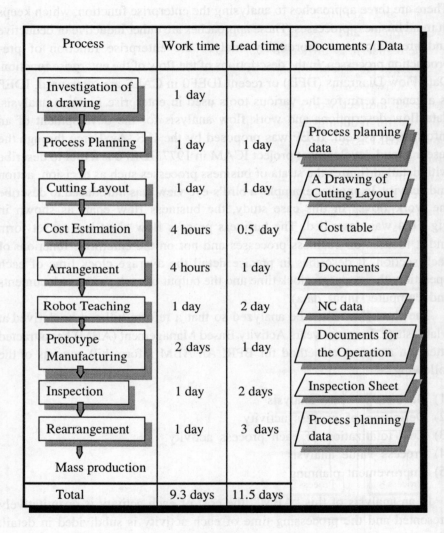

Process	Work time	Lead time	Documents / Data
Investigation of a drawing	1 day		
Process Planning	1 day	1 day	Process planning data
Cutting Layout	1 day	1 day	A Drawing of Cutting Layout
Cost Estimation	4 hours	0.5 day	Cost table
Arrangement	4 hours	1 day	Documents
Robot Teaching	1 day	2 day	NC data
Prototype Manufacturing	2 days	1 day	Documents for the Operation
Inspection	1 day	2 days	Inspection Sheet
Rearrangement	1 day	3 days	Process planning data
Mass production			
Total	9.3 days	11.5 days	

Fig. 16.4. An example of the business flow chart.

after they have been classified into two categories of added value and non-added value activities or its three categories of core, support, accompaniment activity and examined. It is said that general activity consists of 30% core, 35% support, and 35% accompaniment. However, in practice, there is the problem that it is difficult to estimate the value of V for each activity. Moreover, the establishment of a system that collects the man hours of every activity over a long time period in order to know the real activity value of indirect work, can be troublesome. Therefore, because a quick solution for reducing the cost of indirect work was required, in this case study, ABM is regarded only as a future theme. It should be understood that such a value analysis is not an objective but rather a tool to derive a reform bill, where in order to derive a reform bill, a deductive approach, as well as the inductive one mentioned above is needed. The methods of analysis that were adopted in this study are as follows. Namely, the business

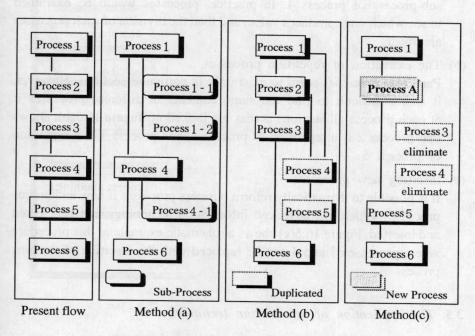

Fig. 16.5. Three methods to analysing the business flow.

process flow chart is renewed using the following three methods of (a) (b) and (c) (see Fig. 16.5), where (a) and (b) are inductive analysis methods and (c) is a deductive analysis method.

(a) Classification of the main processes and sub-processes
   The processes are divided into the following categories;
   (1) Main processes; essential processes
   (2) Incidental sub-processes; sub-processes that accompany the main process
   (3) Exposition sub-processes; exposition processes for the third party

   By making these classifications, omissions and computerisation of sub-processes can be examined at later stages. Figure 16.5(a) shows a schematic drawing of this method. In this drawing, processes 2 and 3 are incidental sub-processes of process 1, and process 5 is an exposition sub-process of process 4. In practice, processes would be examined to see which ones produces value, and then the division of such processes are made.

(b) The extraction of repetition processes
   Particular processes seem to exist only in particular sections. However, it is not difficult to find the same contents in different processes if at each process all sections across are looked at. Figure 16.5(b), shows that process 2 is a repetition of process 4, and process 1 is a repetition of process 5.

(c) Inserting new processes
   It is possible to dramatically reform business processes if new and unique processes which use advanced information technology can be created and inserted. Figure 16.5(c) shows a schematic example of this procedure where processes 3 and 4 can be replaced with the insertion of the new process A.

3.5. *The application of information technology*

After analysing the business flows explained above, the application of information technology to each process is investigated. At the same time, it is very important to evaluate the extent to which information technology matures. The final shape of the business process flow is arranged in this way. Introduction plans and development plans of the application software must be discussed by considering the effect of investment. In addition, discussions must be made to decide if a direct application of a software package, a customisation of a software package or a development of new software is better. Infrastructure such as computer network preparations and unification of database systems must be examined, too.

In this case study, all the project teams had to keep to a budget in the investment of information technology. As a result, a new business process flow was established. As mentioned earlier, a characteristic of the cost reduction activity by IT in this study was that it was a middle–up approach and a gradual procedure rather than a top–down drastic procedure like Hammer's BPR. Of course, good leadership of understanding executives were also necessary as the background. The cost reduction activity by IT that is described here should be applicable to many other Japanese companies.

4. Results of the Case Study and Discussions

In this case study, five project teams namely, an infrastructure, a pre-production process of castings, a pre-production process of machining, a pre-production process of sheet metal welding and a pre-production process of assembling were set up and cost reduction activities by IT were applied. The result of the cost reduction activities by IT in the pre-production process of castings is mentioned as an example in the following.

4.1. *Baseline assessment of the pre-production process*

When a component is designed by using castings in the design division, detailed drawings are sent to the foundry division and productivity examination and cost estimations are made. If the design division estimates the cost and appoints a delivery date, the foundry division starts up the regular pre-production process. This business process is used in Komatsu Ltd. where the foundry division operates as a supplier of raw materials

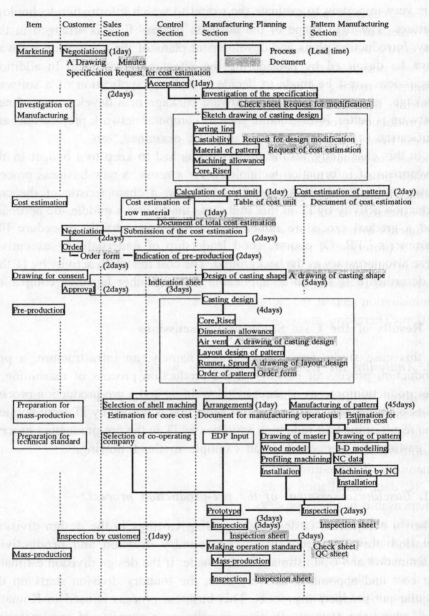

Fig. 16.6. A flow chart of the business processes for manufacturing of castings.

and sells castings to other companies. Competition is fierce in this market and orders are usually placed with the company if the foundry division can satisfy the requirements of QCD (quality, cost, delivery).

Shape design, casting design for runners and risers, cost estimation, mould design, the making of operation instruction for mould and casting manufacturing, the making of inspection sheets, etc. are all important parts of pre-production processes of castings. A summary of the pre-production process flow is described in Fig. 16.6. It is recognised that there are many processes to manufacturing a casting and that a lot of documents are created in each process. When a customer makes an inquiry, preliminaries of a business transaction are started and a reply document, which includes the cost estimation is submitted. If the customer actually places the order, the documents mentioned above are created and the mould is manufactured. After a prototype is manufactured and various examinations are passed, mass production starts. However, before mass production starts, a lot of information is passed between the customer, the business department, the administration section, the casting design section and the mould manufacturing section. Therefore, many documents are created and are referred to.

4.2. Analysing the flow of the business process

The three methods to analysing the business process, (a), (b) and (c) mentioned earlier, have been applied to the flow chart of Fig. 16.6 and the result is shown in Fig. 16.7. When method (a) was applied, specification examinations, cost estimations, casting shape designs, casting designs, generation of three-dimensional models for mould production, generation of NC data, installation of moulds, and inspections were all regarded as indispensable business processes. The remaining business processes were regarded as incidental processes or exposition processes. When method (b) was applied, a part of the final casting design was regarded as a repetition of the sketched casting design used in cost estimation. Moreover, a process for drawing the casting shape was not necessary because it was already included in the drawing of the casting design. A sketch casting design is made only to estimate the product cost of the inquired order and the details

Present Flow	Method (a)			Method (b)	Method (c)
Process	Main	Sub	Exposition	(Duplicated)	(New process)
1 Registration			O		
2 Investigation of	O				
3 Sketch drawing of casting design		O		*⌐	
4 Calculation of cost unit	O			%⌐	Eliminate
5 Cost estimation of pattern		O			Eliminate
6 Cost estimation of raw	O			%⌐	Eliminate
7 Document for negotiation			O		Eliminate
8 Indication of pre-production			O		
9 Design of casting shape	O			#⌐	CAD system
10 Casting design	O			*⌐ #⌐	Solid model
11 Order of pattern			O		Solid model
12 Drawing pattern design		O		+⌐	
13 3-D modeling	O			+⌐	Eliminate
14 NC data generation	O				
15 Machining by NC	O				
16 Installation of pattern	O				
17 Inspection of pattern	O				
18 Arrangement for		O			
19 Manufacturing of a	O				CAE
20 Inspection of the prototype	O			&⌐	
21 Inspection by the customer			O	&⌐	Eliminate
22 Making the documents for manufacturing operations	O	O			
23 Mass-production	O				Database

Fig. 16.7. An example of the flow analysis.

of a casting design are determined only after an order has been placed. Of course, the first sketch of the casting design is succeeded by the final casting design. Therefore, two pieces of drawings are generated but only one is used. The process should be improved to give a final drawing of the casting design by adding several pieces of information to a sketch drawing of the casting design. In addition, it would be useful to predict the possibility of order so that details of the casting design can be investigated from the early stages.

When method (c) was applied, "accurate cost estimation systems in the sales division", "CAD systems customized for casting design", "solid models for mould production" and "CAE for predictions of the casting quality before actual manufacturing"[7] were regarded as candidates for investment. It also pointed out that cost estimation should be made as often as possible by the sales division. For this process, the creation of a new cost estimation system by which the sales division can accurately estimate a cost by considering the production line, the yield, material costs and the cost of the mould was expected. Moreover, master models or surface models for NC machining were considered unnecessary if a solid model made by 3D-CAD can be received and easily handled. Drawings by 2D-CAD are also unnecessary. With the use of computer simulation the trial and error procedure can be minimized by optimizing the casting design on a computer.

4.3. *Examinations and enforcement of the plans to reform the business process*

As mentioned earlier, several reform ideas have appeared. For technology to be applied in these reforms, the scale of investment and expected effects (in terms of both economical efficiency and potential) must be understood. Middle range objectives are also necessary in order to start the reform activity in the proper manner. In this case study, a cost estimation system for the sales division which was connected to the database of factories and a specially customized CAD system for efficient casting design was developed. The objective of this new cost estimation system was to minimize both the work hours needed in cost estimation and the lead time in the replacement of the time consumed. The conventional method required a lot of time in exchanging information between the sales division and the factories.

The sales division and the factories must prepare and maintain detailed cost tables through a network system. A keyword can be given for the retrieval of information such as the name of an item, its dimensions (weight, volume, wall thickness), its functions, the applicable model, etc. For the retrieval of a caricature, it is necessary to handle the image data on a database system. Detailed Weight Cost Tables (WCT) were also prepared for each item and were classified in terms of group technology. It was important

380 Japanese Cost Management

to build up suitable WCT for each production line, mould size, and material, etc. because it allowed costs to be more accurately estimated. By using this new cost estimation system, the lead-time from the time of inquiry until the submission of a document to the customer fell by 1/10 and the work hours used in cost estimation was reduced by half.

The customised CAD system for casting design was useful in reducing drawing costs by large amounts. This was made possible because efficient drawings were made using semi-automatic drawing which were operated by part-time CAD operators. In this study, a method to make a drawing of casting designs which could not only include the casting shape but could also distinguish between them at a later stage was adopted in the following way.

(1) The machining surface in the design section was classified using different colors so that they could be distinguished at a later stage and the elements of the surface were given identification data.
(2) A casting designer (skilled engineer) drew a plan indicating the positions of risers, machining surfaces and cores as well as the types.
(3) A CAD operator completed the casting design on a computer which were based on the plans drawn by the skilled engineer. At the same time, the product shape, risers, cores, machining surfaces were classified.
(4) Drawings of the casting shape and the casting design were automatically printed out by extracting the necessary data.

Furthermore, a parametric design function was added to automatically draw a part geometry for component groups of similar geometry. Compared to the conventional process where a skilled engineer would have to draw a rough design and later, complete these drawings of casting shape and casting design by himself, a customized CAD system efficiently separates these processes. As part-time workers are more than sufficient in operating customized CAD systems, a work improvement of 40% or more was achieved. Therefore it is possible to plan cost at the design stage, and, as the next step, a system integration that allows CAD to connect with cost table is expected. This illustrates how a new flow of the business process can be designed using information technology.

Suitable IT tools were selected and developed with the consideration of the investment effect not only for casting design, but also for the pre-production processes of machining, sheet metal welding and assembling. An engineering database system for the pre-production process was constructed in order to find the most appropriate data in the shortest possible time. In addition, a process planning system was developed to output NC data for machining centers. EDI for CAD data was started up in order to exchange information of geometry for cutting up metal sheets. Also, investigations were made into off-line teaching systems for welding robots and a flexible assembling preparation system for mass production was developed. At the same time, an infrastructure for a computer network which included a basic software environment, such as GroupWare for all the companies in the company network was prepared. Also, a system of one computer for one white-collar worker was established. Finally, it was very important to consider how to process into manufacturing data the CAD data that was generated in the design division at an earlier stage and more efficiently.

References

1. Fujiwara, T., J., Japan Society for the Study of Office Automation, Vol. 15, No. 3, 1994, 193–198,
2. Hanaoka, S., J., Japan Society for the Study of Office Automation, Vol. 15, No. 3, 1994, 187–192.
3. Ito, J. & Yamamoto, K., Decision Making and Information Strategy (Hakuto-shobo, Japan, 1996).
4. Hammer, M. & Champy, J., Reengineering the Corporation (Nicholdas Brealey Publishing, USA, 1993).
5. Research Committee for Future's Wages, More Efficient White Collar Working and the Wage Control (Employment Information Centre, Japan, 1994).
6. Manganelli, R. L. & Klein, M. M., Reengineering Handbook (American Management Association, USA, 1994).
7. Nagasaka, Y. & Isoya, T., Proceeding of Japan Industrial Management Association, November, 1994, 46–47.
8. Nagata, K., Proceeding of Japan Industrial Management Association, May, 1994, 1.

9. Nikkei Business, Japanese Reengineering (Japan Economical Newspaper Press, Japan, 1994).
10. Sakurai, T., Control of Indirect Cost (Chuokeizai-sya, Japan, 1996).
11. Shimada, T., J. of Japan Society for the Study of Office Automation, Vol. 15, No. 3, 1994, 165–172.
12. Toyama, A., J. of Japan Society for the Study of Office Automation, Vol. 15, No. 3, 1994, 206–213.
13. Watanabe, J., Reengineering in Practice (Nikkagiren, Japan, 1994).
14. Yoshida, T., J. of Japan Society for the Study of Office Automation, Vol. 15, No. 3, 1994, 199–205.

Part 6
Cost Management from
Marketing Strategy

Chapter 17

Strategic Control of Marketing Activities Using the ABC System

NOBORU OGURA

1. Introduction

Most expenditure for non-manufacturing activities is treated as normal period costs. However, under recent marketing concepts such as brand equity and customer relations, marketing activities are perceived to serve a strategic rather than an operating function. Restating this in a management accounting context, some parts of marketing costs should be capitalized in obtaining increased sales revenue in future years as well as in the current year.

However, Lorange has pointed out the difficulties that occur when controlling both strategic and operational functions with a single budgetary system. Budget variances usually reflect inefficiencies in operating activities. To meet his budget, a department manager would delay attaining his strategic objectives. Without adequate understanding of strategic objectives, a manager might take the strategic budgets as "gifts" to allow him some slack in addition to his budget. In either case, the planned strategy would be partially accomplished.[1]

Lorange suggested the modification of budgetary control systems by linking budgets more tightly to the strategic programs and dividing budgets into two parts: one plan of resources for operating activities, and one for strategic activities. He then forecasted the limitation of his dual strategic/ operating budgetary system. First, setting a budget only once or twice per

385

year is inadequate for adjusting strategic programs to changes in the environment. Second, budget control process is inward looking and ignores environmental changes. In order to overcome these problems, he proposed four control measures.

Though the dual strategic/operating budgetary system was well designed for planning and setting the budget, it still has some problems in calculating budget variances and controlling strategic activities. One critical problem is a difficulty in separating the actual use of resources for strategy implementation from resources used in operating activities. It is easier to estimate the level of resources needed for implementing the strategy than it is to measure the resources that have been used in strategy. Thus, a variance between budget and the actual use of resources is too arbitrary and less useful in controlling the implementation of strategic programs by a departmental manager.

A solution to the above problem has been introduced by a Japanese manufacturer that devised an activity-based cost system to distinguish the expenses used for strategic programs from those used for operating purposes, and to assign the strategic expenses to each of the strategic objectives.

2. Overview of the Company

K Foods Corporation processes and sells various kinds of fermented foods in Japan. In recent years, K Foods has expanded its market to the West Pacific Area, including China, Southeast Asia, and Australia. Exports have been increasing for ten years and K Foods has constructed and opened overseas plants in China and Australia. On the other hand, imported products have penetrated into the Japanese domestic market to become a significant pressure to K Foods' market share.

By 1990, K Foods had fifteen plants and several sales offices in Japan. Each plant processed and packaged different kinds of food: some were packaged in small cans or bottles for consumer use and others were in bulk cans for restaurants. A sales office dealt with products that came from Japanese plants or were imported. The production headquarters of the company controlled domestic and overseas plants and their marketing headquarters controlled the domestic sales offices. Therefore each plant had few links with sales offices, even those located in the same area.

Though many such plants had been considered necessary for years in order to provide customers with high-quality, fresh products, more than half of the domestic plants were considered to be too small and too obsolete to compete with imported, lower-priced products. The executive board made a long-range plan to discontinue eight old, small plants and to construct a few new plants. They decided at the same time to reorganize two or three other existing plants to try to combine a plant and a sales office in the same area, which would become a regional division. Each of these plants was located in the largest city in a region, and market research showed higher market shares in those cities by 3 to 5 points than other areas. To avoid losing a high market share and to realize higher efficiency than before, a closer association between marketing and production people appeared to be needed.

At the end of 1994, the manager of the Sendai (a major city in North Japan) plant was requested to make a regional strategic program for linking production and marketing functions in that area in preparation of a reorganization to a regional division. The plant manager organized a project team to prepare a strategic program for the future division. This project team consisted of seven managers from various departments, such as purchasing, production, production control, logistic, quality assurance and accounting, in addition to the plant manager.

The project team submitted a strategic program to the company head-quaters in August 1995. This program contained a series of profit goals for the next five years and six categories of strategic objectives, including product quality, customer responsiveness, improvement of transportation, and the training and reassignment of employees (redevelopment of human resources). Each strategic objective was broken down into three or four sub-categories that were assigned year-end goals for the next three years. Finally, the program stated 19 strategic goals that should be attained within the next three years and the year-to-year milestones for those strategic goals. Those goals and milestones were stated quantitatively.

The next task of the project team was to prepare the implementation program for the 19 strategic goals stated above. The team decided to employ an activity-based cost system (ABC system) in order to control the implementation process of the strategic program. The manager of the plant accounting department was responsible for designing the ABC system, and he completed the design of this system in December 1995.

3. The Structure of the ABC System

In preparation for introducing the ABC system, the project team assigned each strategic goal to one or more departments in the Sendai plant and/ or the Sendai sales office. In order to forge a cooperative relationship with the sales office and to provide current market information for the production and transportation departments, customer-related goals were shared between several departments in the plant as well as in the sales office. Responsibility for coordinating the related departments and implementing such a cross-departmental goal was given to one of the members of the project team.

The project team requested each department to restate the goals into activities through which the goals would be attained. Some departments defined one activity corresponding to a goal. Others defined several activities to a goal. In parallel with the strategic activities, each department was required to define the operational activities necessary for day-to-day departmental operations.

The ABC system designed by the plant accounting department had two stages of cost allocation, as most of the standard textbooks advised. The system recorded all costs at the department level before the first stage (see A_1 to A_p in Fig. 17.1). A cost item in a department was considered a resource cost pool. The ABC system allocated department costs in the first stage to the activities in the department in proportion to the consumption of resources by the department (see A_g allocated into b_{g1} to b_{gq} and to c_{g1} to c_{gr}). Some activities were common between departments. Each department had its own cost pool(s) for such common activities in the first stage; therefore all resource costs in a department were to be allocated to the cost pools in that department.

Before the second stage of cost allocation, the costs of all cost pools belonging to an activity were accumulated over the departments (this process is not pictured in chart 1). As stated above, activities were classified into operational and strategic activities. Thus in the second stage, only the costs in operational cost pools were allocated to products and these were used to measure the profitability of products (see B_h allocated into d_{h1} to d_{ht}). Other expenses in strategic activity cost pools in departments were accumulated

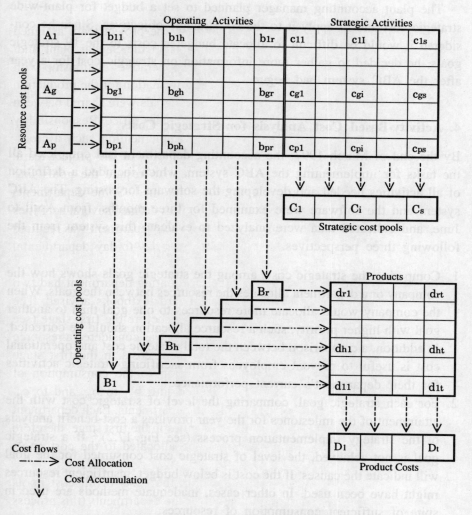

Fig. 17.1. Structure and cost flows in ABC system.

under the strategic goals (see c_{1i} to c_{si} accumulated to C_i) and the total amounts indicated the monthly cost for implementing each of the 19 strategic goals. These strategic costs were to be compared to the budgets that had been estimated necessary for attaining the strategic milestones for the year-end (see C_1 to C_r).

The plant accounting manager planned to set a budget for plant-wide strategic cost and to apply it to the six strategic objectives. Since he considered it would be difficult to allocate budgeted costs to the 19 strategic goals, he decided to gather more information on strategic cost for a year after the ABC system had begun.

4. Activity-Based Cost Analysis for Strategic Costs

By the end of March 1997, the accounting department had completed all the tasks for implementing the ABC system, which included a definition of all activities needed and developing the software for costing. The ABC system and the software were examined for three months, from April to June, and collected data were analyzed to evaluate this system from the following three perspectives.

1. Comparing the strategic costs among the strategic goals shows how the company or a department allocates the resources between the goals. When the company would allocate more resources to one goal than to another goal with higher priority, such a resource allocation should be corrected. In addition, a comparison between the total strategic cost and operational cost is useful to prevent employees from sacrificing strategic activities for their department's current performance.
2. For each strategic goal, comparing the level of strategic cost with the attainment of the milestones for the year provides a cost-benefit analysis of the strategy implementation process (see Fig. 17.2).[2] If a strategic goal is not achieved, the level of strategic cost consumed for the goal will indicate the causes. If the cost is below budget, insufficient resources might have been used. In other cases, inadequate methods are used in spite of sufficient consumption of resources.

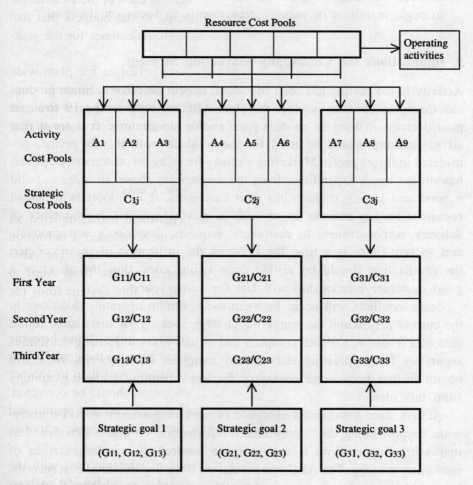

Ah : Costs accumulated in an activity cost pool h.
Cij : Costs accumulated in an strategic cost pool i, in year j.
Gij : A year-end milestone of strategic goal i, in year j.

Fig. 17.2. How to compare strategic costs to strategic goals.

3. For a cross-departmental strategic goal, comparing the strategic costs between the related departments is necessary in order to harmonize the strategic activities in various departments to focus on the goal.

5. Implications for Controlling Marketing Strategy

Activity-based costing has been advocated to provide more accurate product cost than previous cost systems, therefore ABC can help companies to avoid poor decision-making on product price and/or product mix. It assumes that all expenditure would be used for the products sold in this period, not invested in future profit. Marketing strategy focusing on customers, however, has shifted much expenditure from the assumption above. In order to build a good and lasting relationship with customers, it is important to spend resources on key success factor such as product quality, dependability of delivery, responsiveness to customers' requests, developing new products and so on. There is a time lag between the utilization of resources and the results that should be visible from rising sales, thus the effect of a good customer relationship will last for some years.

Some conflicts will occur between the optimum operating decisions in the current period and the marketing strategy looking for sustainable future customer relations. K Foods company had an idea to control strategic activities separately from operating activities by using an ABC system. We could obtain further knowledge necessary for implementing marketing strategy from this idea.

At first, since a successful execution of marketing strategy needs company-wide support along the supply chain, information on other activities than marketing departments is necessary to control the implementation of marketing strategy. The ABC system started from departmental cost records, but could accumulate cross-departmental costs along an activity. Such cost information will be useful for the evaluation in the strategic control process.

Second, implementation of strategy should be evaluated from both viewpoints: how accomplished the strategy is according to the milestone or goal (which in most cases is stated via a non-financial scale), and how much resources have been spent on the strategy. Most organizations monitor the former aspect because many management tools have recently been developed, such as management by objectives, bench marking, TQM, Balanced Scorecard and so on. Accounting researchers are responsible for contributing to support the latter aspect but have paid little attention to such problems. This case will be a starting point for researching cost information for strategic control.

Third, this case has indicated that ABC has such a flexible structure that it can provide various types of cost information corresponding to a different strategy. Activity cost systems for customer analysis or brand analysis have been proposed.[3] Such a design, that would classify costs by customers or by brands, will be desirable in cases where marketing strategies differ among customer groups or among brands. It is essential in such cases for the designer of the cost system to understand all the marketing strategies involved and to define the activities along each strategy.

References

1. Lorange, P., Monitoring Strategic Progress and *ad hoc* Strategy Modification, in Strategic Planning and Control (Blackwell, Oxford, 1993), 142–168.
2. Smith, M., Putting NFIs to Work in a Balanced Scorecard Environment, Management Accounting (UK, March, 1997), 32–35.
3. Kaplan, R. S. & Cooper, R., Cost and Effect (Harvard Business School Press, Boston, 1998), 160–223.

Part 7
Human Factors in
Cost Management

Chapter 18

Japanese Management Style in Achieving Cost Reduction Targets

GUN-YUNG LEE

1. Introduction

There are two sides to the "account system" and the "management system" in Japanese cost management techniques. They are Target costing and Kaizen costing. Target costing contains aspects of an "account system" where the cost elements that are included in the target cost are determined, and the process of achieving the target cost is set. It also has certain aspects of a "management system" which means all the various activities that are undertaken to achieve the target cost provided by the "account system."[24] As this management system is closely related to the management style of Japanese companies and Japanese culture, a synthetic analysis that considers these factors is necessary, compared with the "account system". This necessity is due to the fact that all systems of society, as well as companies, naturally complement each other.

In discussing Japanese cost management techniques, the frame of the management system as a whole needs to be analysed. However, most of the research on Japanese cost management techniques purely focuses on the embodiment of these techniques and does not pay attention to the meaning behind these techniques. Also, the analysis of society, as well as of companies, has been ignored. Therefore, this chapter will study the management system used to promote cost management techniques, and also how Japanese cost management techniques are positioned in relation to the company/society structure.

2. Japanese Cost Management Techniques — Target Costing and Kaizen Costing

Okano[24] compares Japanese cost management with cost management practised in European and American companies as follows. European and American companies consider the function of accounting positively and visualise movements on the shop-floor from a financial viewpoint. However, in Japanese companies, there is a common belief that it is not clear whether or not the movements on the shop-floor can be visualised by the accounting function. Japanese management accounting not only attaches great importance to shop-floor management, such as Just In Time (JIT) or Kaizen activities by positively emphasising the "non-visualisation" side of accounting, but also utilizes non-visualisation by using Target costing together within the process of shop-floor management. This can be called the "backward use" of the non-visualisation of accounting.

As Target costing and Kaizen costing are both used in Japan as cost management techniques, in this chapter, a definition of both techniques will be given.[13] Target costing is a system that "supports the cost reduction process in the developing and designing phase of an entirely new model".

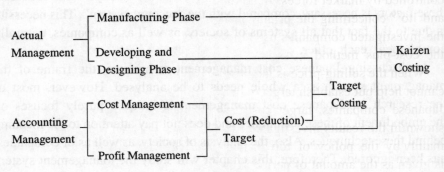

Fig. 18.1. Cost reduction structure.

Kaizen costing is a system that "supports the cost reduction process in the manufacturing phase of the existing product model". In the report entitled "Cost Management (1966)," the industry structure council of the MITI (Ministry of International Trade and Industry) defined cost management as "the management activity which establishes a plan for the cost reduction target and realises it".

If Target costing and Kaizen costing are synthesised together, they can be represented as Fig. 18.1.

Ito[6] points out that the establishment of the target cost in Target costing, by subtracting the necessary profit from the expected selling price of a product, is very similar to the method in the report mentioned above. Thus, it must be noted that the cost management techniques of the 1960s have been preserved in their basic form but have developed into today's Japanese cost management techniques.

3. Cost Reduction Targets and Operating Pressure

3.1. *Cost reduction as a target*

Japanese companies are competing in a keen competitive environment, compared with the companies of other countries. Such a competitive environment has influenced the setting of product prices as well as the quality of products. Thus, when competition is strong, pricing decisions can no longer be controlled by the companies themselves, but instead are controlled by market forces. According to the results investigated by Sakurai and Ito[29] concerning the pricing decisions of Japanese companies, 50% of the investigated companies used the market-pricing method, and 20% used the cost-plus method.

When the selling-price is largely controlled by market factors, companies cannot help but establish target costs according to selling-prices. However, in Japanese companies, target costs are decided based on target profits. As shown in the results investigated by Nishizawa,[21] profit planning is decided mainly by the policy of top management (79.4%) and the profit amount is given as the amount of period profit (94.7%). Thus, when the profit target for a given period is established by top management, the allowable cost is calculated by subtracting that profit amount from the sales amount based on the selling price permitted in the market. The difference between the allowable cost and the estimated cost is the cost reduction target.

The setting of such cost reduction targets differs according to whether or not the targeted product is a new product. For example, in Target costing, the target cost for the development of new products is not only the goal that should accomplish targets such as quality, price, reliability and delivery time corresponding to customer needs, but it is also the goal that should be achieved in order to realise the target profit set up both in the long and mid-term profit plans.[18] In general, such cost reduction targets are established with the acceptance that they are not easily attainable, but must still be accomplished.[31] In Kaizen costing, costs are constantly reduced in the manufacturing phase in order to bridge the gap between the target profit (budgeted profit) and the expected profit of a fiscal period. Therefore, the cost reduction target in Kaizen costing or Target costing is calculated by applying a deductive method to the profit plan that has been decided by top management.[6] This amount is prepared as the "challenge level". In Japanese cost management, the cost reduction target is thus set by top management.

3.2. *Operating pressure*

As discussed earlier, the cost reduction target is calculated based on the targeted period-profit derived from the top–down profit plan. However, the responsibility of achieving these targets is placed entirely on the employees to create new inventions and ideas. Therefore, repetitively setting cost reduction targets in every period eventually has a similar effect to squeezing out a squeezed dust-cloth one more time. One drawback of target costing is that design engineers can suffer from burnout. Kato[7] has pointed out this negative effect of target costing and suggested that the possibility of burnout is high. Burnout can be defined as a state in which the body is fatigued and when a worker cannot respond to excessive and constant stress.

As cost reduction targets are not easily attainable, ideas for achieving them are collected from within the whole company. As a result of this, and because the target becomes "a premise given from top–down decisions", increased pressure is placed on all employees.

As the setting of cost reduction targets are top–down decisions, all employees are under pressure to achieve these targets. This cost reduction process, which is repeated in every period, causes employee stress. Therefore, the formation of a system of alleviating stress is very important. Here, the setting of cost reduction targets by top–down decision and the achievement of these targets can be called "operating pressure".

3.3. *Management by Policy (Hoshin) as a management system for the realisation of cost reduction targets*

There are various definitions of stress. Typical definitions are characteristics of the job environment threatening an individual and the disagreement between personal ability and job demand.[28] The reactions to stress are divided into "eustress" which brings positive and constructive results, and "distress" which brings negative and destructive results. Therefore, stress must be managed to prevent distress and maximise eustress.[28] It is said that the stress caused by complicated objectives can be reduced by breaking down the objectives into simpler ones by effective decision making.

One characteristic of the Japanese management system of cost reduction is that the cost reduction target, as an operating pressure, can be simplified and assigned as simpler targets by using "Management by Policy (MBP)," a technique of total quality control (TQC). Thus, complicated objectives are simplified into low-rank objectives that can be simply executed by a chain of objective-related means. In this way, simplified objectives can be accomplished by the improvement activities of middle management and shop-floor workers. This is a management style where the organisation as a whole bears the pressure of achieving the target because an "operating pressure by top–down decision" is sequentially placed on all the levels within the organisation.

Imai[5] compares MBP with the management styles of European and American companies. In European and American companies, planning is considered to be the work of managers. Therefore, if a subordinate participates in planning, the territory of a manager is considered to be violated. MBP is different from the Western management style in that it allows the participation of lower-rank managers in the setting and development of objectives.

In Japanese companies, MBP is used in various cost management practices, such as Target costing and Kaizen costing. For example, in Kaizen costing at Toyota Motors, the cost reduction amount in each factory is imposed on all departments, and the cost reduction amount of each department is then imposed on all sections. The amount imposed on each section is further imposed on all groups by deploying the objective. In other words, the distribution of objectives to each department, each section and each group in a factory is carried out by MBP where the contents of objective deployment are decided in cost conferences by each class.[14] Nissan Motors also uses MBP as a method of TCR (Total Cost Reduction). This is a cost reduction activity set as normal activities by MBP in each department. This is also an activity that realises cost reduction targets by connecting the objectives to actions and acting towards the achievement of the objectives.[7] TDK, the electrical materials manufacturer, also emphasises the effectiveness of MBP as a device of Ideal Production System (IPS).[10] The top management of the factory establishes an ideal cost as the target for the following three-year period. The active objectives of each department are set up by the distribution of this ideal cost, and then objectives are set out for the whole factory. As the cost-down themes and objectives are deployed through almost the whole factory, all the employees in the factory have a responsibility to accomplish the target.

The above can be seen in Fig. 18.2, which shows cost reduction targets, given by a top–down decision, as executed by MBP.

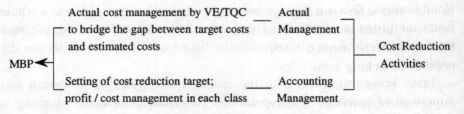

Fig. 18.2. MBP as the execution means of the cost reduction target.

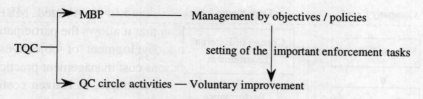

Fig. 18.3. The relationship between MBP and QC circle activities in TQC.

3.4. *MBP and Management by Objectives (MBO)*

The worry that TQC is breaking down is often heard these days. Thus, the Japan Technology Association changed its name from TQC to TQM in April 1996 in order to strengthen the function of management and to strengthen the connection between the vision, the corporate strategy and the policy. TQC is the method that manages the improvement activities by MBP and quality control (QC) circle activities as shown in Fig. 18.3. That is, both the deployment of objectives/policies and the activities to realise the deployed objectives are very important in TQC.

The TQC term-study sub-committee of the Japan Technology Association defines MBP as shown in Box 18.1.[19]

Box 18.1

MBP consists of the activities carried out with the co-operation of the whole company organization in order to efficiently accomplish policies, after the long and mid-term management plans and short-term management policies have been established, based on the basic policy of management.

MBP is a management method to accomplish the objectives determined in mid- and short-term management plans where these objectives are also deployed further into sub organisations by a chain of objective-related means. MBP is thus the method that makes the objectives (managerial items) and policies (checking items) deploy mutually from top management down to supervisors and shop-floor workers. MBP also consists of aggressive improvement activities that are carried out in order to modify situations and to innovate new future situations. However, it differs from the daily

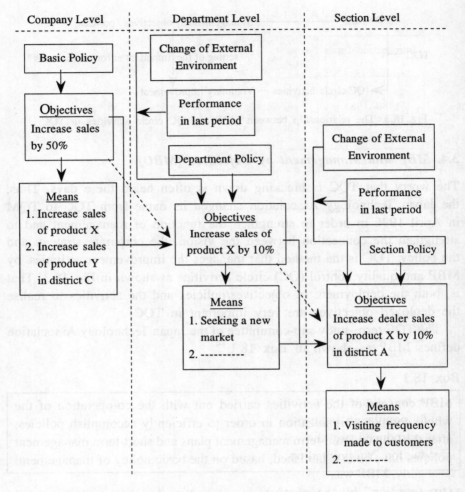

Fig. 18.4. The connection of objectives–means relation for the policy deployment.[25]

management that continuously maintains and manages the work in each department and it also differs from the improvement activities carried out as necessary.[15]

The reality of the use of MBP in Japanese companies will be confirmed using Yui's investigation.[32] This investigation reported that about 91%

Table 18.1. Organisations enforcing MBP.

Introduction times	Number of companies	TQC promotion room	Planning department	Others
−1979	31	6	20	5
1980−1984	21	13	8	0
1985−	23	9	10	4
No answer	3	0	2	1
Total	78	28	40	10

Table 18.2. The relationship between mid-term management plans and one-year policies.

Introduction time	Number of companies	Clear	Relatively clear	Not very clear	Vague	Others
−1979	31	11	16	4	0	0
1980−1984	21	7	8	4	1	1
1985−	23	3	14	6	0	0
No answer	3	0	2	1	0	0
Total	78	21	40	15	1	1

of the investigated companies enforced MBP, confirming that MBP was already popular in Japanese companies. The organisations where MBP has been introduced are shown in Table 18.1 according to the time of MBP introduction. Yui pointed out that in companies where the introduction times were early, MBP was separated from TQC and managed as "MBP = business administration" by the planning departments.

Table 18.2 shows the extent to which there is a clear relationship between the companies' one-year policies and their mid-term plans. From this table, about 78% of investigated companies have a clear connection which implies that their policies are closely connected and promoted with their mid-term management plans.

In the relationship between MBP and budgeting, about 88% of the investigated companies showed that there was a close or relatively close

Table 18.3. MBP and budgeting.

	Number
Closely connected	30
Relatively closely connected	37
Vaguely connected	8
Intentionally separated	0
Others	1
Total	76

Table 18.4. MBP and QC circle activities.

	Number
Formally connected	15
Connected as a result	39
Vaguely connected	17
Not connected	2
Others	5
Total	78

connection between their one-year policies and budgeting. This can be seen in Table 18.3. Table 18.4 shows that MBP is also connected in some way with QC circle activities, another technique of TQC. This may be because the execution of policies depends on the QC circle activities.

However, as for management by objectives (MBO), Drucker[3] (who used the abbreviation, MBO) insisted on MBO's effectiveness on the basis that the real merits of MBO were its conversion from "management by rule" to "management by self-control". MBO is promoted in the following four ways:[4]

1. The objectives that are to be accomplished in any performance evaluation period are clearly given.

2. A subordinate attempts to achieve the objectives, and a superior officer supports this in various ways so that the subordinate can act effectively.
3. Performance is evaluated and compared with the set objectives.
4. If the results of the evaluation interviews show a need for improvement, then corrective action is taken under the mutual agreement of a superior officer and his/her subordinate.

MBO was introduced into Japanese companies in around 1965,[20] and the term MBP was used for the first time as a TQC activity of Bridgestone Tire Co., Ltd. in 1968.[16] It is said that "MBP is the improvement of MBO techniques" where the objectives are accomplished by QC techniques. It is also said to be the result of the search by Japanese companies for a synthetic management system moving towards TQC from statistical quality control (SQC).[15] After that time, these two techniques came to mutually influence each other. However, there was confusion between the two terms. Akao[2] pointed out that, in many cases, the activities carried out by MBP were, during the early stages of its usage, called MBO. The differences between MBP and MBO can be summarised as follows[11,15]:

• The objectives in MBP are established based on the policies of superior officers, whereas in MBO, objectives are established by only those people concerned with the achievement of these objectives. Therefore, the former can be considered as a form of top–down decision making.
• MBP is a QC approach that emphasises the management of processes and provides management with criteria for management items or levels. However, MBO does not prescribe criteria regarding the methods of achieving the objectives.
• In MBO, emphasis is placed more on the individual, but in MBP, this emphasis is placed more on the managers and sub-organisations.
• MBP particularly emphasises the Check-Action stages of the Plan-Do-Check-Action management cycle. If objectives have not been accomplished, the cause will be analysed and corrective action will be taken. In MBO, however, the management cycle is to Plan-Do-See where the results are used only as supplementary data of performance evaluation.

When these techniques are compared, it can be seen that MBO acts as an incentive and its system of performance evaluation emphasises self-motivation. However, in MBP, a weight is placed on those processes which create the results or the deployment of joint objectives. It has been pointed out that the majority of MBO programs being used emphasise the duty itself or the person in charge, implying that MBO does not sufficiently recognise the mutual dependence of duties and team activities.[4]

4. Japanese Performance Evaluation — Process Evaluation

One feature of the Japanese duty execution system is that every employee has a flexible and broad range of duties. This means that because of its vague form, the duty area of each employee overlaps with the duties of others, and the relationship between worker-groups and managers is united.[30] Furthermore, it is believed that such a range of responsibility is particularly important when there is a change in the environment. Nomura[22] made the following comparison between Japanese and German companies. In Germany, both labour and management were in opposition to an enforcement of a strict job evaluation where newly created duties were evaluated and allocated in terms of wage ranks. However, because the Japanese wage system places emphasis on the individual, such opposition between the labour-force and management did not occur, and innovations were carried out smoothly.

In the Japanese style of management the range of duties are vague and the wage system is mainly based on the worker's personal factors. Therefore, the management system in order to accomplish cost reduction targets is not only effective when a joint objective is deployed into the lower classes by MBP, but it also allows for the continuous improvement of each class of employee. Otsubo,[26] who has had experience as a manager, pointed out that in many cases, Japanese performance evaluations were carried out based on informal factors, such as efforts to keep to rule, manner, posture in the workplace and work effort, rather than formal factors. This is because a characteristic of Japanese performance evaluation systems is process evaluation. Japanese wages are not based on performance, because within the Japanese evaluation system, there is a seniority wage system.

However, in economic depressions, with the double blows of the strong yen and the collapse of the economic "bubble", a shift from the traditional seniority wage system to a payment system based on performance was instigated. Although office workers were the main targets of this, the method of execution was through the MBO system. The reason why MBO has come into the spotlight again is because of the low productivity of office workers and management classes. According to a survey in 1995 concerning "an important personnel system for the improvement of management classes",[17] 87% of those asked thought that the introduction of an MBO system was important and 81% agreed on the importance of a combined MBO and reward system. There is a growing need to clarify the relationship between performance and rewards through MBO because there are difficulties in establishing objectives for the office workers and management classes. Additionally there is no clear relationship between the individual objectives and the main company objective. Furthermore, the Policy Information & Research Division of the Labour Minister Secretariat[27] had predicted that "lifetime employment" would be maintained for mainstay workers, but that shifts from the traditional seniority wage system to a payment system based on performance would continue to grow because labour costs were increasing, evaluation intervals were being reduced and a greater emphasis was being placed on performance.

However, according to the investigation carried out in 1,014 companies by the Aichi-ken Manager Association in March 1994,[1] the criteria of performance evaluation differ according to different posts. This is presented in Table 18.5 below.

Table 18.5. Performance evaluation criteria related to the post.

Post \ Criteria	Degree of challenge	Degree of objective achievement	Quality of job	Quality of task	Improvement of duties
General employees	4.0	3.9	7.0	6.7	2.6
Intermediate post	3.9	5.3	7.0	4.8	3.8
Supervisor post	4.0	7.4	5.7	3.0	5.2
Management class	4.3	9.5	4.9	2.4	4.7

Table 18.5 shows rankings in the importance of different performance evaluation criteria for different work posts. The scale of ranking ranges from zero to ten where zero represents "no importance" and ten represents "very important". This table shows that the higher posts are strongly evaluated by the achievement of objectives, but the lower posts are mainly evaluated by the quality of the job and the quantities of the tasks carried out. Thus, as Otsubo pointed out, the lower-ranked posts are evaluated by the job itself, but the higher-ranked posts show a characteristic of MBO which is evaluation in terms of the achievement of objectives.

5. The Administration Structure of Japanese Corporate Society

5.1. *Cost reduction targets and improvement activities*

As mentioned earlier, Japanese cost reduction targets are carried out by the following processes. Firstly, the cost reduction target is decided by top management and is given in the form of an "operating pressure". The target, as an operating pressure, is then simplified and assigned by MBP through a chain of objectives-means relationships. However, such processes will not operate efficiently if employees are not committed to their company and do not voluntarily participate in improvement efforts. This phenomena is strongly related to the Japanese performance evaluation system where a vague range of duties and a human-centred long-term evaluation method make possible the setting of common objectives and joint responsibilities so that objectives can be accomplished through the employees' efforts. These efforts to make improvements will lead to an improvement of MBP itself. Any improvements made will also be continuously improved upon in the following period. However, this effect will cease if no structure exists where employees can voluntarily participate in improvement efforts. Box 18.2 explains such voluntary improvement efforts of employees by describing the self-analysis of an electricity company employee.[9]

Suzuki[30] expresses the feelings of such workers and describes the administration structure as follows. Enforced objectives are first given to workers, then they realise that they cannot help but follow. In other words, because

Box 18.2

I participate in and observe QC circle activities every day at work and have come to feel strongly that neither the words "voluntary" nor "involuntary," can accurately describe these activities. Even though QC circle activities are sometimes carried out unwillingly, it would be incorrect to call them "involuntary". Accordingly, it would also be untrue to say that they are carried out voluntarily and with enthusiasm. Although these activities are unpleasant at first, as you carry them out, a desire to work gradually grows within you and a certain degree of both pleasure and satisfaction can be experienced. In theory, I do not have to participate in any QC circle activity if I find it unpleasant. However, this is not possible in practice. To not participate would be to disrupt the rules of the workplace and would mean being expelled from the company. There is a control structure in the workplace which expects individuals not to venture too far from the group. Therefore, because I cannot be left out, I cannot help but be dragged in. However, because getting left out would be painful, I might as well participate positively and maybe enjoy it.

workers experience a degree of independence that is allowed within a restricted range, participation later develops and the compulsion to resist fades. When a demand for cost reduction is made, under the precondition that this must be accomplished, some small independence is eventually found for individuals. This may be understood on the basis that QC circle activities remove the obstacles to the realisation of objectives and ultimately lead to improvements. However, the argument proposed by Suzuki overlooks the function of motivation in companies where the operating pressure given by top management is simplified and assigned by MBP.

So far, this study has analysed the processes by which objectives are assigned by MBP and accomplished by the efforts of employees. The idea that workers' efforts are voluntary can be explained by the Japanese system of performance evaluation. However, Japanese culture and the structure of corporate society must also be considered.

5.2. *The structure of Japanese corporate society*

When discussing the structure of Japanese corporate society, it is often necessary to explain Japanese culture, because the individual behavioural patterns of employers and employees are influenced by the social culture. Many cases are explained from a standpoint of group behavioural patterns in discussions of the corporate society in relation to Japanese culture. However, this chapter will explain the corporate society structure by referring to the Japanese Confucian moral principle, "on to on-gaeshi" (a favour and its repayment). It is thought that both the employees' commitment towards their company and their source of loyalty are based on this Confucian principle of the old Samurai society. This principle promotes an exchange of favours and states that the receiver of a favour is obliged to honour a repayment.

In Japan, the relationship between parents and children is considered to be relative and conditional in terms of the parents' efforts of raising children and the children's obligation to repay the favour.[8] This practice of receiving a favour is accompanied by the obligation of repayment and is an extension of the feudal relationship between a feudal lord and his subordinates.[8] Of course, it would be unfair to explain today's corporate management by this relationship only. However, it is thought that these cultural sides have been a moral influence in restricting the behaviour of employees in Japanese corporate society. An investigation by The Policy Information & Research Division of the Labour Minister Secretariat,[27] concluded that employees develop a commitment towards their company and have a strong work-ethic for their jobs because corporate growth would guarantee their long-term employment. This suggests that employees' commitment towards their company is secured only by their lifetime employment. Therefore, in Japanese companies, the traditional values of "on to on-gaeshi" exists as the company's culture base and it can be said that lifetime employment and employees' commitment towards their company are the terms of exchange in this exchange relationship.[12]

As discussed in an OECD report,[23] the reason why the Japanese employment system is beneficial to both employers and productivity is because of the employees' commitment towards their company rather than their jobs. However, one weakness of the Japanese employment system is that it restricts the freedom of change of occupation due to social and moral pressures. The Japanese management system, which includes lifetime employment under the traditional cultural foundation of a favour and its repayment, has formed the closed corporate society. The "moral pressure" of the traditional cultural foundation of "on to on-gaeshi" not only raises the employees' commitment towards their company but also makes the corporate culture one of voluntary improvement.

The Policy Information & Research Division of the Labour Minister Secretariat concluded that both personnel evaluation and employee selection over a long-term period based on the lifetime employment system has given employees a desire for promotion and helped them maintain the motivation for work.[27]

6. Conclusion

In Japanese companies, target costs or improvement costs are established based on top–down decisions as the target is derived deductively from the profit plan. MBP is used as a means of achieving the target where the target is reduced into simpler, lower-ranked targets. Therefore, MBP is an effective means of achieving the targets set by top management. However, the targets assigned by MBP are ultimately achieved through the efforts of employees based on their commitment towards the company. Therefore, the process of evaluation is a prolonged incentive and is effective in performance evaluation.

These days, "empowerment" attracts increased attention as the main management control method. The concept of empowerment is that each employee acts voluntarily through an understanding of the company mission based on the corporation's ideology. That is, empowerment may be interpreted as the employees' commitment towards their company and working towards common values. Thus, voluntary improvement is promoted by employee empowerment. Although both common values and employees' commitment towards their company, as characteristics of empowerment, differ from nation to nation, in Japanese companies, empowerment is strongly encouraged and built up by Japanese management and culture.

References

1. Aichi-ken Keieisya Kyokai, Keiei-romu, November, 1994, 9–11.
2. Akao, Y., ed., Hoshin-kanri Katsuyo no Jissai (Nihon Kikaku-kyokai, 1989), 4.
3. Drucker, P., The Practice of Management (Harper & Brothers, 1954).
4. Hayashi, S., Keiei-jitsumu, October, 1992, 40–53.
5. Imai, M., Kaizen (Kodansya, 1988), 270–271.
6. Ito, H., Kigyo-kaikei, Vol. 44, No. 8, 1992, 17–24.
7. Kato, Y., Genka-kikaku (Nihon Keizai-shinbunsya, 1993), 137, 285.
8. Kawashima, T., Nihon-syakai no Kazokuteki Kosei (Nihon Hyoronsya, 1977).
9. Keizai-hyoron Betssatsu, Nihon-teki Roshi-kankei no Hikari to Kage (Nihon Hyoronsya, 1982), 130–131.
10. Kojyo-kanri, June, 1993, 43–50.
11. Kuwada, H., Syogaku Ronsyu, Vol. 16, No. 3 (Osaka Gakuin-daigaku, 1990), 187–210.
12. Lee, G., International Economic Discussion Paper No. 74 (School of Economics Nagoya University, 1994).
13. Monden, Y., Journal of Management Accounting Reseach, Vol. 3, 1991, 16–34.
14. Monden, Y., Kagaku-kyosoryoku wo Tsukeru Genka-kikaku to Genka-kaizen no Giho (Toyokeizaishinbosya, 1994), 232.
15. Nakada, H., ed., TQM-jidai no Senryaku-teki Hoshin-kanri (Nikkagiren, 1996), 4, 12, 99.
16. Naya, K., TQC-suishin no Tameno Hoshin-kanri (Nikkagiren, 1982), 23.
17. Nemoto, T., JMA Manejimento Rebyu, May, 1996, 24–27.
18. Nihon Kaikei Kenkyu-gakkai Dai 53 Daikai Tokubetsu-iinkai, 1994.
19. Nikkagiren MC-yogo Kento Syo-iinkai, Hinsitus-kanri, March, 1988, 47–50.
20. Nikkeiren Kohobu, ed., Mokuhyo-kanri Seido-jireisyu (Nikkeiren Kohobu, 1994), 11.
21. Nishizawa, O., Nihon-kanrikaikei-gakkai Dai 5 kai Zenkoku-daikai, 1995.
22. Nomura, M., Syushin-koyo (Iwanami-syoten, 1994), 122–123.
23. OECD, Tainichi Rodo Hokokusyo (Nihon Rodo-kyokai, 1972).
24. Okano, H., Nihonteki-kanrikaikei no Tenkai (Chuo-keizaisya, 1995), 98–100, 118–120.
25. Orita, Y., Hoshin-kanri no Susumekata (Bijinesu O-mu, 1984).
26. Otsubo, M., Sosiki-kagaku, Vol. 28, No. 4, 1995, 66–75.

27. Rodo-daijin Kanpo Seisaku-chosabu, ed., Nihon-teki Koyo-seido no Genjyo to Tenbo (Okura-syo Insatsu-kyoku, 1995), 13–15.

28. Ryu, K., Stress Management (Boeki-keieisya, 1992), 84–90.

29. Sakurai, M. & Ito, K., Kigyo-kaikei, Vol. 38, No. 11, 1986, 41–52.

30. Suzuki, Y., Nihon-teki Seisan-sisutemu to Kigyo-syakai (Hokkaido-daigaku Tosyo-kankokai, 1994), 254–265.

31. Tanaka, M., Genka-kikaku no Riron to Jissen (Chuo-keizaisya, 1995), 48.

32. Yui, H., Keieigaku-ronsyu (Ryukoku-daigaku, 1993), 43–52.

Chapter 19

A Management System for the Simultaneous Attainment of Customer Satisfaction and Employee Satisfaction

KAZUKI HAMADA

1. Introduction

One of the changes in the corporate environment in recent years has been the intensification of competition among companies. If all the attributes of a certain product and the level of customer service in different companies are the same, competition among companies is determined by price. However, because such price competition promotes a price-cutting war, this is not good for companies. Therefore, each company tries to develop higher functional products and higher quality products than those of other companies in order to evade this price competition, and thus the competition of quality differentiation is promoted. This tendency promotes an increased product range within a company and, soon, companies need more funds and holding stocks than before. As a result, companies raise their fund efficiency, and measures for shortening the production–sales cycle become necessary for stock reduction.

Shortening the appointed date of delivery has positive effects on production, such as an improvement in productivity by the rejection of wastes etc., in addition to having a positive effect on sales such as an increase in reliability for customers, the setting of higher prices, etc. Work improvements become necessary in order to shorten appointed delivery dates, and there is an increased probability that these improvements are connected with improvements in responsiveness and flexibility of employees. On the other hand, because the merits of quickly receiving the product which a buyer has ordered are high on the buyer's side, the buyer demands further reductions to delivery periods.

Because other companies aim to produce many kinds of products for the same reasons, the market has diversified greatly. This accelerates the early obsolescence of a product and shortens its life cycle. Therefore, companies proceed with a concurrent development which is called a rugby-type development, and need to shorten the development cycles of new products.

Technological innovation is particularly intense in the electronics industry. It is profitable for companies that the starting point of development draws near to the marketing point to make products with higher functionality and lower costs, because the company can utilize the latest technologies. If a company shortens its development cycle, risks will be reduced, because it is sufficient to predict customers' needs for the near future. Furthermore, a company can have the advantage of the establishment of standards and the advantage of having taken the initiative in innovation. Shortening the appointed date of delivery and the development cycle is a time competition.

As mentioned above, currently, competition between companies occurs on prices, quality and time, and companies need to win these competitions to gain competitive advantages. Of course the shortening of the production time influences a quality and price differentiation, and a quality differentiation influences price and time; therefore price, quality and time are mutually related and these mutual relationships also influence the competitive edge.

Another change of company environment is the advancement of the information-intensive society. By several different kinds of media, a customer today can get information on products throughout the world, and the customer can get everything he or she wants from more or less anywhere. An employee also can get information on markets and activity processes in "real time".

Such things give power to customers and employees and the situation becomes one where customers take the leading roles of markets and employees take the responsibilities of process implementations.

Systems and processes need flexibility and innovations because the responsiveness to customers is important in today's information-intensive society. This also means that the degree of independent actions of each employee becomes higher. Therefore the role of the manager cannot help changing into an empowerment from top–down form of control. Empowerment means that managers transfer their authority to their subordinates and they thus motivate subordinates.

If the above two changes in the company environment are considered, it seems that currently companies are concentrating on ways to motivate employees and to provide products and services which satisfy customers by organizational innovation to win cost competitions, differentiation competitions and time competitions.

The purpose of this chapter is to approach this subject from the view of management accounting. Therefore, I will examine from various angles how the various factors concerning customers and employees that bring competitive advantages are considered. Then I will consider the method of TP (total productivity) management, which is a method of greatly improving factors of price, quality, and the appointed date of delivery related to CS (customer satisfaction) and factors of ES (employee satisfaction).

2. Factors Concerning Customers and Employees for Competitive Advantage

The factors that must be considered in the planning of company strategy are as follows:

(1) sensitive reaction to customers' needs
(2) profitability
(3) quality
(4) innovation of systems and processes
(5) flexibility of systems and processes.

(1) is the most important factor for it brings competitive advantages, and (5) relates to the improvement of employees' solutions to problems and their sensitive reactions in various situations.

Appropriate evaluation systems are necessary for the balanced attainment of strategic goals, and some companies execute this management method by "balanced scorecard". This management method is a top–down type method basically that sets an attainment goal and evaluates performance from the points of view of customers, business processes, innovation and learning, and financial affairs, taking into consideration the business idea and the business vision. For example, Ref. 1.

(1) indexes of customer relationship: appointed date of delivery, quality, price (cost), customer service, etc.
(2) indexes of business processes: process time, quality, productivity, cost, etc.
(3) indexes of innovation, organizational learning and human resources: technological and organizational innovation, education and training of employees, employee satisfaction, etc.
(4) financial indexes: profitability, growth rate, indexes of stockholder relationship, etc.

Of these indexes, the indexes of customer relationship and employee relationship are the most important. The balanced scorecard also included financial indexes and non-financial indexes, external indexes and internal indexes, past attainment indexes and prospective attainment indexes, objective indexes and subjective indexes. For companies, the balanced attainment of those indexes is important. Management by such balanced scorecards is a method adopted against the criticism that the performance evaluation system in companies has depended too heavily on financial indexes until now and the wrong solutions have been selected because of this. For example, if companies depend too much on financial indexes, they try to keep surplus stocks in order to raise production efficiency, and to purchase materials of lower quality in order to lower material costs and also to reduce the education/training costs of employees.

As financial indexes are clear and objective, they are fair indexes in this sense. However, it is important to evaluate and to control invisible assets for attaining strategic goals. Even if a company attains CS and ES, it is also important for a company to attain its financial goals. Therefore financial indexes are also contained in the indexes of balanced scorecard.

It is important to note that, at first, balanced scorecards were only used to stress performance evaluation, but in recent years balanced scorecards have also been used for various other situations, as follows. For example,

(1) They are useful in making company strategies and plans.
(2) They promote the joint ownership of appropriate information.
(3) It is useful in order to keep co-ordination among individuals, organizations and departments in order to attain a common goal. They also make clear that much contact becomes necessary.
(4) They are useful to attain simultaneously conflicting goals set up in a long-term plan.

Four aspects of balanced scorecards are shown to be cause–result relationships in Fig. 19.1. For example, if a company is going to increase its profit and its rate of return on capital, it must increase CS and customer loyalty. In addition, keeping to appointed delivery dates, quality improvement and price-reducing by cost reduction become necessary for CS and the increase of customer loyalty. The appointed date of delivery, quality and cost are influenced by the degree of production and sales process improvement. This improvement of processes is attained by more competent employees, and ES becomes a premise for this. In this way, if the indexes

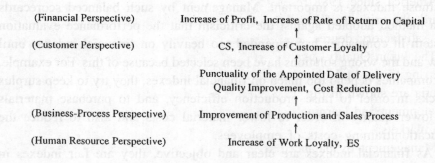

Fig. 19.1. Relationship between cause and result.

(Direction and Driving Force) (Operation System)   (Goals and Results)

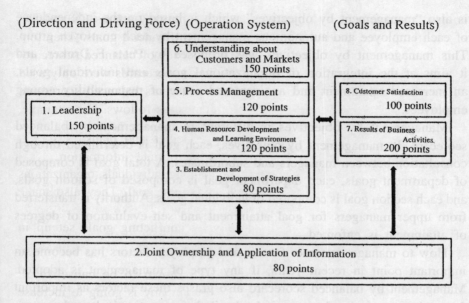

Fig. 19.2. Framework of Japan Quality Award (1997 fiscal year). From Ref. 2, p. 14.

of balanced scorecards are adjusted to show relationship between cause and result, this resembles the way of thinking of a service–profit chain. Service–profit chain is a way of thinking that relates profitability, customer loyalty, ES, worker loyalty and productivity.

The criteria of the Malcolm Baldrige National Quality Award commended in America since 1988 resemble those of a balanced scorecard. For this award, the criteria of human resource development and customer priority and satisfactory degree are also given high marks.

The Japan Quality Award[2] was established in Japan in December 1995, referring to the Malcolm Baldrige National Quality Award. The evaluation criteria are shown in Fig. 19.2. High grades are offered in human resource development and learning environment and understanding about customers and markets.

Management by balanced scorecard has been carried out originally as a top–down type management with regard to employees. By contrast, there is also "management by objectives" which is based on the independence of each employee and autonomous management by each employee group. This management by objectives was proposed by Peter F. Druker, and it aims at the integration of organizational goals and individual goals, an increased attainment and an increased sense of responsibility among employees.

Management by objectives is different to management by balanced scorecard. In management by objectives, each goal is determined through consultation between managers and subordinates. A total goal is composed of department goals, each department goal is composed of section goals, and each section goal is composed of individual goals. Authority is transferred from upper managers for goal attainment and self-evaluation of degrees of attainment is enforced.

How to manage customer factors and employee factors has become an important point in recent years, if any type of management is adopted. Management by balanced scorecard also grasps these factors as important factors in strategy development and a detailed examination is done; however, for execution, the strategy must be more specific.

With management by objectives, the goal is to take the motivation of employees into account, and measures are examined at each level in order to make goals more specific. However, there is one weak point, that by too much emphasis on employee participation, the integration between a total goal and the goals of each level becomes difficult and the fulfillment of goals decreases. Therefore I will now discuss the method of TP management as an advanced method of mixing management advantages by using both balanced scorecard and management by objectives, and I will consider these in detail in the following section.

3. TP Management to Aim at the Balanced Attainment of Goals

TP management is defined by Professor Masao Akiba as follows:[3]

(1) It shows the concrete attainment of goals and the concrete efficiency criteria to execute correctly and effectively the subjects for productivity improvement,

(2) It adopts the top–down type/priority system of management,
(3) It clarifies how each activity within a division is connected directly with the attainment goals and explains how better to contribute towards the effective realization of the attainment goals,
(4) It effectively builds highly motivated and vital arrangements of actions,
(5) It is a management technique which drastically improves the nature of production and attains the given goals through a united effort.

The basic type of TP management is shown in Fig. 19.3. As shown in this figure, TP management attaches importance to a "total" viewpoint and, within this management, objective setting, objective deployment, measures selection, organization system and implementation management there are five important pillars.

Figure 19.3 is limited to showing production activities. For example, let us suppose that productivity improvement is established as an overall objective. The objectives to attain this are listed systematically by the story-type chart. The objective of the lowest rank is each individual objective and this is the part objective for the overall objective attainment. Therefore, as the overall objective is achieved by the attainments of all the individual objectives, managers can calculate contribution rates to the overall achievement of each objective.

After individual objectives have been decided, the measures to attain these objectives, with respect to the varieties of products, manufacturing processes and materials are examined. After these measures have been selected, the individual results that will be gained by adopting these measures are forecast. By checking these results with the individual objectives, concrete implementation targets are decided. The activity centers in charge of these implementation targets are decided. It is considered how staff are concerned with these lines, and thus the organization system is decided. The necessity of a corporation that can exceed obstacles to its organization is recognized by this layout. An implementation schedule is decided for implementation targets, and the implementation management toward the target attainment is carried out. In this way, objectives and measures are set out logically and specifically, problems decrease and it becomes clear what managers should do. As objectives and measures are set out by using matrixes, the

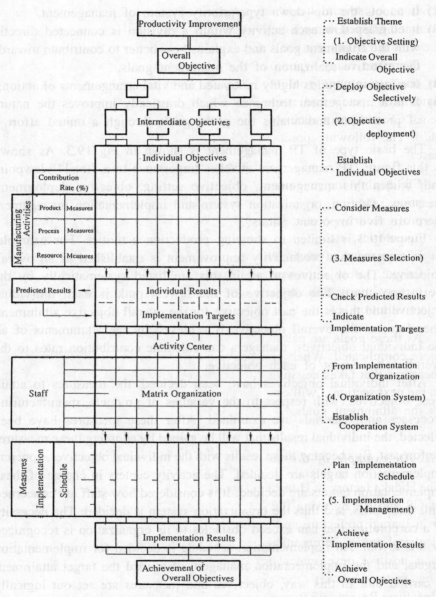

Fig. 19.3. The overall structure of TP management. From Ref. 3, p. 28.

relations of several items are clarified and the total constitution can be seen and grasped immediately. Since it is easy to relate one matrix to another, the characteristics can be utilized in the setting out of this plan.

There are many types of TP management. Some types pay attention to one attainment goal (e.g. "CS", "profit security", "ES", "factory innovation", etc.) and some pay attention to the joint attainment goals (e.g. "CS and profit security", "CS and ES", "CS and factory innovation", etc.). The following points are established as intermediate goals in each case:

1. CS: quality improvement, shortening appointed delivery dates, cutting prices, etc.
2. profit security: cost reduction, increasing production volume, decreasing inventories, etc.
3. ES: increase of motivation, increased personnel activity, decrease in fatigue, safety improvements, etc.
4. factory innovation: technical improvements, improvement in factory constitution, etc.

As those goals are parallel or inter-relational, their breakdown becomes more complicated. When goals have mutual relationships, the selection of measures that takes negative effects into account becomes more important. In the next section, I will consider the ways in which CS and ES are decided as the attainment goals.

3.1. *An example of the simultaneous attainment of CS and ES*

The Hidaka factory of Hitachi Cable Co. Ltd.[4] is an example of the integration of CS and ES by using the TP management method. The Hidaka factory is in Ibaragi prefecture and the factory mainly produces electric cables for electrical power, communications and electronic machinery. In recent years their positive development into the field of information has carried out. This factory has set "the attainment of a good factory" as a company objective. By using TP management, the factory intended to increase CS by quality improvement, cutting prices (cost reduction), service improvements (shortening the appointed date of delivery, increase of production) and the increase of ES by improving work environments and the education/training of employees.

Some aspects of CS and ES conflict in the short-term, however, they have a positive relationship in the long-term, as a service-profit chain shows. The growth of a company cannot be attained without CS, and CS is supported by ES. For example, if a company introduces CIM in order to improve its working environment, this brings positive effects for ES (such as the reduction of working hours, and the decrease of work-related accidents) as well as leading to positive effects for CS (such as an increased product reliability, cost reductions and the shortening of appointed delivery dates). There are also many cases where a company has promoted the improvement of employee ability, along with company morale, by introducing education systems in order to promote employee self-improvement and have therefore attained cost reduction and an improvement of productivity as a result. Furthermore, technological development is necessary for CS, and there have been some cases where the improvement of morale in employees is initiated through technological development in a company.

Figure 19.4 shows a way of integrating CS and ES. First, various factors of customers' needs are evaluated and analyzed, and their contribution rate and contribution value are calculated by each factor. Similarly, factors of employees' needs are evaluated and analyzed, and their contribution rate and contribution value are also calculated by each factor. It is then necessary to consider what kinds of measures must be selected to increase the evaluation factors of high contribution values for CS and ES using the distribution diagram of product function deployment. Operational measures are decided with regard to whether cost goals and service goals are attained.

Figure 19.5 shows in detail the analysis of CS factors and the computation of contribution values taken from Fig. 19.4. At first, the expectations for quality improvement are decided by customers' needs, and the frequencies of these items are examined and ranked in A, B, C, etc. order. Then the relations between the expectation items and the evaluation factors are analyzed and marked by symbols such as ◎, ○, △ etc. In Fig. 19.5 for rank A, ◎ is 5 points, ○ is 4 points, △ is 3 points, for rank B, ◎ is 4 points,

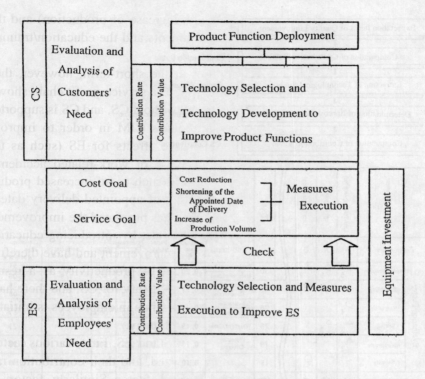

Fig. 19.4. Framework of integration of CS and ES. From Ref. 4, p. 71.

O is 3 points, △ is 2 points. The total points for each evaluation factor are calculated and the contribution rate is also calculated. Furthermore, technology subjects for evaluation factors are extracted and improvement goals are also decided. Improvement coefficients are decided on this basis and each contribution value is decided by the multiplication of a contribution rate, a factor weight and finally an improvement coefficient. The contribution value is the one for CS in the case of the attainment of the technological goal. The total contribution value of each factor is 1.73 in Fig. 19.5. This means that CS would become 1.73 times greater than at present if measures were executed entirely according to the goals.

The analysis of ES factors and the calculation of contribution values are done in the same way as the analysis of customer evaluation factors and the

Expectation Items of Quality Improvement

↓

Computation of Contribution Rate — Contribution Rate : a

↓

Extraction of Technological Subjects — Factor Weight : b

↓

Determination of Improvement Coefficient — Improvement Coefficient : e

↓

Computation of Contribution Value — CS Contribution Value : N=a×b×e

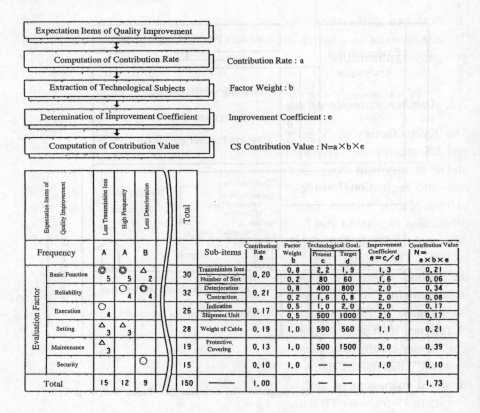

Expectation Items of Quality Improvement → Frequency	Less Transmission loss A	High Frequency A	Less Deterioration B	Total	Evaluation Factor	Sub-items	Contribution Rate a	Factor Weight b	Technological Goal Present c	Target d	Improvement Coefficient e=c/d	Contribution Value N= a×b×e
Basic Function	◎ 5	◎ 5	△ 2	30		Transmission loss	0.20	0.8	2.2	1.9	1.3	0.21
						Number of Sort		0.2	80	60	1.6	0.06
Reliability		○ 4	◎ 4	32		Deterioration	0.21	0.8	400	800	2.0	0.34
						Contraction		0.2	1.6	0.8	2.0	0.08
Execution	○ 4			26		Indication	0.17	0.5	1.0	2.0	2.0	0.17
						Shipment Unit		0.5	500	1000	2.0	0.17
Setting	△ 3	△ 3		28		Weight of Cable	0.19	1.0	590	560	1.1	0.21
Maintenance	△ 3			19		Protective Covering	0.13	1.0	500	1500	3.0	0.39
Security			○	15			0.10	1.0	—	—	1.0	0.10
Total	15	12	9	150			1.00		—	—		1.73

Fig. 19.5. Analysis of customer evaluation factors and calculation of contribution values. From Ref. 4, p. 71.

calculation of contribution values. First, improvement items are arranged and marks are given for the evaluation factors by consideration of their frequencies. The contribution rates are calculated and contribution values for ES are calculated on the basis of these and improvement coefficients.

Measures to attain the goals of costs, appointed delivery dates and production volume are decided by using the contribution values for CS and ES with the distribution diagram of product function deployment. Based on the operation plan, the allocation of equipment investment is decided afterwards.

As shown above, the Hidaka factory of the Hitachi Cable Co. Ltd. cites TP management as a major management technique in managing the whole company synthetically.

3.2. *Another example of the simultaneous attainment of CS and ES*

The Kyoto factory of N company is another example of simultaneous CS and ES attainment.[5] The Kyoto factory is a core factory of the N group, and its factory is in charge of the development and production of commercial cars and recreational vehicles. The production bases of N company are in two places, Shonan factory and Kyoto factory; the latter is the only production factory in the Kinki zone. In this factory, K-TAP (Kyoto Total Approach to Productivity), which is real total management, was introduced in 1991. The second stage of this activity is currently being executed. In the second stage, just as in the first stage, the increase of CS (quality improvement, cost reduction, shortening appointed delivery dates, etc.) and the increase of ES (increase of employees' comfort, reduction in feelings of fatigue, increased feelings of attainment, etc.) are the two objectives. The factory claims to have achieved the goal of the factory being "connected by heart" and makes much of their attainments such as the establishment of speed management and cost reduction.

Figure 19.6 shows TP management in Kyoto factory. In this figure, goals relating to cost, quality and the appointed date of delivery are broken down into individual goals as shown. Measures to attain these goals have been examined from viewpoints of design, plan, work and control. The examination of what influence the measures have on ES is also carried out. Furthermore, if the measures are executed, they can be examined where the charge posts are.

This method is called "Simulation Rolling". It predicts and evaluates in what kind of position there is the excavation/enforcement situation of measures of comparison with each goal, as developed in this factory. Using this method, managers will be able to predict precisely whether the factory will be able to attain goals of a set term and what kinds of measures should be executed in the next fiscal year. They will be able to calculate precisely

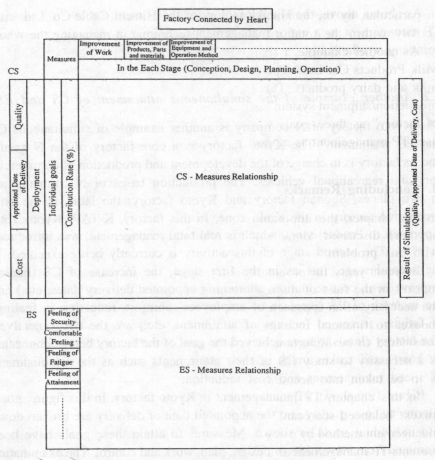

Fig. 19.6. TP management in Kyoto Factory. From Ref. 5, p. 16.

what degree of influence the cost reduction in each small group will give to costs all over the factory. Simulations are carried out each week by small groups and the evaluation of these results, the revision of goals and the provision of extra measures are carried out immediately, thus giving a real-time management.

The Kyoto factory mentioned above also uses TP management as a method that succeeds in focusing individual activities on a total corporate goal and, in particular, by the technique of simulation rolling, the position of each activity within the total management structure is determined.

As another example, I shall consider the Atugi factory of Snow Brand Milk Products Co. Ltd.[6] The Atugi factory is a mainstay factory producing milk and dairy products. This factory has set the "establishment of flexible production/shipment system" as a general goal, and "CS", "ES" and "renewal of factory" as three goals which should be considered. This factory also uses TP management as a general method of managing the entire company.

4. Concluding Remarks

In this chapter, the importance of CS and ES in company management has been discussed, along with how management accounting should cope with this problem.

In recent years, the problems of using only financial indexes as attainment indexes in the field of management accounting have been pointed out and the necessity of an approach by balanced scorecard, which adds operational indexes to financial indexes, is emphasized. Indexes of CS and ES are considered to be important in this balanced scorecard. This means that it is a necessity to study CS and ES if the field of management accounting is to be taken into account.

In this chapter, TP management has been discussed as a method that mixes "balanced scorecard" and management by objectives, and a general management method by using these theories has been described. This chapter presents TP management as a method that precedes management by balanced scorecard. Recently, the definition of balanced scorecard has changed to include not only the indexes for performance evaluation but also measures for communicating and coordinating strategies. This means that management by balanced scorecard and TP management both require a similar way of thinking.

Therefore both methods have many common points, and the advantages of using them are as follows:

1. They are useful to give a constant framework for organizational innovation and goal attainments.

2. They are useful for employees to clarify the processes that goals are decided upon.
3. They are useful for employees to precisely communicate the goals.
4. They are useful for employees to improve the understanding of a goal.
5. They are useful to maintain co-ordination between goals and not to attain partial opimisation, but to attain total optimisation.
6. They are useful to maintain co-ordination between goals and measures.
7. They promote learning about the relationship between goals and measures by leaving records for others to learn from.

Thus, both management methods have many advantages but it should be understood that the "balanced scorecard" method only arranges and lists the important points for strategy developments and attainment evaluations.

Although it is difficult to compare the two methods, as their focal points are different, it seems that TP management has more advantages than the management by balanced scorecard, as shown below:

1. TP management is useful to clarify logically the relationships between goals (vertical relationships and horizontal relationships) because the breaking down of goals is done systematically.
2. It is easy to take action and to innovate organizations because TP management shows more systematically the relations between goals and measures taken.
3. TP management clarifies how a change of measure and a part goal have influences over a total goal.

The method of TP management has, of course, not been studied in the field of management accounting but in the field of business administration and industrial engineering. However, I believe that management accounting methods can be further improved by introducing TP management into the field of management accounting.

References

1. Kaplan, R. S. & Norton, D. P., The Balanced Scorecard (Harvard Business School Press, Boston, 1996).

2. Ajikata, M., Criterion of Japan Quality Award (Nikkan- Kogyo Sinbunsha, Tokyo, 1997).
3. Akiba, M., Implementation Method of TP Management (Nihon Noritu Kyokai Management Center, Tokyo, 1994).
4. Seki, S., Nakazato, K., Nakahigasi, F. & Sago, H., Rapid Advance of the Hidaka Factory of Hitachi Cable Co. Ltd. by the Achievement of CS and ES, Kojyo Kanri, D38-9, 1992, 68–75.
5. Kaji, H., Special Award of TP Management: Kyoto Factory of Nissan Shatai Co. Ltd. JMA Management Review, D2-6, 1996, 14–17.
6. Koyanagi, H. & Sasaki, D., Establishment of Production/Sales System to Fit the Various/Variable Production and High Frequency Deliveries, Kojyo Kanri, D39-12, 1993, 74–80.

Part 8
Cost Management in Budgetary Control System

Chapter 20

Profit Evaluation Measures for the Division Managers in Japanese Decentralized Company — Focusing on Controllable and Corporate Costs

NORIKO HOSHI and YASUHIRO MONDEN

1. Introduction

In this paper we establish and then examine the hypotheses concerning the relationship between the use of profit measures for evaluating divisional performance and organizational performance in Japanese companies. For this purpose, we will relate the costs controllable by the divisional manager along with those not controlled by him, such as central head-office or corporate costs. When companies adopt a diversification strategy to operate various activities, its business will become complicated which will lead them to adopt a decentralized organization system. Usually these divisions function as profit centers and, since these are not independent companies, divisional managers must periodically report the divisional performance (that is, the periodic profit) to the company's top management. The top management uses this periodic profit figure to evaluate the divisional performance in two ways: (1) to evaluate the division manager's performance,

437

(2) to evaluate the division's performance. From existing literature, it is found that the profit measure normally used to evaluate a divisional manager's performance differs from that of a division: while the "profit before head-office or corporate cost" is used in the former situation, "profit after head-office or corporate cost" is used in the latter. David Solomon[10] argues that the most suitable income figure for use in appraising the performance of divisional management, and also for use by divisional executives in guiding their decisions, is controllable residual income before tax, arrived at after deducting controllable division overheads, depreciation, property taxes and insurance on controllable fixed assets. He added that to guide top management in its decisions relating to a division, the most appropriate figure seems to be net residual income, arrived at after subtracting non-controlled divisional overheads and incremental central expenses chargeable to the division. However, in Japanese companies it is actually seen that divisional managers are evaluated by the "profit after head-office or corporate cost."

Accordingly, the main purpose of this chapter is to analyze the Japanese practice of evaluating division manager's performance measures through a questionnaire survey, and also to clarify why such practice is undertaken in Japan.

2. Conventional Theory on the Controllable Profit and the Profit after Allocating Corporate Costs

Generally, there are four concepts relating to the periodic profit of a division. Similar concepts are also offered by Horngren *et al.*[2]

Contribution Margin is sales revenues minus the total variable costs of production and sales.

Controllable Profit is the contribution margin minus all divisional fixed costs that are (1) directly traceable to the division and (2) controllable by the divisional manager. This measure includes the cost of providing such services as indirect labor, indirect materials, and utilities. These are called managed capacity costs. The division manager can reduce these costs by streamlining operations or by reducing complexity and diversity in product lines and marketing channels.[3]

Contribution Margin to Corporate Costs and Profit is controllable profit minus the divisional fixed costs not controlled by the division manager. This represents the estimated contribution that the division is making to corporate profit and capacity-related costs that provide general purpose capacity, such as administrative and office resources. This includes the committed capacity costs.

Net Income Before Tax is calculated by subtracting general management (or corporate) costs and service departments costs from the contribution margin to corporate costs and profit. These costs are common capacity costs outside the division. However, while distinguishing between corporate cost and company-wide service department costs, the latter is allocated almost in proportion to the degree of service used by each division, but the former is fixed.

These profit concepts are illustrated in Fig. 20.1.

In calculating divisional net income before tax, many companies arbitrarily allocate all capacity-related costs incurred at the corporate level to their divisions. Since the profits generated by divisions must exceed centrally incurred costs before the company becomes profitable, there is considerable interest in allocating these costs in order to identify each division's contribution to the company.[3] It may not be relevant to use this profit measure in evaluating a division manager's performance since this includes the costs over which he has no control.

Contribution profit to corporate costs and profit represents the contribution to cover corporate costs and profit. It evaluates the performance of the divisions more than it does the performance of the division manager. Some of the division's committed capacity-related cost, which a division manager cannot control, such as depreciation, property tax, factory space, warehouses, machinery, administrative personnel and managers' salary may result from past investment decisions made by top management. Unless

	Total	Division 1	Division 2
		(Hundred million yen)	
Sales Revenues	7,600	3,000	4,600
Variable cost of sales	2,700	1,000	1,700
Divisional variable selling and management costs	300	100	200
Contribution margin	4,600	1,900	2,700
Divisional fixed costs controllable by division manager	2,000	800	1,200
Controllable profit	2,600	1,100	1,500
Divisional fixed costs uncontrollable by division manager	1,500	500	1,000
Contribution margin for corporate costs and profit	1,100	600	500
Fixed costs allocated outside division	500	150	350
Income before income taxes	600	450	150

Fig. 20.1. Division income statement and four profit concepts.

the divisional manager is given authority to restructure the investments of key personnel in the division, these costs are not controllable and hence may not be appropriate in evaluating the manager's performance.[3] This profit figure provides useful information for the top management to decide on the disposal of the division.

Controllable profit is perhaps the best performance measure of a divisional manager's performance because it measures a manager's ability to use effectively the resources under his control and authority. An important limitation of this measure is the difficulty in distinguishing between controllable and non-controllable capacity-related costs. For example, depreciation, insurance, and property taxes on fixed assets would be controllable if the division managers had the authority to dispose of these assets but would not be controllable if they did not have this discretion.[3]

Contribution margin is not pertinent to performance evaluation; rather it provides the divisional manager with information to take short-term decisions on production, sales, product mix, price-setting etc. This measure is meaningful to order to understand how to control revenues and costs that vary with the use of capacity within the division. It does not include costs over which the division manager has control.

3. Performance Evaluation Measures under Increased Division Manager Authority: A Proposal

When a divisional manager, as the head of the investment center, possesses the decision authority to make new business projects and invest in new equipment, not only the working capital but also the investment in fixed assets becomes controlled by him. Even though the authority is narrow, some degree of divisional manager's influence is recognized in determining the fixed investment within the amount of the accumulated depreciation and retained earnings. In Japanese companies, until recently, the head-office took key decisions when an existing division went into a large-scale new business due to the expansion of its internal funds. However, in many cases, the original draft of the newly formed business is proposed by the divisional manager. Here the influential power of the divisional manager relating to the overall fixed assets of the division is recognized.

In recent years, however, the transfer of authority to the divisional manager has gone hand in hand with increasing diversification and globalization. In a decentralized organization having a so-called "in-house-company system," the divisional manager holds the authority in fixed assets investment, and the division is called an investment center. Here the divisional manager has substantial influential power and decision-making authority regarding fixed assets investments. In this way, in an investment center having the company system, each individual uncontrolled fixed cost will become controlled, where the divisional manager holds the decision authority regarding investment in fixed assets. Thus the amount of controllable profit will conform with the amount of contribution margin to the corporate costs and profit as shown in Fig. 20.2. However, the fixed costs of a division

	(Hundred million yen)		
	Total	Division 1	Division 2
Sales Revenues	7,600	3,000	4,600
Variable cost of sales	2,700	1,000	1,700
Divisional variable selling and management costs	300	100	200
Contribution margin	4,600	1,900	2,700
Divisional fixed costs controllable by division manager	3,970	1,430	2,540
Controllable profit	630	470	160
Divisional fixed costs uncontrollable by division manager	0	0	0
Contribution margin for corporate costs and profit	630	470	160
Fixed costs allocated outside division	30	20	10
Income before income taxes	600	450	150

Fig. 20.2. Profits under the increased division manager authority.

do not become entirely controlled. For example, a divisional manager cannot decide his own salary.

Besides, as more and more of the corporate service functions (such as distribution and purchasing) and corporate personnel affairs which have so far been managed by the head-office are transferred to the divisions, and as the ratio of corporate costs to sales becomes smaller, the divisional controllable profit will be closer to the divisional operating profit or net profit before tax. In this case, to evaluate the performance of a divisional manager, it is appropriate to use the net profit before tax as shown in Fig. 20.2.

In this chapter, we will investigate whether — and how far — the proposal as mentioned above is really followed in Japanese companies. By using a questionnaire survey, we will further clarify what measures should be adopted for evaluating performance in the current situation.

4. Hypotheses

In hypotheses development, we focused on the following three points regarding how the measures for evaluating divisional manager's performance change with the expansion of his authority:

(1) The effect of the degree of decentralization on the investment decision-making authority of the divisional manager as well as on the ratio of corporate costs.
(2) The effect of the investment decision-making authority of the divisional manager as well as the ratio of corporate costs on the profit measure used to evaluate the performance of the divisional manager.
(3) The effect of the profit measure used to evaluate the performance of the divisional manager and the ratio of corporate costs on the company performance.

In conjunction with the above three points, the hypotheses can be formulated in the following way:

4.1. *The effect of the degree of decentralization on the investment decision-making authority of the division manager as well as on the ratio of corporate costs*

As the adoption of the division-based system becomes more common, the consciousness of decentralization also becomes popular in companies, and top management will be more inclined to transfer greater authority to the divisional manager. Accordingly, the following hypothesis can be formulated.

Hypothesis 1: As the adoption of the division-based system is increased, the investment decision-making authority of the divisional manager will be expanded.

In a company where the division-based system is adopted at a lower level, the ratio of corporate costs becomes higher since, in most companies, the divisions have to depend on the head-office for maintaining personnel affairs and other service-related functions such as power supply, purchase, product planning, transportation, information processing, research and development and so on. On the other hand, where the division-based system is adopted at a higher level, the service functions and the corporate coordination function will be transferred to the division and consequently the ratio of corporate costs will become smaller. From this viewpoint, hypothesis 2 can be formed.

Hypothesis 2: The ratio of corporate costs will be lower in companies where the division-based system is adopted at a higher level. Conversely, the ratio of the corporate costs will be higher for companies where the division-based system is adopted at a lower level.

4.2. *The effect of the investment decision-making authority of the divisional manager as well as the ratio of corporate costs on the profit measure used to evaluate the performance of divisional manager*

In a division-based company, when the investment decision-making authority of a divisional manager is strengthened and the degree of decentralization become higher, the service functions (such as power supply, purchasing, product planning, transportation, information processing, research, etc.) and the corporate coordination functions (such as high-level personnel or financial affairs) which have so far been handled by the head-office will be transferred to the divisions. Consequently, the ratio of corporate cost will become smaller and the range of the controllable cost of a divisional manager will be increased. Since each of the divisional traceable fixed costs becomes controllable, the amount of uncontrolled fixed cost such as depreciation of division equipment will be reduced. In this way, as the amount of controllable profit gets closer to the amount of net profit before tax, in most companies the profit after allocating corporate costs is used to evaluate the divisional manager's performance. With this background the following three hypotheses may be developed:

Hypothesis 3: When the divisional manager holds greater investment decision-making authority, in most companies the profit after allocating the corporate cost is used to evaluate the performance of the divisional manager.

Hypothesis 4: Where the ratio of corporate costs is smaller, in most companies the profit after allocating the corporate cost is used to evaluate the performance of the divisional manager.

Hypothesis 5: Where the divisional manager holds greater investment authority, in most companies the ratio of corporate costs becomes smaller.

4.3. *The effect of the profit measure used to evaluate the performance of the divisional manager and the ratio of corporate costs on the company performance*

The amount of controllable costs will be increased in a division functioning as an investment center due to the extended authority of the divisional manger in using the divisional assets. To evaluate the performance of these managers, the profit after allocating the corporate costs can be used. Next, as the divisional managers will be able to think more about the effective use of assets, the total asset turnover ratio will be improved. Therefore, the following two hypotheses may be constructed:

Hypothesis 6: The total asset turnover ratio is enhanced in companies where the ratio of corporate costs is smaller and the profit after allocating the corporate costs is used for evaluating the divisional manager's performance. On the contrary, the total asset turnover ratio decreases in companies where the ratio of corporate costs is larger and the profit after allocating the corporate costs is used for evaluating the divisional manager's performance.

Hypothesis 7: The total asset turnover ratio gets worse in companies where the ratio of corporate costs is smaller and the controllable profit is used for evaluating the divisional manager's performance. Conversely, the total asset turnover ratio is improved in companies where the ratio of corporate costs is smaller and the profit after allocating the corporate costs is used for evaluating the divisional manager's performance.

5. Verification of Hypotheses

Questionnaires were mailed to 1,296 companies on 3rd October 1997 whose stocks are listed at the Tokyo Stock Exchange. Three hundred and nine

Table 20.1. Collection of questionnaire.

Industry types	Sent	Received	Effective answers received	Rate of effective answers
Manufacturing	866	226	224	25.9%
Non-manufacturing	430	82	80	18.6%
Others		1	0	0.0%
Total	1,296	309	304	23.5%

companies responded by the deadline of 17th November 1997, of which five responses could not be used due to their incomplete answers. The response rate is thus 23.84% and the effective response rate is 23.46%. Table 20.1 gives this information in detail.

In handling company performance data, the companies were divided into successful and unsuccessful groups to remove the effects of industry differences by using the method as adopted by Varandarajan and Ramanujam.[16] To do this, the industry median values of return on total assets and sales growth rate were calculated. A company is regarded as a successful company if both of the returns on total assets and sales growth rate are greater than their respective median values. Companies are considered as unsuccessful if any one of the returns on total assets or the sales growth rate is lower than their respective median values. In other words, a company is called unsuccessful if the value of at least one of the above measures is less than its median value. We categorized successful companies as "1" and unsuccessful companies as "0".

5.1. *Verification of Hypothesis 1*

Table 20.2 exhibits the results of the chi-square test along with the cross-table showing the relationship between the degree of the adoption of the division-based system and the degree of the divisional manager's investment decision-making authority.

Table 20.2. The relationship between the degree of adoption of division-based system and the degree of investment decision authority of a division manager.

		The degree of investment decision authority of a division manager		
		small	big	
The degree of adoption of division-based system	low	5 45.5%	6 54.5%	11 100%
	high	9 24.3%	28 75.7%	37 100%
		14 29.2%	34 70.8%	48 100%

	Value	Degree of freedom	Significant probability
Chi-square	1.832	1	.176

Question 7 of the questionnaire was used to ascertain the degree of adoption of decentralization and question 36 was used for the extent of the investment decision-making authority of the divisional manager. The chi-square value is 1.83 with a significance level of 17.6%. That means that hypothesis 1 cannot be rejected at 10% level of significance. However, since the authors could theoretically explain and justify the hypothesis, and the statistical significance level (0.176) is below 20%, the original theoretical hypothesis is supported sufficiently by data and statistics. Therefore it may be said that as the degree of adoption of the division-based system is increased, the investment decision-making authority of the division manager will be extended.

5.2. *Verification of Hypothesis 2*

Table 20.3 displays the results of the chi-square test along with the cross-table presenting the relationship between the degree of adoption of the division-based system and the ratio of corporate costs.

Here question 7 was used for the degree of adoption of the division-based system and question 23 was used for the size of the corporate costs ratio. The chi-square value is 4.81 with a 2.8% level of significance. The results show that the null hypothesis cannot be accepted. Therefore, it can be said that the degree of decentralization is related to the ratio of corporate costs. In the cross-table, it is apparent that 63.6% of the companies belong to the group with a high degree of decentralization and lower corporate costs ratio. On the other hand, 36.4% of the companies belong to the group with a higher level of decentralization and larger corporate costs ratio. Again, 51.1% of companies have a lower degree of decentralization and larger

Table 20.3. The relationship between the degree of division-based system adoption and the corporate costs ratio.

		The corporate costs ratio		
		small	big	
The degree of adoption of division-based system	low	45 48.9%	47 51.1%	92 100%
	high	84 63.6%	48 36.4%	132 100%
		129 57.6%	95 42.4%	224 100%

	Value	Degree of freedom	Significant probability
Chi-square	4.812	1	.028

corporate costs ratio. On the other hand, 48.9% companies belong to the group of lower degree of decentralization and corporate costs ratio. Hence hypothesis 2 is proved by the results. Accordingly, it can be said that the ratio of the corporate costs will be lower for companies where the division-based system is adopted to a higher degree. Conversely, the ratio of the corporate costs will be higher for companies where the division-based system is adopted at a lower level.

5.3. *Verification of Hypothesis 3*

The relationship between a divisional manager's investment decision-making authority and the profit measure for evaluating his performance is shown in Table 20.4.

Question 36 is used for the size of a divisional manager's decision-making authority while question 11 is used for the proportion of the companies using profit after allocating corporate costs for evaluating a divisional manager's performance. The chi-square value is found to be 4.852 with 2.8% level of significance. The null hypothesis cannot be accepted. That means that a divisional manager's investment decision-making authority is related to the profit measure used to evaluate his performance. According to the actual frequency as shown in the cross-table (Table 20.4) it is seen that, irrespective of the size of the decision-making authority, a large number of companies use the profit after allocating corporate cost. When the size of investment decision-making authority is large, around 90% of the companies use profit after allocating corporate cost and the remaining 10% use controllable profit. Again, when the size of investment decision-making authority is small, about 61.5% of the companies use profit after allocating corporate cost and the remaining 38.5% use controllable profit. When the investment decision-making authority is extended, the difference between the proportion of the companies using the profit measures was comparatively large. Thus, hypothesis 3 cannot be rejected. That is to say, when the divisional manager holds greater investment decision-making authority, in most companies the profit after allocating the corporate cost is used to evaluate the performance of the divisional manager.

Table 20.4. The cross table and chi-square test of the relationship between investment decision authority of a division manager and the profit measure to evaluate his performance.

		The profit measures used to evaluate a division manager		
		Controll-able profit	Profit after allocating corporate costs	
The degree of investment decision authority of a division manager	small	5 38.5%	8 61.5%	13 100%
	big	3 10%	27 90%	30 100%
		8 18.6%	35 81.4%	43 100%

	Value	Degree of freedom	Significant probability
Chi-square	4.852	1	.028

5.4. *Verification of Hypothesis 4*

Table 20.5 shows the results of the chi-square test as well as the cross-table presenting the relationship between the size of the ratio of corporate costs and the profit measure used to evaluate the divisional manager's performance.

Question 23 is used to find out the size of corporate costs ratio and question 11 is used to find the proportion of the companies using profit after allocating corporate costs for evaluating a divisional manager's performance. The chi-square value is found to be 12.664 with 0.00% level of significance. The null hypothesis cannot thus be accepted. That means

Table 20.5. The relationship between the ratio of the corporate costs and the profit measure to evaluate a division manager.

		The profit measure to evaluate a division manager		
		Controll-able profit	Profit after allocating the corporate costs	
The ratio of corporate costs	small	26 22%	92 78%	118 100%
	big	38 45.8%	45 54.2%	83 100%
		64 31.8%	137 68.2%	201 100%

	Value	Degree of freedom	Significant probability
Chi-square	12.664	1	.000

that the corporate costs ratio is related to the profit measure used to evaluate his performance. According to the actual frequency shown in the cross-table (Table 20.5) it is seen that, irrespective of the size of the corporate costs ratio, a large number of companies use the profit after allocating corporate cost. When the size of the corporate costs ratio is large, about 54.2% of companies use profit after allocating corporate cost and the remaining 22% use controllable profit. However, this difference is not significant. Again, when the corporate costs ratio is small, about 78% of companies use profit after allocating corporate cost and the remaining 38.5% use controllable profit. That means that when the corporate costs ratio is small, a large number of companies use the profit after allocating corporate costs. Hypothesis 3 is substantiated by these results. Therefore, where the ratio of corporate costs is smaller, in most companies the profit after allocating the corporate cost is used to evaluate the performance of the divisional manager.

5.5. *Verification of Hypothesis 5*

Table 20.6 shows the results of the chi-square test along with the cross-table presenting the relationship between the size of a divisional manager's investment decision-making authority and the size of the ratio of corporate costs.

Question 36 was used for the size of the divisional manager's decision-making authority while Question 23 was used to find out the size of corporate costs ratio. The chi-square value is 1.93 with 16.5% level of significance.

Table 20.6. The relationship between investment decision authority of a division manager and the ratio of the corporate costs.

		The ratio of corporate costs		
		small	big	
The investment decision authority of division manager	small	7 53.8%	6 46.2%	13 100%
	big	24 75%	8 25%	32 100%
		31 68.9%	14 31.1%	45 100%

	Value	Degree of freedom	Significant probability
Chi-square	1.930	1	.165

That means that null hypothesis cannot be rejected at 10% level of significance. However, since the authors could theoretically explain and justify the hypothesis, and the statistical significance level (0.165) is below 20%, the original theoretical hypothesis is supported sufficiently by data and statistics. Therefore it may be said that where the divisional manager holds greater investment authority, in most companies the ratio of corporate costs becomes smaller.

5.6. *Verification of Hypothesis 6*

Table 20.7 shows the results of the chi-square test including the cross-table presenting the relationship between the total asset turnover ratio and the corporate costs ratio of companies where profit after allocating corporate costs is used for evaluating a divisional manager's performance.

Table 20.7. The relationship between the ratio of the corporate costs of the companies using profit after allocating corporate costs to evaluate division managers and the total assets turnover ratio.

		Total assets turnover ratio		
		Unsuccessful	Successful	
The ratio of the corporate costs of the company using profit after allocating the corporate costs to evaluate a division manager	small	34 37.4%	57 62.6%	91 100%
	big	24 53.3%	21 46.7%	45 100%
		58 42.6%	78 57.4%	136 100%

	Value	Degree of freedom	Significant probability
Chi-square	3.140	1	.076

Question 23 is used for the proportion of the companies with higher corporate costs ratio and question 11 is used for the companies that use profit after allocating corporate costs for evaluating a divisional manager's performance. For data relating to asset turnover ratio we used published company data.[15] The chi-square value is found to be 3.14 with 7.6% level of significance. The null hypothesis cannot be accepted. That means that the total asset turnover ratio is related to the size of the corporate costs ratio of companies where profit after allocating corporate costs is used to evaluate a divisional manager's performance. It is evident that about 62.2% of companies have a higher total asset turnover ratio when the ratio of corporate costs is smaller than companies using profit after allocating corporate costs, and the remaining 37.4% belong to the lower total asset turnover ratio group. The difference between these groups is significant. On the other hand, about 53.3% of companies have a higher total asset turnover ratio when the ratio of corporate costs is bigger for companies using the profit after allocating corporate costs, and the remaining 46.7% belong to the lower total asset turnover ratio group. There are only three companies whose total asset turnover ratio is worse than the others. Hence hypothesis 6 is supported by the results. Therefore, the total asset turnover ratio is enhanced in companies where the ratio of corporate costs is smaller and the profit after allocating the corporate costs is used for evaluating a divisional manager's performance. On the contrary, the total asset turnover ratio is decreased in companies where the ratio of corporate costs is larger and the profit after allocating the corporate costs is used for evaluating the divisional manager's performance.

5.7. Verification of Hypothesis 7

Table 20.8 shows the results of the chi-square test along with the cross-table showing the relationship between the total asset turnover ratio and the use of the profit measures for evaluating the divisional manager's performance in companies with a lower corporate costs ratio.

Questions 23 and 11 were used respectively for companies which had a lower corporate costs ratio and companies using profit after allocating

Table 20.8. The relationship between the profit measure used for evaluating of the division manager in the companies whose ratios of the corporate costs are small and total assets turnover ratio.

		Total assets turnover ratio		
		Unsuccessful	Successful	
The profit measure used for evaluating the division managers in the compaies whose ratios of the corporate costs are small	The controllable profit	14 53.8%	12 46.2%	26 100%
	The profit after allocating of the corporate costs	34 37.4%	57 62.6%	91 100%
		48 41%	69 59%	117 100%

	Value	Degree of freedom	Significant probability
Chi-square	2.271	1	.132

corporate costs to evaluate a divisional manager's performance. Data relating to total asset turnover is available from published company data. The chi-square value is 2.271 with the significance level of 13.2%. This means that null hypothesis cannot be rejected at 10% level of significance. However, since the authors could theoretically explain and justify the hypothesis, and the statistical significance level (0.132) is below 20%, the original theoretical hypothesis is supported sufficiently by data and statistics. Therefore it may be said that the total asset turnover ratio gets worse in companies where the ratio of corporate costs is smaller and the controllable profit is used for evaluating a divisional manager's performance. Conversely, the total asset turnover ratio is improved in companies where the ratio of corporate costs is smaller and the profit after allocating the corporate costs is used for evaluating a divisional manager's performance.

6. Conclusion

If a company adopts a division-based system it should mean that their divisions are functioning highly efficiently, not only as profit centers but also as investment centers. In the present empirical study it was confirmed that under the wider decision-making authority of the divisional manager when the division undertakes many functional activities (that is, when the ratio of corporate costs is small), the total asset turnover ratio of a company will get better if the profit after allocating corporate costs is used for evaluating the divisional manager's performance. The causal relationships established through the verification of the variables is portrayed in Fig. 20.3.

One of the main purposes for evaluating a divisional manager's performance is to motivate him to increase his efforts to achieve his division's target. An essential characteristic of a performance evaluation measure is to provide a standard to evaluate the efficiency of the divisional manager in controlling the resources at his discretion in the prevailing business environment.

The investment decision-making authority of the division manager will be increased as the degree of adopting division-based systems is increased

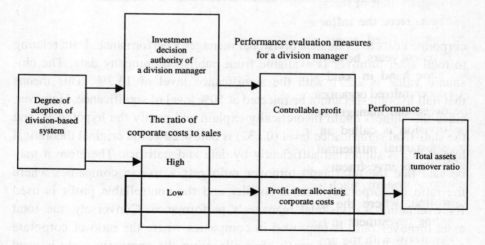

Fig. 20.3. Causal relationship among variables.

due to the diversification of business activities. As a result, investment decisions which have so far been made by head-office will be transferred to the divisional manager and, in this way, the amount of his controllable resources will be increased. Furthermore, other service functions such as purchasing, distribution and head-office co-ordination functions such as personnel affairs will progressively be transferred to the divisions. The controllable costs of a divisional manager will be increased as the proportion of corporate costs to sales becomes smaller. In this way, by efficiently using the enlarged controllable profit and by employing the appropriate profit measure to evaluate this, the divisional manager will make every effort to achieve his organizational objectives. Therefore, when a company's business activities diversify, the head-office will give the investment decision-making authority to the divisional manager. Furthermore, the head-office or central functions will be transferred as far possible to the divisional manager and the profit after allocating the corporate costs will be used for evaluating his performance. In this way, the company-wide profit, that is, total asset turnover ratio, will be improved.

When businesses are not diversified, the degree of adopting a division-based system and the investment decision-making authority will be lower. As a result, since the ratio of corporate costs will become larger, it will be effective to evaluate a divisional manager by the controllable profit under his narrowed controllable range. However, due to the insufficiency of data it was not possible to investigate this aspect of research and thus this may be an interesting topic for future research.

Appendix

• Variables relating to the structure of decentralized organization

Degree of adoption of division-based system

Question 7. How wide is the degree of adopting division-based system in your company in comparison to centralized production and sales organization? Please circle the appropriate number.

Decentralization |———+———+———+———+———+———| Operate almost as
is not adopted   Mainly   Mid-level   Mainly   division excepting
    at all   Functional   Divisionalised   the head-office
                                                                    system

- **Variable relating to performance evaluation of division manager**

  Profit measures for evaluating division manager

  Question 11. From the following, which profit measure is used for evaluating the division manager's performance?

  1. Controllable profit
  2. Profit after allocating corporate costs
  3. Others (   )

- **Variable relating to the corporate costs and service departments**

  Ratio of corporate costs to sales

  Question 23. Please circle one of the following options relating to the present situation and the tendency of the ratio of corporate costs to sales.

  1. Less than 1%   (1) Increase   (2) Decrease
                           (3) No change   (4) Others

  2. 1% — Less than 3%   (1) Increase   (2) Decrease
                           (3) No change   (4) Others

  3. 3% — Less than 5%   (1) Increase   (2) Decrease
                           (3) No change   (4) Others

  4. 5% — Less than 10%   (1) Increase   (2) Decrease
                           (3) No change   (4) Others

  5. More than 10%   (1) Increase   (2) Decrease
                           (3) No change   (4) Others

- **Variable relating to the investment decision-making authority of the division manager**

  Size of the investment decision-making authority of division manager

Question 36. To what degree do the divisions of your company hold authority for making decisions on how to use its own capital (for example, equipment investments, new businesses, related company investments, specially restrictions on investment in long-term funds)? Please circle the appropriate number.

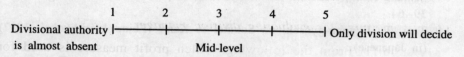

- Variable relating to company performance

Total assets turnover ratio

Data was obtained from the published company data as mentioned in Ref. 15.

References

1. Chandler, A. D. Jr., Strategy and Structure (MIT Press, 1962).
2. Horngren, C. T., Foster, G. & Datar, S. M., Cost Accounting: A Managerial Emphasis, 9th edition, (Prentice Hall, 1997).
3. Kaplan, R. S. & Atkinson, A. A., Advanced Management Accounting, 3rd edition, (Prentice Hall, 1998).
4. Kobayashi, T., Kyotsuhi no Haibun to Gyoseki-hyoka, Kokumin Keizai Zasshi (in Japanese), Vol. 143, No. 3, 1981, 57–74.
5. Kobayashi, T., Kyotsuhi-haibun no Mokuteki to Tokusei, Kokumin Keizai Zasshi (in Japanese), Vol. 146, No. 3, 1982, 35–52.
6. Kobayashi, T., Kanrikaike ni okeru Kanrikano Gainen, Kokumin Keizai Zasshi (in Japanese), Vol. 146, No. 3, 1982, 35–52.
7. Kubota, O., Kanrikaikei (Shinpan) (Yuhikaku, 1976) (in Japanese).
8. Rumelt, R. P., Strategy, Structure and Economic Performance (Harvard Business School, 1974).
9. Shibata, G. & Nakahashi, K., Keieikanri no Riron to Jissai (Tokyo-joho-shuppan, 1997) (in Japanese).
10. Solomon, D., Divisional Performance: Measurement and Control (Irwin, 1965), 82–83.

11. Tani, T., Soshiki-kozo to Honbuhi no Haifu, Kaikei (in Japanese), Vol. 124, No. 2, 1983, 17–30.
12. Tani, T., Jigyobu-gyoseki Kanrikaikei no Kiso (Kunimoto-shobo, 1983) (in Japanese).
13. Tani, T., Wagakuni Kigyo ni okeru Honshahi Kyotsuhi Haibun Shisutemu no Sentaku Kodo, Kokumin Keizai Zasshi (in Japanese), Vol. 153, No. 1, 1986, 39–64.
14. Tani, T., Jigyobu-gyoseki no Sokutei to Kanri (Zeimu-keiri-kyokai, 1987) (in Japanese).
15. Toyo-keizai-shinposha, Kaisha Shikiho 1997nen 3shu/Kakigo (Toyo-keizai-shinposha, 1997) (in Japanese).
16. Varadarajan, P. R. & Ramanujam, V., The Corporate Performance Conundrum; A Synthesis of Contemporary Views and an Expansion, Journal of Management Studies, Vol. 20, No. 5, September, 1990, 463–483.
17. Zimmerman, J. L., The Costs and Benefits of Cost Allocations, The Accounting Review, Vol. 54, No. 3, July, 1979, 504–521.

Chapter 21

Culture and Budget Control Practices: A Study of Manufacturing Companies in U.S.A. and Japan

SUSUMU UENO*

This study reports the results of an empirical study which examined the cultural influence on budget control practices in the United States and Japan. The two countries were selected as research sites because a number of previous studies provided reasons to suspect cultural differences between U.S. and Japanese management control practices which are considered relevant to the present issues. A framework for developing hypotheses is formulated in this study by matching Hofstede's cultural dimensions with the three basic functions of budget control systems, that is (1) communication and coordination,(2) planning and (3) performance evaluation. Data was collected, using a questionnaire survey, to test the six hypotheses from the managers of 70 U.S. and 149 Japanese major manufacturing companies in the summer of 1990. The results of analysis supported four hypotheses developed from the Individualism–Collectivism dimension, revealing that U.S. companies, compared to Japanese companies, used formal communication and coordination to a greater extent, built budget slack to a greater extent, practiced controllability of

*Business Address: 8-9-1, Okamoto, Higashi-nadaku, Kobe-city, 658-8501 Japan.
E-mail: ueno@konan-u.ac.jp
Research Interests: Management and accounting control practices of MNE's, cross-cultural studies, research methodology in social science.

budgets to a greater extent, and used long-term performance measures to a lesser extent. The results were inconclusive in regard to the other two hypotheses that tap the extent of using long-range planning and structuring of budgetary processes.

In spite of the importance of budget control systems as a key subset of management control systems, only a few empirical studies[2,3,7,9] have focused upon comparisons between U.S. and Japanese budget control practices. These studies did provide valuable insights into both budget control practices and managers' attitudes toward such practices. However none of them has confirmed the hypothesis that cultural characteristics affect budget control practices. Culture provides the cognitive premises for an individual within a group and sets preconditions for human behavior. This study therefore views budget control practices as being contingent upon the national culture in which the company operates. Thus the main research question explored in this study is:

To what extent do the specific aspects of budget control practices vary between the United States and Japan which can be attributed to specific dimensions of cultural difference?

Two cultural variables that have been selected as explanatory variables for this investigation are Individualism–Collectivism and Uncertain Avoidance, these will be explained later. The specific aspects of budget control practices to be studied are formal communication and coordination, planning time-horizons, structuring of budgetary processes, budget slack, controllability of budget and performance evaluation time-horizons.

1. Theoretical Framework and Hypotheses

Culture may be defined as a system of meaning, including patterns of ideas and values that contribute to shaping individual and collective behavior.[25] Various theorists have provided their favorite lists of the major dimensions of cultural validations.

Hofstede[10,11] studied work-related values, obtaining responses from members of one multinational company (IBM) operating in 50 different countries across two points in time (around 1968 and 1972). He empirically established the cultural differences in four organizationally relevant dimensions; Power Distance, Uncertainty Avoidance, Individualism–Collectivism, and Masculinity–Femininity. Previous empirical studies have validated his work. The framework in this study accordingly draws upon Hofstede's work. It is formulated by matching Hofstede's cultural dimensions with the three basic functions of budget control systems, that is, (1) communication and coordination, (2) planning and (3) performance evaluation.

Since the immediate interest here is in terms of U.S.–Japan comparisons, this study will offer an explanation of how values placed by managers on specific cultural dimensions, as delineated by Hofstede, affect the particular aspects of budget control practices, by focusing on the cultural dimensions in which the United States and Japan differ most, that is, Individualism–Collectivism and Uncertainty Avoidance. Two nations' scores on the above two cultural dimensions indicate that the Japanese (1) tend to view themselves in collectivistic rather than in individualistic terms and (2) have a high need to avoid uncertainty. In contrast, Americans view themselves in individualistic rather than in collectivistic terms and have a relatively low need to avoid uncertainty.

1.1. *Communication and coordination*

Communication and coordination refers to the extent to which organizational subunits get involved in the budgetary process. Since budgets are developed for an entire company, communication and coordination is essential in budgeting.

In a collectivistic society, organizational policies and practices are established and expected to be followed by members out of their sense of loyalty and duty to the system. Because employees already have in mind the "bigger picture" and work together, managers in such a society do not need to spend much time and effort in ensuring that the goals of the organization are achieved. In an individualistic society, managers look at their own self-interest[24] and are eager to maximize their own opportunities for advancement. Individuals in such a society are active agents themselves and are more independent from their organizations.[11] Managers, therefore, have a greater need to bring things out into the open both to clarify the situation and to make sure that everyone explicitly understands the organization's goals and their roles. In other words, manager in an individualistic society have to use formal communication and coordination in budgetary processes to a greater extent than managers in a collective society. Hence:

H1: U.S. companies use formal communication and coordination in budget planning processes to a greater extent than Japanese companies.

1.2. *Planning*

The budgetary planning, both short- and long-range, determines what people are going to do, how they are going to do it, and who is going to do it. Uncertainty Avoidance or the need to avoid uncertainty is likely to have an impact on planning time-horizons.

In a strong Uncertainty Avoidance society, the budget serves, among other things, to act as an agent for reducing anxiety over a long period of time. Thus, managers in a strong Uncertainty Avoidance society would tend to spend much time and effort in formulating long-range budgets that cover broad time-horizons in addition to having budgets that cover a year or less. Japanese managers, being strong on Uncertainty Avoidance, will tend to resort to the uncertainty reduction mode and build the budget from broad time-horizons in order to reduce their anxiety about the future. Hence:

H2: Japanese companies use broad time-horizons in budget planning processes to a greater extent than U.S. companies.

Uncertainty Avoidance also has an impact on the structuring of budgetary processes. Structuring of budgetary processes refers to the extent to which procedures and rules are considered to be important for formulating budgets. According to Hofstede,[10] an organization reduces internal uncertainty

— caused by the unpredictability of the behavior of its members and stakeholders — by setting rules and procedures. Managers in a strong Uncertainty Avoidance society feel high stress in unstructured situations and, therefore, attempt to overcome the unpredictability of the behavior of their subordinates by setting procedures and rules. Since formalized rules and procedures are embedded in budget manuals, managers would develop and follow the budget manuals to a great extent in order to reduce the level of their anxiety. Hence:

H3: Japanese companies structure budget planning processes to a greater extent than U.S. companies.

Individualism–Collectivism and Uncertainty Avoidance have an impact on budget slack building. Budget slack can be defined as a deliberately created difference between the honest budget estimate and the submitted budget figure that is padded.

In an individualistic society, performance evaluation is based on the achievements of the individual. The evaluation, then, must meet one's calculative value of being perceived as an effective performer. Therefore, managers tend to create budget slack to be sure of accomplishing the results within their budgets and to be evaluated positively. In a collectivistic society, in contrast, performance evaluation is based on group-achievements. Managers in such a culture will tend to feel less pressure for personally meeting their goals and, therefore, would feel less compulsion for building budget slack.

The Uncertainty Avoidance dimension is also likely to play a role in determining the manager's behavior in slack building. Budget slack is understood as an ex ante concept, insulating managers against the effects of unpredicted events as they are able to draw on the surplus resources in adverse time.[19] Japanese managers with a very high score on the Uncertainty Avoidance Index would feel great tension from the effects of unpredicted events and are likely to be more motivated to create slack into the budget.

It is very difficult to speculate on the direction of this hypothesis because the two cultural dimensions, namely, Individualism–Collectivism and Uncertainty Avoidance, lead to conflicting views about the practices in budget slack building. However, it should be noted that the building of budget slack is tied closely to performance evaluation. If a manager ends up overspending his budget, he is likely to be evaluated by his superiors in unfavorable terms. This indicates that Individualism–Collectivism might prevail over Uncertainty Avoidance. Therefore, the following hypothesis is formulated:

> H4: U.S. companies build slack into budgets to a greater extent
> than Japanese companies.

1.3. *Performance evaluation*

For control systems to work effectively, evaluation should be conducted in the light of verifiable and objective goals, and controls should be tailored to positions.

In an individualistic society, the expending of effort should lead to the intended results. Budget control systems in such a culture can provide a valid basis only when they incorporate the calculative value of an individual and measure his real accomplishments. In contrast, in a collectivistic society, performance evaluation is based on group achievements wherein the performance is evaluated less for one's own sake and more for the sake of the group. This approach indicates that a manager in an individualistic society feels a greater need to be in charge of the controllability of budgets. Controllability of budgets in this study refers to the extent which personnel within the management control system should be charged or credited only for items within their control.[16] Hence:

> H5: U.S. companies practice controllability of budgets to a
> greater extent than Japanese companies.

Many decisions that managers make today influence a company's performance over a certain period of time, and the results of these decisions sometimes may not be reflected in the current performance evaluation. Conversely, current performance data may reflect in part the impact of the events and decisions from previous periods.[1,15]

In an individualistic society, people constantly seek greater advancement for themselves, and evaluation has to appeal to the calculative value of an individual. In such a society, people tend to have a short-term view of their jobs and lack a feeling of identification with their companies. These attitudes indicate that employees in an organization prefer to be evaluated at shorter intervals and expect immediate rewards on the basis of their efforts devoted to short-term operations. In a collectivistic society, evaluation has to appeal to the moralistic value of an individual; that is, evaluation is based on group- or organization-based achievements.[24] People in such a society would behave in a manner which leads to the acquisition of collective outcomes that provide shared benefits.[32] They would not be keen on being evaluated at short intervals, but wait for the longer time period when group achievement can become evident. Thus,

> H6: Japanese companies use broad evaluation time-horizons to a greater extent than U.S. companies.

2. Research Method

2.1. *Population and sample*

Manufacturing companies listed on the major stock exchanges in the United States and Japan with an annual sales over a certain specified volume formed the population for the study; that is, in the United States, companies with a 1988 sales volume of over $100 billion and, in Japan, companies with a 1988 sales volume of over 100 billion Yen (1 US$ = 125.90 Yen on December 31, 1988) provided the basis for the study. A total of 452 large manufacturing companies in the United States and Japan (205 U.S. and 247 Japanese companies) were identified.

A copy of the questionnaire was mailed, with a self-addressed stamped return envelope, to each of the U.S. and Japanese controllers or other senior managers at his company address in the summer of 1990. A total of 219 responses were received, with a total response rate of 48.5 percent. In the United States, 70 of the 205 companies responded, providing a response rate of 34.1 percent. In Japan, 149 of the 247 companies responded, providing a response rate of 60.3 percent.

In the sample, attributes, such as company size, industry, position or status, period in the current position, age, and tenure with the company were also examined because the structure and the functions of an organization might be closely related to these attributes.[6,14,22,28]

2.2. *Survey instruments*

The questionnaire incorporating 30 statements (Appendix), measuring the six budget-related variables described later, was developed for testing the six hypotheses proposed earlier. In developing the questionnaire items, a number of previous works were drawn upon.[4,5,7,10,13,18,20,26,27] Each of the 30 statements were graded on a 5-point Likert-type scale ranging from "strongly disagree (= 1)" to "strongly agree (= 5)," to measure the extent to which each item in the questionnaire was true for their organization. To reduce response bias, some items were negatively worded.

The six budget-related variables that constitute the dependent variables of this research are as follows:

1. Communication and Coordination: the extent to which organizational subunits are involved formally, that is, the process of formal communication and coordination in budgetary planning.
2. The Importance of Long-Range Planning: the time-frame of budget plans and the use of long-range (three years or more) versus short-range (no more than one year) planning.
3. Structuring of Budgetary Processes: the extent to which actual procedures and rules are fundamental to the formulation of budgets.
4. Budget Slack: the extent to which slack is built into the budget.
5. Controllability of Budgets: the extent to which managers are charged or credited only for items within their control.
6. Short-Term Versus Long-Term Performance: the extent of company practices toward budget performance evaluation as they relate to the short-term (current year) or long-term (three years or more).

Since a familiar obstacle to cross-cultural survey research is that measures which support a particular hypothesis of underlying concepts in one country may fail to do so in another,[14] it is essential to ensure conceptual equivalence of the measure.[8,12,23] Thus, factor analyses of the items measuring the variables were performed separately on both the U.S. and Japanese samples to determine the components of an additive measure for each of the six variables.

Table 21.1 shows both the final items that constituted measures and the Cronbach's alpha reliability for the six variables. As can be seen from

Table 21.1. Results of reliability test (Cronbach's alpha).

Variables	U.S.A	Japan
V1: Communication-coordination (items 2,3,4)	0.591	0.619
V2: The importance of long-range planning (items 6-10)	0.724	0.734
V3: Structuring of budgetary processes (items 11-15)	0.832	0.769
V4: Budget slack (items 16-20)	0.823	0.808
V5: Controllability of budgets (items 21,22,23)	0.350	0.404
V6: Short-term versus long-term performance (items 26,28,29)	0.764	0.650

Table 21.2. Means and standard deviation of variables and results of T-test.

	U.S.A.		Japan		T-test
	Mean	S.D.	Mean	S.D.	P-value
Communication and coordination (V1)[a]	4.03	0.758	3.70	0.647	0.001
The importance of long-range planning (V2)[b]	3.51	0.738	3.52	0.607	0.965
Structuring of budgetary processes (V3)[c]	2.95	0.852	2.90	0.621	0.700
Budget slack (V4)[d]	3.08	0.712	2.89	0.557	0.049
Controllability of budget (V5)[e]	3.42	0.640	3.17	0.545	0.003
Short-term versus long-term performance (V6)[f]	2.80	0.783	3.11	0.544	0.003

Notes: (a) V1 = (item 2 + item 3 + item 4) ÷ 3
      (b) V2 = (item 6 + _____ + item 10) ÷ 5
      (c) V3 = (item 11 + _____ + item 15) ÷ 5
      (d) V4 = (item 16 + _____ + item 20) ÷ 5
      (e) V5 = (item 21 + item 22 + item 23) ÷ 3
      (f) V6 = (item 26 + item 28 + item 29) ÷ 3

the table, five measures (Communication and Coordination, The Importance of Long-Range Planning, Structuring of Budgetary Processes, Budget Slack and Short-Term versus Long-Term Performance) were safely above the lower limits of acceptability that are usually considered to be 0.50 or 0.60. The means and standard deviations of these variables are reported in Table 21.2.

3. Results and Discussions

The hypotheses were examined by performing T-test at the 0.05 level of confidence. Table 21.2 summarizes the results that are discussed below.

The first hypothesis, H1, developed from the perspective of the Individualism–Collectivism dimension, states that U.S. companies will use formal communication and coordination in budget planning processes to a greater extent than Japanese companies. The difference in the means of the two samples (4.03 for the U.S. and 3.70 for Japan) was significant in the hypothesized direction ($t = 3.26$, $p = 0.001$). This not only supports our hypothesis but is also congruent with the findings of Hawkins[9] and Asada.[2]

The second hypothesis, H2, developed from the perspective of the Uncertainty Avoidance dimension, states that Japanese companies will use broad time-horizons in budget planning processes to a greater extent than U.S. companies. However the hypothesis was not supported because the means of the two samples (3.51 for the U.S. and 3.52 for Japan) were not significantly different ($t = -0.04$, $p = 0.965$). In addition, the result runs counter to the findings of Daley *et al.*[7]

The third hypothesis, H3, developed from the perspective of the Uncertainty Avoidance dimension, states that Japanese companies will structure budget planning processes to a greater extent than U.S. companies. This hypotheses was not supported because the means of the two samples (2.95 for the U.S. and 2.90 for Japan) were not significantly different ($t = 0.39$, $p = 0.700$).

The fourth hypothesis, H4, developed from the perspective of the Individualism–Collectivism dimension, states that U.S. companies will build slack into budgets to a greater extent than Japanese companies. The difference in the means of the two samples (3.08 for the U.S. and 2.89 for Japan) was significant in the hypothesized direction ($t = 1.99$, $p = 0.049$).

The fifth hypothesis, H5, developed from the perspective of the Individualism–Collectivism dimension, states that U.S. companies will practice controllability of budgets to a greater extent than Japanese companies. The difference in the means of the two samples (3.42 for the U.S. and 3.17 for Japan) was significant in the hypothesized direction ($t = 2.98$, $p = 0.003$). This hypothesis however was not tested in a rigorous fashion because of the poor reliability of the measure.

The last hypothesis, H6, developed from the perspective of the Individualism–Collectivism dimension, states that Japanese companies will use broad evaluation time–horizons to a greater extent than U.S. companies. The difference in the means of the two samples (2.80 for the U.S. and 3.11 for Japan) was significant in the hypothesized direction ($t = -2.99$, $p = 0.003$).

The findings to this point supported the four hypotheses developed from the Individualism–Collectivism dimension. The results however were equivocal for the other two hypotheses developed from the Uncertainty Avoidance dimension. This implies that the conceptual framework has been better formalized from the Individualism–Collectivism dimension and incorrectly conceptualized from the Uncertainty Avoidance dimension.

A number of studies have looked at the effects of contextual variables such as size, production technology, and the manager's authority levels and functional area in the organization. Tracy and Azumi[28] reported that many relationships between context and structure were quite similar between Japanese and Western companies. Therefore samples attributes also seem to have important implications for the present study.

Although the U.S. and Japanese samples seemed to be comparable, closer examination of the sample attributes revealed the significant mean difference in company size ($t = 3.18$, $p = 0.003$): the average number of employees in the U.S. companies was considerably larger than that of their Japanese counterparts.[29] Since larger organizations tend to have more specialization, more standardization and more formalization than smaller organizations, it is essential to isolate variance in the dependent variables that might be presumably caused by size. Therefore multiple regression analyses were carried out including size as a control. In the regression equations, budget-related variables constituted dependent variables. The independent variables included were one cultural variable and one control variable.

As shown in Table 21.3, all of the six equations reported the predicted signs on the coefficient estimates of culture, but *t*-values of the coefficient estimates were insignificant at the 0.05 level, except for the use of short-term versus long-term performance measure ($p = 0.002$). None of the *t*-value of the co-efficient estimates of size in the equations was significant at the 0.05 level.

With respect to communication and coordination, the coefficient estimate of culture was significant only at the 0.10 level ($p = 0.085$), but not at the 0.05 level. The coefficient estimate of size in the equation was also insignificant although organization theory suggests that size matters to formal communication and coordination.

Table 21.3. Results of regression analysis of budget control practices on culture and number of employees.

*significant at the 0.05 level
**significant at the 0.01 level
***significant at the 0.001 level

	Standardized regression coefficients (beta)		Adjusted R^2	F-value
	Culture (US = 1, Japan = 0)	Log of number of employees[a]		
V1[b]	0.161	0.064	0.032	4.062*
V2[c]	−0.051	0.109	−0.003	0.693
V3[d]	−0.034	0.153	0.007	1.660
V4[e]	0.097	0.024	0.002	1.187
V5[f]	0.101	0.113	0.026	3.474*
V6[g]	−0.286**	0.012	0.067	7.626***

Notes: (a) Numeric transformations were performed on values of number of employees by taking the natural logarithms of the values.
(b) (V1) = Communication and coordination
(c) (V2) = The importance of long-range planning
(d) (V3) = Structuring of budgetary processes
(e) (V4) = Budget slack
(f) (V5) = Controllability of budgets
(g) (V6) = Short-term versus long-term performance

The commonly held assumption that Japanese companies use broader planning time-horizons than U.S. companies was not substantiated by the result. Although we have no ready explanation at hand, U.S. and/or Japanese managers, for some reason, might have changed their preferences for planning time-horizons. Convergent theorists indeed suggest that Japanese seem to moving closer to the American model, whereas Americans may be moving closer to Japanese.

This study formulated the hypothesis, H3, from the Uncertainty Avoidance perspective, however, literature on bureaucracy often implies that it is the size that influences the structure of an organization.[6,22] If this is so, U.S. companies should have a greater need for a complex system of formal rules and procedures. This conjecture is totally the opposite of our hypothesis. The coefficient estimate of size in the regression equation was insignificant. The equivocal result indicates that individualism and rationalism in American society might have intervened on the effect of Uncertainty Avoidance on structuring budgetary processes.

When size was controlled, the effect of culture on building budget slack was insignificant. This indicates that the effect of Individualism–Collectivism on budget slack building behavior of managers was not very strong, and that the effect might be moderated by the effect of Uncertainty Avoidance. Indeed, managers often insulate against the effects of unpredictable events by building budget slack as they are able to draw on surplus resources in times of adversity.

It is perplexing that the hypothesis based on the Individualism–Collectivism dimension that Japanese companies would prefer long-term performance evaluation more than U.S. companies was supported, but a similar long term versus short-term difference postulated in the planning time-horizon from an Uncertainty Avoidance perspective did not hold water. This leads us to conjeture that it is possible that the Individualism–Collectivism dimension is a stronger predictor of budget control practices than the Uncertainty Avoidance dimension.

4. Conclusions

This paper examined the relationship between national culture and a number of budget control practices. It was theorized that the Individualism–Collectivism and the Uncertainty Avoidance dimensions of culture identified by Hofstede will have an influence on several budget control practices.

The results of analysis supported four hypotheses developed from the Individualism–Collectivism dimension, revealing that U.S. companies, compared to Japanese companies, used formal communication and coordination to a greater extent, built budget slack to a greater extent, practiced controllability of budget to a great extent, and used long-term performance measures to a lesser extent. The results were equivocal for the other two hypotheses which tap the extent of using long-range planning and structuring of budgetary processes. When company size was controlled, only one hypothesis that taps the extent of using long-term versus short-term performance measure was supported.

The results can be explained in several ways. A first possible explanation is that the conceptual framework might have been better formulated from the Individual–Collectivism dimension and incorrectly conceptualized from the Uncertainty Avoidance dimension, as addressed before. A second possible explanation is that today the four-dimensional model delineated by Hofstede almost twenty years ago does not represent the ultimate truth about the subject. About possible long-term trends of cultural dimensions, Hofstede indeed suggests that individualism will increase and the Power Distance norm will decrease as long as national wealth increases, and that uncertainty avoidance fluctuates over time with a 25–40 year wave length.

Limitations exist in this study. First, the sampling design restricts generalizability in as much as one cannot be sure that the samples obtained were representative of the culture. Because of the narrow sample, the results and conclusions relate only to a group of large manufacturing organizations in the United States and Japan. Another potential problem is non-response bias. This type of bias might be considered a problem in the U.S. where the response rate was low (34.1%) compared to Japan (60.3%). Measurements might also have caused a problem: they might not adequately capture the concepts of the theories.

Despite the above imperfections, it is believed that the research design and measurement procedures produced a reasonably meaningful test of the research question stated at the outset.

Appendix

QUESTIONNAIRE

Company name _____ Your name _____

Section 1

Your age _____

Your functional position or title

_____

Length of time with the company _____ years

Length of time in your present position _____ years

Section 11

Below are 30 statements which refer to various facts of the budget control practices. Please circle the number that is most appropriate for each item as it pertains to your company, using the following scale.

The response scale is:

Strongly   Strongly
Disagree.   Disagree   Neutral   Agree   Agree.
1 .... 2 .... 3 .... 4 5

A. <u>COMMUNICATION AND COORDINATION:</u> This refers to the extent to which organizational subunits get involved in the budgetary process.

1. In our company, a necessary requirement of an annual budget is that it is formulated by the group it affects.

1 2 3 4 5

2. In our company, the development of annual budgets is a long-drawn process with several levels of management participating in it.

1 2 3 4 5

Strongly Disagree.	Disagree	Neutral	Agree	Strongly Agree.
1	2	3	4	5

3. In our company, corporate budgets are formulated by integrating divisional budgets developed by budget committees at the divisional level.

1   2   3   4   5

4. In our company, budgets are formulated after joint discussions with the managers concerned.

1   2   3   4   5

5. In formulating a divisional budget, we usually do not spend too much time and effort for obtaining inputs from the employees concerned.

1   2   3   4   5

B. <u>THE IMPORTANCE OF LONG-RANGE PLANNING:</u> This refers to the time-frame of budget plans in your organization. Planning time-horizons are categorized as short-range if the planning covers one year or less, and long-range if the planning covers three years or more.

6. In our company, short-range budgets are developed only after elaborate discussions of long-range budgets.

1   2   3   4   5

7. In our company, long-range financial planning has been deliberately pursued to deal with future uncertainty.

1   2   3   4   5

8. In our company, long-range budgets are formulated comprehensively, covering every functional area of the firm.

1   2   3   4   5

9. Long-range budgets are not considered to be very important in our company.

1   2   3   4   5

10. Our company does not spend much time and effort to formulate long-range budgets.

1   2   3   4   5

Strongly
Disagree.   Disagree   Neutral   Agree   Strongly
Agree.

1 .... 2 .... 3 .... 4 5

C. <u>STRUCTURING OF BUDGETARY PROCESS:</u> This refers to the extent to which procedures and rules are considered to be important for formulating budgets.

11. In our company, detailed procedures and rules have been established to develop long-range budgets.

1 2 3 4 5

12. While developing budgets, budgets manuals are referred to and followed throughout in our company.

1 2 3 4 5

13. In our company, those who do not follow the rules and procedures as set forth in the budget manual, are admonished.

1 2 3 4 5

14. Budget manuals are not comprehensive in our company, covering every functional area of the firm.

1 2 3 4 5

15. Our company does not adhere strictly to budget manuals while formulating budgets.

1 2 3 4 5

D. <u>BUDGET SLACK:</u> Budget slack is defined as a deliberately created difference between the true budget estimate and the submitted budget figure.

16. In our company, managers usually build some slack in the budget.

1 2 3 4 5

17. In our company, managers usually try to build as much slack as possible in the budget so as to have access to extra resources.

1 2 3 4 5

18. In our company, managers build slack in the budget to do things that otherwise cannot be done.

1 2 3 4 5

Strongly Disagree.	Disagree	Neutral	Agree	Strongly Agree.
1	2	3	4	5

19. In our company, managers build budget slack to prepare for future uncertainty.

1 2 3 4 5

20. In our company, managers do not have the tendency to build budget slack.

1 2 3 4 5

E. <u>CONTROLLABILITY OF BUDGETS:</u> This refers to the extent to which managers within the budgetary control system are charged or credited only for items within their control.

21. While developing divisional budgets, managers sufficiently distinguish controllable and non-controllable items and managers are charged or credited only for the items under their control.

1 2 3 4 5

22. Our company practices flexible manufacturing overhead budgets to a large extent.

1 2 3 4 5

23. Our company practices responsibility accounting to a great extent.

1 2 3 4 5

24. In our company, managers will absolutely refuse to be held accountable for any unfavorable budget variance when they do not have full control.

1 2 3 4 5

25. In our company, divisional budgets include items which may not be under the direct control of the divisional managers.

1 2 3 4 5

F. <u>SHORT-TERM VERSUS LONG-TERM PERFORMANCE:</u> This refers to the evaluation of short-term and long-term performance of managers as they relate to budgets. Short-term is defined as performance which covers one year or less, and long-term covers three years or more.

Strongly
Disagree.   Disagree   Neutral   Agree   Strongly
Agree.

1 .... 2 .... 3 .... 4 5

26. In our company, managers are evaluated basically on their long-term performance.

                                                                1   2   3   4   5

27. In our company, an exceptional performance in the short-term does not necessarily deserve as much reward as consistent good performance over the long-term.

                                                                  1   2   3   4   5

28. In our company, importance is attached more to short-term performance than to long-term performance.

                                                                  1   2   3   4   5

29. In our company, long-term budget performance is seldom used as: a criterion for evaluating managers.

                                                                  1   2   3   4   5

30. The manager who has an unfavorable short-term budget variance is not evaluated negatively in our company.

                                                                  1   2   3   4   5

Thank you for completing this questionnaire. Would you please check to see that you have responded to all the questions?

____ I want to receive a copy of the research summary.

____ I do not want to receive a copy of the research summary.

References

1. Anthony, R. N., Management Accounting Principles, Illinois, (Richard D. Irwin, 1965).
2. Asada, T., Yosan Kanri System no Nichibei Kigyo Hikaku ni Tsuite (1) (A Comparison of Budget Control Systems Between the U.S. and Japan (2)), Kigyo-Kaikei, Vol. 41, No. 4, 1989a, 99–106.

3. Asada, T., Yosan Kanri System no Nichibei Kigyo Hikaku ni Tsuite (1) (A Comparison of Budget Control Systems Between the U.S. and Japan (2)), Kigyo-Kaikei, Vol. 41, No. 5, 1989b, 113–121.

4. Birnberg, J. G. & Snodgrass, C., Culture and Control, Accounting, Organizations and Society, Vol. 13, No. 5, 1988, 447–464.

5. Bruns, W. J. & Waterhouse, J. H., Budgetary Control and Organization Structure, Journal of Accounting Research, Autumn, 1975, 177–203.

6. Child, J., Predicting and Understanding Organizational Structure, Administrative Science Quarterly, June, 1973, 168–185.

7. Daley, L, Jiambalvo, J., Sundem, G. L. & Kondo, Y., Attitudes Toward Financial Control Systems in the United States and Japan, Journal of International Business Studies, Fall, 1985, 91–110.

8. England, G. W. & Harpaz, I., Some Methodological and Analytic Considerations in Cross-National Comparative Research, Journal of International Business Studies, Fall, 1983, 49–59.

9. Hawkins, C. E., A Comparative Study of the Management Accounting Practices of Individual Companies in the United States and Japan, Michigan, U.M.I., 1983.

10. Hofstede, G., Culture's Consequence: International Differences in Work Related Values, London, Sage, 1980.

11. Hofstede, G., The Cultural Relativity of Organizational Practices and Theories, Journal of International Business Studies, Fall, 1983, 75–90.

12. Hui, C. H. & Triandis, H. C., Measurement in Cross-Culture Psychology, Journal of Cross-Cultural Psychology, Vol. 16, No. 2, 1985, 131–152.

13. Kenis, I., Effects of Budgetary Goal Characteristics on Managerial Attitudes and Performances, The Accounting Review, October, 1979, 707–721.

14. Lincoln, J. R. & Kalleberg, A. L., Work Organization and Workforce Commitment: A Study of Plants and Employees in the U.S. and Japan, American Sociological Review, Vol. 50, 1985, 738–760.

15. Magee, R., Advanced Managerial Accounting, New York (Harper & Row, Publishers, 1986).

16. McNally, G. M., Responsibility Accounting and Organizational Control: Some Perspectives and Prospects, Journal of Business Finance and Accounting, Vol. 7, No. 2, 1980, 165–181.

17. Merchant, K. A., The Design of the Corporate Budgeting System: Influences on Managerial Behavior and Performance, The Accounting Review, October, 1981, 813–829.

18. Milani, K., The Relationship of Participation in Budget-Setting to Industrial Supervisor Performance and Attitudes: A Field Study, The Accounting Review, April, 1975, 274–284.

19. Nandan, C., Responsibility Accounting and Controllability, Accounting and Business Research, Summer, 1986, 189–198.

20. Onsi, M., Factor Analysis of Behavioral Variables Affecting Budgetary Slack, The Accounting Review, July, 1973, 535–548.

21. Otley, D. T., Budget Use and Managerial Performance, Journal of Accounting Research, Spring, 1978, 122–149.

22. Pough D. S., Hickson, D. J., Hinings, C. R. & Turner, C., The Context of Organizational Structures, Administrative Science Quarterly, March, 1969, 91–114.

23. Sekaran, U., Methodological Theoretical Issues and Advancements in Cross — Cultural Research, Journal of International Business Studies, Fall, 1983, 61–74.

24. Sekaran, U. & Snodgrass, C. R., A Model for Examining Organizational Effectiveness Cross-Culturally, Advances in International Comparative Management, Vol. 1, 1986, 211–232.

25. Seror, A. C., Cross-Cultural Organizational Analysis: Research Methods and the Aston Program, International Studies of Management & Organization, Vol. 18, No. 3, 1988, 31–43.

26. Simons, R., Accounting Control Systems and Business Strategy: An Empirical Analysis, Accounting, Organizations and Society, Vol. 12, No. 4, 1987, 357–374.

27. Swieringa, R. J. & Moncur, R. H., Some Effects of Participative Budgeting on Managerial Behavior, New York, National Association of Accountant, 1975.

28. Tracy, P. & Azumi, K., Determinants of Administrative Control: A Test of a Theory with Japanese Factories, American Sociological Review, Vol. 41, February, 1976, 80–94.

29. Ueno, S., The Influence of Culture on Budget Control Practices in the U.S.A. and Japan: An Empirical Study, Michigan, U.M.I., 1992.

30. Ueno, S. & Wu, F. H., The Comparative Influence of Culture on Budget Control Practices in the United States and Japan, The International Journal of Accounting, Vol. 28, No. 1, 1993, 17–39.

31. Ueno, S. & Sekaran, U., The Influence of Culture on Budget Control Practices in the U.S.A. and Japan: An Empirical Study, Journal of International Business Studies, Vol. 23, No. 4, 1992, 659–674.

32. Wagner, J. A. & Moch, M. K., Individualism–Collectivism: Concept and Measure, Group & Organization Studies: An International Journal, September, 1986, 280–303.

Index

483